D0646490

AVENGERS

WRITER: **JONATHAN HICKMAN**

AVENGERS #35

PENCILERS: **JIM CHEUNG, PACO MEDINA, NICK BRADSHAW & DUSTIN WEAVER**

INKERS: **MARK MORALES, GUILLERMO ORTEGA, JUAN VLASCO, NICK BRADSHAW & DUSTIN WEAVER**

COLOR ARTISTS: **FRANK MARTIN & DAVID CURIEL**

LETTERER: **VC'S CORY PETIT**

COVER ART: **JIM CHEUNG & JUSTIN PONSOR**

NEW AVENGERS #24

ARTIST: **VALERIO SCHITI**

COLOR ARTISTS: **FRANK MARTIN & DAVID CURIEL**

LETTERER: **VC'S JOE CARAMAGNA**

COVER ART: **GABRIELE DELL'OTTO**

AVENGERS #36

ARTIST: **STEFANO CASELLI**

COLOR ARTIST: **FRANK MARTIN**

LETTERER: **VC'S CORY PETIT**

COVER ART: **STUART IMMONEN, WADE VON GRAWBADGER & MARTE GRACIA**

NEW AVENGERS #25

ARTIST: **KEV WALKER**

COLOR ARTISTS: **FRANK MARTIN & DAVID CURIEL**

LETTERER: **VC'S JOE CARAMAGNA**

COVER ART: **BUTCH GUICE & MATTHEW WILSON**

AVENGERS #37

ARTIST: **MIKE DEODATO**

COLOR ARTIST: **FRANK MARTIN**

LETTERER: **VC'S CORY PETIT**

COVER ART: **JAMIE MCKELVIE**

ASSISTANT EDITOR: **JAKE THOMAS** EDITORS: **TOM BREVOORT** WITH **WIL MOSS**

AVENGERS CREATED BY STAN LEE & JACK KIRBY

COLLECTION EDITOR: **JENNIFER GRÜNWALD** ASSISTANT EDITOR: **SARAH BRUNSTAD**
ASSOCIATE MANAGING EDITOR: **ALEX STARBUCK** EDITOR, SPECIAL PROJECTS: **MARK D. BEAZLEY**
SENIOR EDITOR, SPECIAL PROJECTS: **JEFF YOUNGQUIST** SVP PRINT, SALES & MARKETING: **DAVID GABRIEL**

EDITOR IN CHIEF: **AXEL ALONSO** CHIEF CREATIVE OFFICER: **JOE QUESADA**
PUBLISHER: **DAN BUCKLEY** EXECUTIVE PRODUCER: **ALAN FINE**

ENGERS: TIME RUNS OUT VOL. 1. Contains material originally published in magazine form as AVENGERS #35-37 and NEW AVENGERS #24-25. First printing 2015. ISBN# 978-0-7851-9341-8. Published by MARVEL ORLDWIDE, INC., a subsidiary of MARVEL ENTERTAINMENT, LLC. OFFICE OF PUBLICATION: 135 West 50th Street, New York, NY 10020. Copyright © 2015 Marvel Characters, Inc. All rights reserved. All characters tured in this issue and the distinctive names and likenesses thereof, and all related indicia are trademarks of Marvel Characters, Inc. No similarity between any of the names, characters, persons, and/or institutions his magazine with those of any living or dead person or institution is intended, and any such similarity which may exist is purely coincidental. **Printed in the U.S.A.** ALAN FINE, EVP - Office of the President, Marvel rldwide, Inc. and EVP & CMO Marvel Characters B.V.; DAN BUCKLEY, Publisher & President - Print, Animation & Digital Divisions; JOE QUESADA, Chief Creative Officer; TOM BREVOORT, SVP of Publishing; DAVID BOGART, P of Operations & Procurement, Publishing; C.B. CEBULSKI, SVP of Creator & Content Development; DAVID GABRIEL, SVP Print, Sales & Marketing; JIM O'KEEFE, VP of Operations & Logistics; DAN CARR, Executive ector of Publishing Technology; SUSAN CRESPI, Editorial Operations Manager; ALEX MORALES, Publishing Operations Manager; STAN LEE, Chairman Emeritus. For information regarding advertising in Marvel Comics n Marvel.com, please contact Niza Disla, Director of Marvel Partnerships, at ndisla@marvel.com. For Marvel subscription inquiries, please call 800-217-9158. **Manufactured between 11/14/2014 and 12/28/2014**
R.R. DONNELLEY, INC., SALEM, VA, USA.

987654321

"THE THREE AVENGERS"

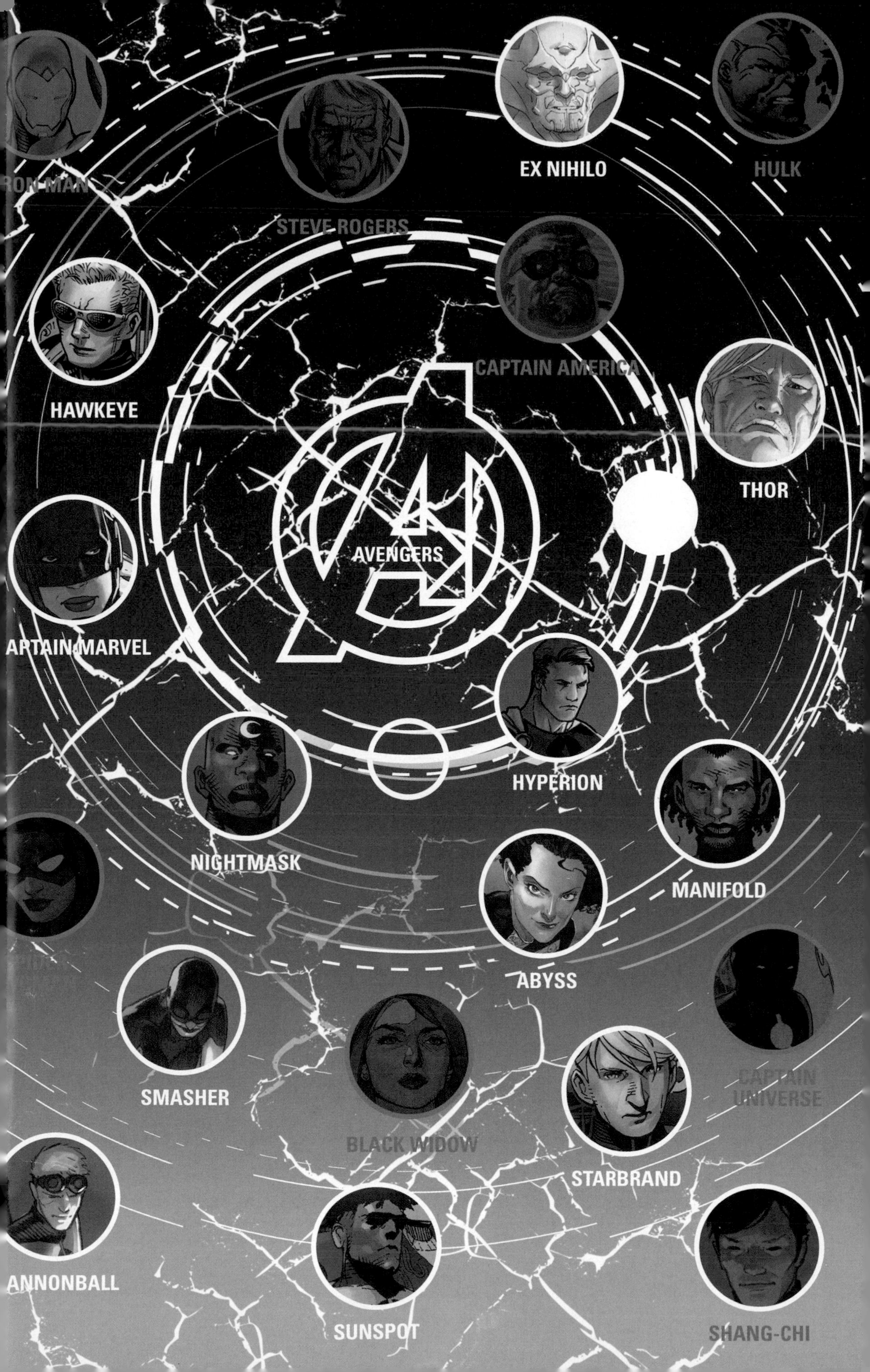

RON MAN
STEVE ROGERS
EX NIHILO
HULK
CAPTAIN AMERICA
HAWKEYE
THOR
AVENGERS
APTAIN MARVEL
HYPERION
NIGHTMASK
MANIFOLD
ABYSS
SMASHER
BLACK WIDOW
CAPTAIN UNIVERSE
STARBRAND
ANNONBALL
SUNSPOT
SHANG-CHI

PREVIOUSLY IN AVENGERS

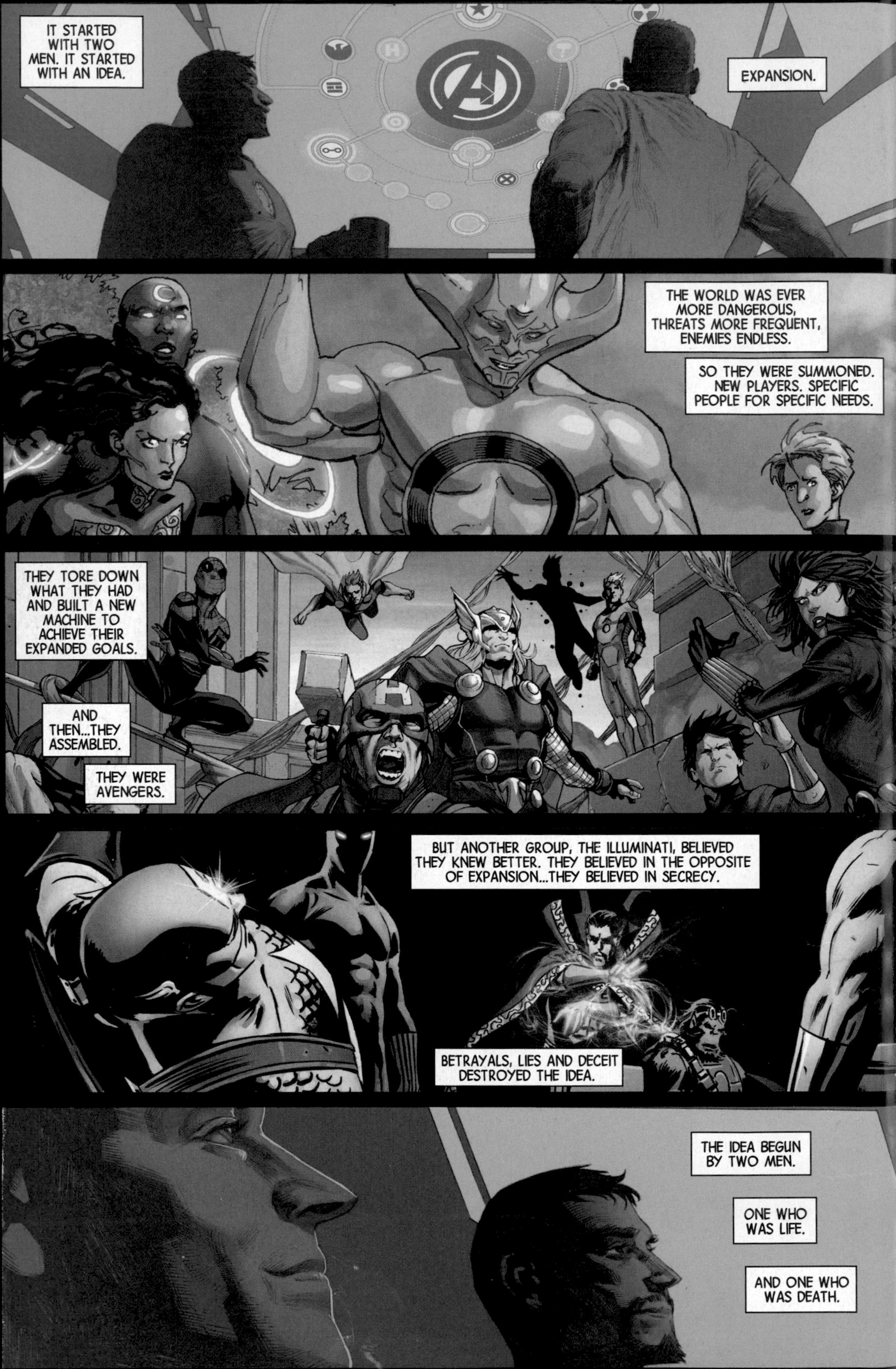
IT STARTED WITH TWO MEN. IT STARTED WITH AN IDEA.
EXPANSION.
THE WORLD WAS EVER MORE DANGEROUS, THREATS MORE FREQUENT, ENEMIES ENDLESS.
SO THEY WERE SUMMONED. NEW PLAYERS. SPECIFIC PEOPLE FOR SPECIFIC NEEDS.
THEY TORE DOWN WHAT THEY HAD AND BUILT A NEW MACHINE TO ACHIEVE THEIR EXPANDED GOALS.
AND THEN...THEY ASSEMBLED.
THEY WERE AVENGERS.
BUT ANOTHER GROUP, THE ILLUMINATI, BELIEVED THEY KNEW BETTER. THEY BELIEVED IN THE OPPOSITE OF EXPANSION...THEY BELIEVED IN SECRECY.
BETRAYALS, LIES AND DECEIT DESTROYED THE IDEA.
THE IDEA BEGUN BY TWO MEN.
ONE WHO WAS LIFE.
AND ONE WHO WAS DEATH.

EIGHT MONTHS LATER

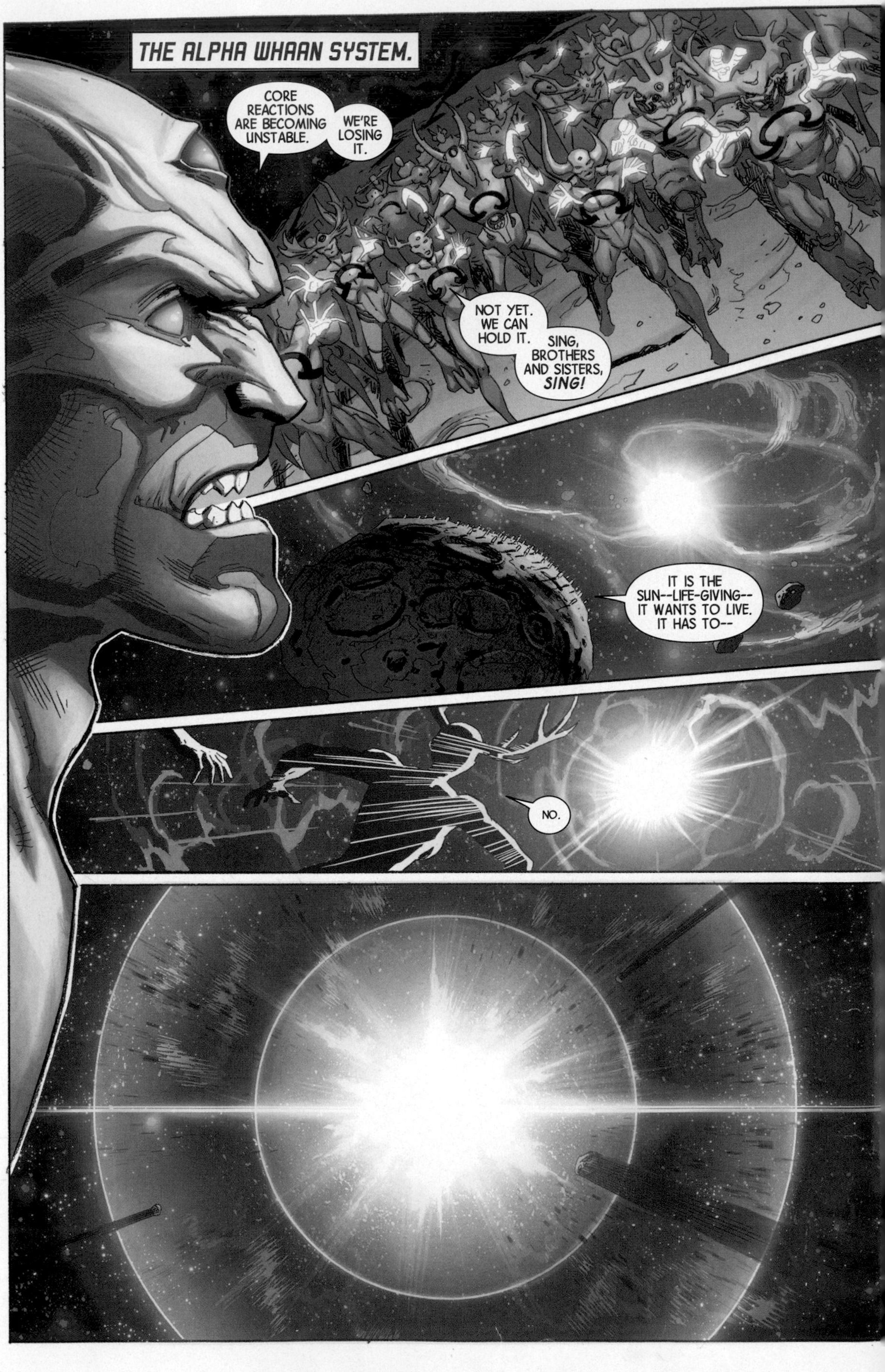
THE ALPHA WHAAN SYSTEM.
CORE REACTIONS ARE BECOMING UNSTABLE.
WE'RE LOSING IT.
NOT YET. WE CAN HOLD IT.
SING, BROTHERS AND SISTERS, SING!
IT IS THE SUN--LIFE-GIVING-- IT WANTS TO LIVE. IT HAS TO--
NO.

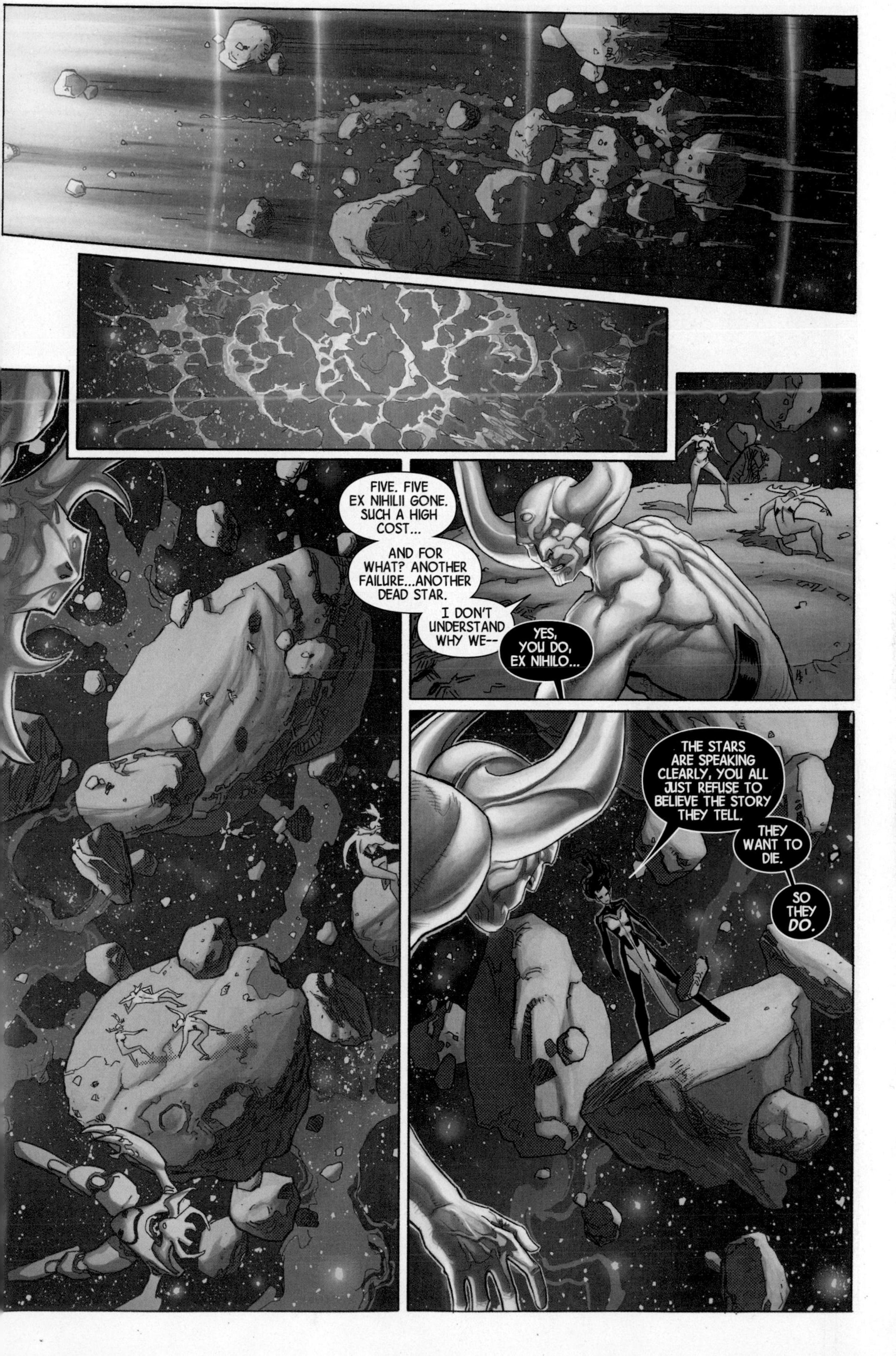
FIVE. FIVE EX NIHILII GONE. SUCH A HIGH COST...
AND FOR WHAT? ANOTHER FAILURE...ANOTHER DEAD STAR.
I DON'T UNDERSTAND WHY WE--
YES, YOU DO, EX NIHILO...
THE STARS ARE SPEAKING CLEARLY, YOU ALL JUST REFUSE TO BELIEVE THE STORY THEY TELL.
THEY WANT TO DIE.
SO THEY DO.

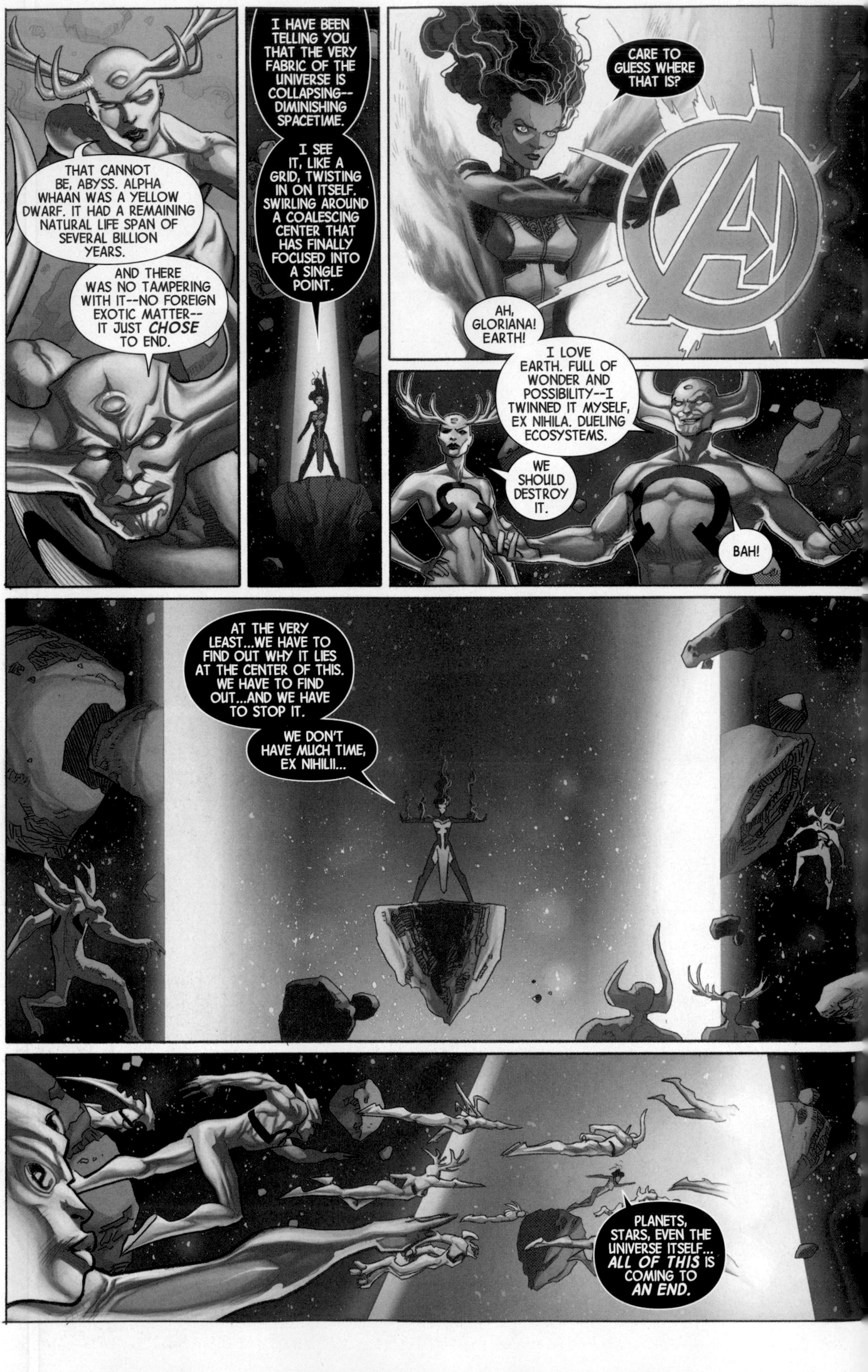
THAT CANNOT BE, ABYSS. ALPHA WHAAN WAS A YELLOW DWARF. IT HAD A REMAINING NATURAL LIFE SPAN OF SEVERAL BILLION YEARS.
AND THERE WAS NO TAMPERING WITH IT--NO FOREIGN EXOTIC MATTER--IT JUST *CHOSE* TO END.
I HAVE BEEN TELLING YOU THAT THE VERY FABRIC OF THE UNIVERSE IS COLLAPSING--DIMINISHING SPACETIME.
I SEE IT, LIKE A GRID, TWISTING IN ON ITSELF. SWIRLING AROUND A COALESCING CENTER THAT HAS FINALLY FOCUSED INTO A SINGLE POINT.
CARE TO GUESS WHERE THAT IS?
AH, GLORIANA! EARTH!
I LOVE EARTH. FULL OF WONDER AND POSSIBILITY--I TWINNED IT MYSELF, EX NIHILA. DUELING ECOSYSTEMS.
WE SHOULD DESTROY IT.
BAH!
AT THE VERY LEAST...WE HAVE TO FIND OUT WHY IT LIES AT THE CENTER OF THIS. WE HAVE TO FIND OUT...AND WE HAVE TO STOP IT.
WE DON'T HAVE MUCH TIME, EX NIHILI...
PLANETS, STARS, EVEN THE UNIVERSE ITSELF... *ALL OF THIS* IS COMING TO *AN END.*

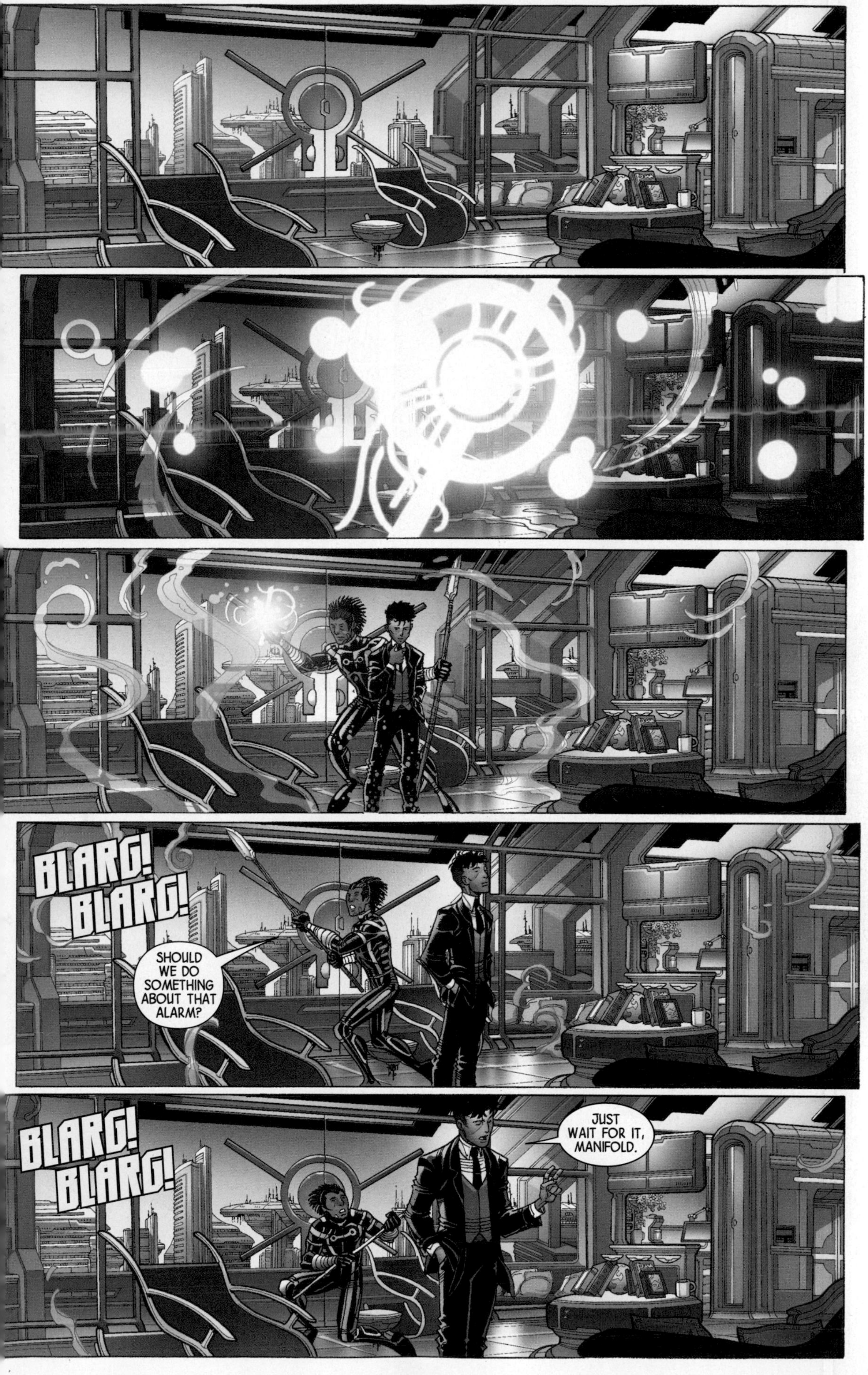
BLARG! BLARG!
SHOULD WE DO SOMETHING ABOUT THAT ALARM?
BLARG! BLARG!
JUST WAIT FOR IT, MANIFOLD.

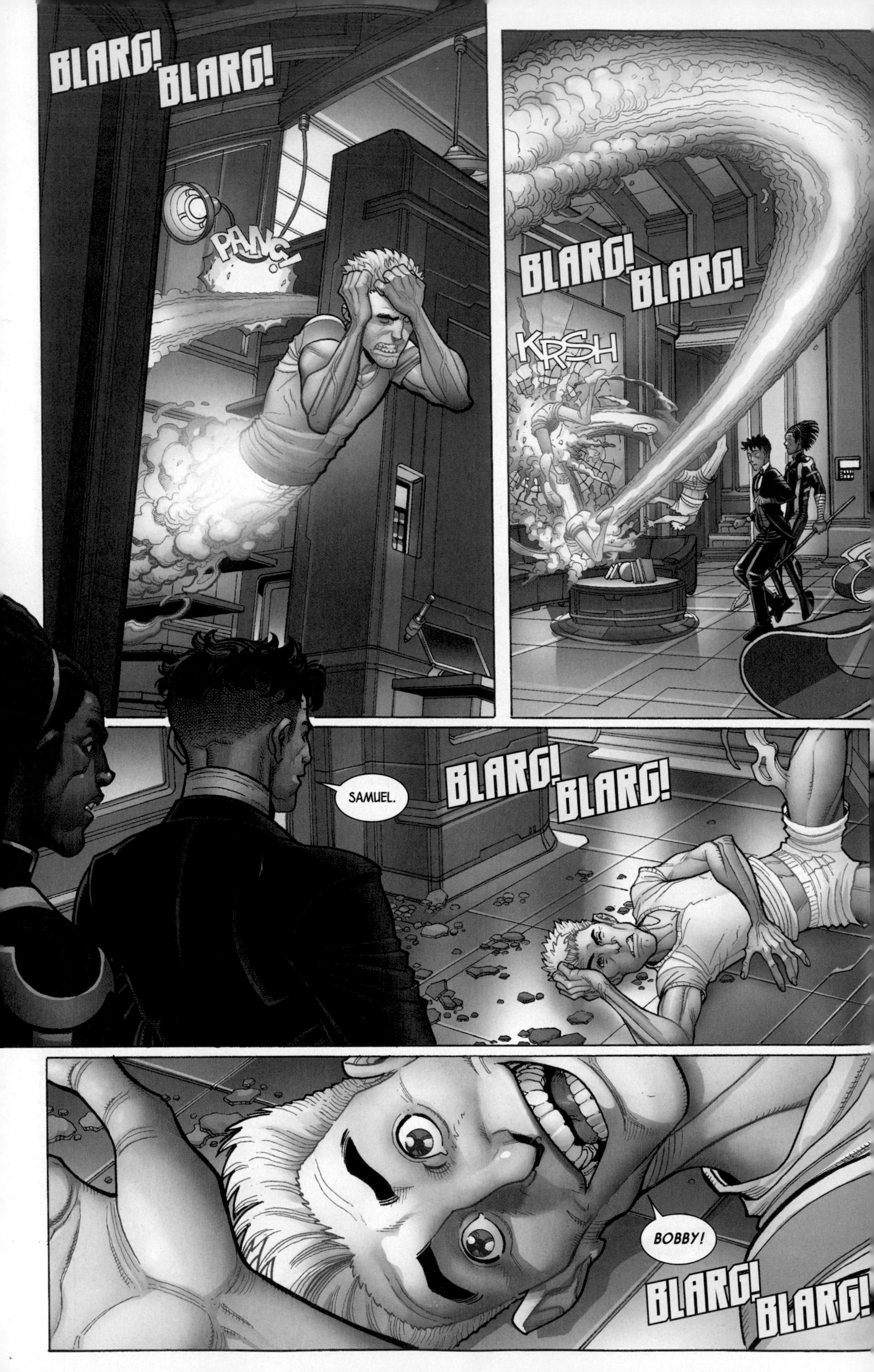
BLARG! BLARG!
PANG!
BLARG! BLARG!
KRSH
SAMUEL.
BLARG! BLARG!
BOBBY!
BLARG! BLARG!

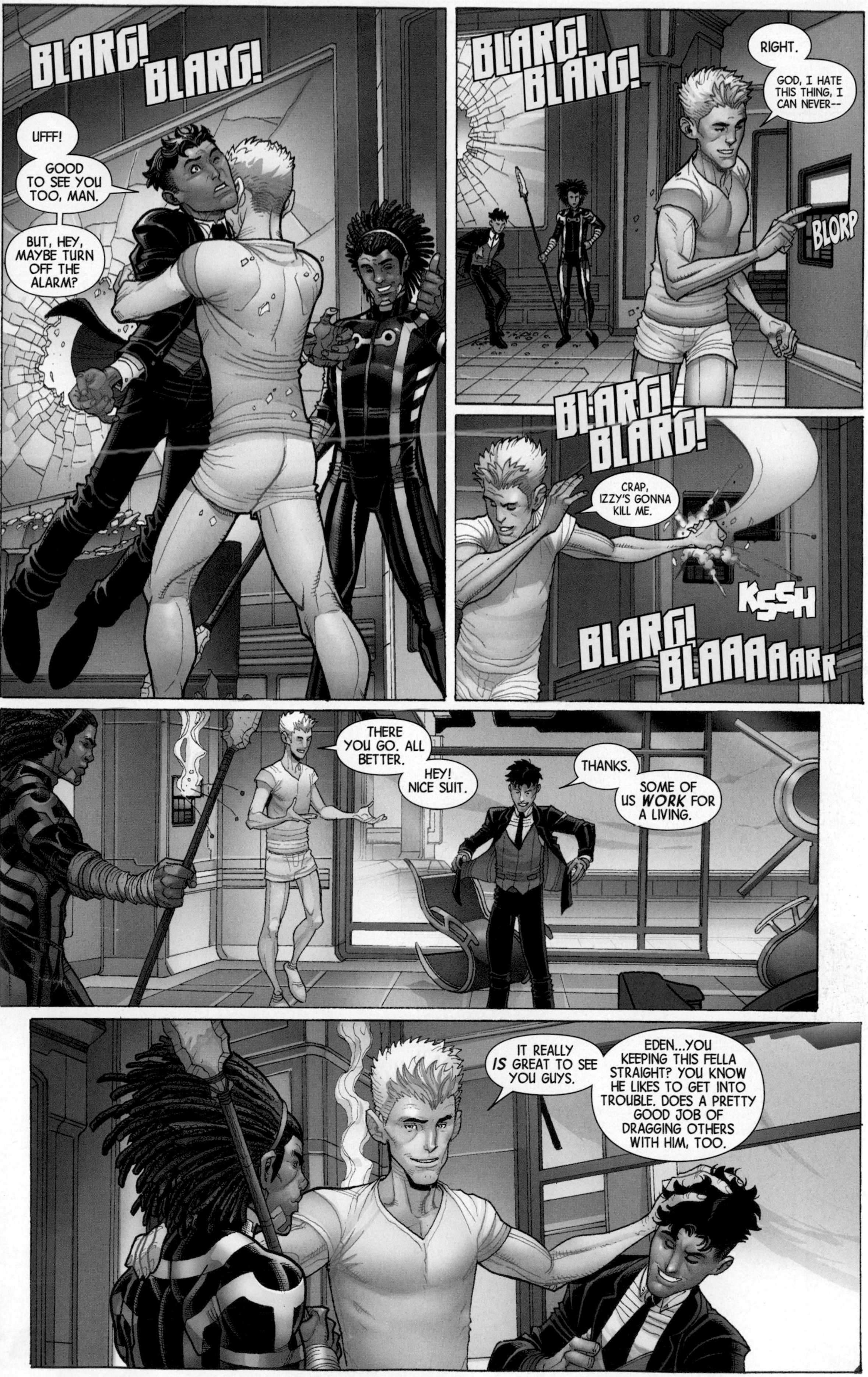
BLARG! BLARG!
UFFF!
GOOD TO SEE YOU TOO, MAN.
BUT, HEY, MAYBE TURN OFF THE ALARM?
BLARG! BLARG!
RIGHT.
GOD, I HATE THIS THING, I CAN NEVER--
BLORP
BLARG! BLARG!
CRAP, IZZY'S GONNA KILL ME.
KSSH
BLARG! BLAAAAARR
THERE YOU GO. ALL BETTER.
HEY! NICE SUIT.
THANKS.
SOME OF US WORK FOR A LIVING.
IT REALLY IS GREAT TO SEE YOU GUYS.
EDEN...YOU KEEPING THIS FELLA STRAIGHT? YOU KNOW HE LIKES TO GET INTO TROUBLE. DOES A PRETTY GOOD JOB OF DRAGGING OTHERS WITH HIM, TOO.

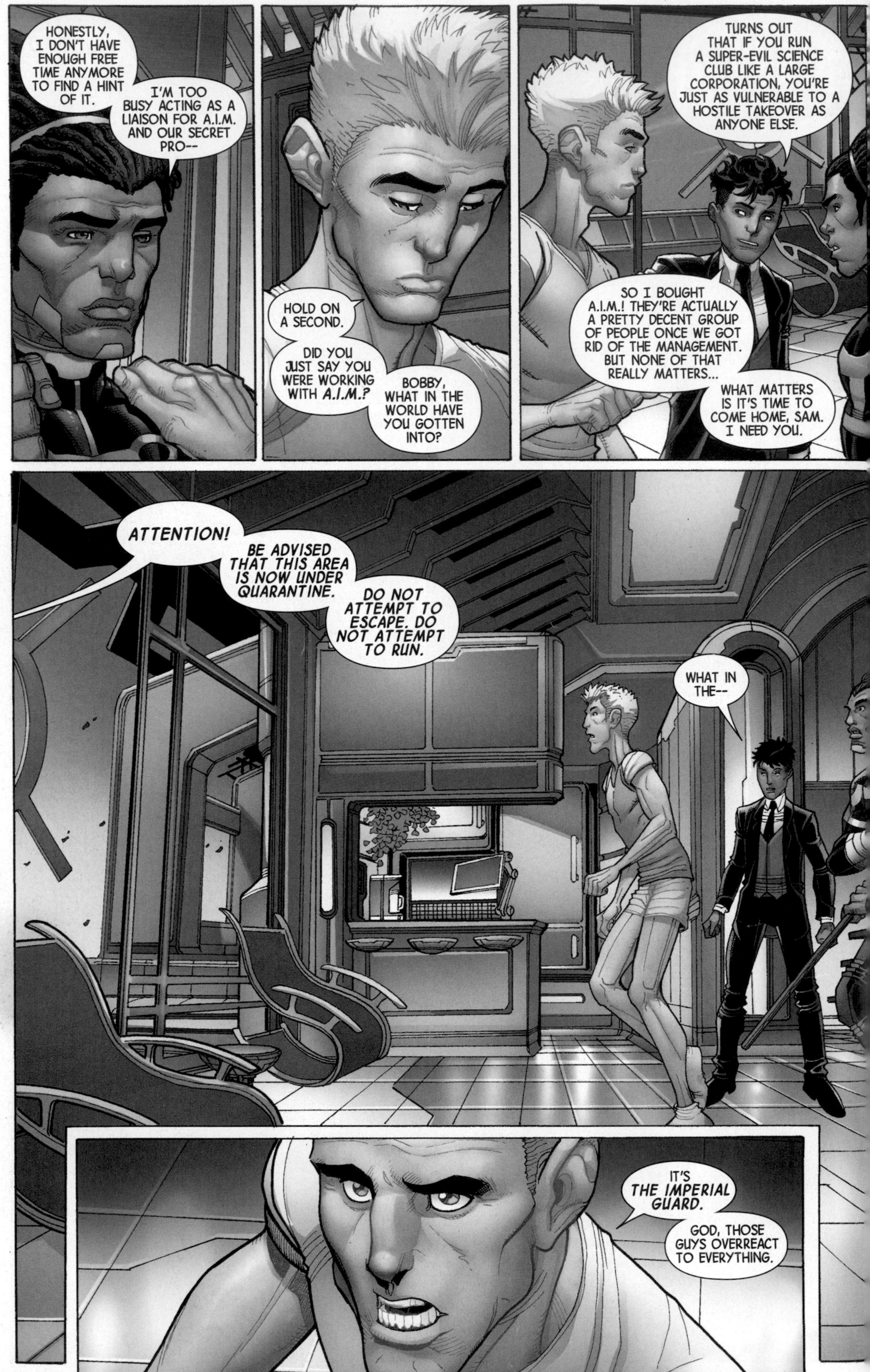
HONESTLY, I DON'T HAVE ENOUGH FREE TIME ANYMORE TO FIND A HINT OF IT.
I'M TOO BUSY ACTING AS A LIAISON FOR A.I.M. AND OUR SECRET PRO--
HOLD ON A SECOND.
DID YOU JUST SAY YOU WERE WORKING WITH A.I.M.?
BOBBY, WHAT IN THE WORLD HAVE YOU GOTTEN INTO?
TURNS OUT THAT IF YOU RUN A SUPER-EVIL SCIENCE CLUB LIKE A LARGE CORPORATION, YOU'RE JUST AS VULNERABLE TO A HOSTILE TAKEOVER AS ANYONE ELSE.
SO I BOUGHT A.I.M.! THEY'RE ACTUALLY A PRETTY DECENT GROUP OF PEOPLE ONCE WE GOT RID OF THE MANAGEMENT. BUT NONE OF THAT REALLY MATTERS...
WHAT MATTERS IS IT'S TIME TO COME HOME, SAM. I NEED YOU.
ATTENTION!
BE ADVISED THAT THIS AREA IS NOW UNDER QUARANTINE.
DO NOT ATTEMPT TO ESCAPE. DO NOT ATTEMPT TO RUN.
WHAT IN THE--
IT'S THE IMPERIAL GUARD.
GOD, THOSE GUYS OVERREACT TO EVERYTHING.

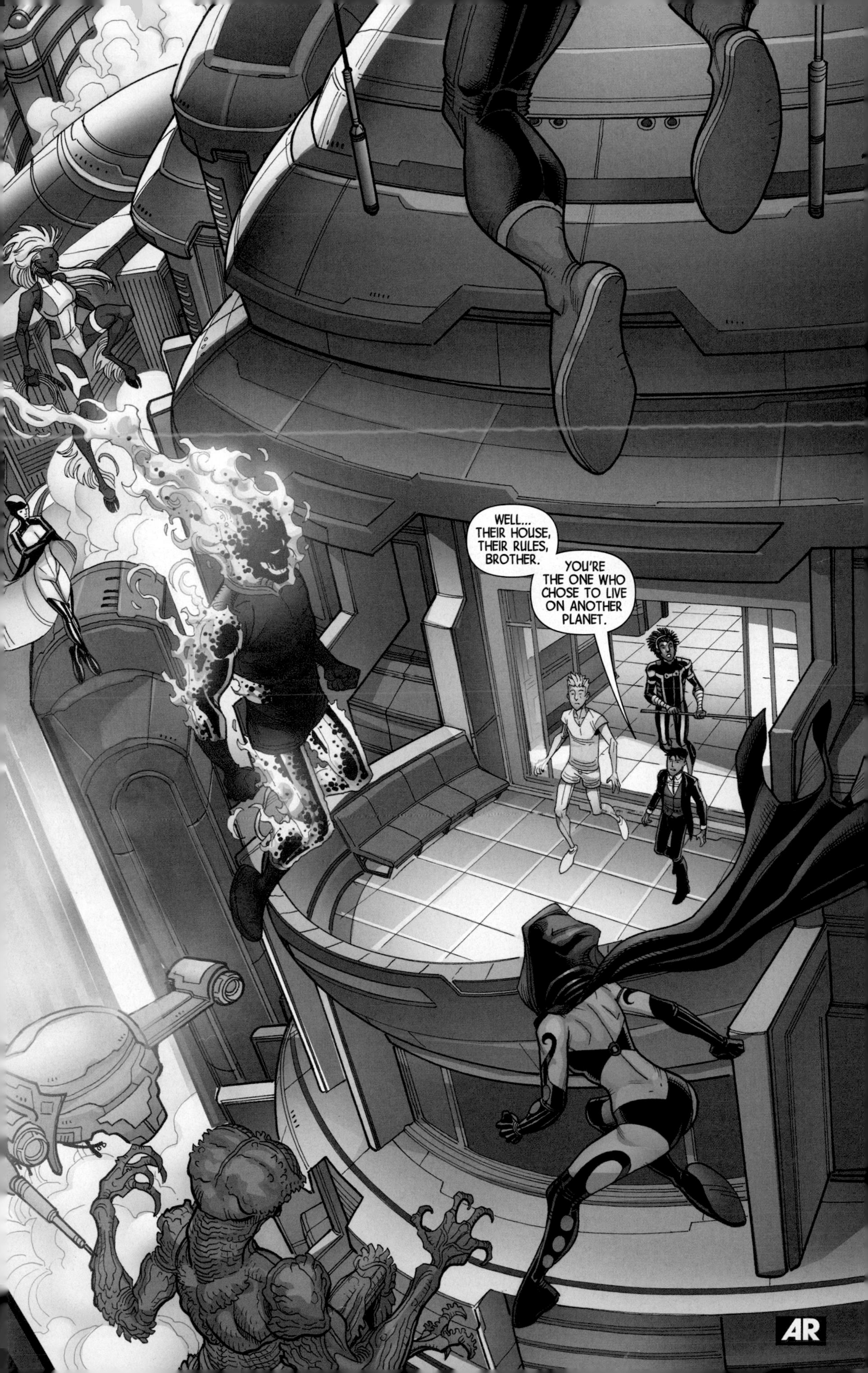
WELL... THEIR HOUSE, THEIR RULES, BROTHER.
YOU'RE THE ONE WHO CHOSE TO LIVE ON ANOTHER PLANET.

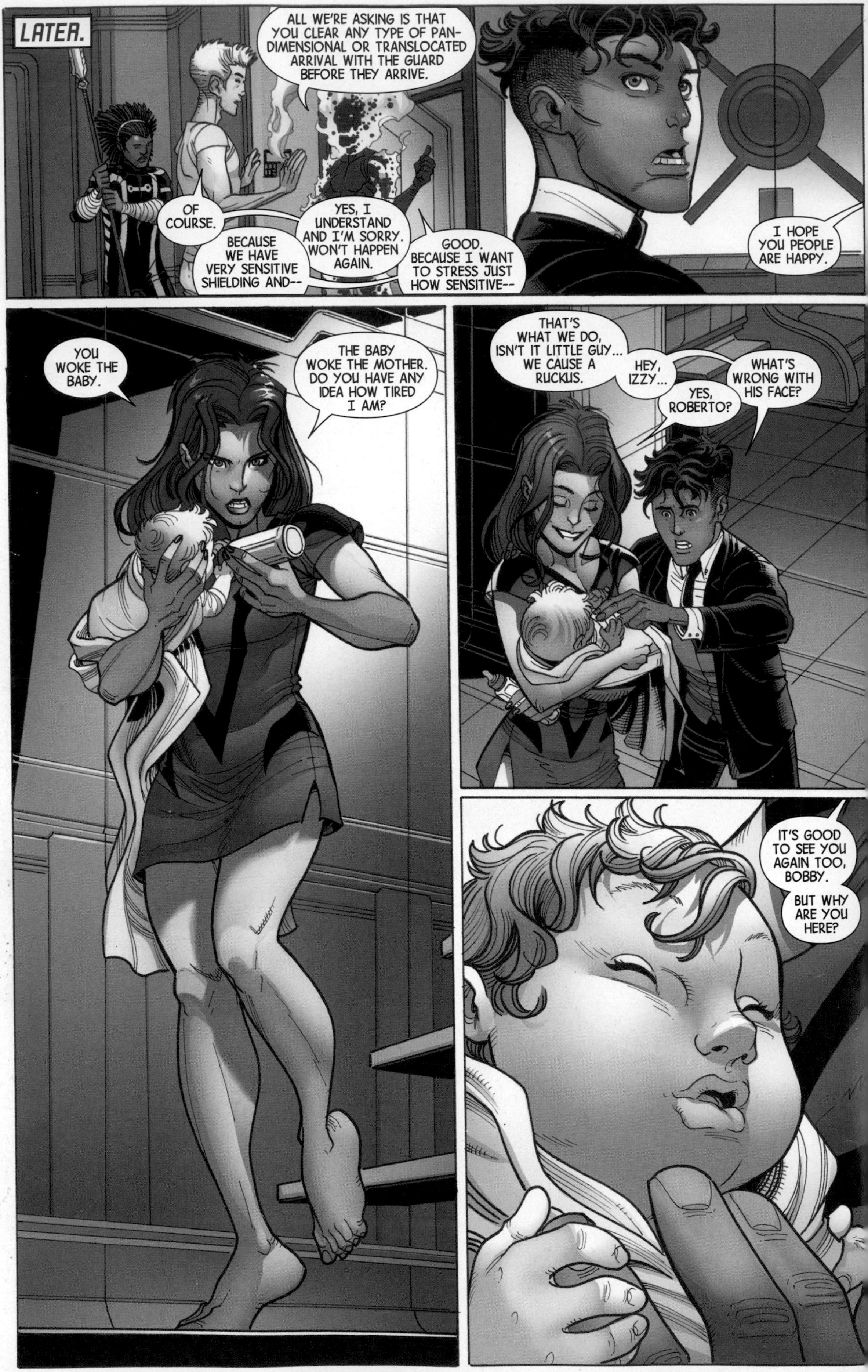
LATER.
ALL WE'RE ASKING IS THAT YOU CLEAR ANY TYPE OF PAN-DIMENSIONAL OR TRANSLOCATED ARRIVAL WITH THE GUARD BEFORE THEY ARRIVE.
OF COURSE.
BECAUSE WE HAVE VERY SENSITIVE SHIELDING AND--
YES, I UNDERSTAND AND I'M SORRY. WON'T HAPPEN AGAIN.
GOOD. BECAUSE I WANT TO STRESS JUST HOW SENSITIVE--
I HOPE YOU PEOPLE ARE HAPPY.
YOU WOKE THE BABY.
THE BABY WOKE THE MOTHER. DO YOU HAVE ANY IDEA HOW TIRED I AM?
THAT'S WHAT WE DO, ISN'T IT LITTLE GUY... WE CAUSE A RUCKUS.
HEY, IZZY...
YES, ROBERTO?
WHAT'S WRONG WITH HIS FACE?
IT'S GOOD TO SEE YOU AGAIN TOO, BOBBY.
BUT WHY ARE YOU HERE?

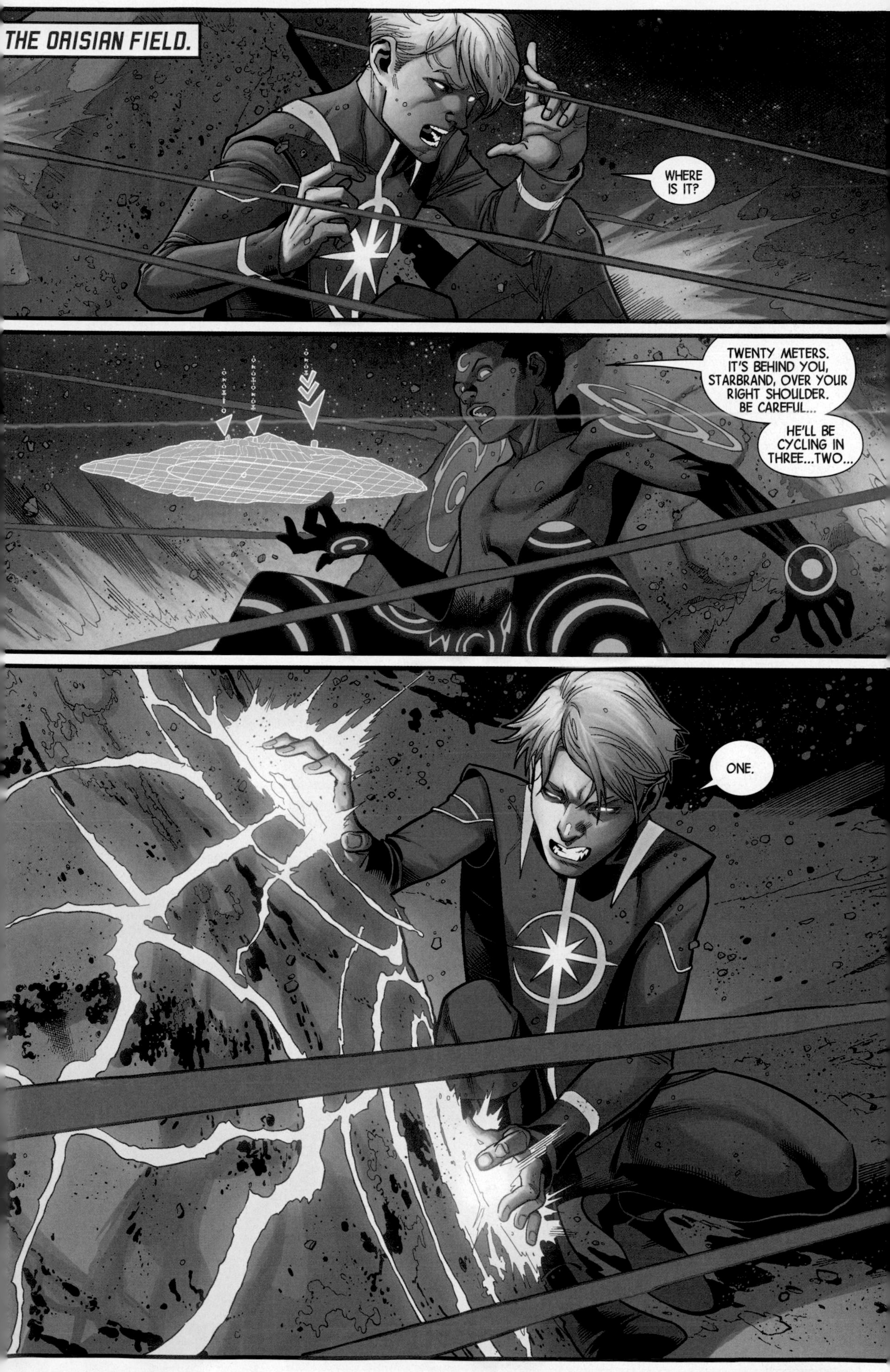
THE ORISIAN FIELD.
WHERE IS IT?
TWENTY METERS. IT'S BEHIND YOU, STARBRAND, OVER YOUR RIGHT SHOULDER. BE CAREFUL...
HE'LL BE CYCLING IN THREE...TWO...
ONE.

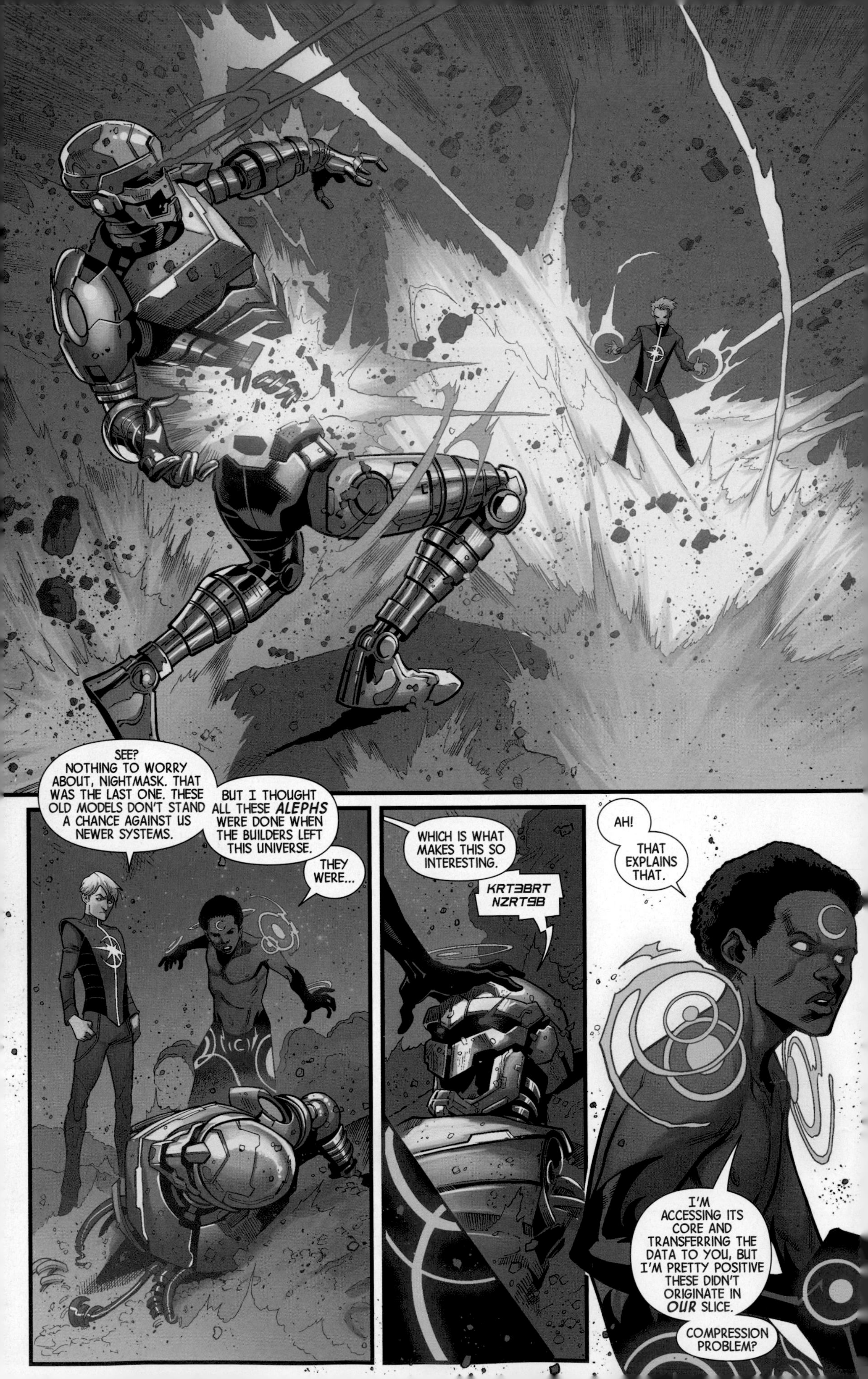
SEE? NOTHING TO WORRY ABOUT, NIGHTMASK. THAT WAS THE LAST ONE. THESE OLD MODELS DON'T STAND A CHANCE AGAINST US NEWER SYSTEMS.
BUT I THOUGHT ALL THESE ALEPHS WERE DONE WHEN THE BUILDERS LEFT THIS UNIVERSE.
THEY WERE...
WHICH IS WHAT MAKES THIS SO INTERESTING.
KRT3BRT NZRT9B
AH!
THAT EXPLAINS THAT.
I'M ACCESSING ITS CORE AND TRANSFERRING THE DATA TO YOU, BUT I'M PRETTY POSITIVE THESE DIDN'T ORIGINATE IN OUR SLICE.
COMPRESSION PROBLEM?

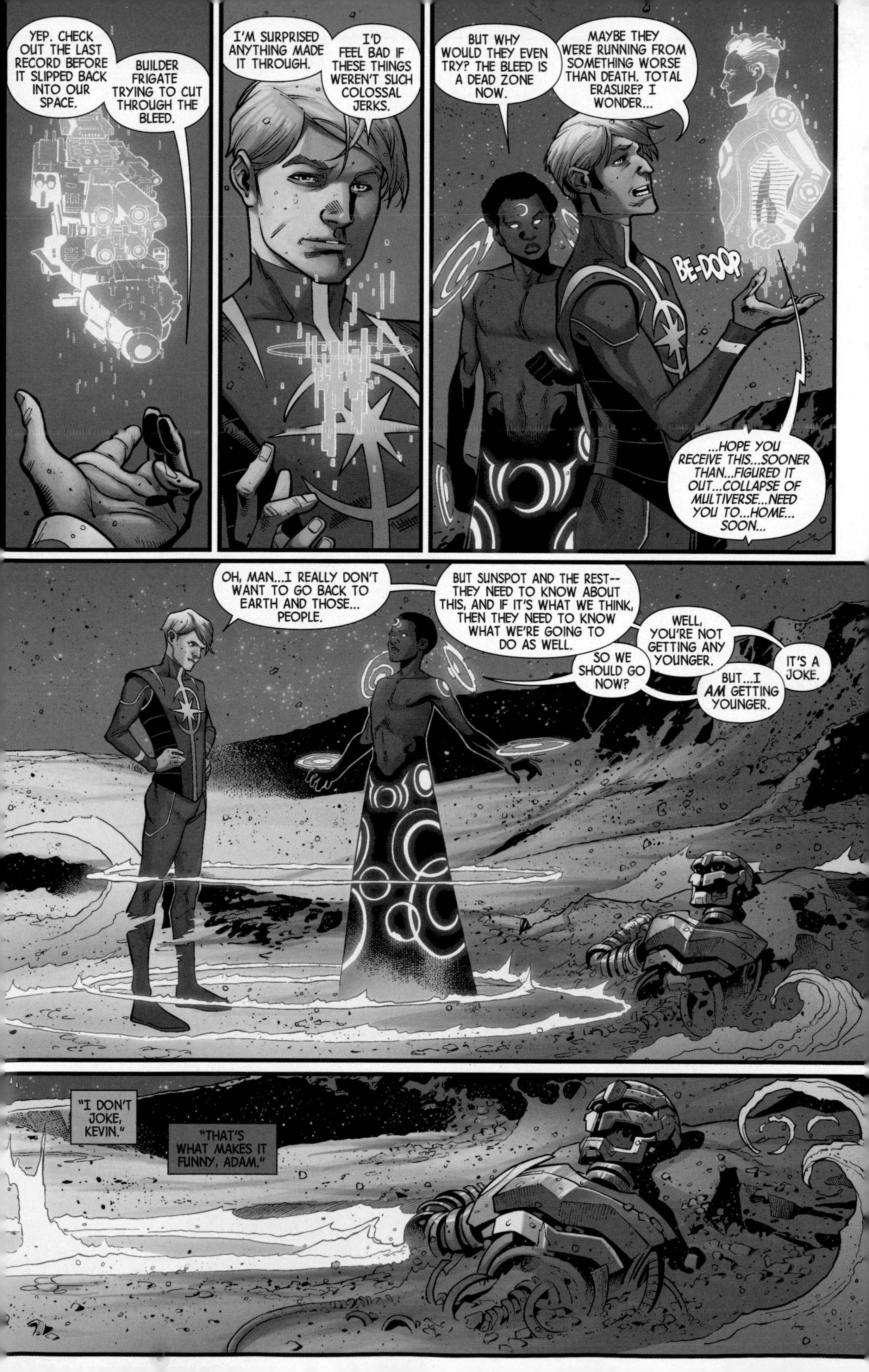
YEP. CHECK OUT THE LAST RECORD BEFORE IT SLIPPED BACK INTO OUR SPACE.
BUILDER FRIGATE TRYING TO CUT THROUGH THE BLEED.
I'M SURPRISED ANYTHING MADE IT THROUGH.
I'D FEEL BAD IF THESE THINGS WEREN'T SUCH COLOSSAL JERKS.
BUT WHY WOULD THEY EVEN TRY? THE BLEED IS A DEAD ZONE NOW.
MAYBE THEY WERE RUNNING FROM SOMETHING WORSE THAN DEATH. TOTAL ERASURE? I WONDER...
BE-DOOP
...HOPE YOU RECEIVE THIS...SOONER THAN...FIGURED IT OUT...COLLAPSE OF MULTIVERSE...NEED YOU TO...HOME... SOON...
OH, MAN...I REALLY DON'T WANT TO GO BACK TO EARTH AND THOSE... PEOPLE.
BUT SUNSPOT AND THE REST-- THEY NEED TO KNOW ABOUT THIS, AND IF IT'S WHAT WE THINK, THEN THEY NEED TO KNOW WHAT WE'RE GOING TO DO AS WELL.
SO WE SHOULD GO NOW?
WELL, YOU'RE NOT GETTING ANY YOUNGER.
BUT...I AM GETTING YOUNGER.
IT'S A JOKE.
"I DON'T JOKE, KEVIN."
"THAT'S WHAT MAKES IT FUNNY, ADAM."

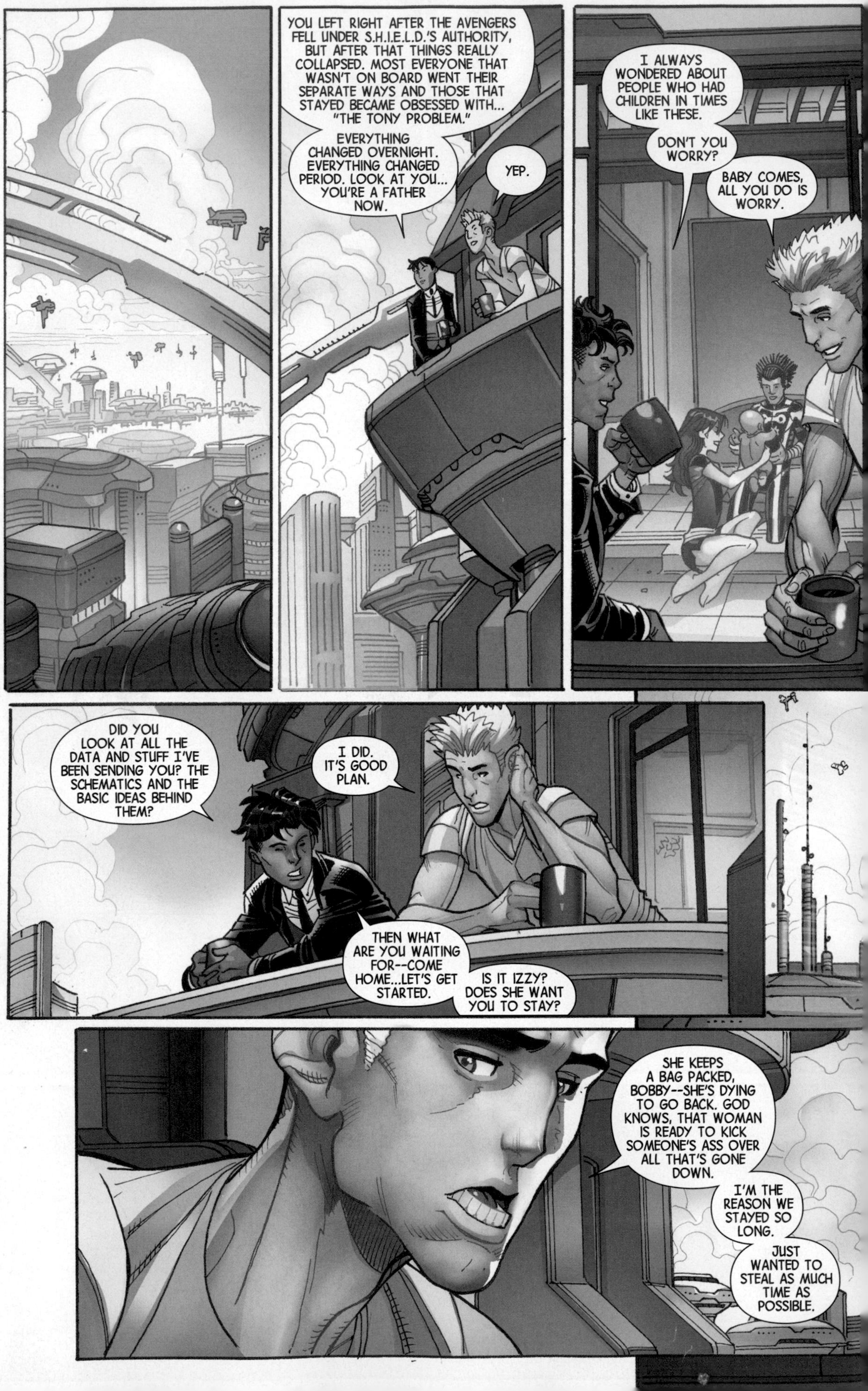
YOU LEFT RIGHT AFTER THE AVENGERS FELL UNDER S.H.I.E.L.D.'S AUTHORITY, BUT AFTER THAT THINGS REALLY COLLAPSED. MOST EVERYONE THAT WASN'T ON BOARD WENT THEIR SEPARATE WAYS AND THOSE THAT STAYED BECAME OBSESSED WITH... "THE TONY PROBLEM."
EVERYTHING CHANGED OVERNIGHT. EVERYTHING CHANGED PERIOD. LOOK AT YOU... YOU'RE A FATHER NOW.
YEP.
I ALWAYS WONDERED ABOUT PEOPLE WHO HAD CHILDREN IN TIMES LIKE THESE.
DON'T YOU WORRY?
BABY COMES, ALL YOU DO IS WORRY.
DID YOU LOOK AT ALL THE DATA AND STUFF I'VE BEEN SENDING YOU? THE SCHEMATICS AND THE BASIC IDEAS BEHIND THEM?
I DID. IT'S GOOD PLAN.
THEN WHAT ARE YOU WAITING FOR--COME HOME...LET'S GET STARTED.
IS IT IZZY? DOES SHE WANT YOU TO STAY?
SHE KEEPS A BAG PACKED, BOBBY--SHE'S DYING TO GO BACK. GOD KNOWS, THAT WOMAN IS READY TO KICK SOMEONE'S ASS OVER ALL THAT'S GONE DOWN.
I'M THE REASON WE STAYED SO LONG.
JUST WANTED TO STEAL AS MUCH TIME AS POSSIBLE.

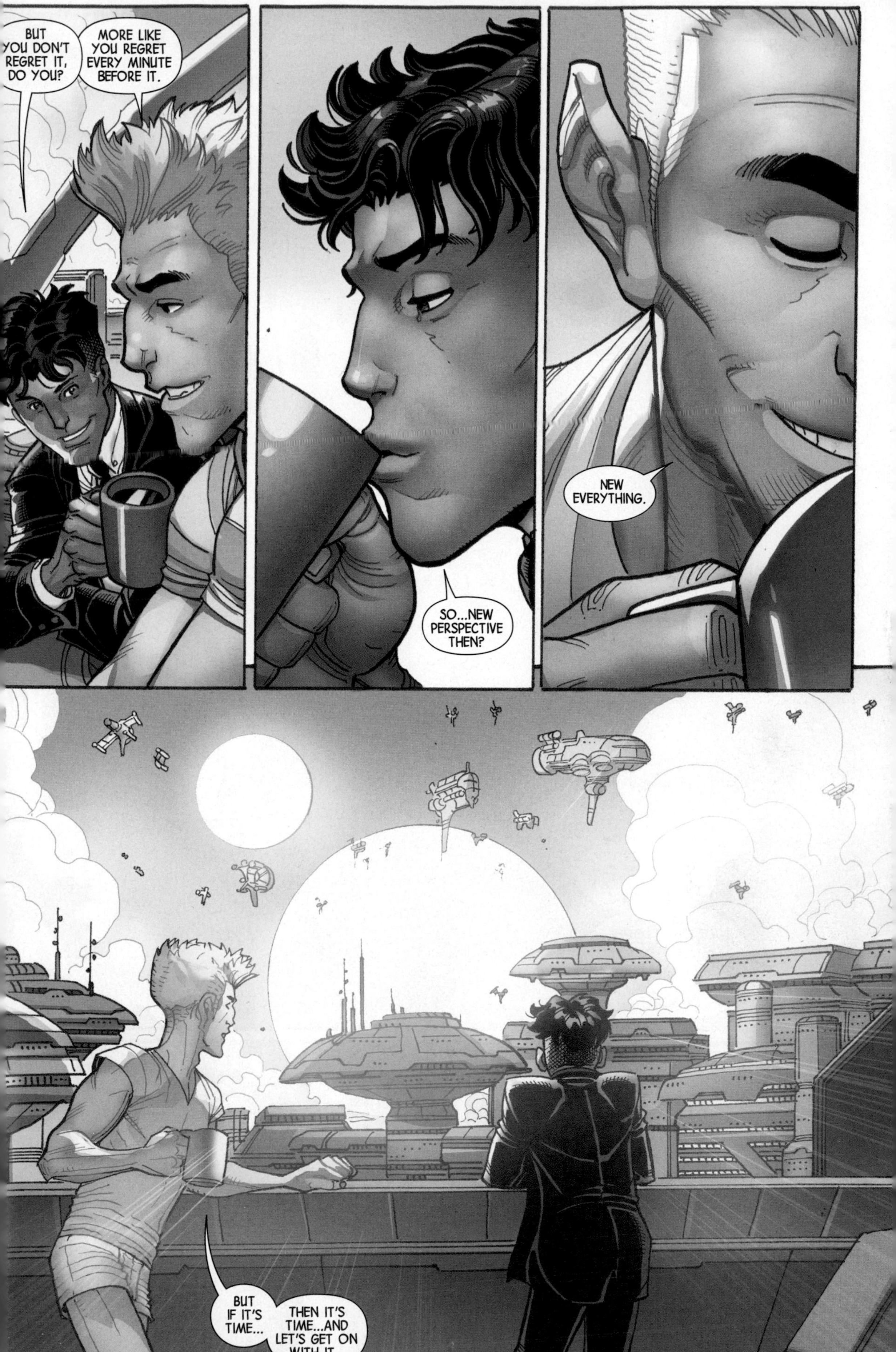
BUT YOU DON'T REGRET IT, DO YOU?
MORE LIKE YOU REGRET EVERY MINUTE BEFORE IT.
SO...NEW PERSPECTIVE THEN?
NEW EVERYTHING.
BUT IF IT'S TIME...
THEN IT'S TIME...AND LET'S GET ON WITH IT.

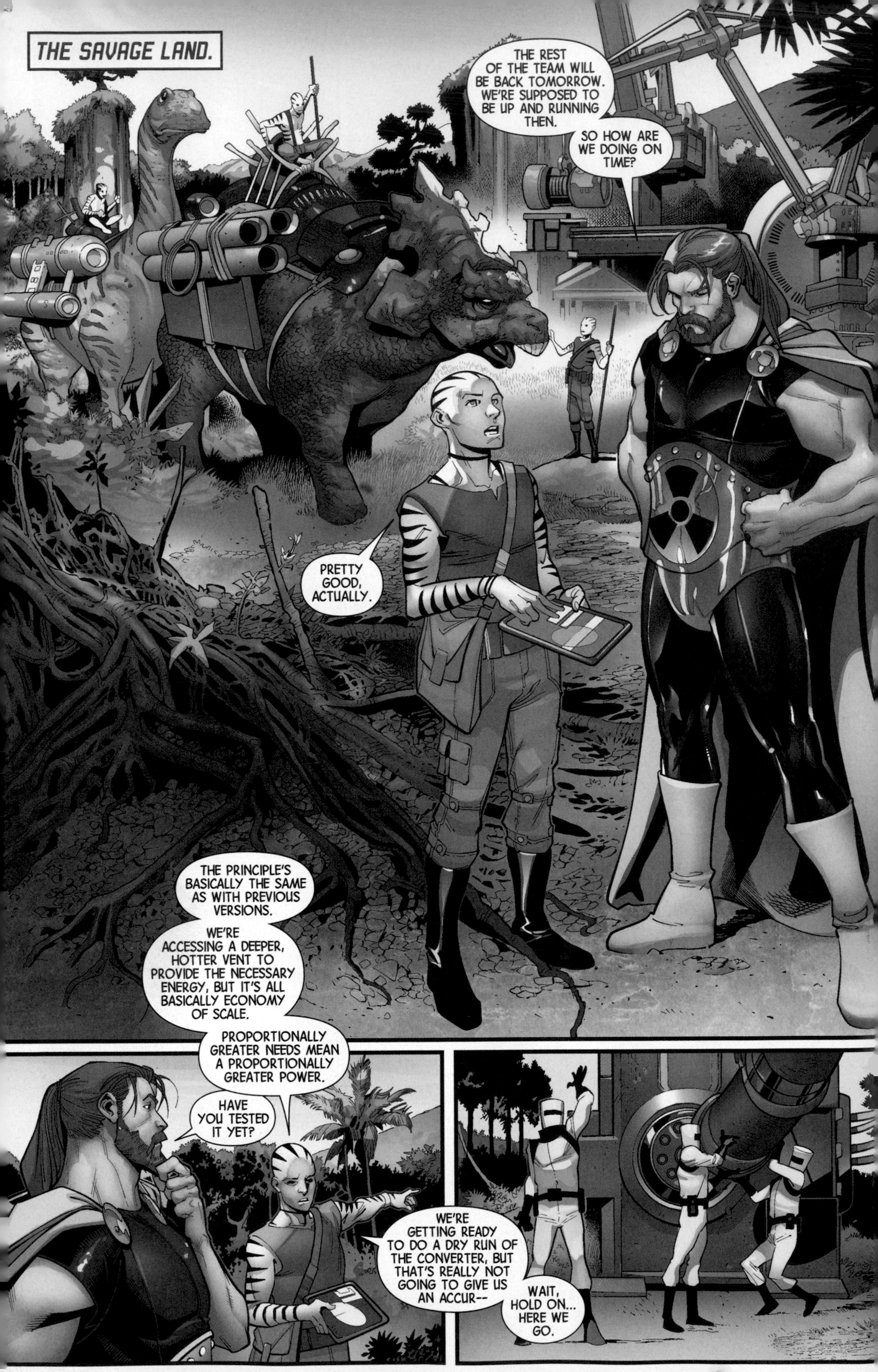
THE SAVAGE LAND.
THE REST OF THE TEAM WILL BE BACK TOMORROW. WE'RE SUPPOSED TO BE UP AND RUNNING THEN.
SO HOW ARE WE DOING ON TIME?
PRETTY GOOD, ACTUALLY.
THE PRINCIPLE'S BASICALLY THE SAME AS WITH PREVIOUS VERSIONS.
WE'RE ACCESSING A DEEPER, HOTTER VENT TO PROVIDE THE NECESSARY ENERGY, BUT IT'S ALL BASICALLY ECONOMY OF SCALE.
PROPORTIONALLY GREATER NEEDS MEAN A PROPORTIONALLY GREATER POWER.
HAVE YOU TESTED IT YET?
WE'RE GETTING READY TO DO A DRY RUN OF THE CONVERTER, BUT THAT'S REALLY NOT GOING TO GIVE US AN ACCUR--
WAIT, HOLD ON... HERE WE GO.

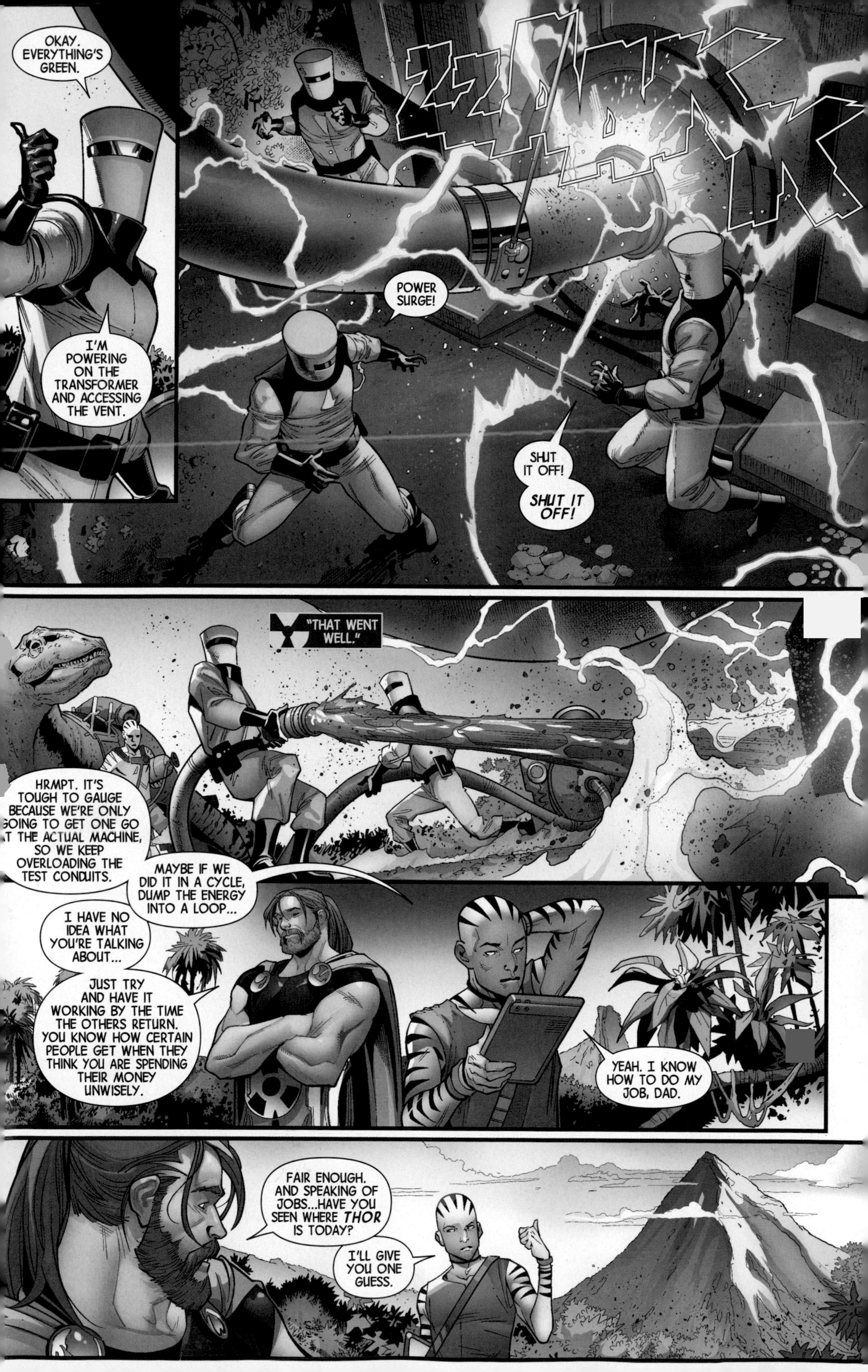
OKAY. EVERYTHING'S GREEN.
I'M POWERING ON THE TRANSFORMER AND ACCESSING THE VENT.
POWER SURGE!
SHUT IT OFF!
SHUT IT OFF!
"THAT WENT WELL."
HRMPT. IT'S TOUGH TO GAUGE BECAUSE WE'RE ONLY GOING TO GET ONE GO AT THE ACTUAL MACHINE, SO WE KEEP OVERLOADING THE TEST CONDUITS.
MAYBE IF WE DID IT IN A CYCLE, DUMP THE ENERGY INTO A LOOP...
I HAVE NO IDEA WHAT YOU'RE TALKING ABOUT...
JUST TRY AND HAVE IT WORKING BY THE TIME THE OTHERS RETURN. YOU KNOW HOW CERTAIN PEOPLE GET WHEN THEY THINK YOU ARE SPENDING THEIR MONEY UNWISELY.
YEAH. I KNOW HOW TO DO MY JOB, DAD.
FAIR ENOUGH. AND SPEAKING OF JOBS...HAVE YOU SEEN WHERE THOR IS TODAY?
I'LL GIVE YOU ONE GUESS.

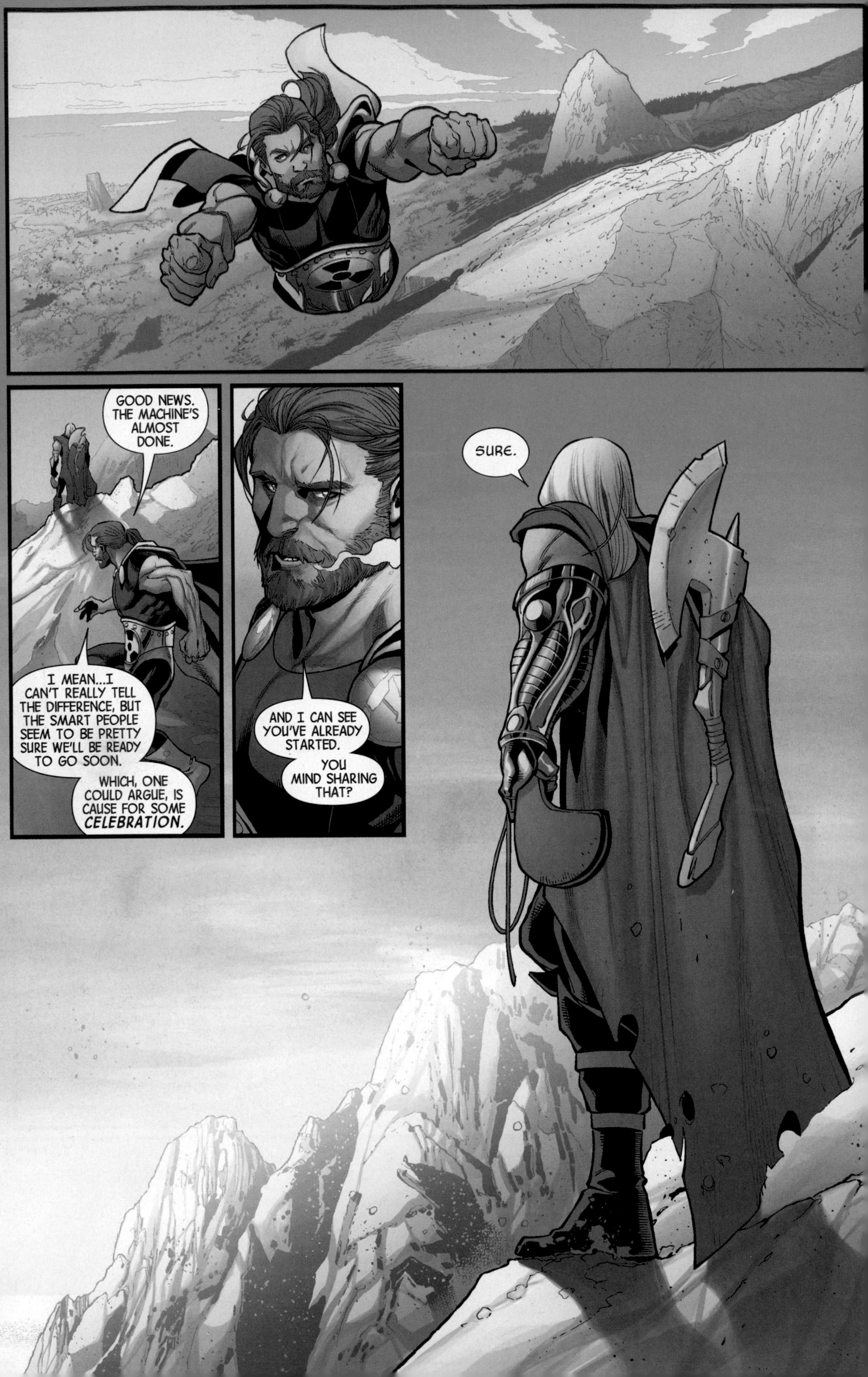
GOOD NEWS. THE MACHINE'S ALMOST DONE.
I MEAN...I CAN'T REALLY TELL THE DIFFERENCE, BUT THE SMART PEOPLE SEEM TO BE PRETTY SURE WE'LL BE READY TO GO SOON.
WHICH, ONE COULD ARGUE, IS CAUSE FOR SOME *CELEBRATION*.
AND I CAN SEE YOU'VE ALREADY STARTED.
YOU MIND SHARING THAT?
SURE.

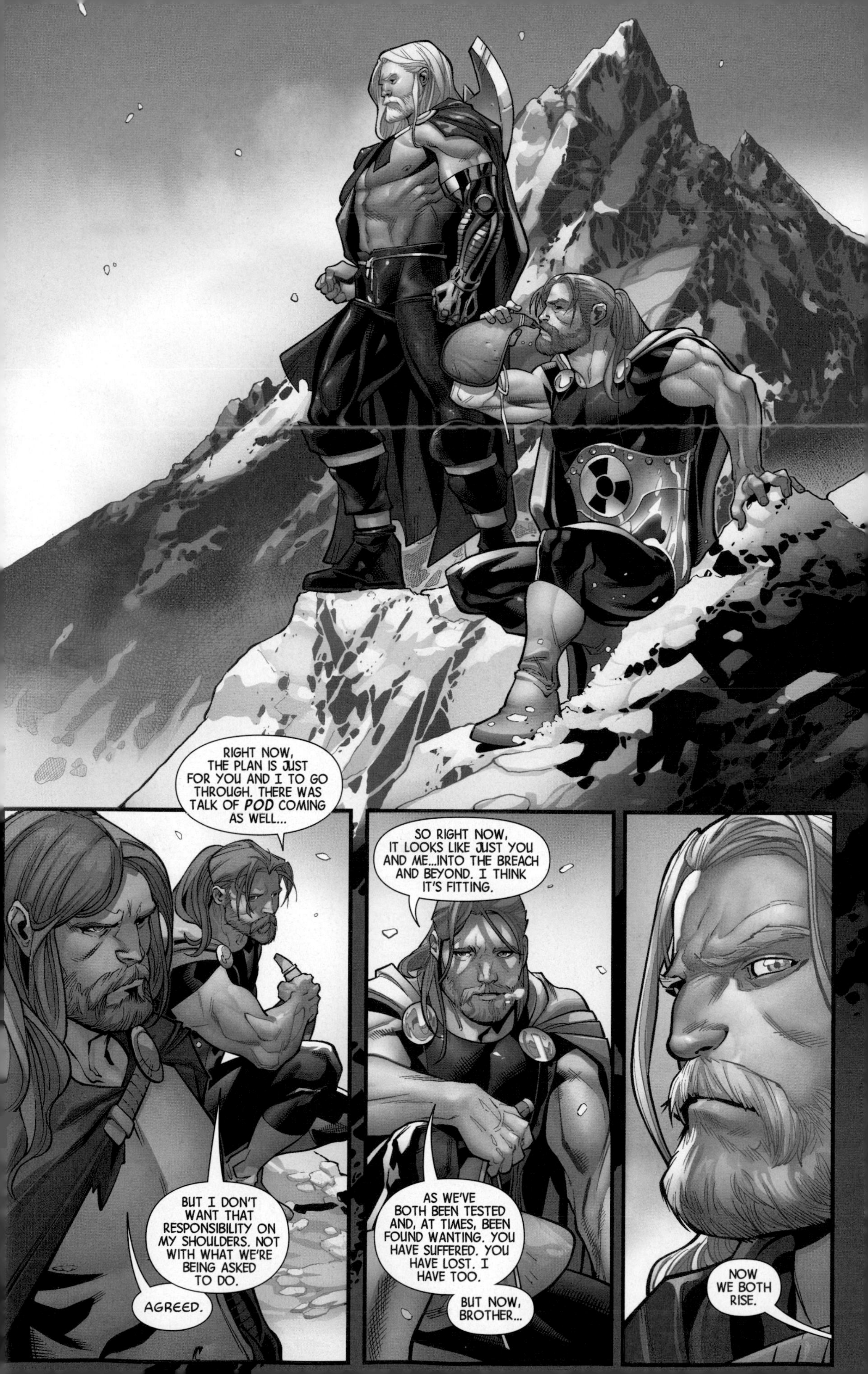
RIGHT NOW, THE PLAN IS JUST FOR YOU AND I TO GO THROUGH. THERE WAS TALK OF *POD* COMING AS WELL...
BUT I DON'T WANT THAT RESPONSIBILITY ON MY SHOULDERS. NOT WITH WHAT WE'RE BEING ASKED TO DO.
AGREED.
SO RIGHT NOW, IT LOOKS LIKE JUST YOU AND ME...INTO THE BREACH AND BEYOND. I THINK IT'S FITTING.
AS WE'VE BOTH BEEN TESTED AND, AT TIMES, BEEN FOUND WANTING. YOU HAVE SUFFERED. YOU HAVE LOST. I HAVE TOO.
BUT NOW, BROTHER...
NOW WE BOTH RISE.

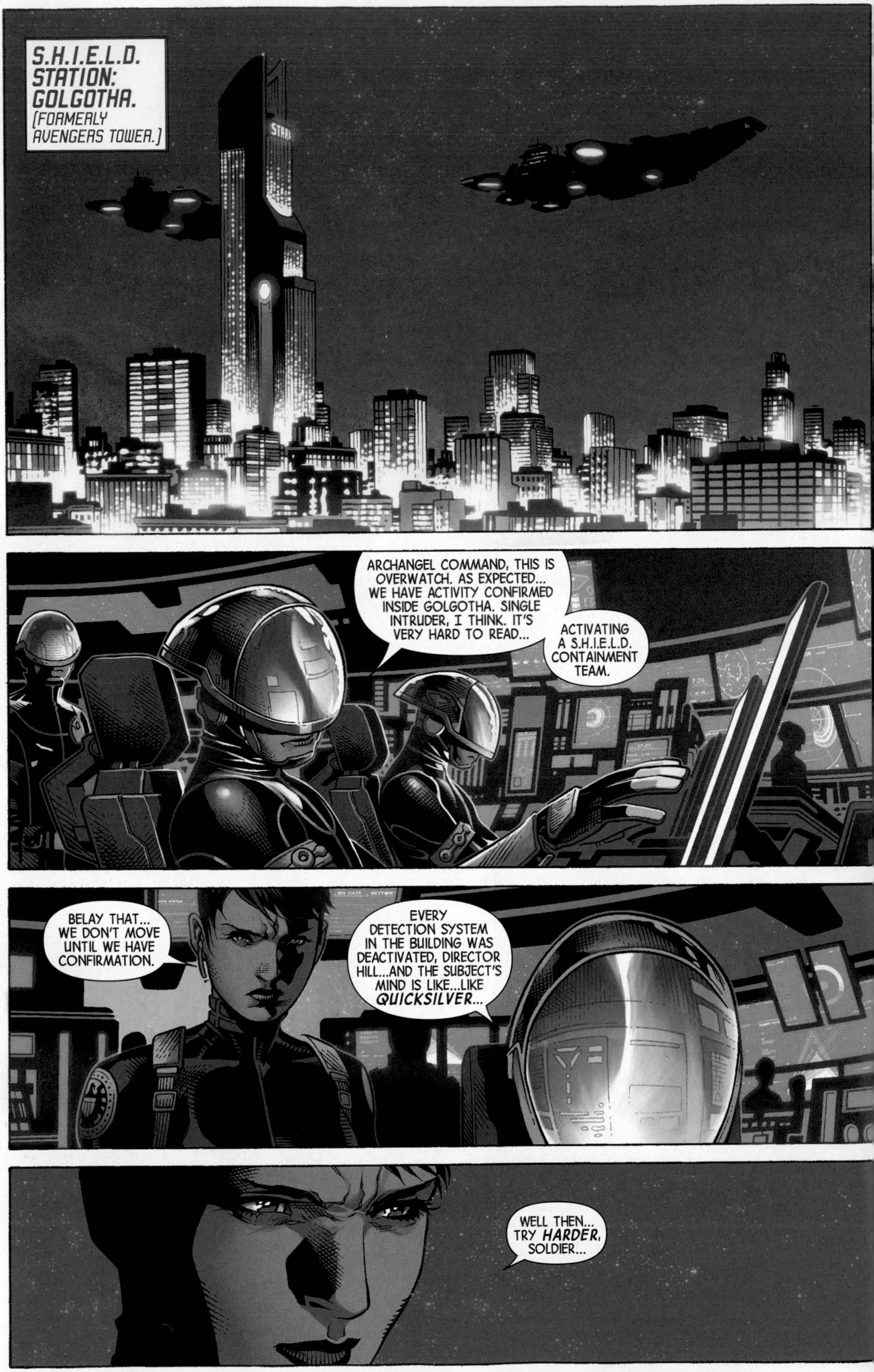
S.H.I.E.L.D. STATION: GOLGOTHA.
[FORMERLY AVENGERS TOWER.]
ARCHANGEL COMMAND, THIS IS OVERWATCH. AS EXPECTED... WE HAVE ACTIVITY CONFIRMED INSIDE GOLGOTHA. SINGLE INTRUDER, I THINK. IT'S VERY HARD TO READ...
ACTIVATING A S.H.I.E.L.D. CONTAINMENT TEAM.
BELAY THAT... WE DON'T MOVE UNTIL WE HAVE CONFIRMATION.
EVERY DETECTION SYSTEM IN THE BUILDING WAS DEACTIVATED, DIRECTOR HILL...AND THE SUBJECT'S MIND IS LIKE...LIKE QUICKSILVER...
WELL THEN... TRY HARDER, SOLDIER...

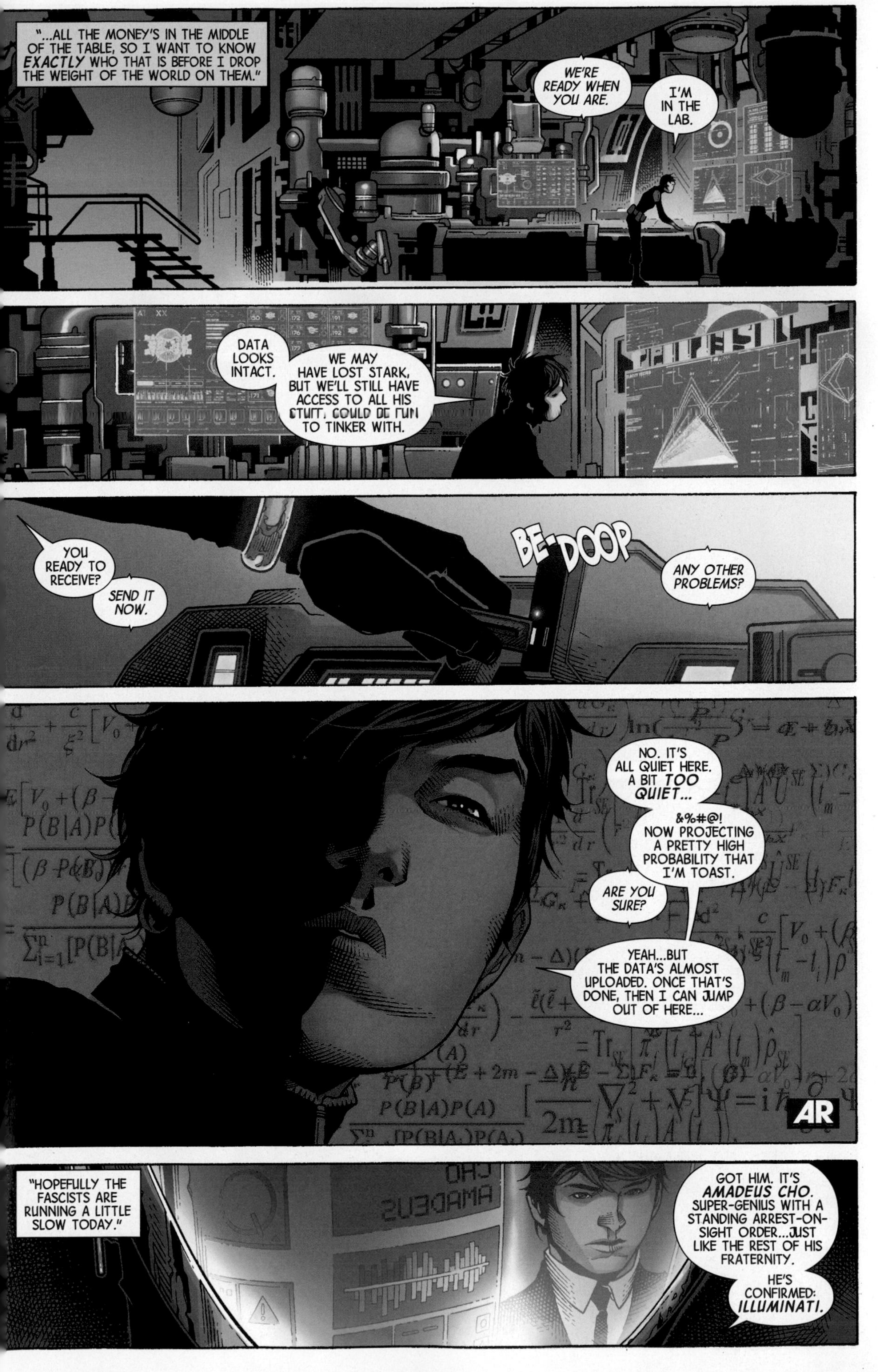
"...ALL THE MONEY'S IN THE MIDDLE OF THE TABLE, SO I WANT TO KNOW EXACTLY WHO THAT IS BEFORE I DROP THE WEIGHT OF THE WORLD ON THEM."
WE'RE READY WHEN YOU ARE.
I'M IN THE LAB.
DATA LOOKS INTACT.
WE MAY HAVE LOST STARK, BUT WE'LL STILL HAVE ACCESS TO ALL HIS STUFF. COULD BE FUN TO TINKER WITH.
YOU READY TO RECEIVE?
SEND IT NOW.
BE-DOOP
ANY OTHER PROBLEMS?
NO. IT'S ALL QUIET HERE. A BIT TOO QUIET...
&%#@! NOW PROJECTING A PRETTY HIGH PROBABILITY THAT I'M TOAST.
ARE YOU SURE?
YEAH...BUT THE DATA'S ALMOST UPLOADED. ONCE THAT'S DONE, THEN I CAN JUMP OUT OF HERE...
AR
"HOPEFULLY THE FASCISTS ARE RUNNING A LITTLE SLOW TODAY."
AMADEUS CHO
GOT HIM. IT'S AMADEUS CHO. SUPER-GENIUS WITH A STANDING ARREST-ON-SIGHT ORDER...JUST LIKE THE REST OF HIS FRATERNITY.
HE'S CONFIRMED: ILLUMINATI.

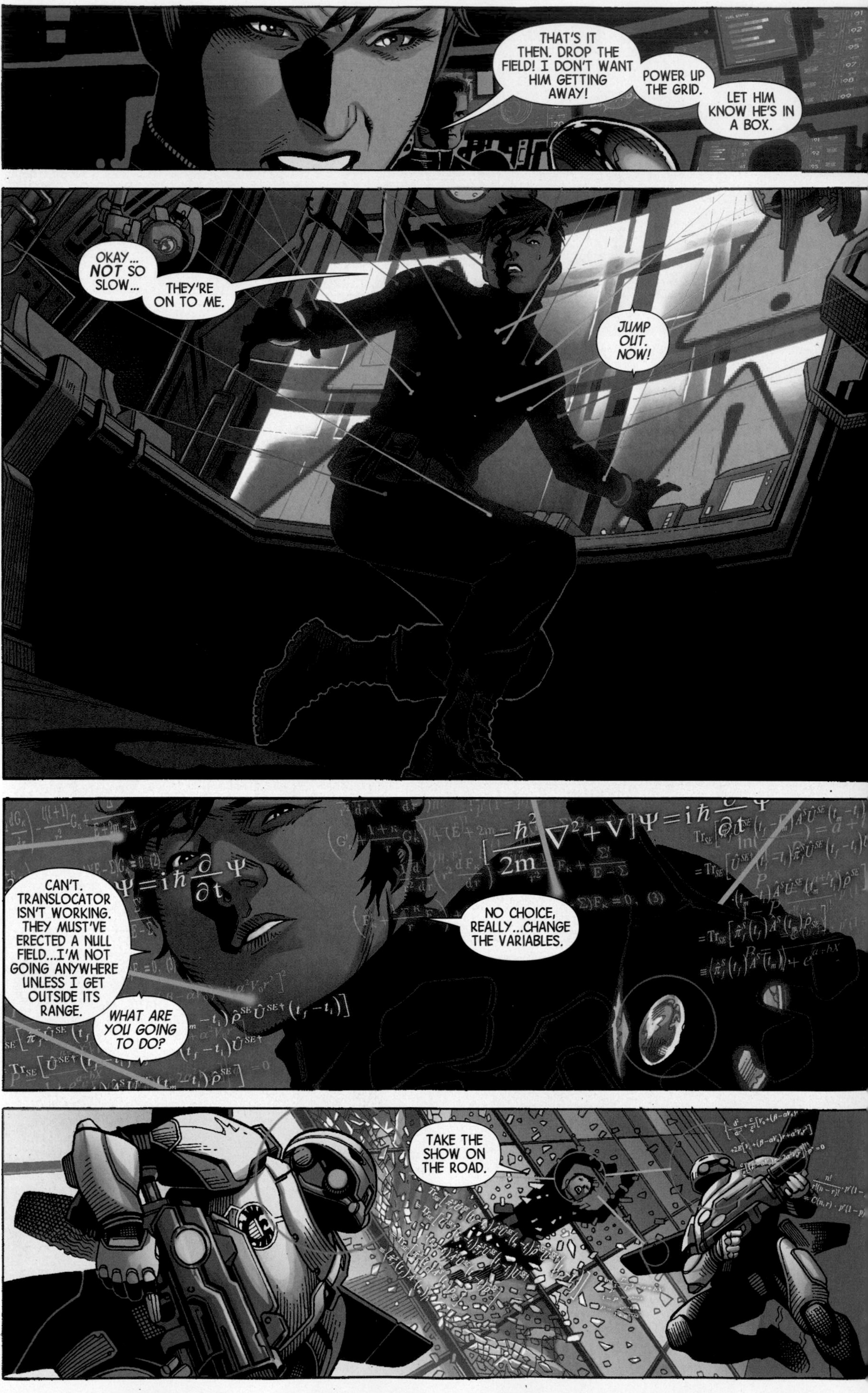

THAT'S IT THEN. DROP THE FIELD! I DON'T WANT HIM GETTING AWAY!
POWER UP THE GRID.
LET HIM KNOW HE'S IN A BOX.
OKAY... NOT SO SLOW...
THEY'RE ON TO ME.
JUMP OUT. NOW!
CAN'T. TRANSLOCATOR ISN'T WORKING. THEY MUST'VE ERECTED A NULL FIELD...I'M NOT GOING ANYWHERE UNLESS I GET OUTSIDE ITS RANGE.
WHAT ARE YOU GOING TO DO?
NO CHOICE, REALLY...CHANGE THE VARIABLES.
TAKE THE SHOW ON THE ROAD.

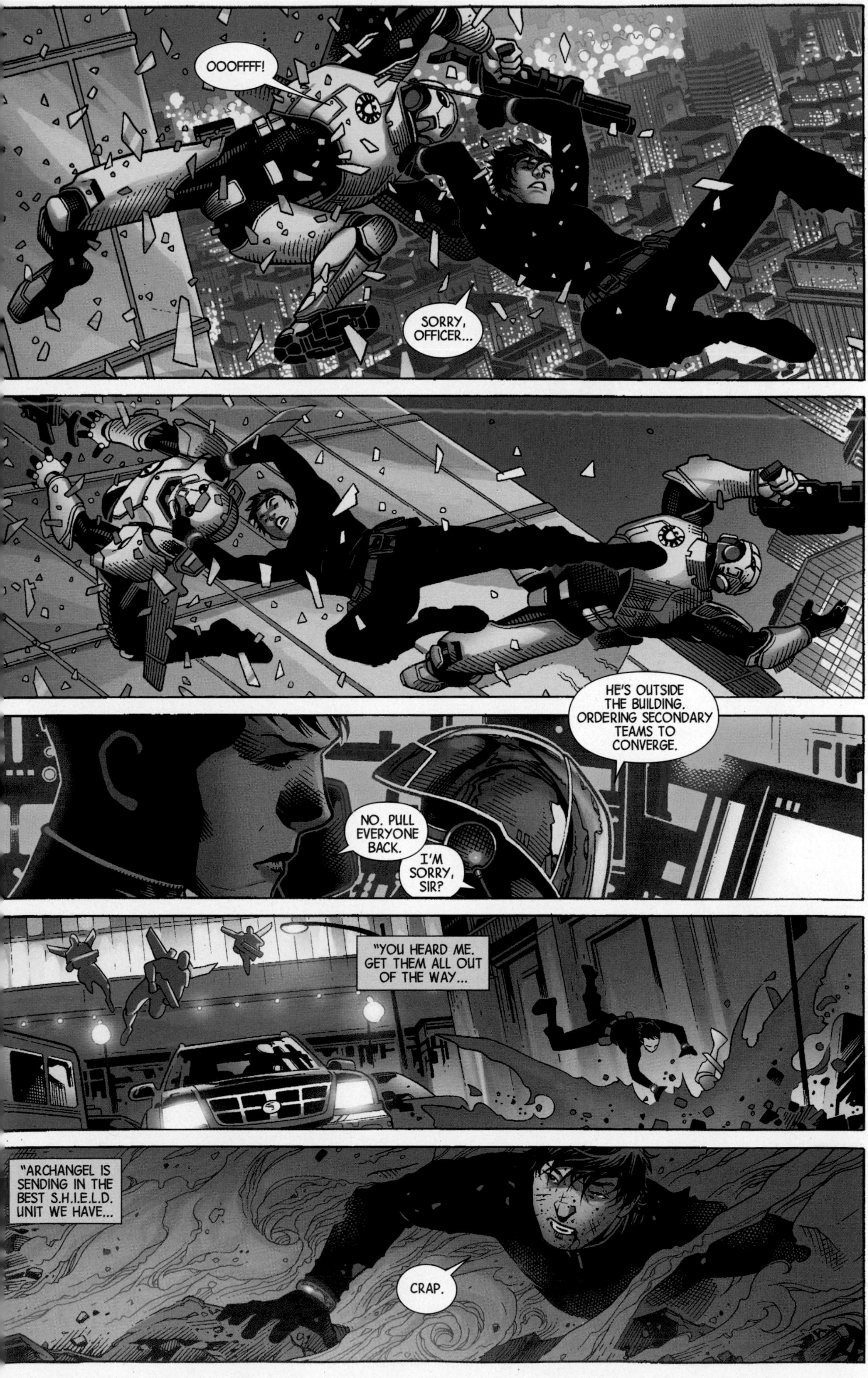
OOOFFFF!
SORRY, OFFICER...
HE'S OUTSIDE THE BUILDING. ORDERING SECONDARY TEAMS TO CONVERGE.
NO. PULL EVERYONE BACK.
I'M SORRY, SIR?
"YOU HEARD ME. GET THEM ALL OUT OF THE WAY...
"ARCHANGEL IS SENDING IN THE BEST S.H.I.E.L.D. UNIT WE HAVE...
CRAP.

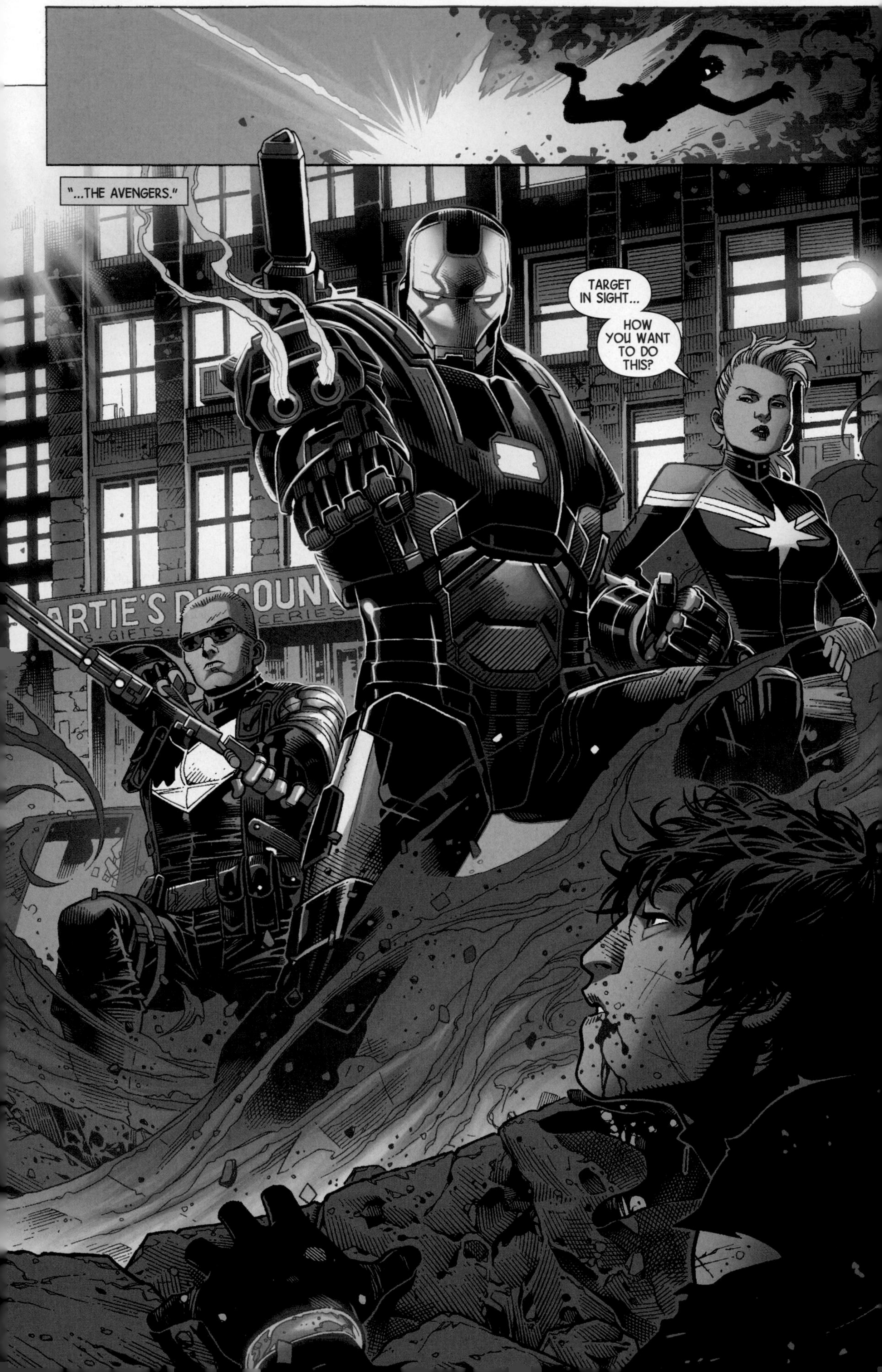
"...THE AVENGERS."
TARGET IN SIGHT...
HOW YOU WANT TO DO THIS?
ARTIE'S DISCOUNT
GIFTS
CERIES

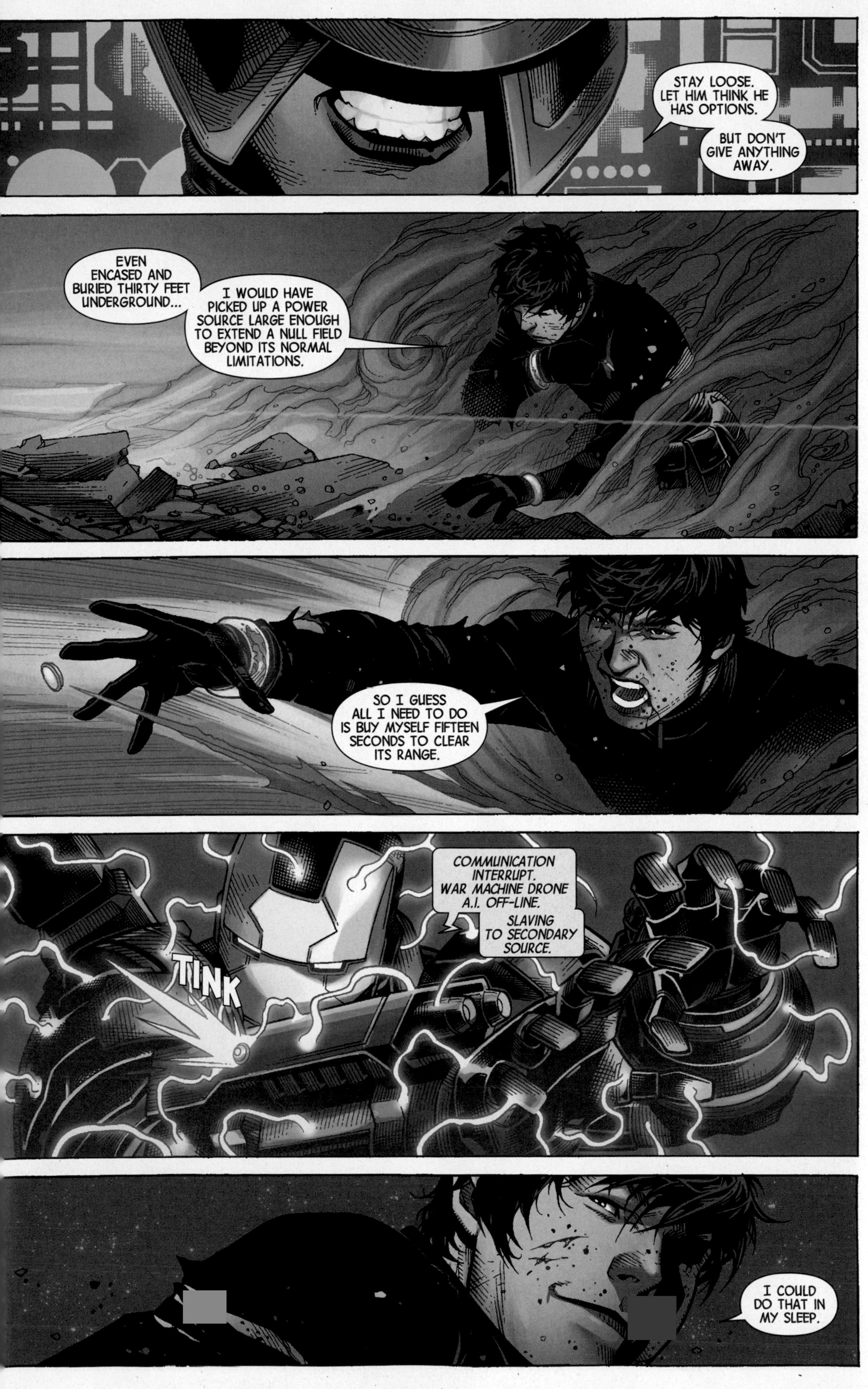
STAY LOOSE. LET HIM THINK HE HAS OPTIONS.
BUT DON'T GIVE ANYTHING AWAY.
EVEN ENCASED AND BURIED THIRTY FEET UNDERGROUND...
I WOULD HAVE PICKED UP A POWER SOURCE LARGE ENOUGH TO EXTEND A NULL FIELD BEYOND ITS NORMAL LIMITATIONS.
SO I GUESS ALL I NEED TO DO IS BUY MYSELF FIFTEEN SECONDS TO CLEAR ITS RANGE.
TINK
COMMUNICATION INTERRUPT. WAR MACHINE DRONE A.I. OFF-LINE.
SLAVING TO SECONDARY SOURCE.
I COULD DO THAT IN MY SLEEP.

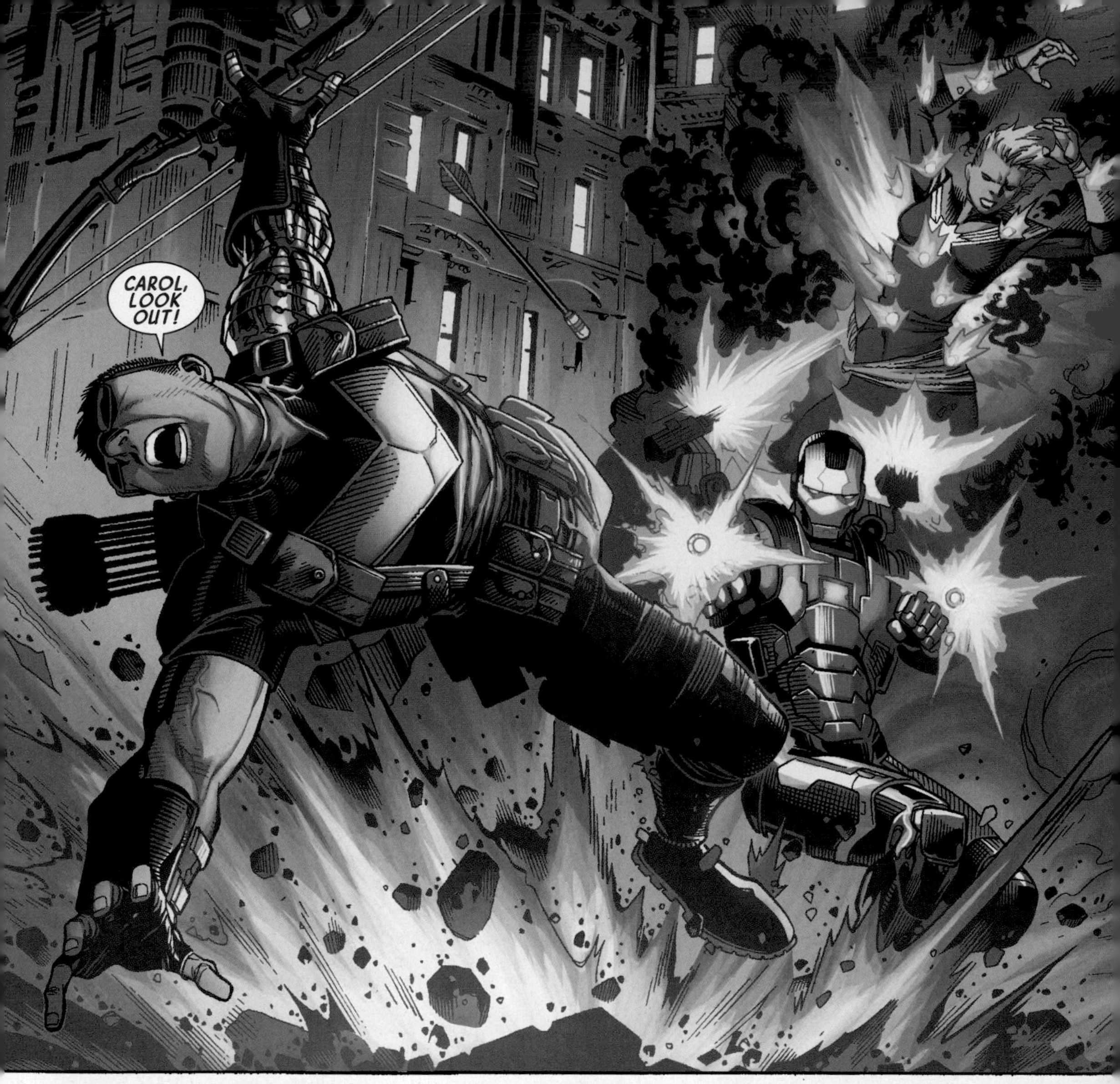
CAROL, LOOK OUT!

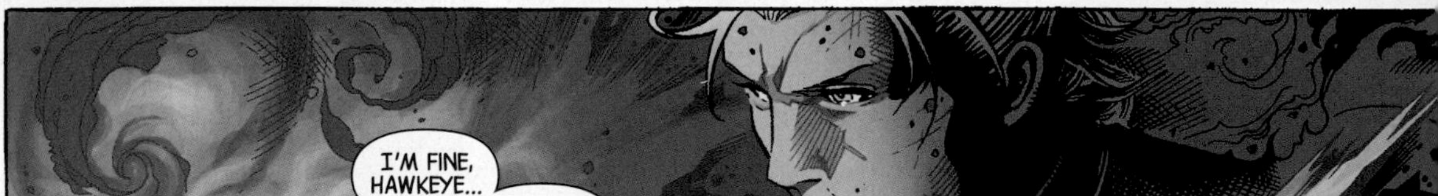
I'M FINE, HAWKEYE...
JUST RUNNING A LITTLE HOT.

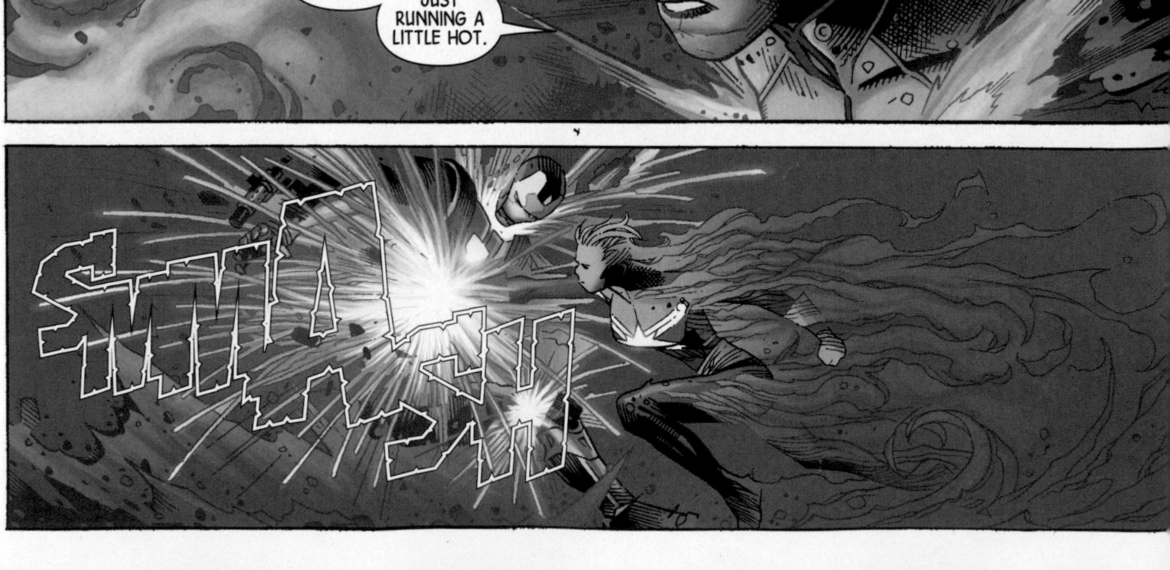

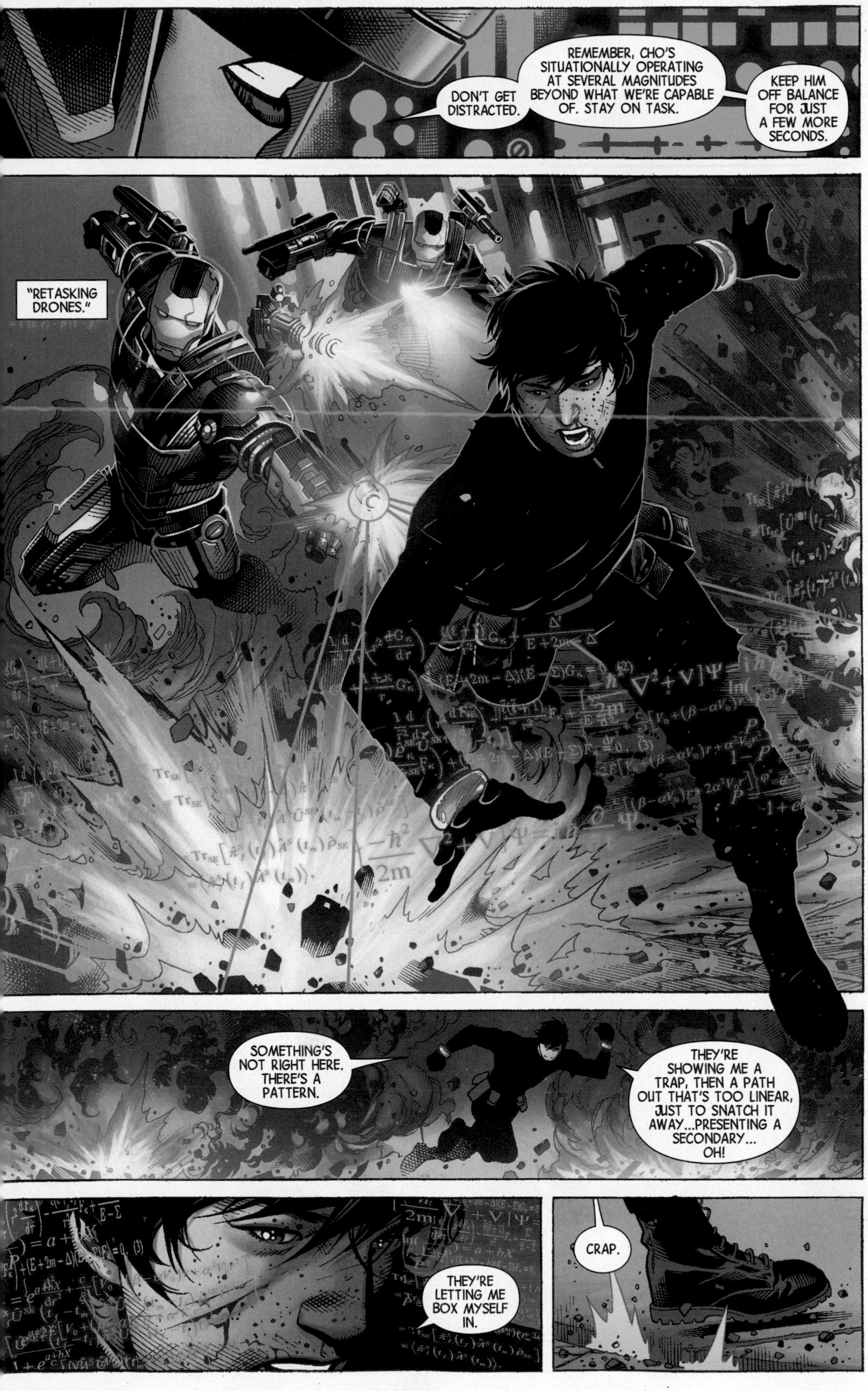
DON'T GET DISTRACTED.
REMEMBER, CHO'S SITUATIONALLY OPERATING AT SEVERAL MAGNITUDES BEYOND WHAT WE'RE CAPABLE OF. STAY ON TASK.
KEEP HIM OFF BALANCE FOR JUST A FEW MORE SECONDS.
"RETASKING DRONES."
SOMETHING'S NOT RIGHT HERE. THERE'S A PATTERN.
THEY'RE SHOWING ME A TRAP, THEN A PATH OUT THAT'S TOO LINEAR, JUST TO SNATCH IT AWAY...PRESENTING A SECONDARY... OH!
THEY'RE LETTING ME BOX MYSELF IN.
CRAP.

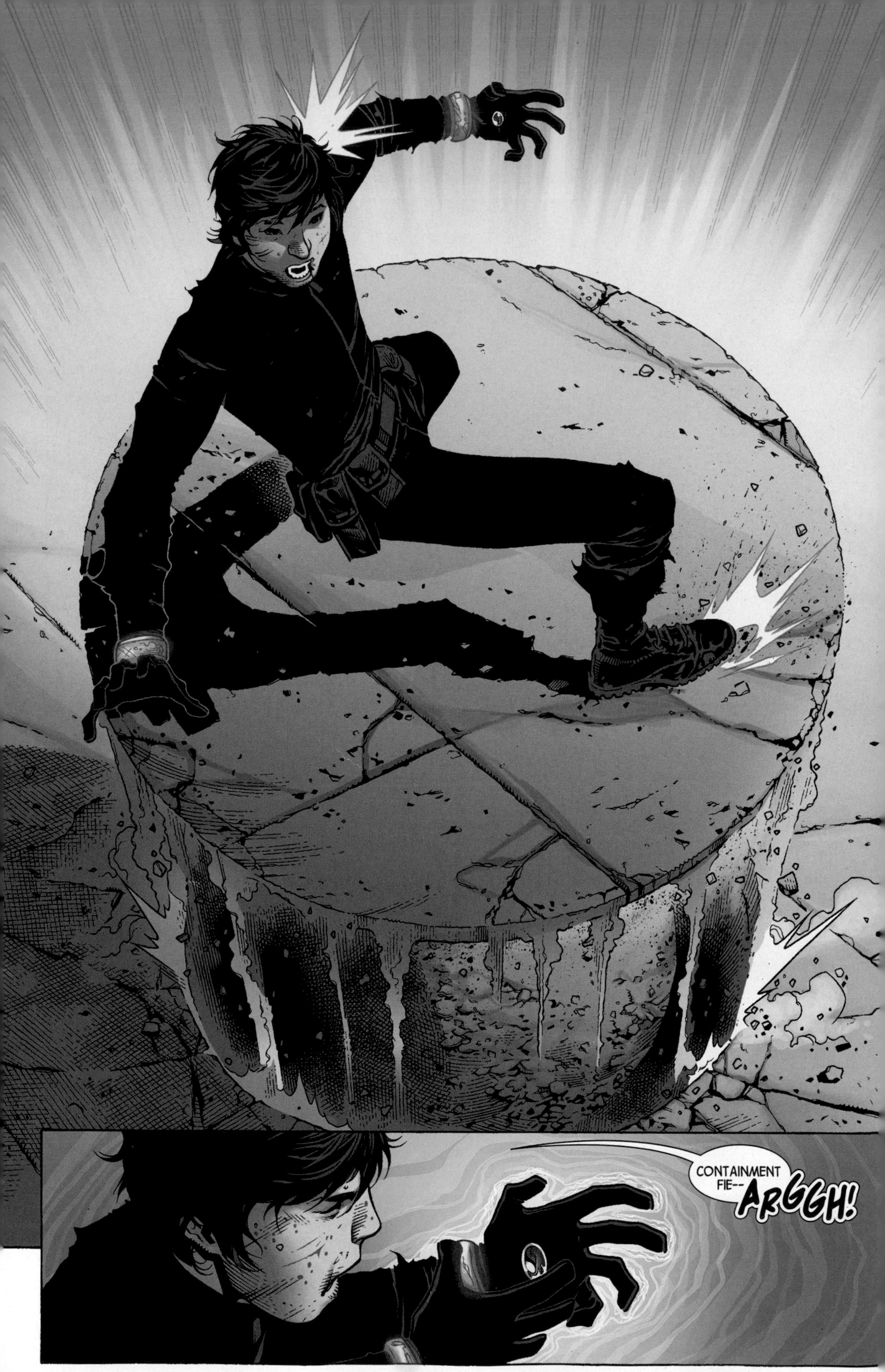
CONTAINMENT FIE--
ARGGH!

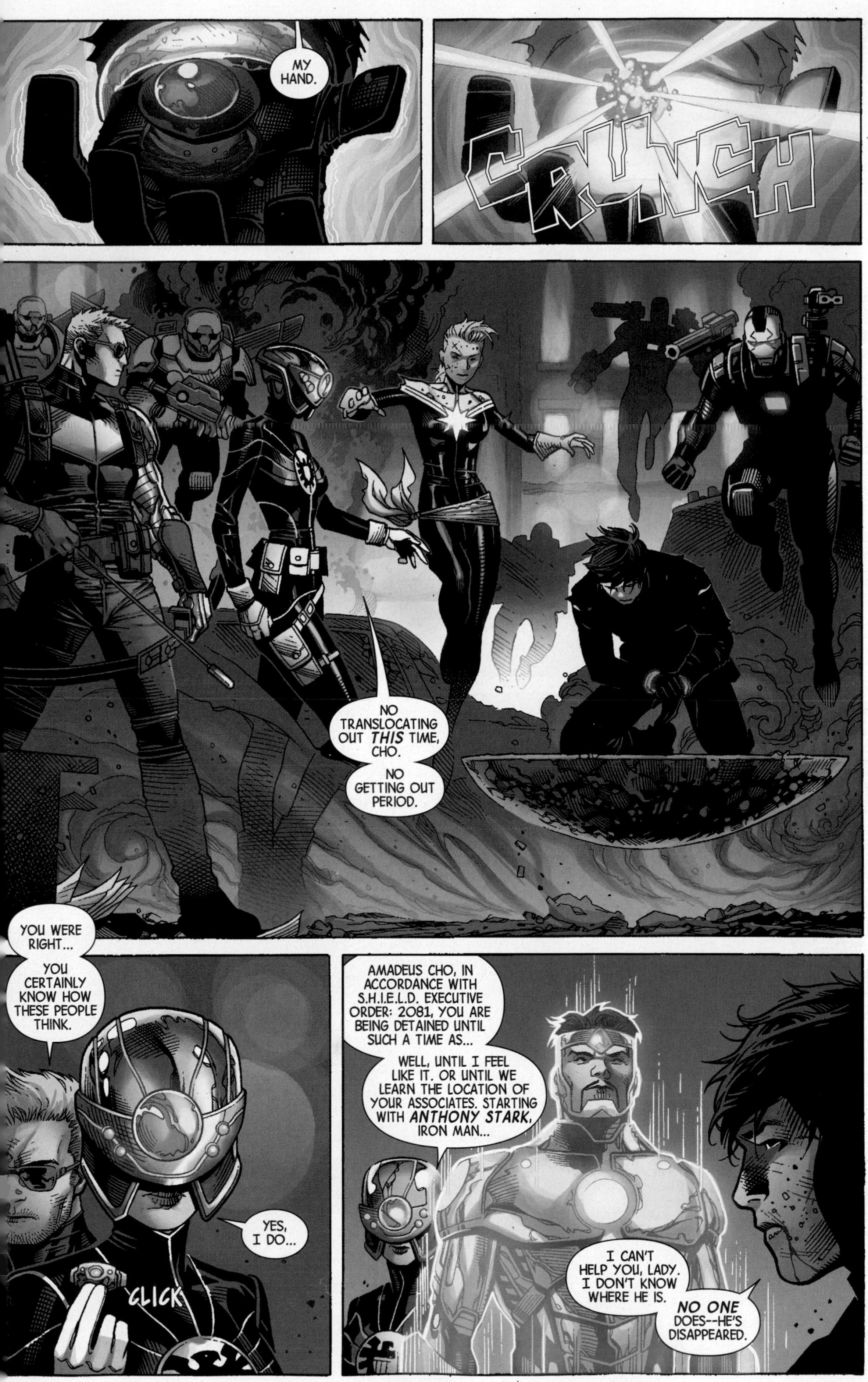
MY HAND.
CRUNCH
NO TRANSLOCATING OUT THIS TIME, CHO.
NO GETTING OUT PERIOD.
YOU WERE RIGHT...
YOU CERTAINLY KNOW HOW THESE PEOPLE THINK.
YES, I DO...
CLICK
AMADEUS CHO, IN ACCORDANCE WITH S.H.I.E.L.D. EXECUTIVE ORDER: 2081, YOU ARE BEING DETAINED UNTIL SUCH A TIME AS...
WELL, UNTIL I FEEL LIKE IT. OR UNTIL WE LEARN THE LOCATION OF YOUR ASSOCIATES. STARTING WITH ANTHONY STARK, IRON MAN...
I CAN'T HELP YOU, LADY. I DON'T KNOW WHERE HE IS.
NO ONE DOES--HE'S DISAPPEARED.

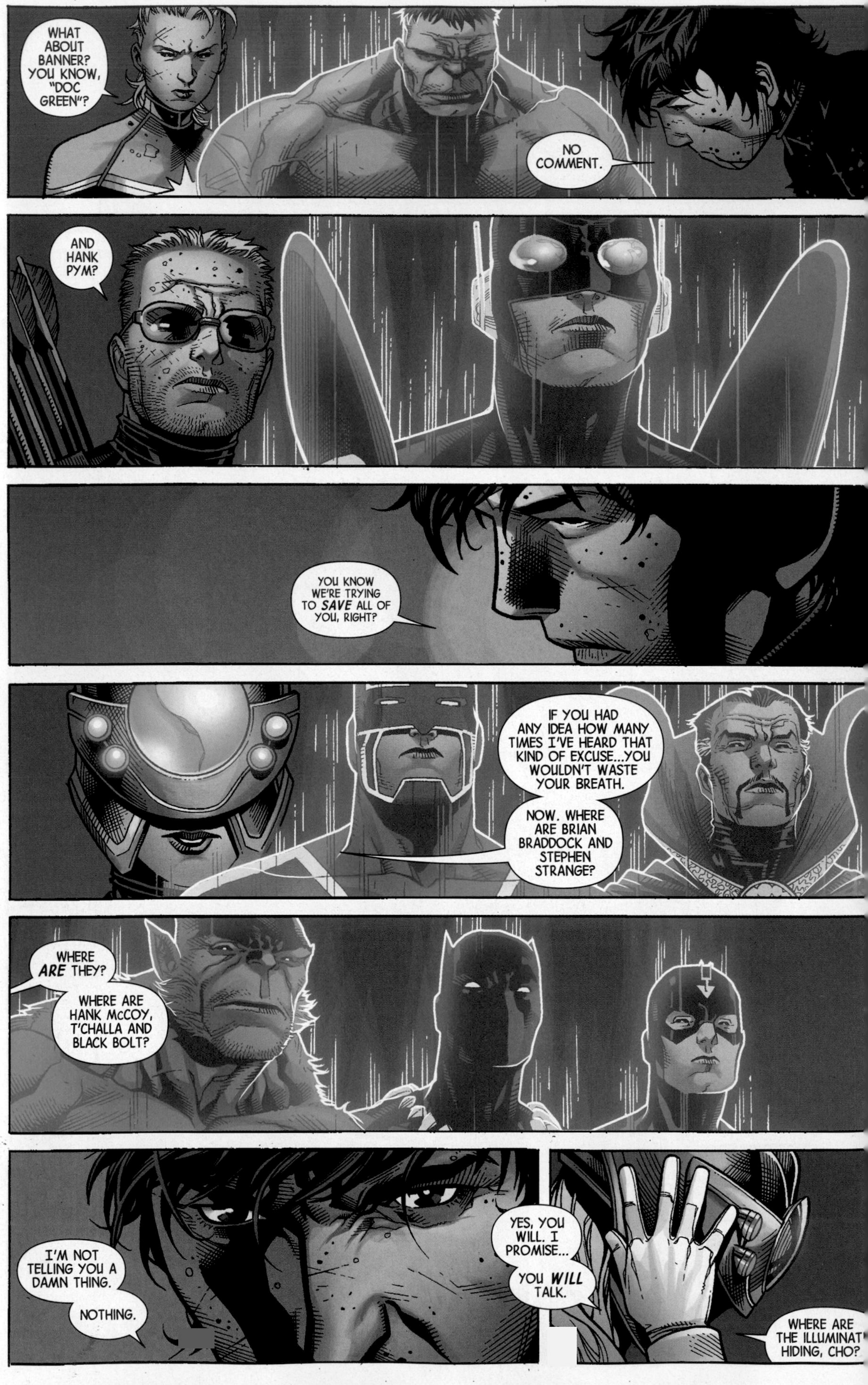
WHAT ABOUT BANNER? YOU KNOW, "DOC GREEN"?
NO COMMENT.
AND HANK PYM?
YOU KNOW WE'RE TRYING TO *SAVE* ALL OF YOU, RIGHT?
IF YOU HAD ANY IDEA HOW MANY TIMES I'VE HEARD THAT KIND OF EXCUSE...YOU WOULDN'T WASTE YOUR BREATH.
NOW. WHERE ARE BRIAN BRADDOCK AND STEPHEN STRANGE?
WHERE *ARE* THEY?
WHERE ARE HANK McCOY, T'CHALLA AND BLACK BOLT?
I'M NOT TELLING YOU A DAMN THING.
NOTHING.
YES, YOU WILL. I PROMISE...
YOU *WILL* TALK.
WHERE ARE THE ILLUMINAT HIDING, CHO?

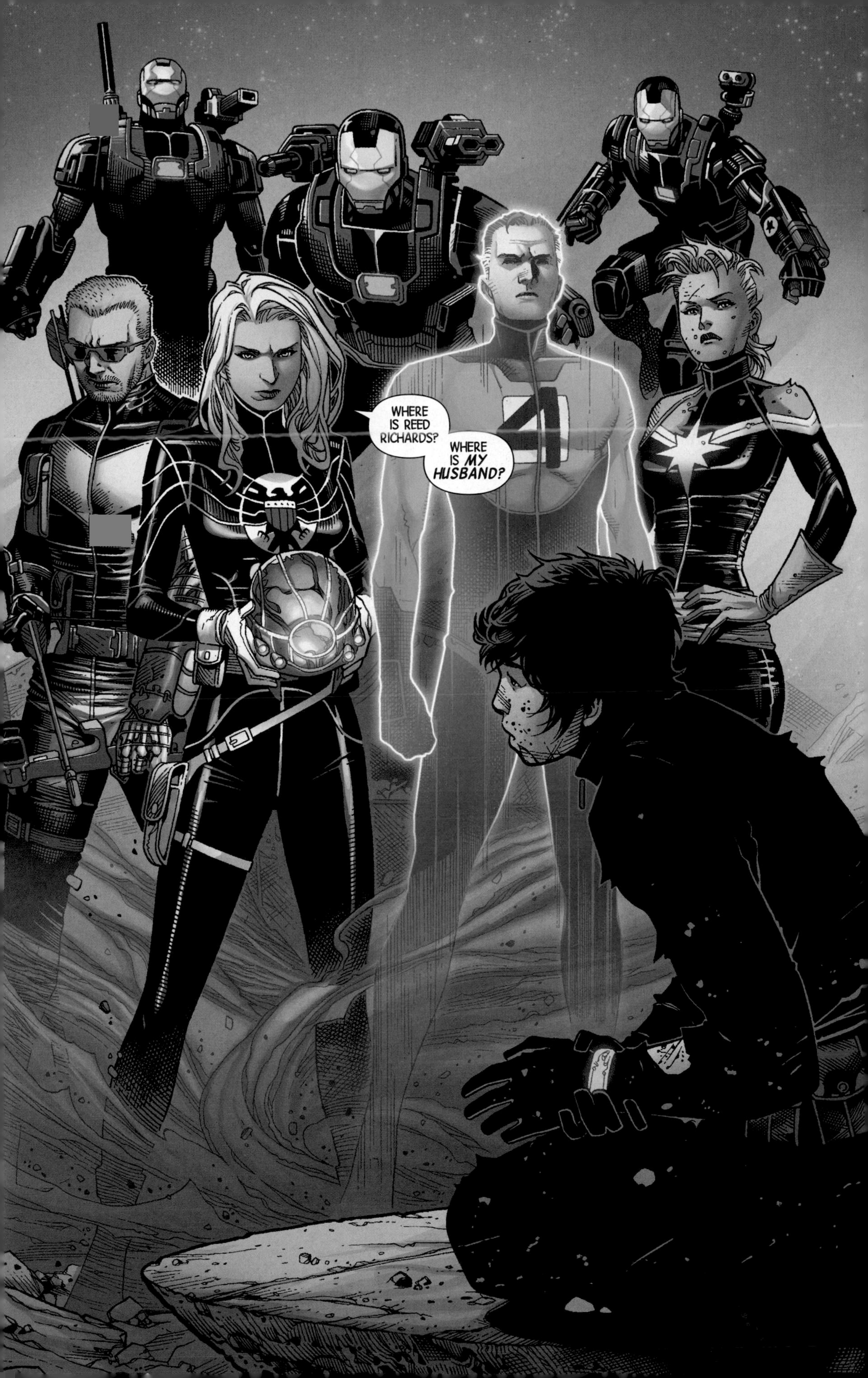
WHERE IS REED RICHARDS?
WHERE IS MY HUSBAND?

"THE CABAL"

THE ILLUMINATI

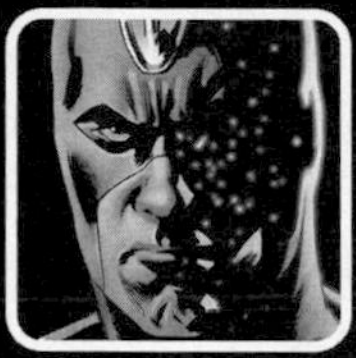

BLACK BOLT
Celestial Messiah

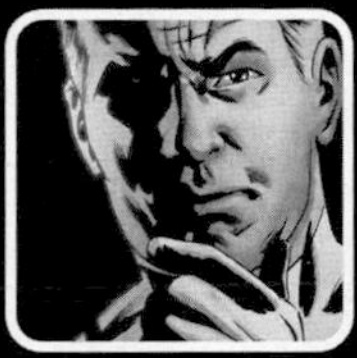

REED RICHARDS
Universal Builder

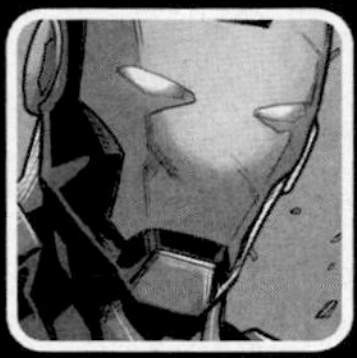

IRON MAN
Master of Machines

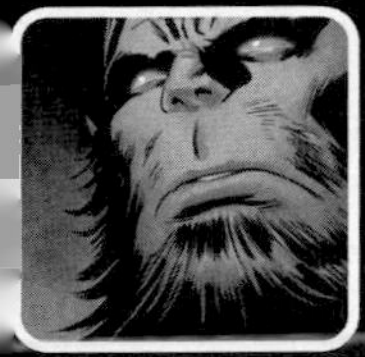

BEAST
Mutant Genius

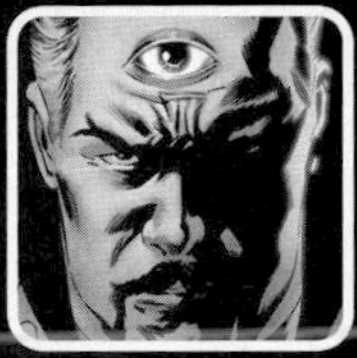

DOCTOR STRANGE
Sorcerer Supreme

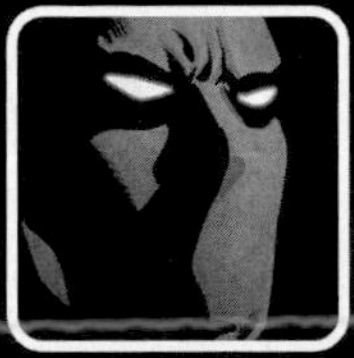

BLACK PANTHER
King of the Dead

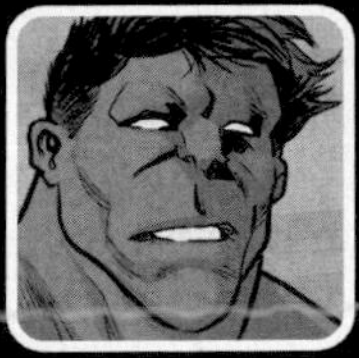

HULK
Strongest There Is

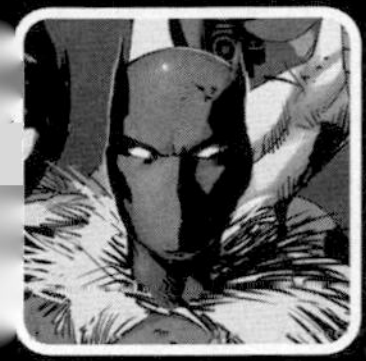

LACK PANTHER (SHURI)
Queen of Wakanda

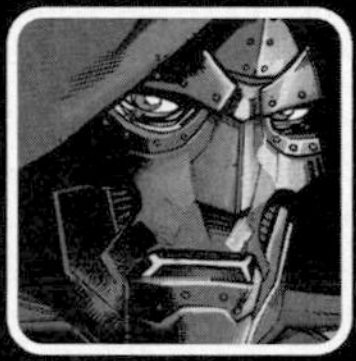

DR. DOOM
Ruler of Latveria

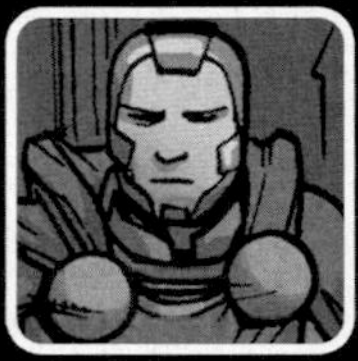

KRISTOFF VERNARD
Doom's Heir

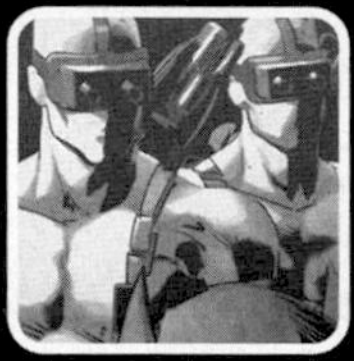

THE HATUT ZERAZE
Wakandan Strike Force

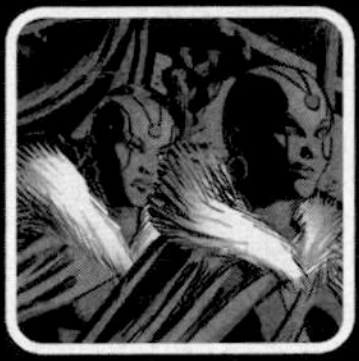

THE DORA MILAJE
Wakandan Royal Bodyguards

THE CABAL

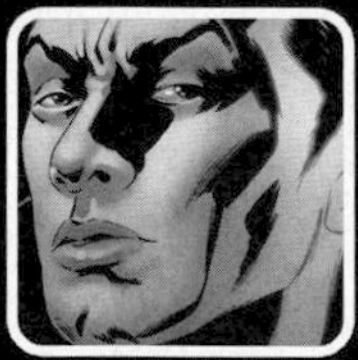

NAMOR
Imperius Rex

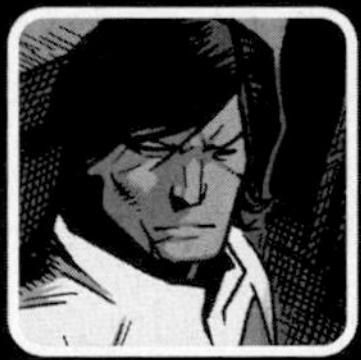

MAXIMUS
Inhuman Madman

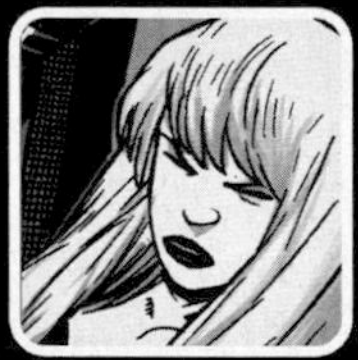

BLACK SWAN
Incursion Survivor

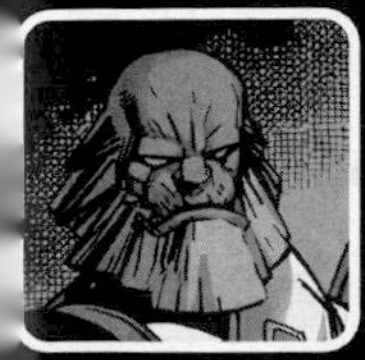

TERRAX
The Truly Enlightened

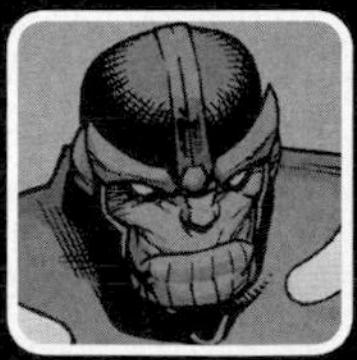

THANOS
The Mad Titan

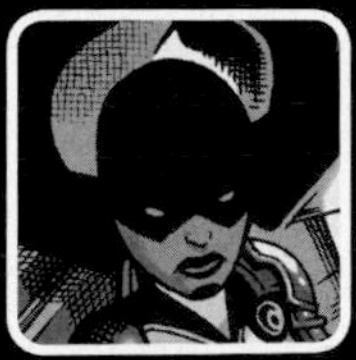

PROXIMA MIDNIGHT
Servant of Thanos

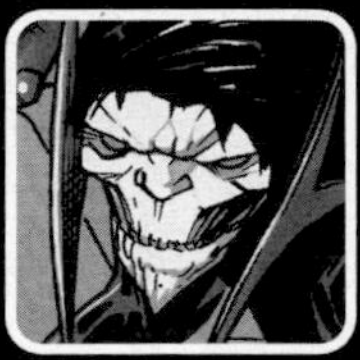

CORVUS GLAIVE
Destroyer of Worlds

PREVIOUSLY IN NEW AVENGERS

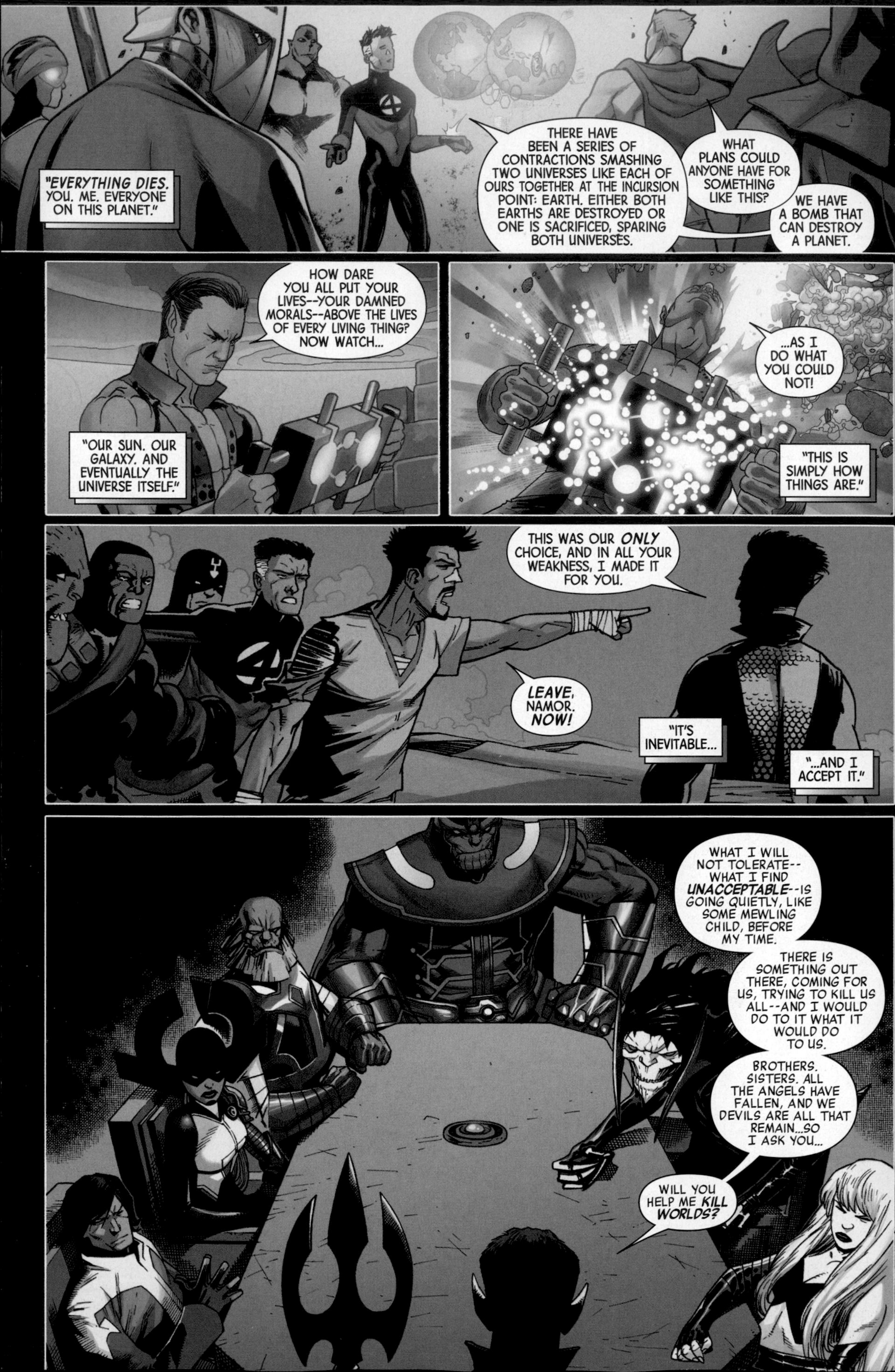

"EVERYTHING DIES. YOU. ME. EVERYONE ON THIS PLANET."
THERE HAVE BEEN A SERIES OF CONTRACTIONS SMASHING TWO UNIVERSES LIKE EACH OF OURS TOGETHER AT THE INCURSION POINT: EARTH. EITHER BOTH EARTHS ARE DESTROYED OR ONE IS SACRIFICED, SPARING BOTH UNIVERSES.
WHAT PLANS COULD ANYONE HAVE FOR SOMETHING LIKE THIS?
WE HAVE A BOMB THAT CAN DESTROY A PLANET.
HOW DARE YOU ALL PUT YOUR LIVES--YOUR DAMNED MORALS--ABOVE THE LIVES OF EVERY LIVING THING? NOW WATCH...
"OUR SUN. OUR GALAXY. AND EVENTUALLY THE UNIVERSE ITSELF."
...AS I DO WHAT YOU COULD NOT!
"THIS IS SIMPLY HOW THINGS ARE."
THIS WAS OUR ONLY CHOICE, AND IN ALL YOUR WEAKNESS, I MADE IT FOR YOU.
LEAVE, NAMOR. NOW!
"IT'S INEVITABLE...
"...AND I ACCEPT IT."
WHAT I WILL NOT TOLERATE--WHAT I FIND UNACCEPTABLE--IS GOING QUIETLY, LIKE SOME MEWLING CHILD, BEFORE MY TIME.
THERE IS SOMETHING OUT THERE, COMING FOR US, TRYING TO KILL US ALL--AND I WOULD DO TO IT WHAT IT WOULD DO TO US.
BROTHERS. SISTERS. ALL THE ANGELS HAVE FALLEN, AND WE DEVILS ARE ALL THAT REMAIN...SO I ASK YOU...
WILL YOU HELP ME KILL WORLDS?

EIGHT MONTHS LATER

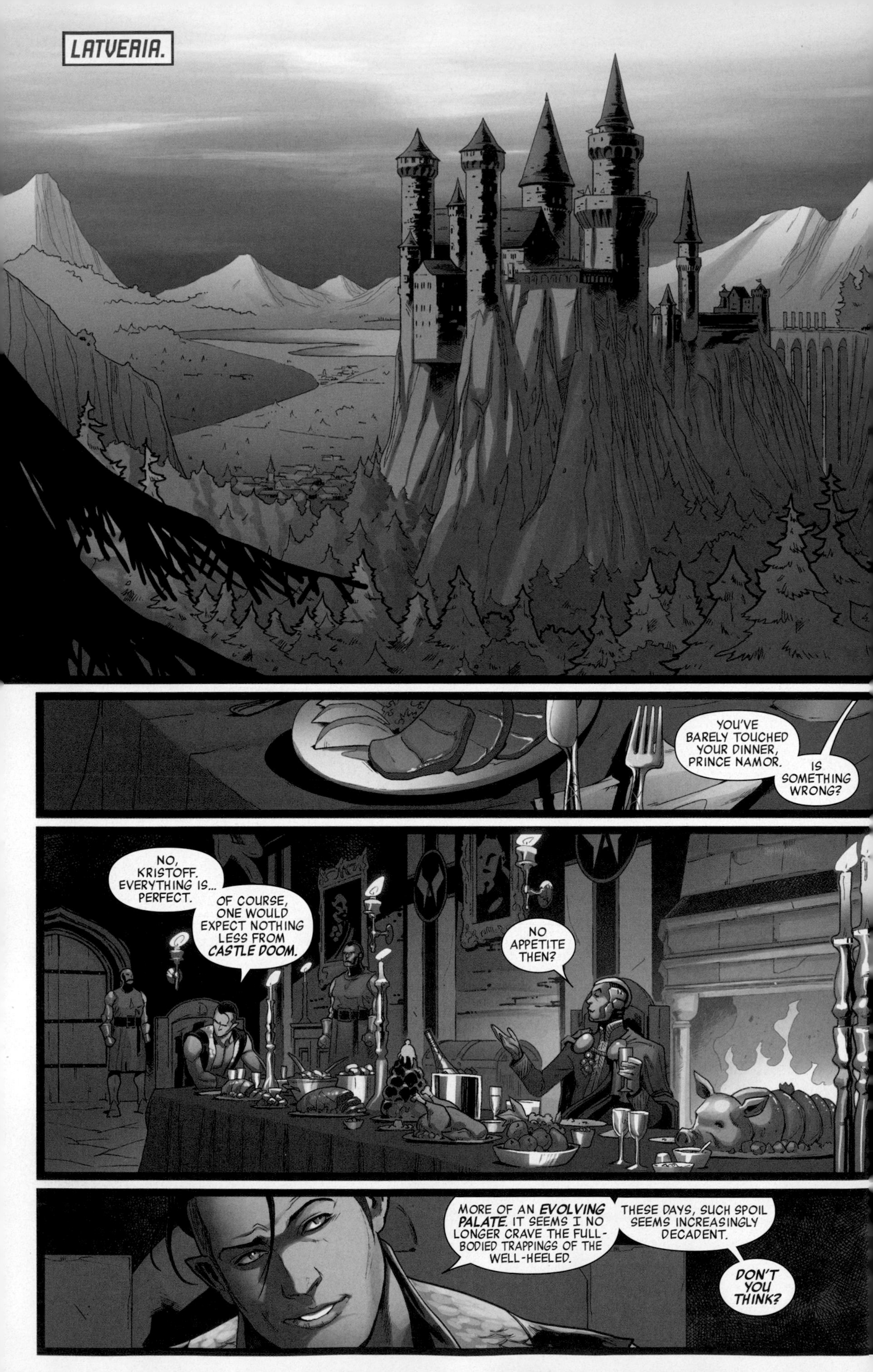
LATVERIA.
YOU'VE BARELY TOUCHED YOUR DINNER, PRINCE NAMOR.
IS SOMETHING WRONG?
NO, KRISTOFF. EVERYTHING IS... PERFECT.
OF COURSE, ONE WOULD EXPECT NOTHING LESS FROM CASTLE DOOM.
NO APPETITE THEN?
MORE OF AN EVOLVING PALATE. IT SEEMS I NO LONGER CRAVE THE FULL-BODIED TRAPPINGS OF THE WELL-HEELED.
THESE DAYS, SUCH SPOIL SEEMS INCREASINGLY DECADENT.
DON'T YOU THINK?

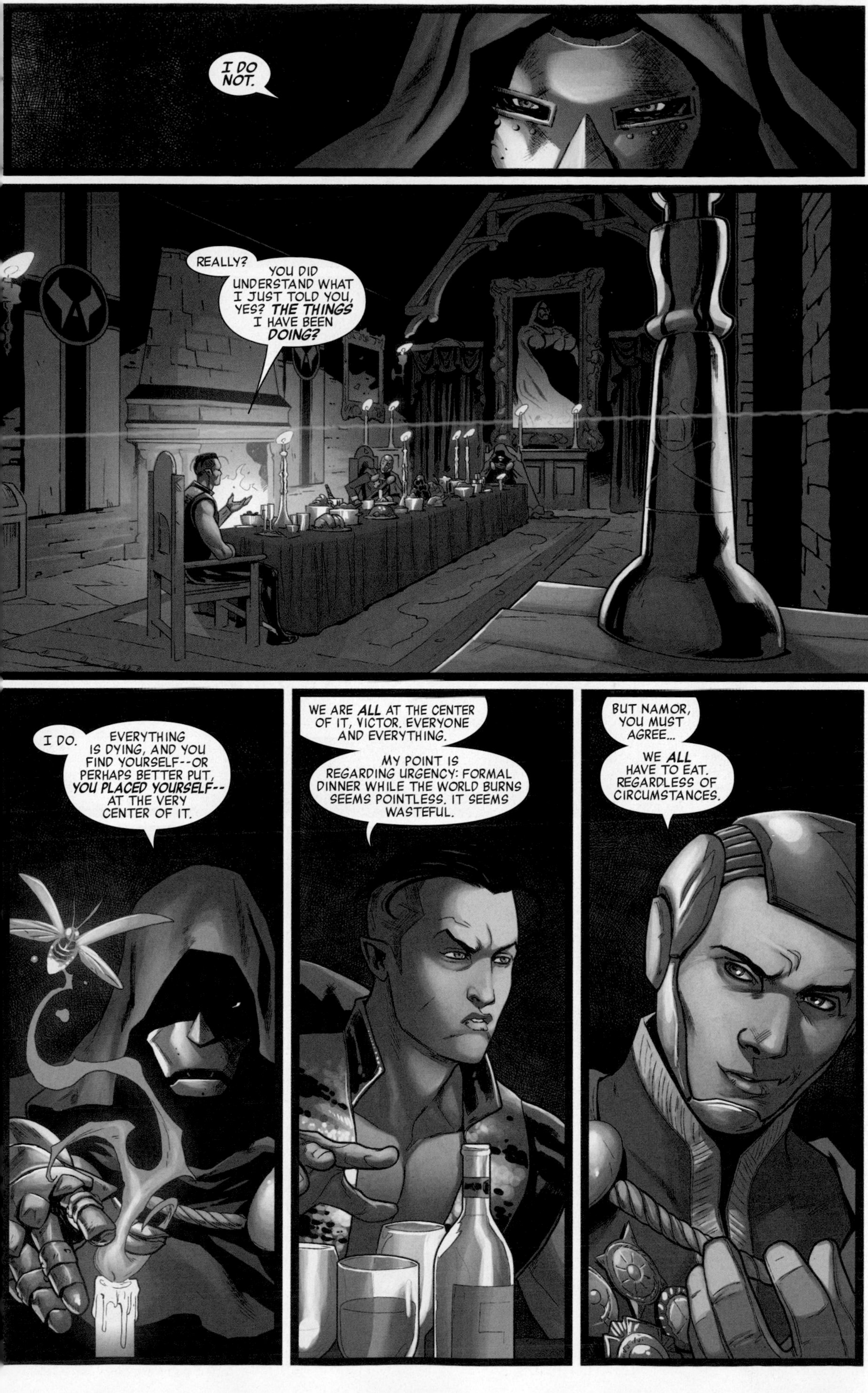
I DO NOT.
REALLY?
YOU DID UNDERSTAND WHAT I JUST TOLD YOU, YES? THE THINGS I HAVE BEEN DOING?
I DO.
EVERYTHING IS DYING, AND YOU FIND YOURSELF--OR PERHAPS BETTER PUT, YOU PLACED YOURSELF--AT THE VERY CENTER OF IT.
WE ARE ALL AT THE CENTER OF IT, VICTOR. EVERYONE AND EVERYTHING.
MY POINT IS REGARDING URGENCY: FORMAL DINNER WHILE THE WORLD BURNS SEEMS POINTLESS. IT SEEMS WASTEFUL.
BUT NAMOR, YOU MUST AGREE...
WE ALL HAVE TO EAT. REGARDLESS OF CIRCUMSTANCES.

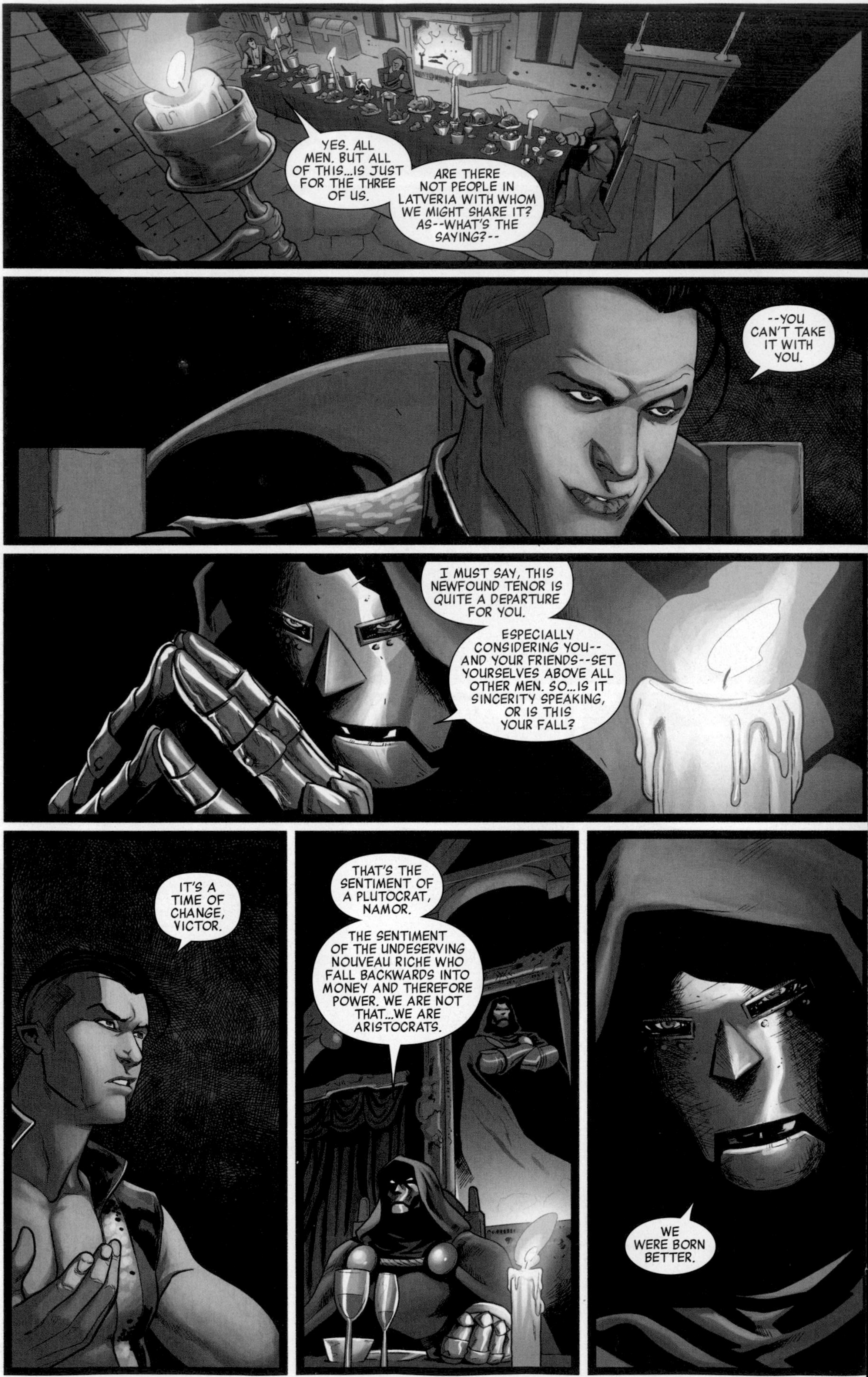
YES. ALL MEN. BUT ALL OF THIS...IS JUST FOR THE THREE OF US.
ARE THERE NOT PEOPLE IN LATVERIA WITH WHOM WE MIGHT SHARE IT? AS--WHAT'S THE SAYING?--
--YOU CAN'T TAKE IT WITH YOU.
I MUST SAY, THIS NEWFOUND TENOR IS QUITE A DEPARTURE FOR YOU.
ESPECIALLY CONSIDERING YOU--AND YOUR FRIENDS--SET YOURSELVES ABOVE ALL OTHER MEN. SO...IS IT SINCERITY SPEAKING, OR IS THIS YOUR FALL?
IT'S A TIME OF CHANGE, VICTOR.
THAT'S THE SENTIMENT OF A PLUTOCRAT, NAMOR.
THE SENTIMENT OF THE UNDESERVING NOUVEAU RICHE WHO FALL BACKWARDS INTO MONEY AND THEREFORE POWER. WE ARE NOT THAT...WE ARE ARISTOCRATS.
WE WERE BORN BETTER.

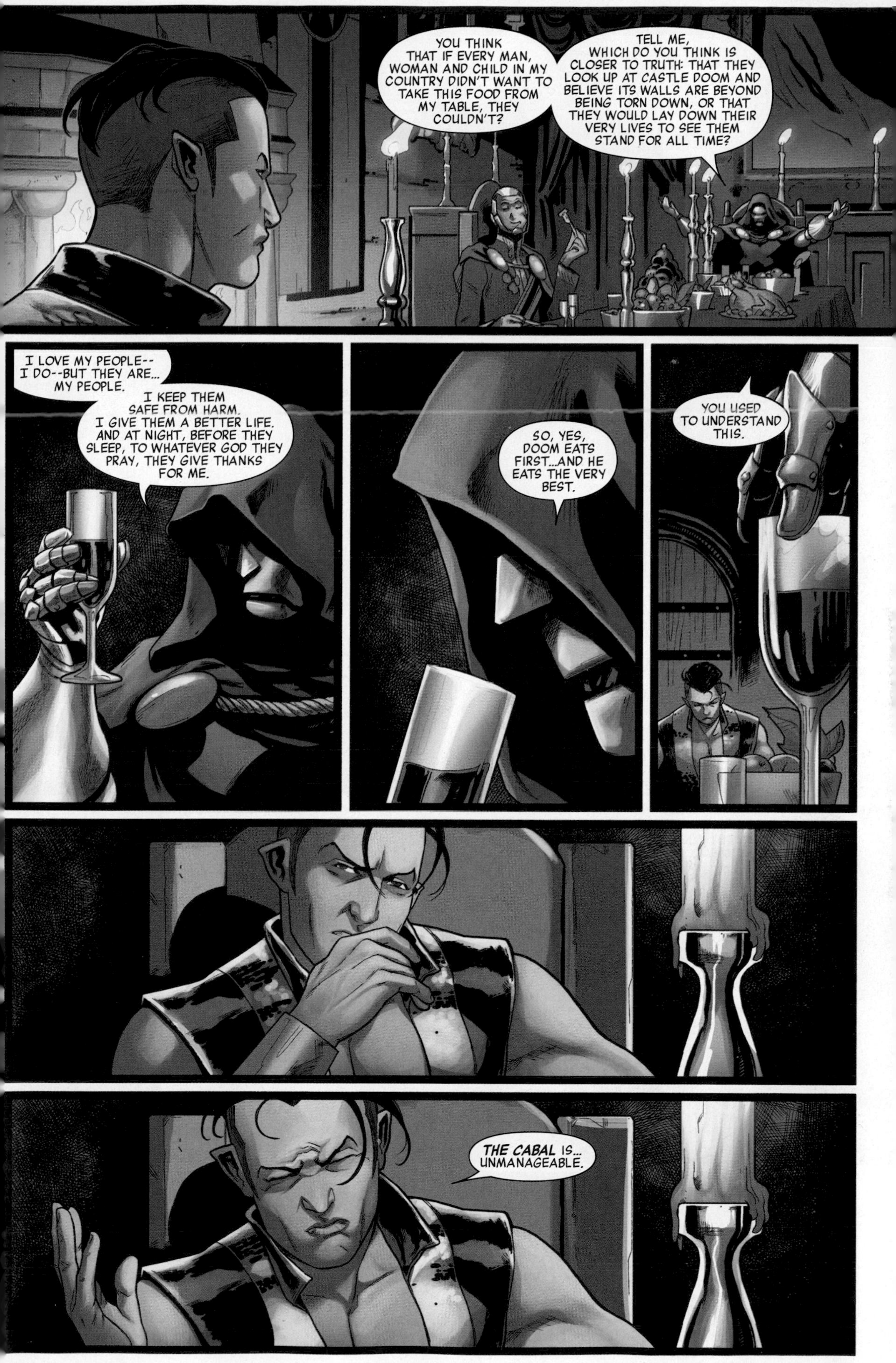
YOU THINK THAT IF EVERY MAN, WOMAN AND CHILD IN MY COUNTRY DIDN'T WANT TO TAKE THIS FOOD FROM MY TABLE, THEY COULDN'T?
TELL ME, WHICH DO YOU THINK IS CLOSER TO TRUTH: THAT THEY LOOK UP AT CASTLE DOOM AND BELIEVE ITS WALLS ARE BEYOND BEING TORN DOWN, OR THAT THEY WOULD LAY DOWN THEIR VERY LIVES TO SEE THEM STAND FOR ALL TIME?
I LOVE MY PEOPLE--I DO--BUT THEY ARE... MY PEOPLE.
I KEEP THEM SAFE FROM HARM. I GIVE THEM A BETTER LIFE. AND AT NIGHT, BEFORE THEY SLEEP, TO WHATEVER GOD THEY PRAY, THEY GIVE THANKS FOR ME.
SO, YES, DOOM EATS FIRST...AND HE EATS THE VERY BEST.
YOU USED TO UNDERSTAND THIS.
THE CABAL IS... UNMANAGEABLE.

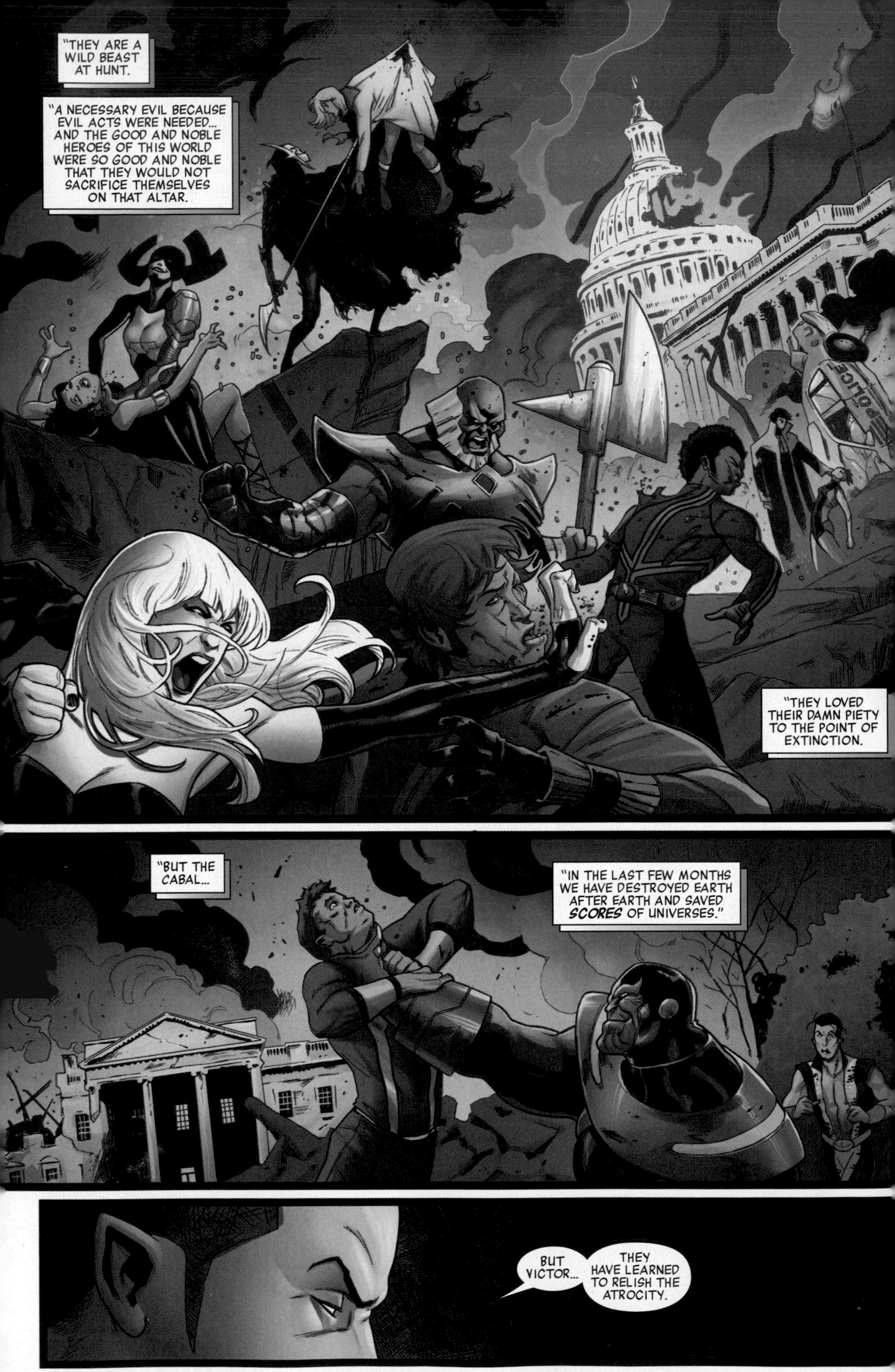
"THEY ARE A WILD BEAST AT HUNT.
"A NECESSARY EVIL BECAUSE EVIL ACTS WERE NEEDED... AND THE GOOD AND NOBLE HEROES OF THIS WORLD WERE SO GOOD AND NOBLE THAT THEY WOULD NOT SACRIFICE THEMSELVES ON THAT ALTAR.
POLICE
"THEY LOVED THEIR DAMN PIETY TO THE POINT OF EXTINCTION.
"BUT THE CABAL...
"IN THE LAST FEW MONTHS WE HAVE DESTROYED EARTH AFTER EARTH AND SAVED *SCORES* OF UNIVERSES."
BUT VICTOR...
THEY HAVE LEARNED TO RELISH THE ATROCITY.

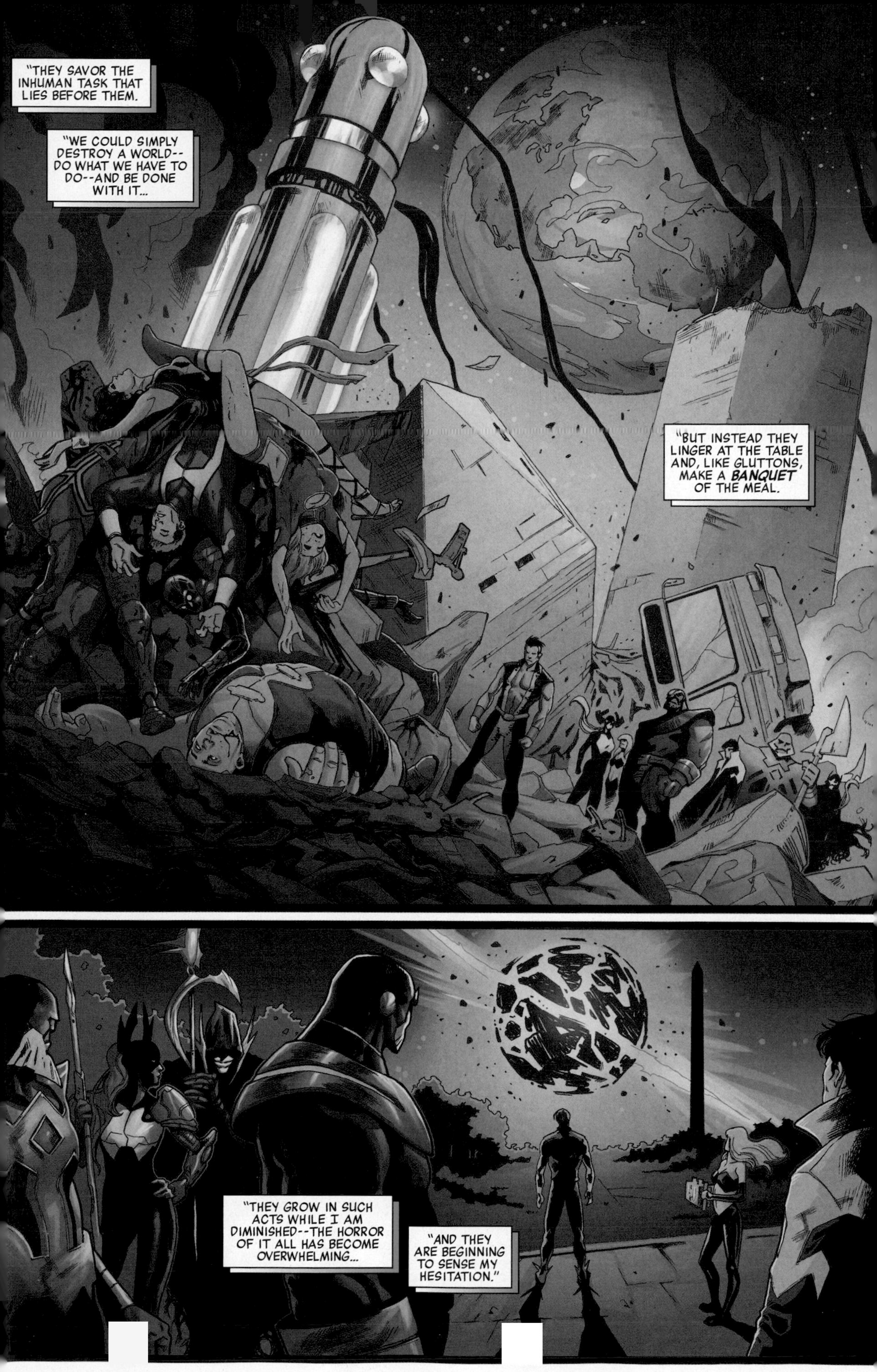
"THEY SAVOR THE INHUMAN TASK THAT LIES BEFORE THEM.
"WE COULD SIMPLY DESTROY A WORLD--DO WHAT WE HAVE TO DO--AND BE DONE WITH IT...
"BUT INSTEAD THEY LINGER AT THE TABLE AND, LIKE GLUTTONS, MAKE A BANQUET OF THE MEAL.
"THEY GROW IN SUCH ACTS WHILE I AM DIMINISHED--THE HORROR OF IT ALL HAS BECOME OVERWHELMING...
"AND THEY ARE BEGINNING TO SENSE MY HESITATION."

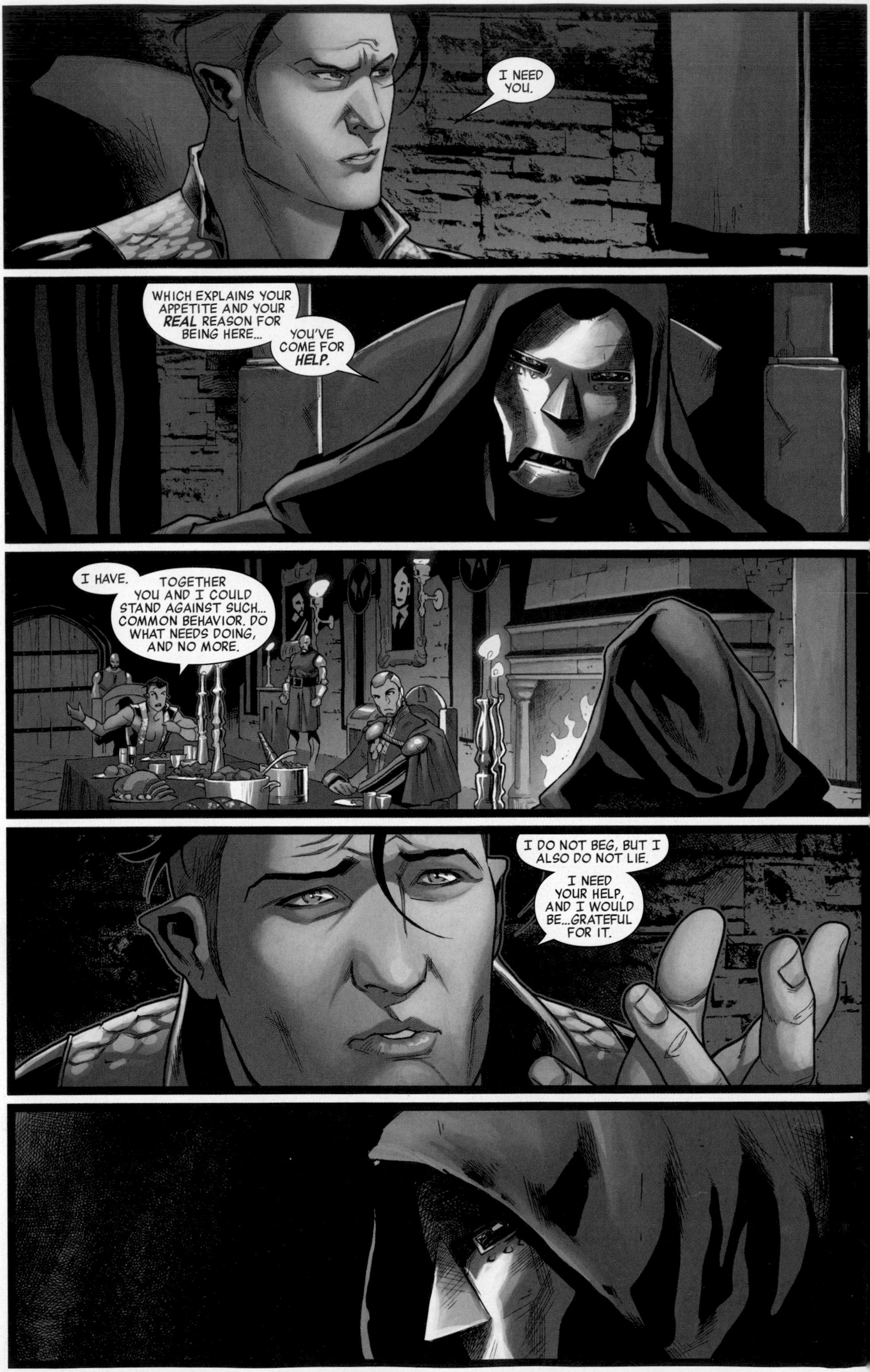
I NEED YOU.
WHICH EXPLAINS YOUR APPETITE AND YOUR REAL REASON FOR BEING HERE...
YOU'VE COME FOR HELP.
I HAVE.
TOGETHER YOU AND I COULD STAND AGAINST SUCH... COMMON BEHAVIOR. DO WHAT NEEDS DOING, AND NO MORE.
I DO NOT BEG, BUT I ALSO DO NOT LIE.
I NEED YOUR HELP, AND I WOULD BE...GRATEFUL FOR IT.

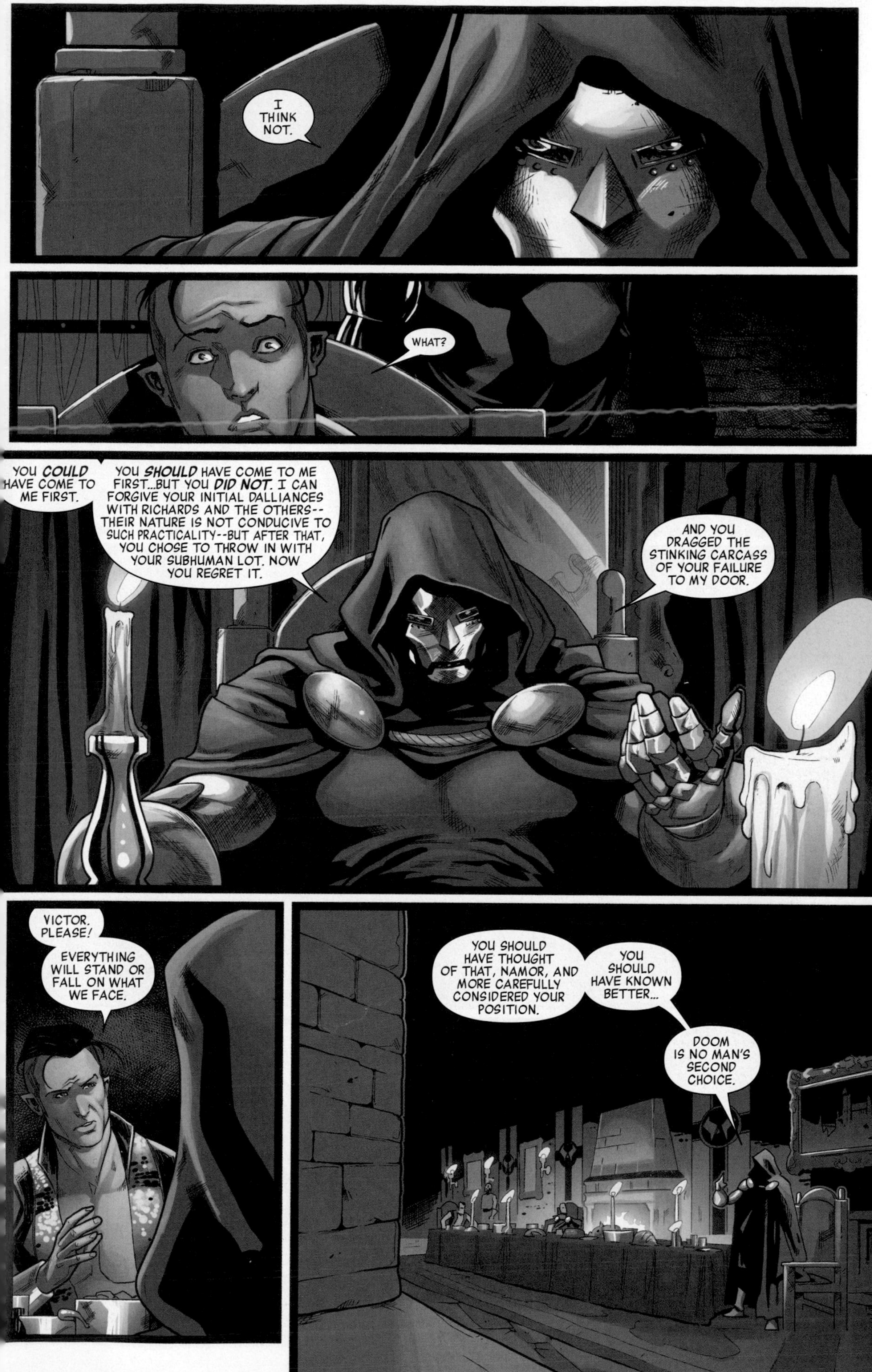
I THINK NOT.
WHAT?
YOU COULD HAVE COME TO ME FIRST.
YOU SHOULD HAVE COME TO ME FIRST...BUT YOU DID NOT. I CAN FORGIVE YOUR INITIAL DALLIANCES WITH RICHARDS AND THE OTHERS--THEIR NATURE IS NOT CONDUCIVE TO SUCH PRACTICALITY--BUT AFTER THAT, YOU CHOSE TO THROW IN WITH YOUR SUBHUMAN LOT. NOW YOU REGRET IT.
AND YOU DRAGGED THE STINKING CARCASS OF YOUR FAILURE TO MY DOOR.
VICTOR. PLEASE!
EVERYTHING WILL STAND OR FALL ON WHAT WE FACE.
YOU SHOULD HAVE THOUGHT OF THAT, NAMOR, AND MORE CAREFULLY CONSIDERED YOUR POSITION.
YOU SHOULD HAVE KNOWN BETTER...
DOOM IS NO MAN'S SECOND CHOICE.

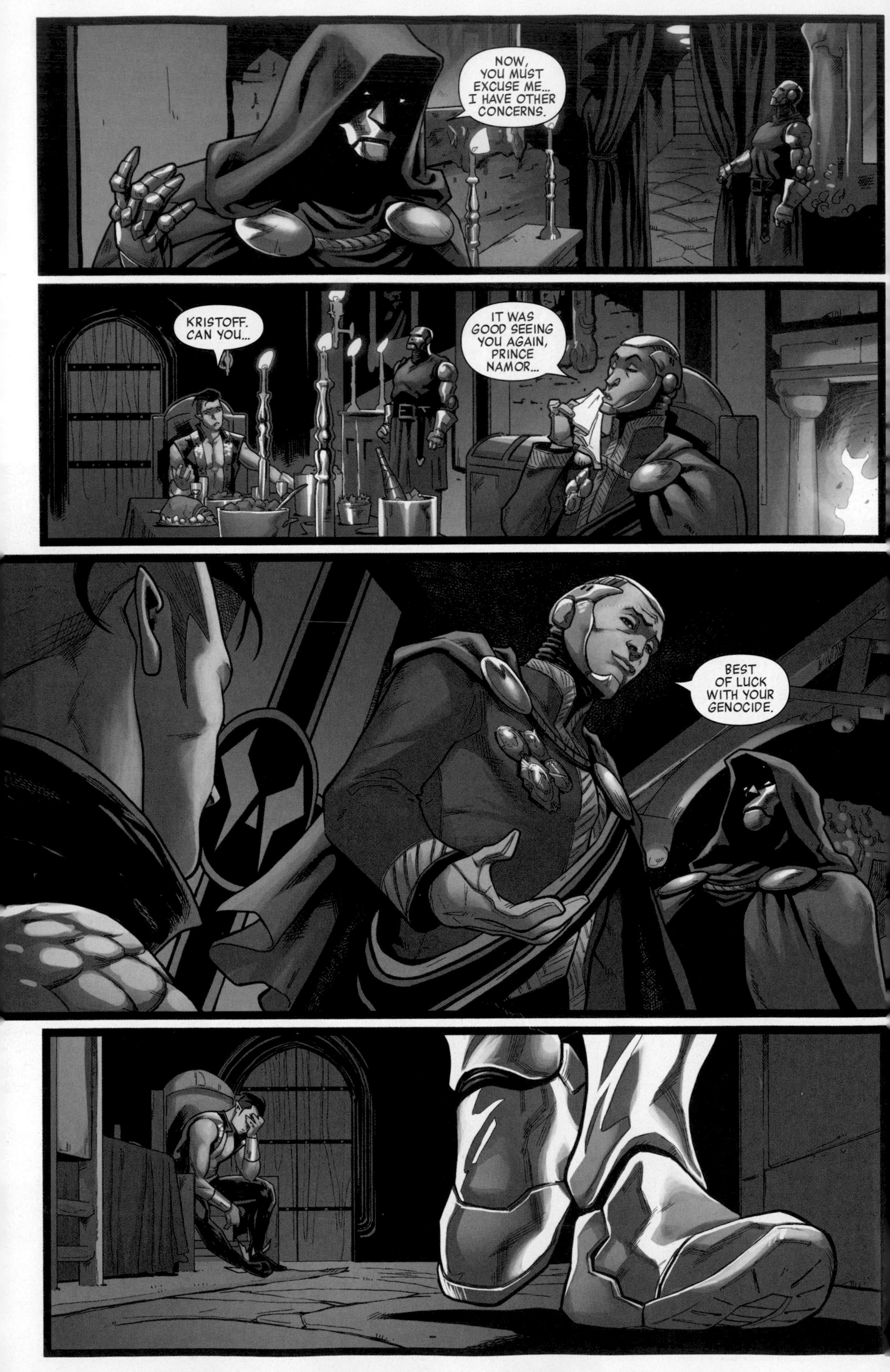
NOW, YOU MUST EXCUSE ME... I HAVE OTHER CONCERNS.
KRISTOFF. CAN YOU...
IT WAS GOOD SEEING YOU AGAIN, PRINCE NAMOR...
BEST OF LUCK WITH YOUR GENOCIDE.

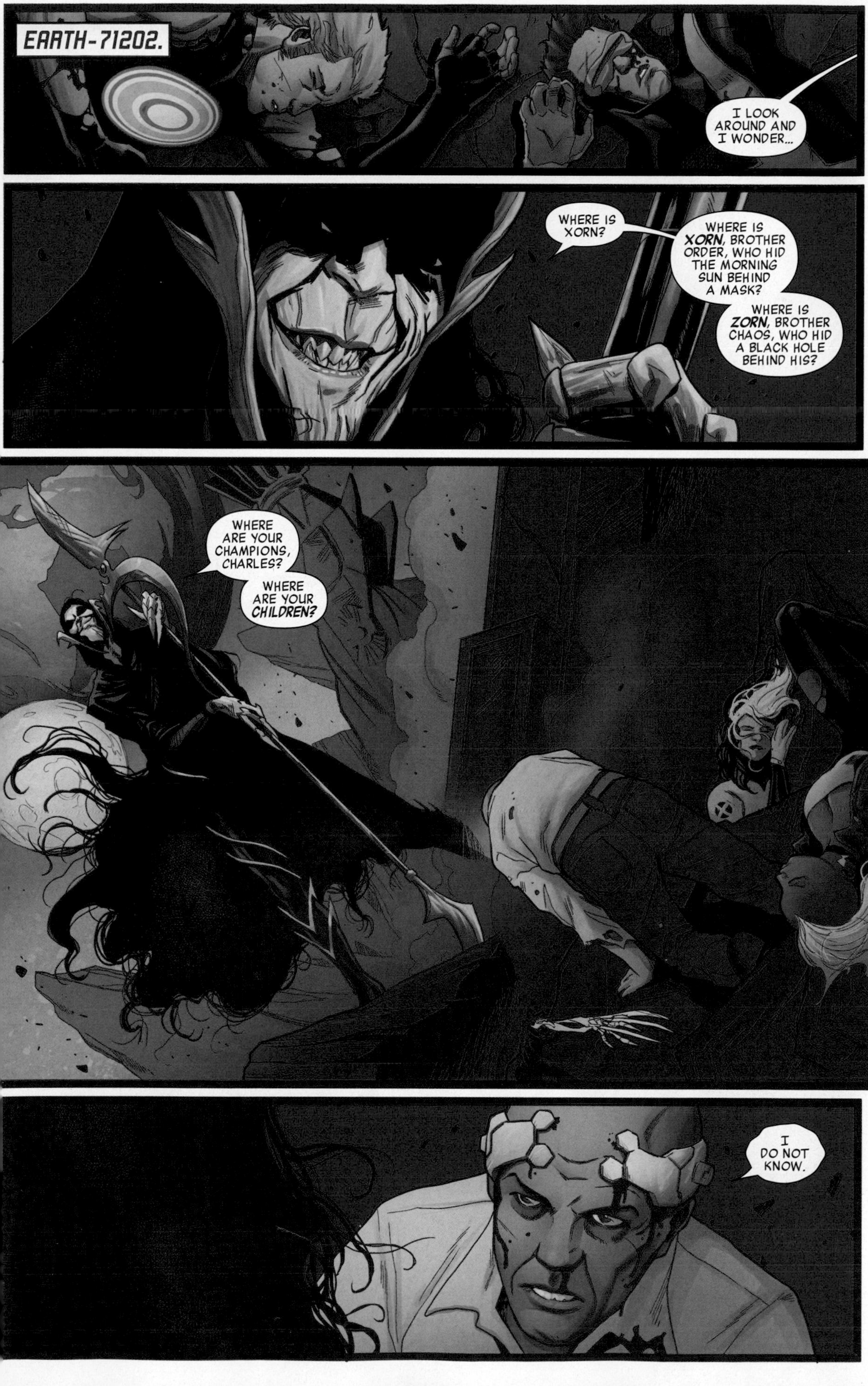
EARTH-71202.
I LOOK AROUND AND I WONDER...
WHERE IS XORN?
WHERE IS XORN, BROTHER ORDER, WHO HID THE MORNING SUN BEHIND A MASK?
WHERE IS ZORN, BROTHER CHAOS, WHO HID A BLACK HOLE BEHIND HIS?
WHERE ARE YOUR CHAMPIONS, CHARLES?
WHERE ARE YOUR CHILDREN?
I DO NOT KNOW.

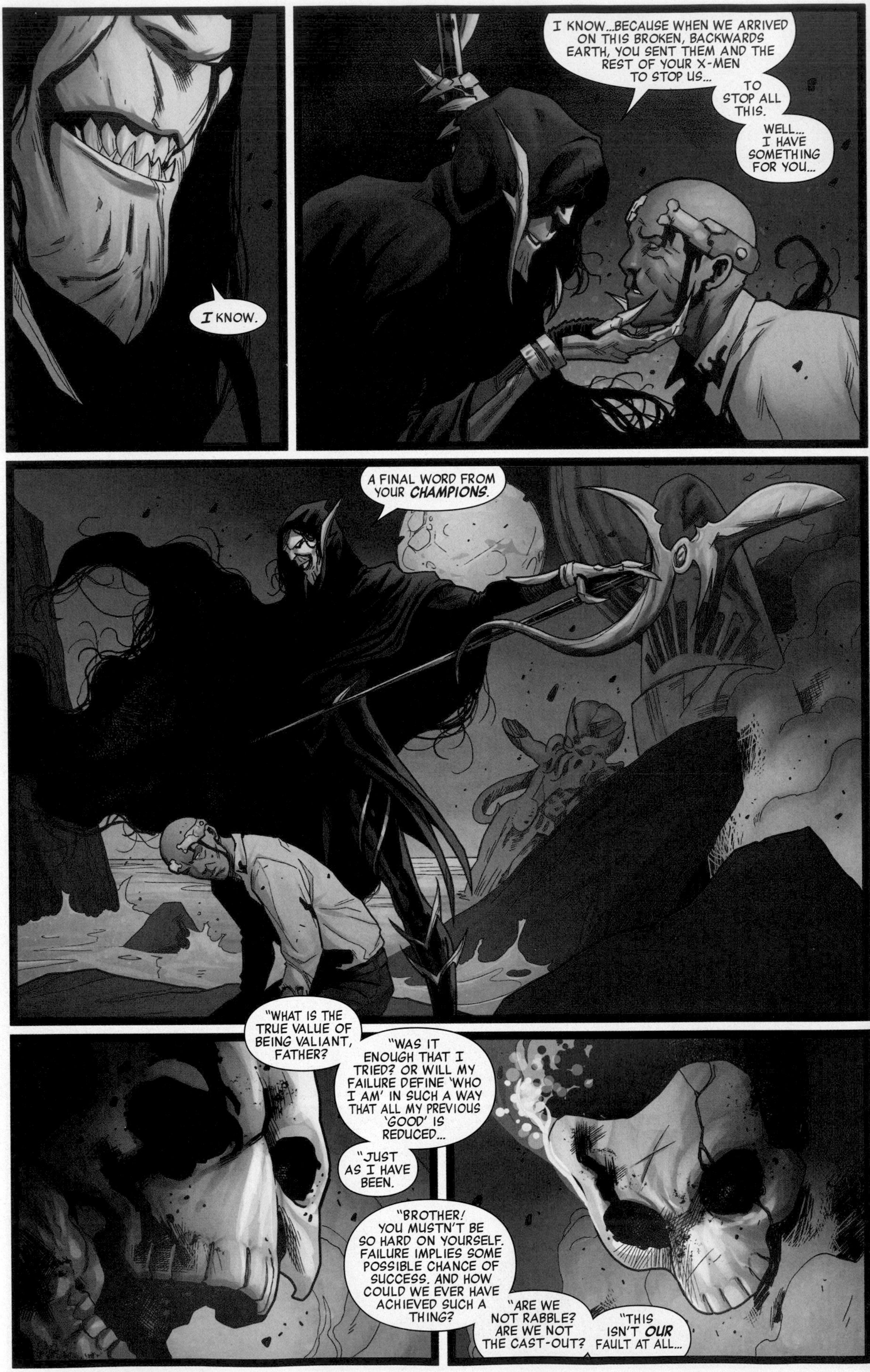
I KNOW.
I KNOW...BECAUSE WHEN WE ARRIVED ON THIS BROKEN, BACKWARDS EARTH, YOU SENT THEM AND THE REST OF YOUR X-MEN TO STOP US...
TO STOP ALL THIS.
WELL... I HAVE SOMETHING FOR YOU...
A FINAL WORD FROM YOUR CHAMPIONS.
"WHAT IS THE TRUE VALUE OF BEING VALIANT, FATHER?
"WAS IT ENOUGH THAT I TRIED? OR WILL MY FAILURE DEFINE 'WHO I AM' IN SUCH A WAY THAT ALL MY PREVIOUS 'GOOD' IS REDUCED...
"JUST AS I HAVE BEEN.
"BROTHER! YOU MUSTN'T BE SO HARD ON YOURSELF. FAILURE IMPLIES SOME POSSIBLE CHANCE OF SUCCESS. AND HOW COULD WE EVER HAVE ACHIEVED SUCH A THING?
"ARE WE NOT RABBLE? ARE WE NOT THE CAST-OUT?
"THIS ISN'T OUR FAULT AT ALL...

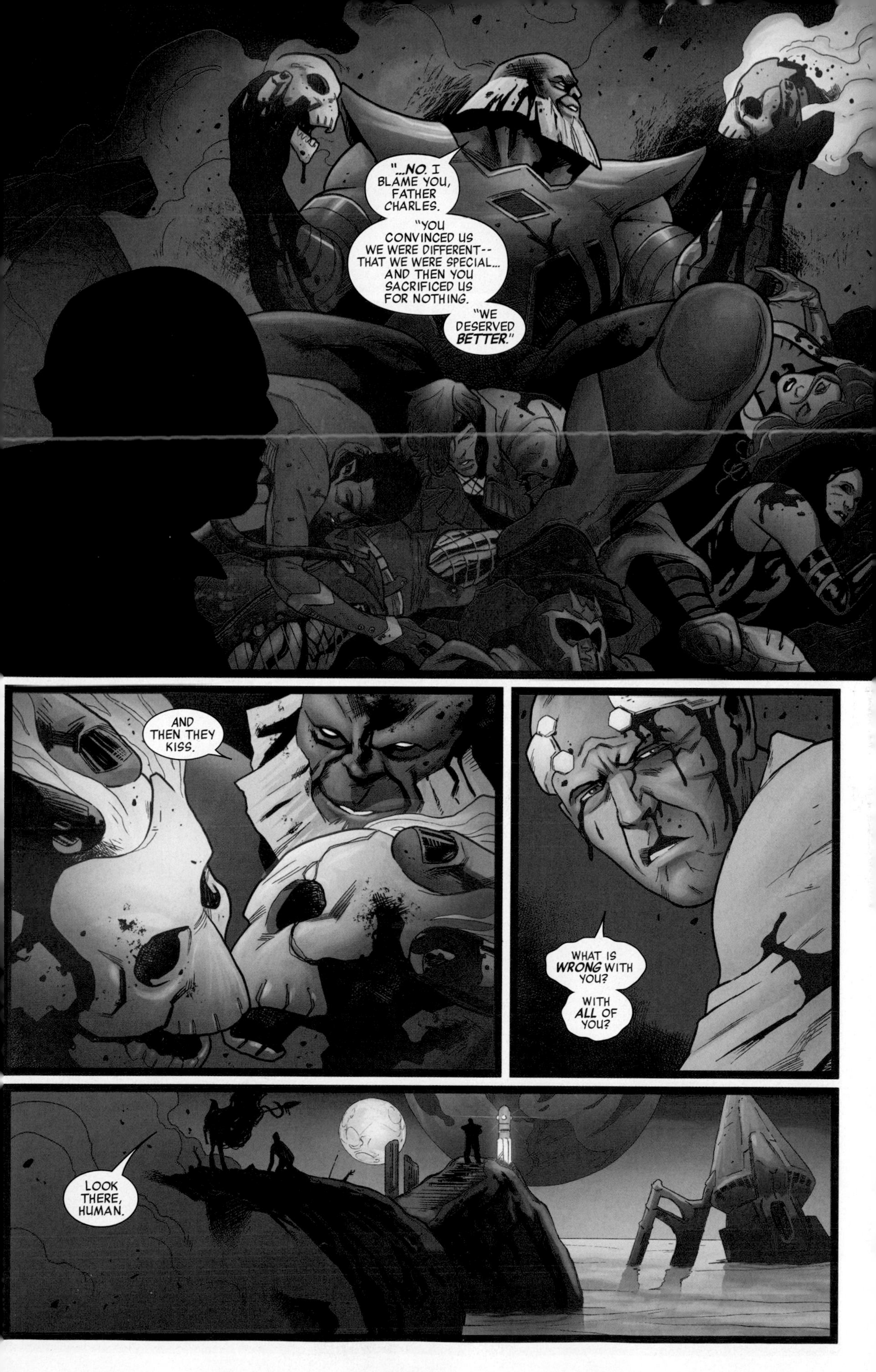
"...NO. I BLAME YOU, FATHER CHARLES.
"YOU CONVINCED US WE WERE DIFFERENT-- THAT WE WERE SPECIAL... AND THEN YOU SACRIFICED US FOR NOTHING.
"WE DESERVED BETTER."
AND THEN THEY KISS.
WHAT IS WRONG WITH YOU?
WITH ALL OF YOU?
LOOK THERE, HUMAN.

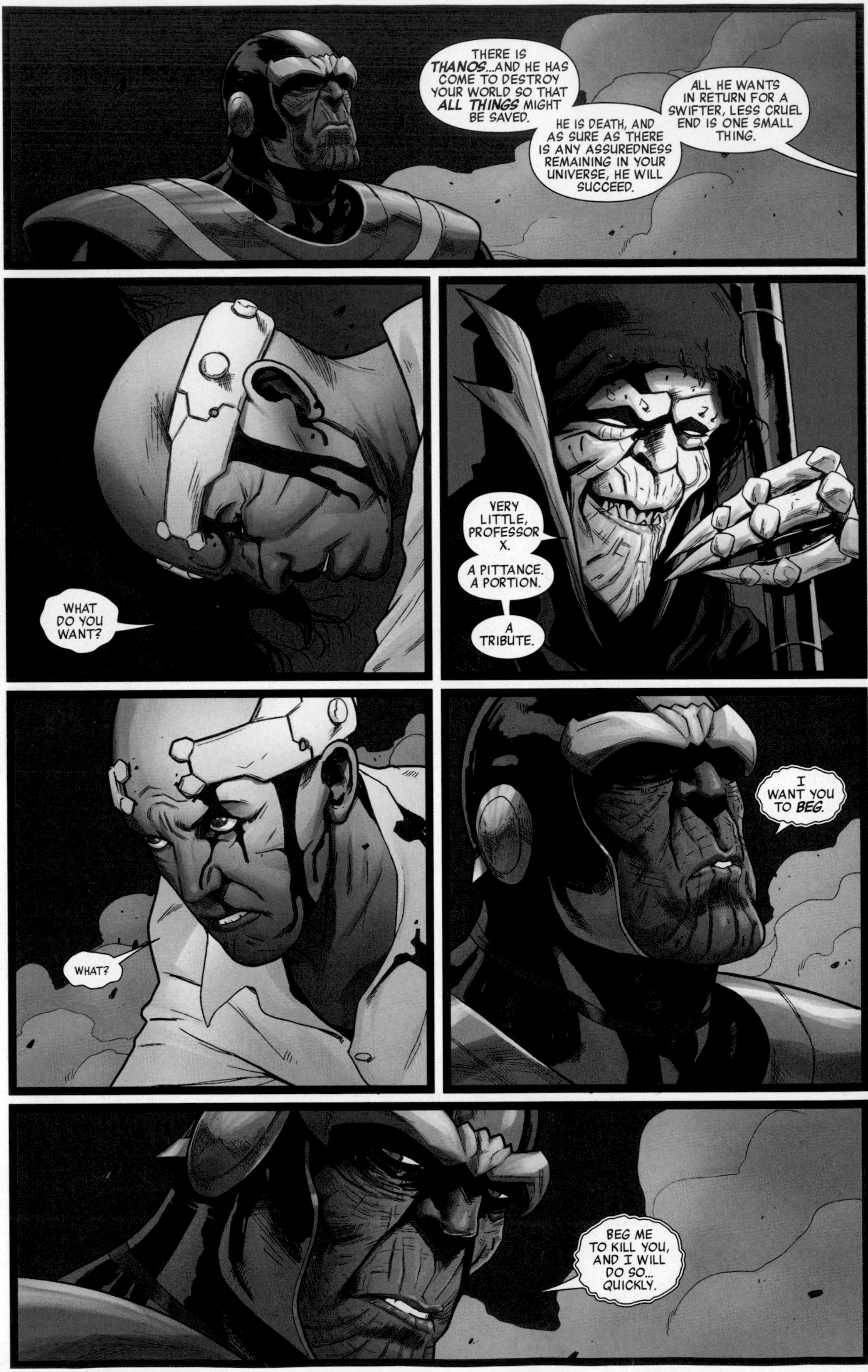
THERE IS THANOS...AND HE HAS COME TO DESTROY YOUR WORLD SO THAT ALL THINGS MIGHT BE SAVED.
HE IS DEATH, AND AS SURE AS THERE IS ANY ASSUREDNESS REMAINING IN YOUR UNIVERSE, HE WILL SUCCEED.
ALL HE WANTS IN RETURN FOR A SWIFTER, LESS CRUEL END IS ONE SMALL THING.
WHAT DO YOU WANT?
VERY LITTLE, PROFESSOR X.
A PITTANCE. A PORTION.
A TRIBUTE.
WHAT?
I WANT YOU TO BEG.
BEG ME TO KILL YOU, AND I WILL DO SO... QUICKLY.

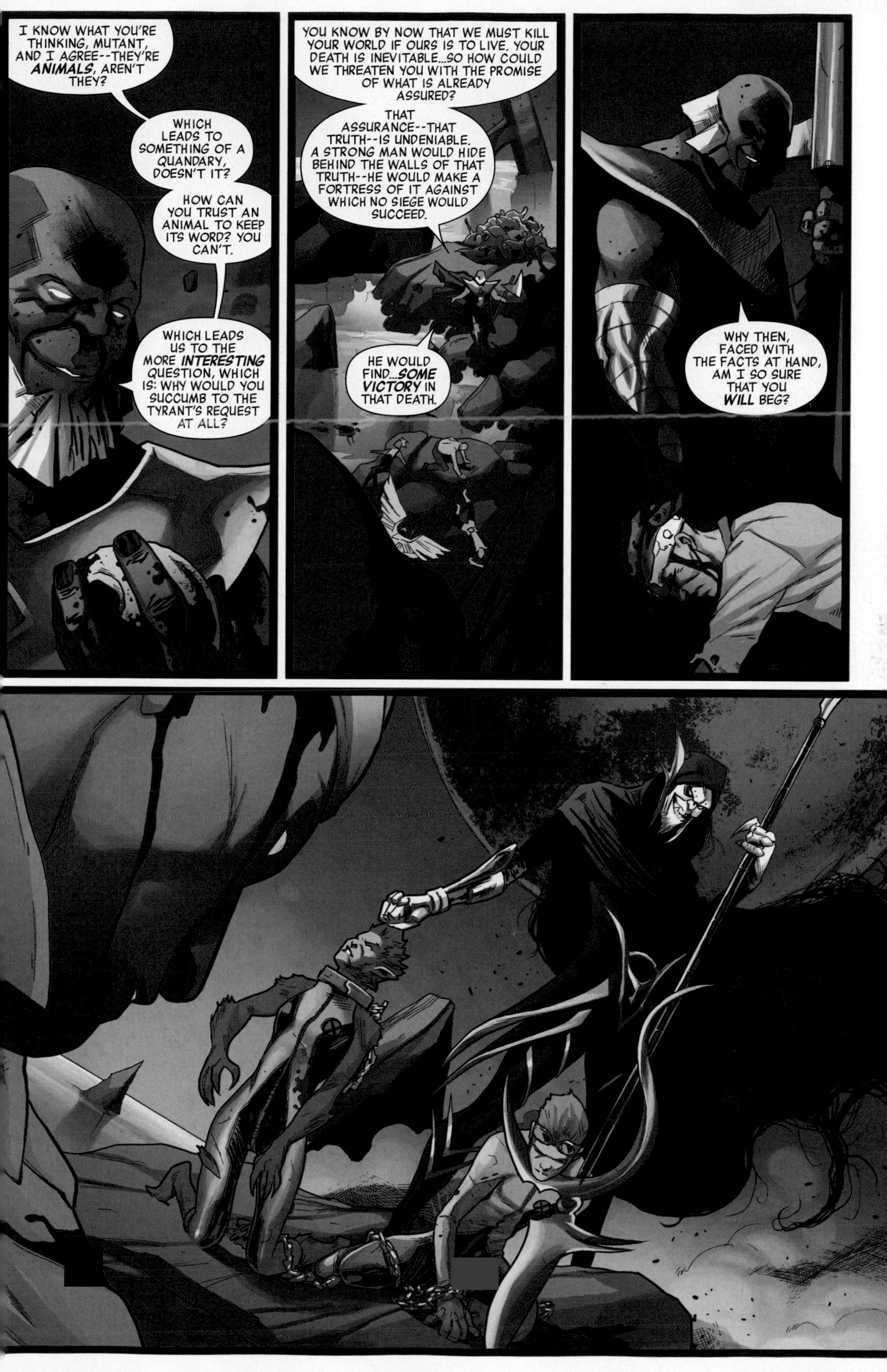
I KNOW WHAT YOU'RE THINKING, MUTANT, AND I AGREE--THEY'RE ANIMALS, AREN'T THEY?
WHICH LEADS TO SOMETHING OF A QUANDARY, DOESN'T IT?
HOW CAN YOU TRUST AN ANIMAL TO KEEP ITS WORD? YOU CAN'T.
WHICH LEADS US TO THE MORE INTERESTING QUESTION, WHICH IS: WHY WOULD YOU SUCCUMB TO THE TYRANT'S REQUEST AT ALL?
YOU KNOW BY NOW THAT WE MUST KILL YOUR WORLD IF OURS IS TO LIVE. YOUR DEATH IS INEVITABLE...SO HOW COULD WE THREATEN YOU WITH THE PROMISE OF WHAT IS ALREADY ASSURED?
THAT ASSURANCE--THAT TRUTH--IS UNDENIABLE. A STRONG MAN WOULD HIDE BEHIND THE WALLS OF THAT TRUTH--HE WOULD MAKE A FORTRESS OF IT AGAINST WHICH NO SIEGE WOULD SUCCEED.
HE WOULD FIND...SOME VICTORY IN THAT DEATH.
WHY THEN, FACED WITH THE FACTS AT HAND, AM I SO SURE THAT YOU WILL BEG?

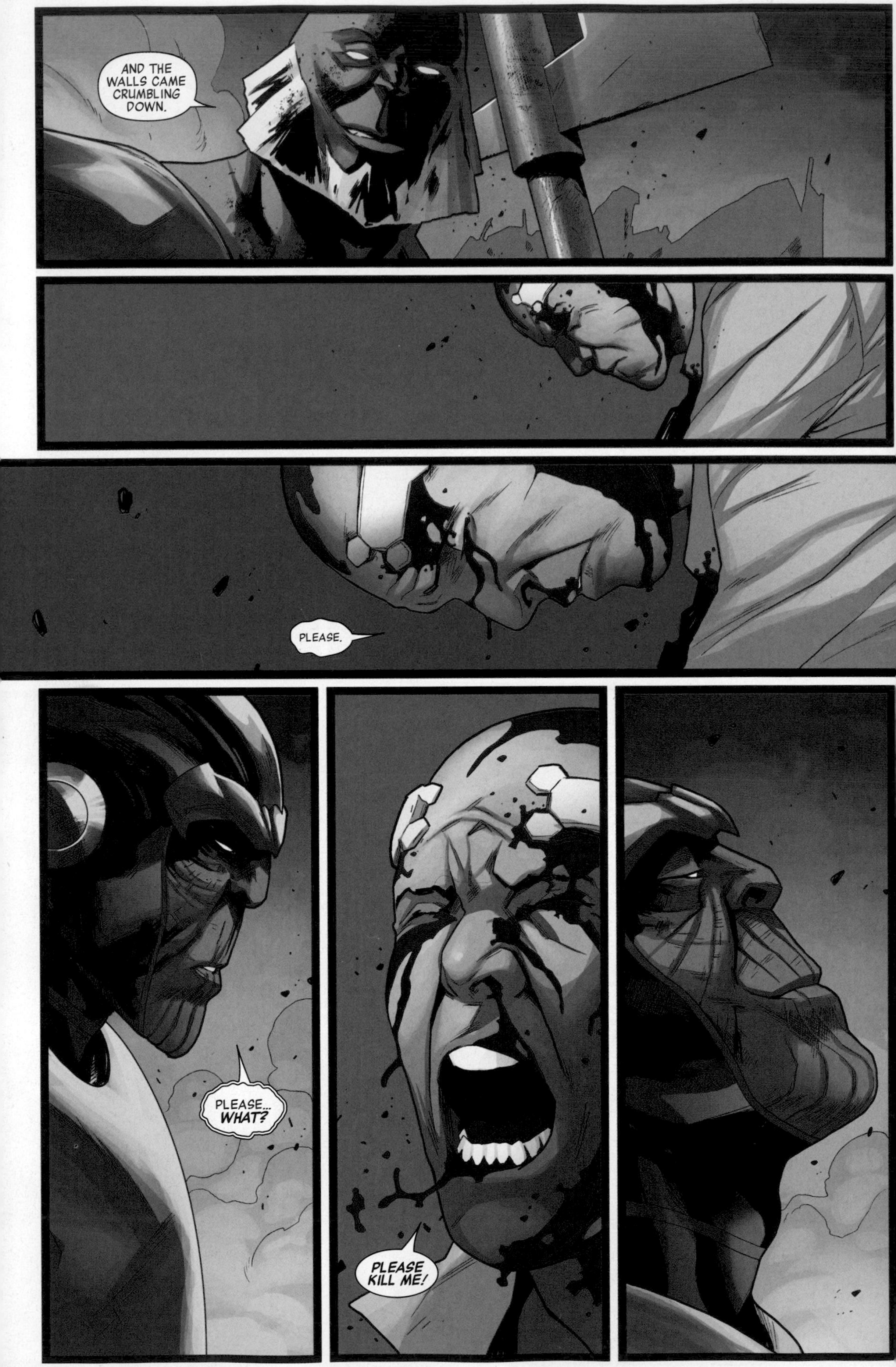
AND THE WALLS CAME CRUMBLING DOWN.
PLEASE.
PLEASE... WHAT?
PLEASE KILL ME!

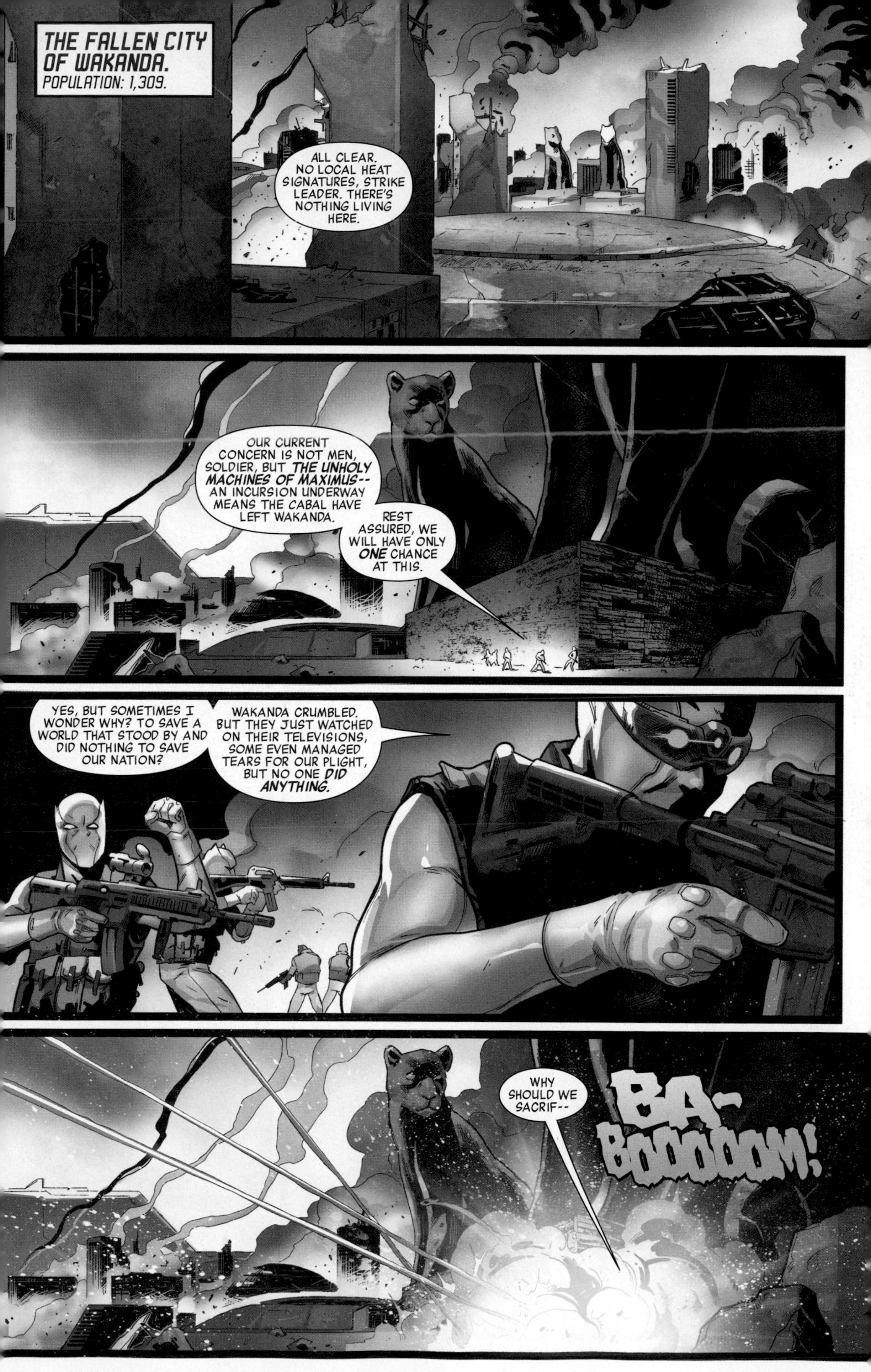
THE FALLEN CITY OF WAKANDA.
POPULATION: 1,309.
ALL CLEAR. NO LOCAL HEAT SIGNATURES, STRIKE LEADER. THERE'S NOTHING LIVING HERE.
OUR CURRENT CONCERN IS NOT MEN, SOLDIER, BUT THE UNHOLY MACHINES OF MAXIMUS-- AN INCURSION UNDERWAY MEANS THE CABAL HAVE LEFT WAKANDA.
REST ASSURED, WE WILL HAVE ONLY ONE CHANCE AT THIS.
YES, BUT SOMETIMES I WONDER WHY? TO SAVE A WORLD THAT STOOD BY AND DID NOTHING TO SAVE OUR NATION?
WAKANDA CRUMBLED. BUT THEY JUST WATCHED ON THEIR TELEVISIONS, SOME EVEN MANAGED TEARS FOR OUR PLIGHT, BUT NO ONE DID ANYTHING.
WHY SHOULD WE SACRIF--
BA-BOOOOOM!

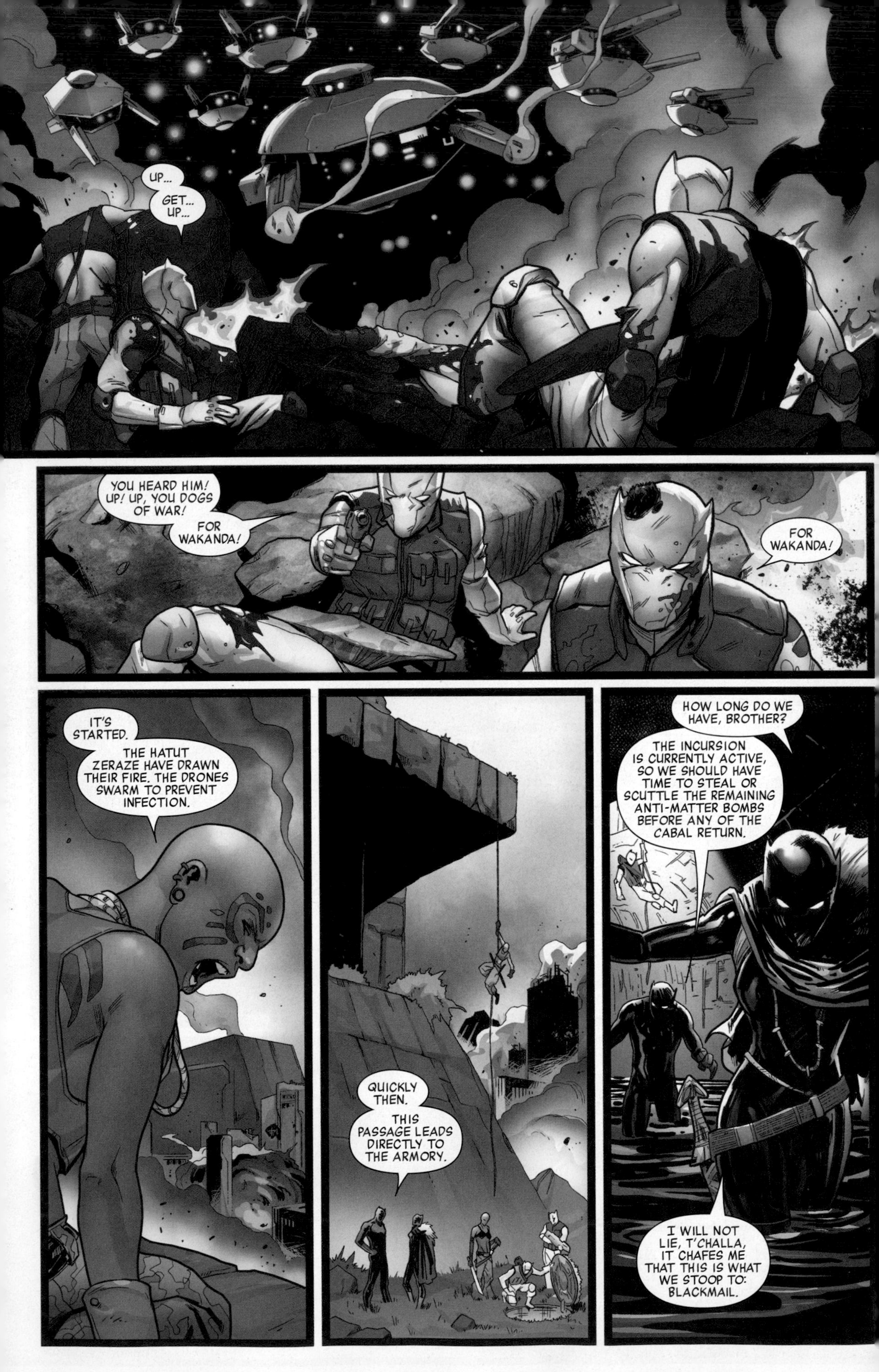
UP...
GET... UP...
YOU HEARD HIM! UP! UP, YOU DOGS OF WAR!
FOR WAKANDA!
FOR WAKANDA!
IT'S STARTED.
THE HATUT ZERAZE HAVE DRAWN THEIR FIRE. THE DRONES SWARM TO PREVENT INFECTION.
QUICKLY THEN.
THIS PASSAGE LEADS DIRECTLY TO THE ARMORY.
HOW LONG DO WE HAVE, BROTHER?
THE INCURSION IS CURRENTLY ACTIVE, SO WE SHOULD HAVE TIME TO STEAL OR SCUTTLE THE REMAINING ANTI-MATTER BOMBS BEFORE ANY OF THE CABAL RETURN.
I WILL NOT LIE, T'CHALLA, IT CHAFES ME THAT THIS IS WHAT WE STOOP TO: BLACKMAIL.

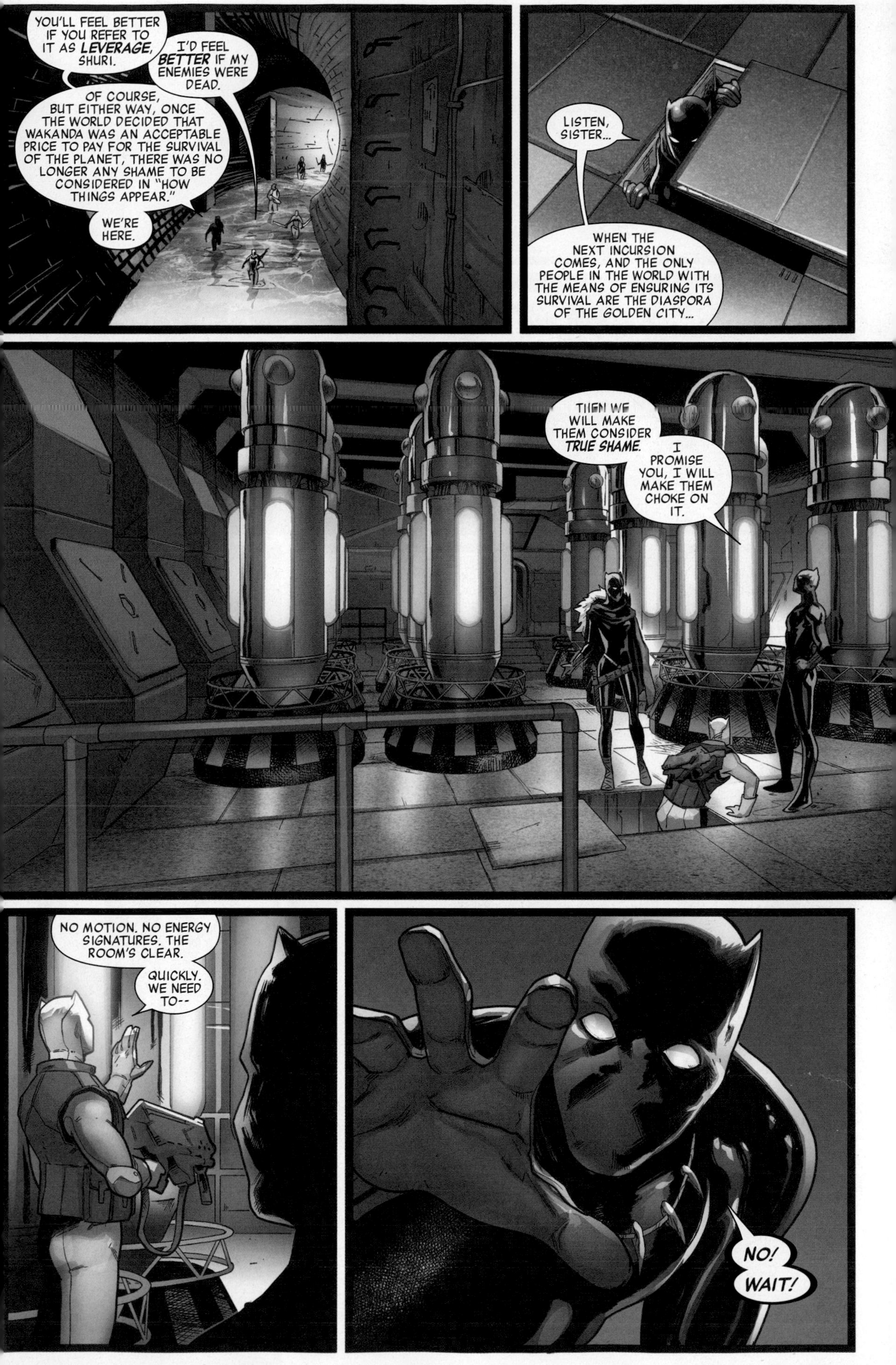

YOU'LL FEEL BETTER IF YOU REFER TO IT AS LEVERAGE, SHURI.
I'D FEEL BETTER IF MY ENEMIES WERE DEAD.
OF COURSE, BUT EITHER WAY, ONCE THE WORLD DECIDED THAT WAKANDA WAS AN ACCEPTABLE PRICE TO PAY FOR THE SURVIVAL OF THE PLANET, THERE WAS NO LONGER ANY SHAME TO BE CONSIDERED IN "HOW THINGS APPEAR."
WE'RE HERE.
LISTEN, SISTER...
WHEN THE NEXT INCURSION COMES, AND THE ONLY PEOPLE IN THE WORLD WITH THE MEANS OF ENSURING ITS SURVIVAL ARE THE DIASPORA OF THE GOLDEN CITY...
THEN WE WILL MAKE THEM CONSIDER TRUE SHAME.
I PROMISE YOU, I WILL MAKE THEM CHOKE ON IT.
NO MOTION. NO ENERGY SIGNATURES. THE ROOM'S CLEAR.
QUICKLY. WE NEED TO--
NO! WAIT!

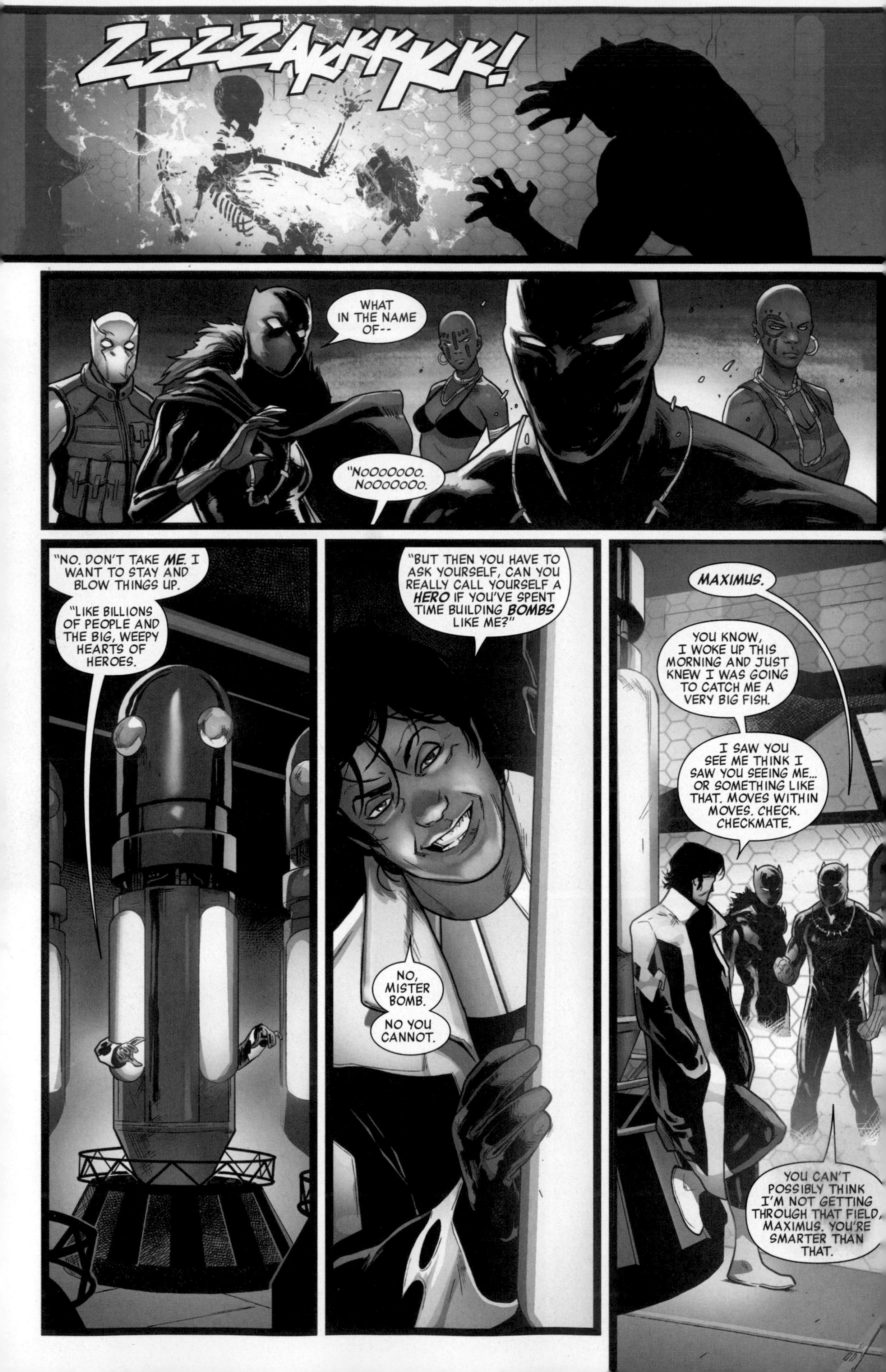
ZZZZAKKKK!
WHAT IN THE NAME OF--
"NOOOOOOO. NOOOOOOO.
"NO. DON'T TAKE *ME*. I WANT TO STAY AND BLOW THINGS UP.
"LIKE BILLIONS OF PEOPLE AND THE BIG, WEEPY HEARTS OF HEROES.
"BUT THEN YOU HAVE TO ASK YOURSELF, CAN YOU REALLY CALL YOURSELF A *HERO* IF YOU'VE SPENT TIME BUILDING *BOMBS* LIKE ME?"
NO, MISTER BOMB.
NO YOU CANNOT.
MAXIMUS.
YOU KNOW, I WOKE UP THIS MORNING AND JUST KNEW I WAS GOING TO CATCH ME A VERY BIG FISH.
I SAW YOU SEE ME THINK I SAW YOU SEEING ME... OR SOMETHING LIKE THAT. MOVES WITHIN MOVES. CHECK. CHECKMATE.
YOU CAN'T POSSIBLY THINK I'M NOT GETTING THROUGH THAT FIELD, MAXIMUS. YOU'RE SMARTER THAN THAT.

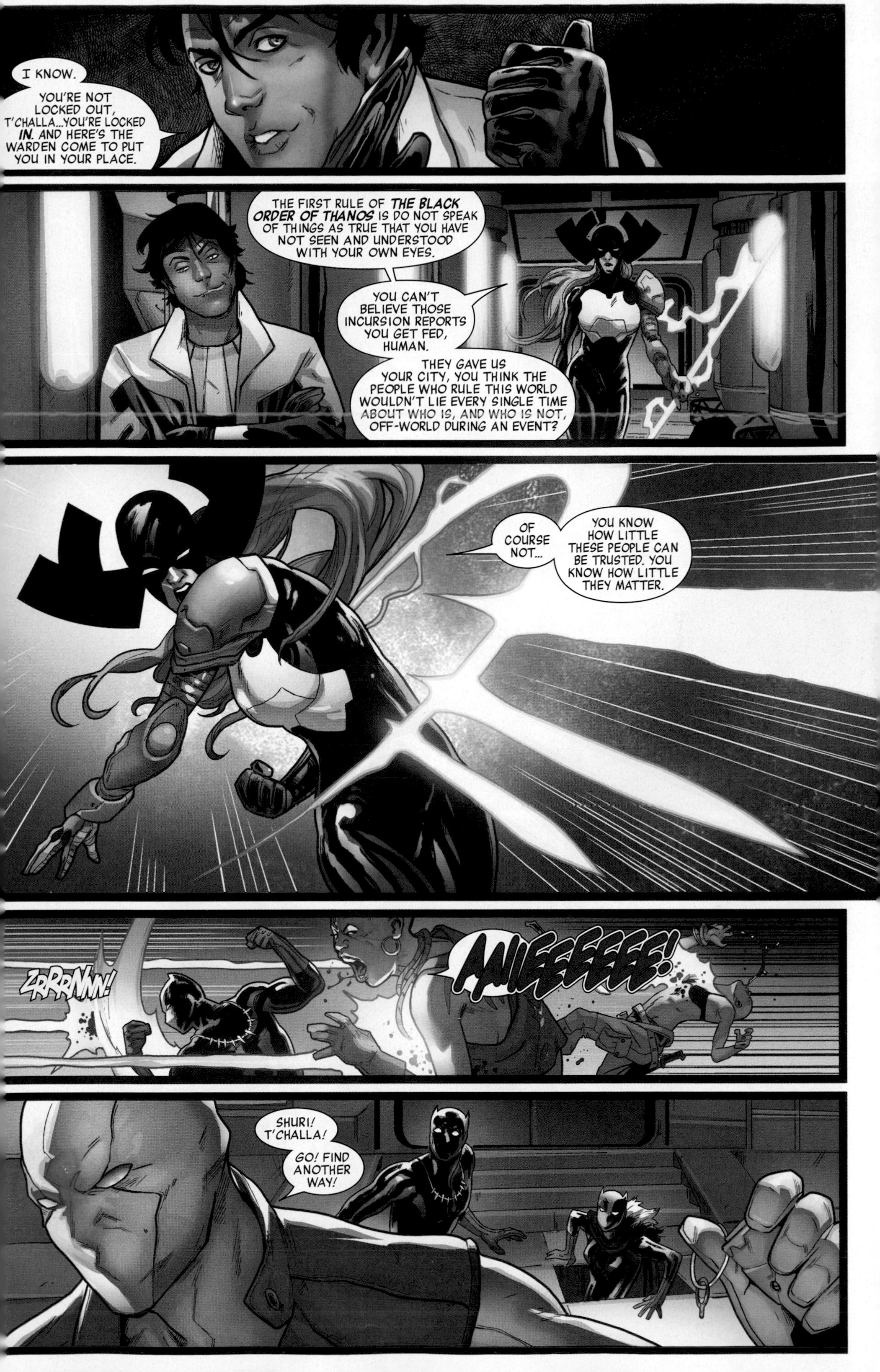
I KNOW.
YOU'RE NOT LOCKED OUT, T'CHALLA...YOU'RE LOCKED IN. AND HERE'S THE WARDEN COME TO PUT YOU IN YOUR PLACE.
THE FIRST RULE OF THE BLACK ORDER OF THANOS IS DO NOT SPEAK OF THINGS AS TRUE THAT YOU HAVE NOT SEEN AND UNDERSTOOD WITH YOUR OWN EYES.
YOU CAN'T BELIEVE THOSE INCURSION REPORTS YOU GET FED, HUMAN.
THEY GAVE US YOUR CITY, YOU THINK THE PEOPLE WHO RULE THIS WORLD WOULDN'T LIE EVERY SINGLE TIME ABOUT WHO IS, AND WHO IS NOT, OFF-WORLD DURING AN EVENT?
OF COURSE NOT...
YOU KNOW HOW LITTLE THESE PEOPLE CAN BE TRUSTED. YOU KNOW HOW LITTLE THEY MATTER.
ZRRRNNN!
AAIIEEEEEEE!
SHURI! T'CHALLA!
GO! FIND ANOTHER WAY!

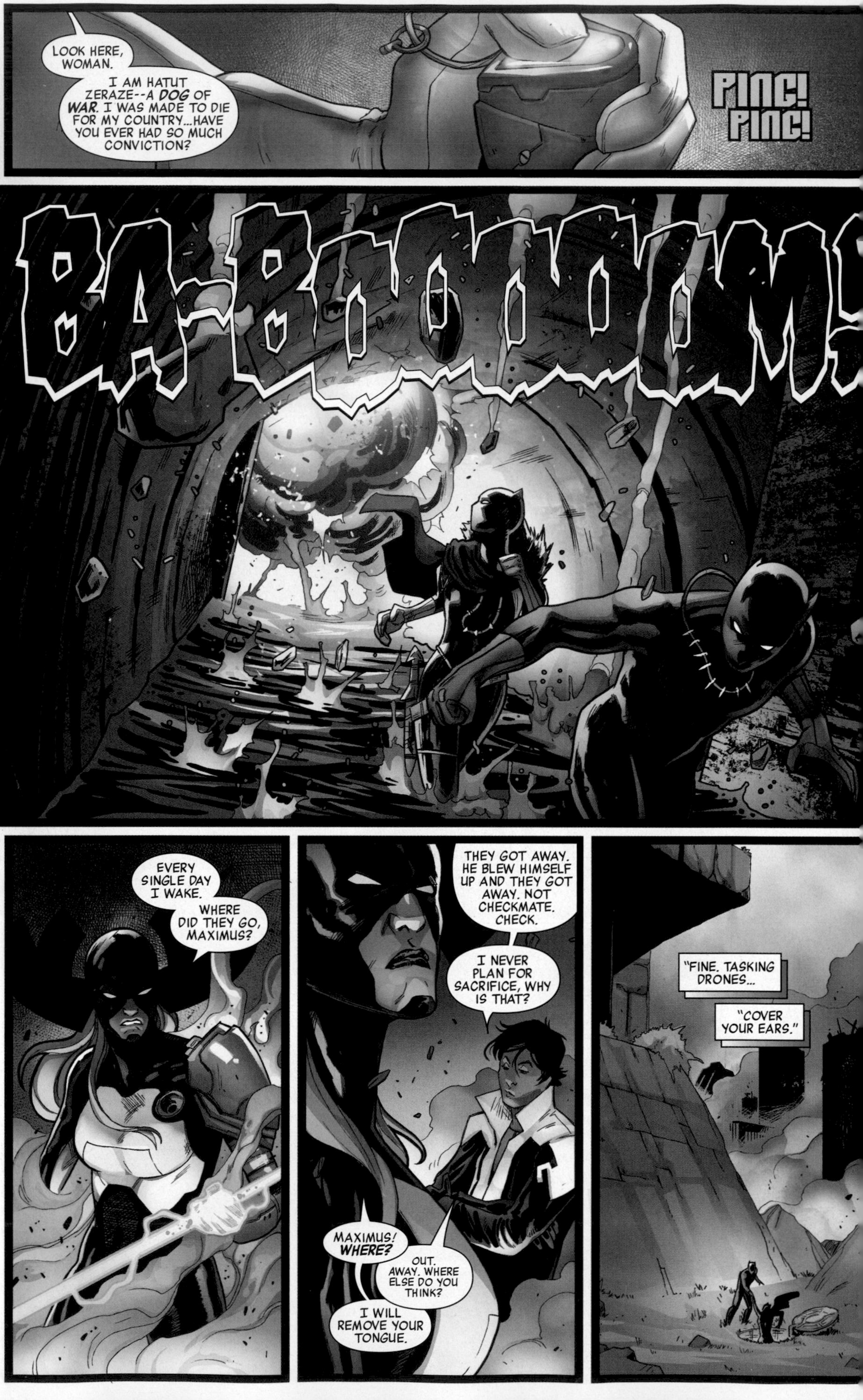
LOOK HERE, WOMAN.
I AM HATUT ZERAZE--A DOG OF WAR. I WAS MADE TO DIE FOR MY COUNTRY...HAVE YOU EVER HAD SO MUCH CONVICTION?
PING! PING!
BA-BOOOOOM!
EVERY SINGLE DAY I WAKE.
WHERE DID THEY GO, MAXIMUS?
THEY GOT AWAY. HE BLEW HIMSELF UP AND THEY GOT AWAY. NOT CHECKMATE. CHECK.
I NEVER PLAN FOR SACRIFICE, WHY IS THAT?
MAXIMUS! WHERE?
OUT. AWAY. WHERE ELSE DO YOU THINK?
I WILL REMOVE YOUR TONGUE.
"FINE. TASKING DRONES...
"COVER YOUR EARS."

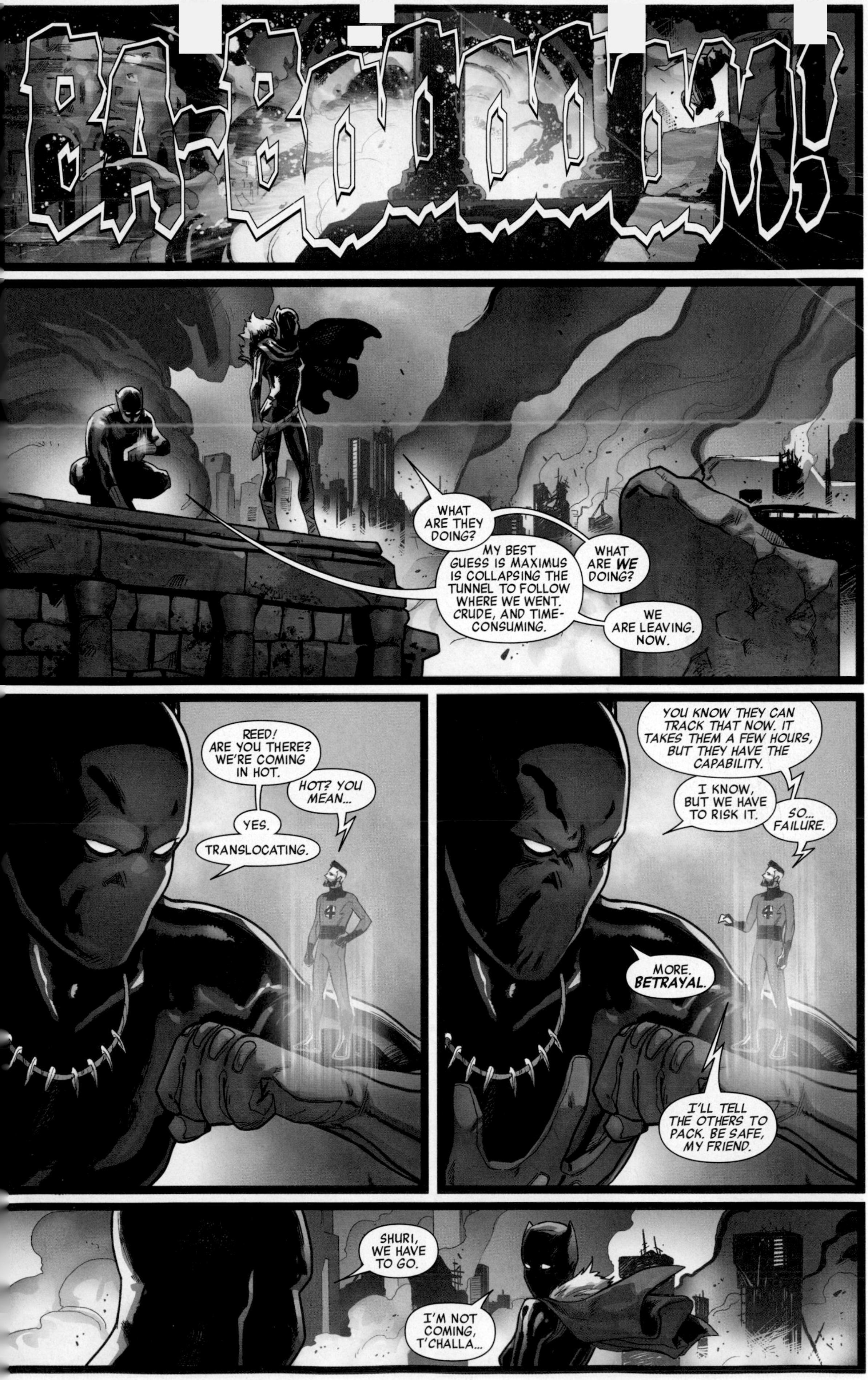
BABOOOOOM!
WHAT ARE THEY DOING?
MY BEST GUESS IS MAXIMUS IS COLLAPSING THE TUNNEL TO FOLLOW WHERE WE WENT. CRUDE, AND TIME-CONSUMING.
WHAT ARE **WE** DOING?
WE ARE LEAVING. NOW.
REED! ARE YOU THERE? WE'RE COMING IN HOT.
HOT? YOU MEAN...
YES.
TRANSLOCATING.
YOU KNOW THEY CAN TRACK THAT NOW. IT TAKES THEM A FEW HOURS, BUT THEY HAVE THE CAPABILITY.
I KNOW, BUT WE HAVE TO RISK IT.
SO... FAILURE.
MORE. **BETRAYAL.**
I'LL TELL THE OTHERS TO PACK. BE SAFE, MY FRIEND.
SHURI, WE HAVE TO GO.
I'M NOT COMING, T'CHALLA...

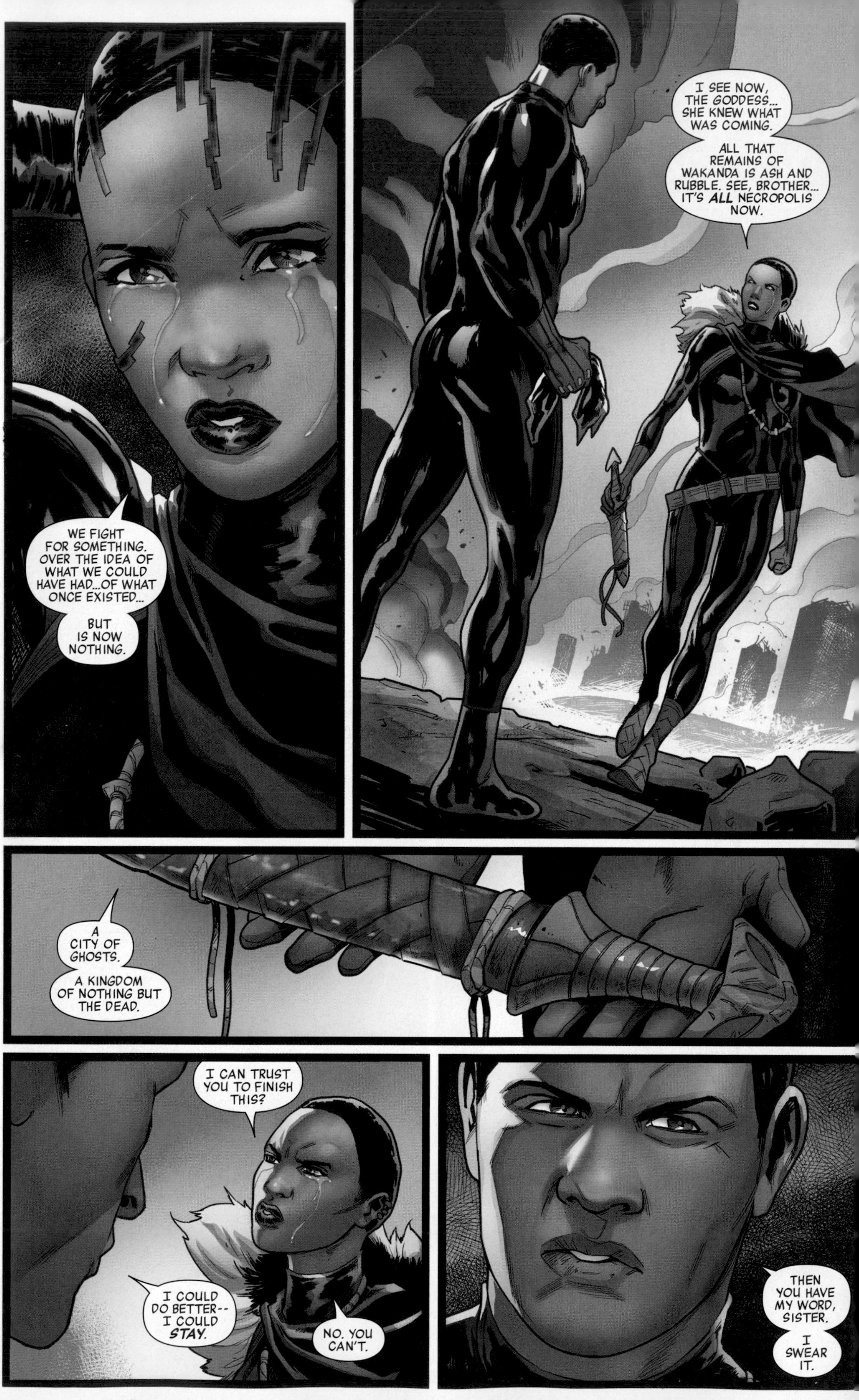

WE FIGHT FOR SOMETHING. OVER THE IDEA OF WHAT WE COULD HAVE HAD...OF WHAT ONCE EXISTED...
BUT IS NOW NOTHING.
I SEE NOW, THE GODDESS... SHE KNEW WHAT WAS COMING.
ALL THAT REMAINS OF WAKANDA IS ASH AND RUBBLE. SEE, BROTHER... IT'S ALL NECROPOLIS NOW.
A CITY OF GHOSTS.
A KINGDOM OF NOTHING BUT THE DEAD.
I CAN TRUST YOU TO FINISH THIS?
I COULD DO BETTER-- I COULD STAY.
NO. YOU CAN'T.
THEN YOU HAVE MY WORD, SISTER.
I SWEAR IT.

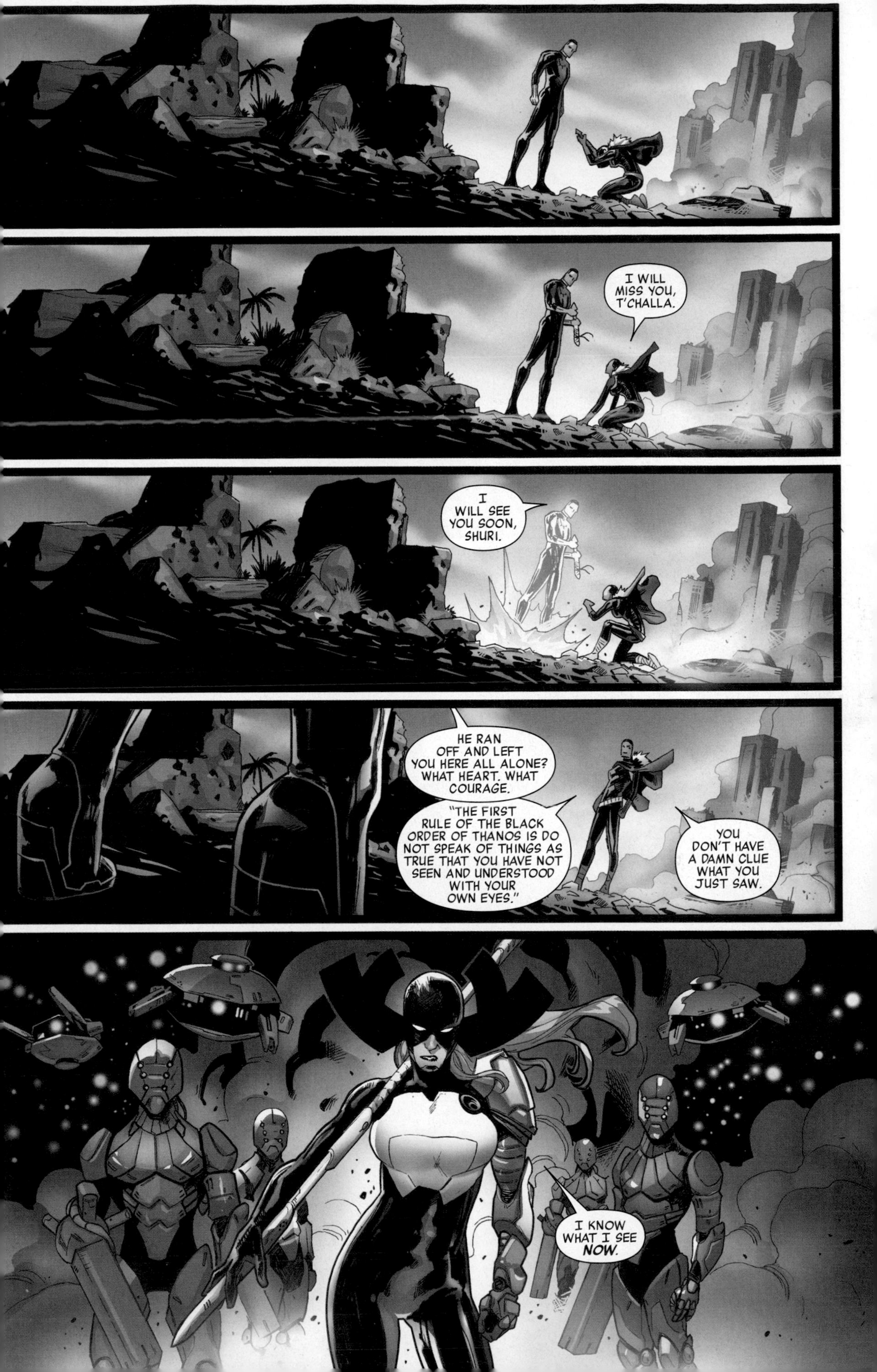
I WILL MISS YOU, T'CHALLA.
I WILL SEE YOU SOON, SHURI.
HE RAN OFF AND LEFT YOU HERE ALL ALONE? WHAT HEART. WHAT COURAGE.
"THE FIRST RULE OF THE BLACK ORDER OF THANOS IS DO NOT SPEAK OF THINGS AS TRUE THAT YOU HAVE NOT SEEN AND UNDERSTOOD WITH YOUR OWN EYES."
YOU DON'T HAVE A DAMN CLUE WHAT YOU JUST SAW.
I KNOW WHAT I SEE *NOW*.

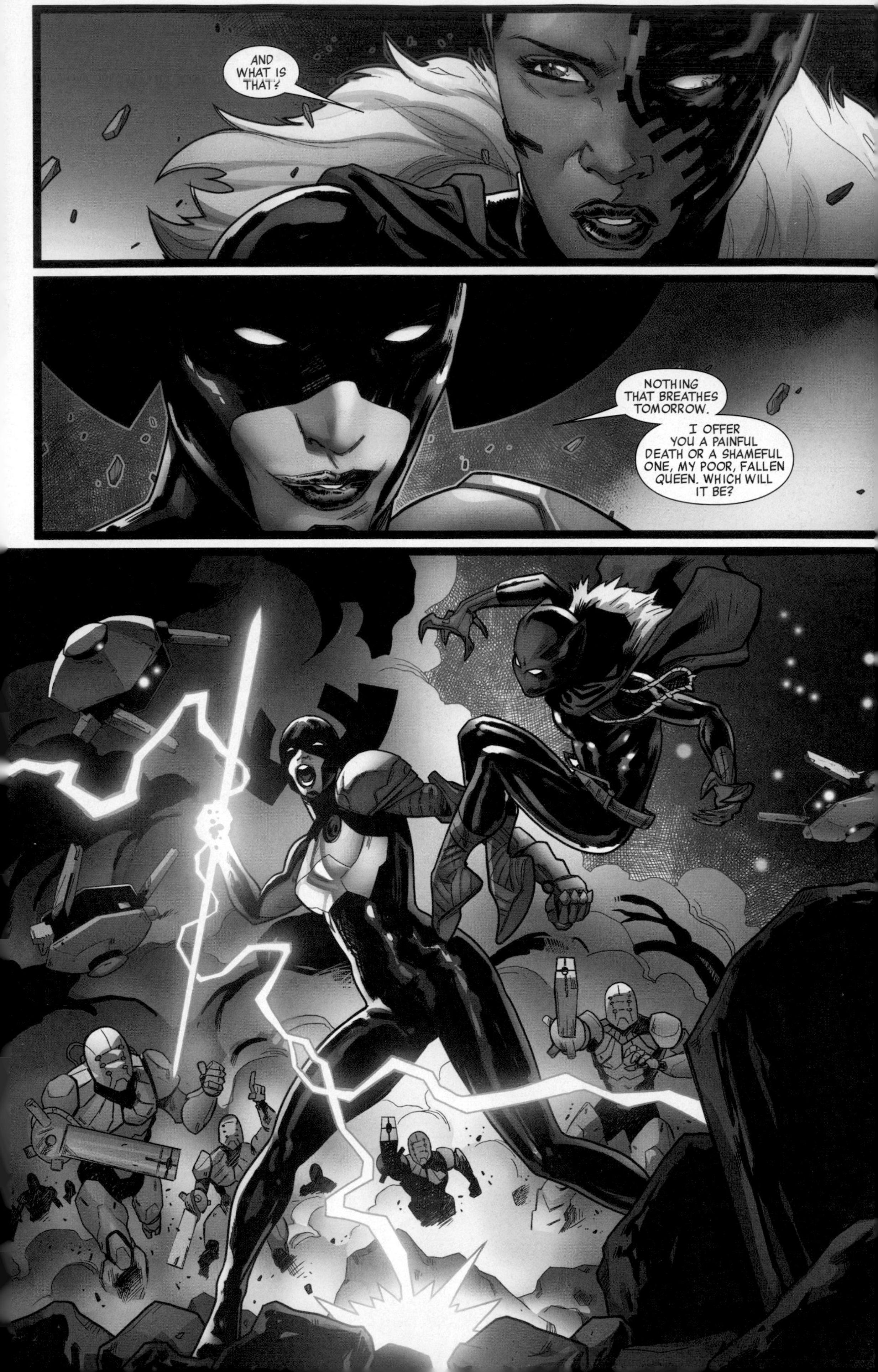
AND WHAT IS THAT?
NOTHING THAT BREATHES TOMORROW.
I OFFER YOU A PAINFUL DEATH OR A SHAMEFUL ONE, MY POOR, FALLEN QUEEN. WHICH WILL IT BE?

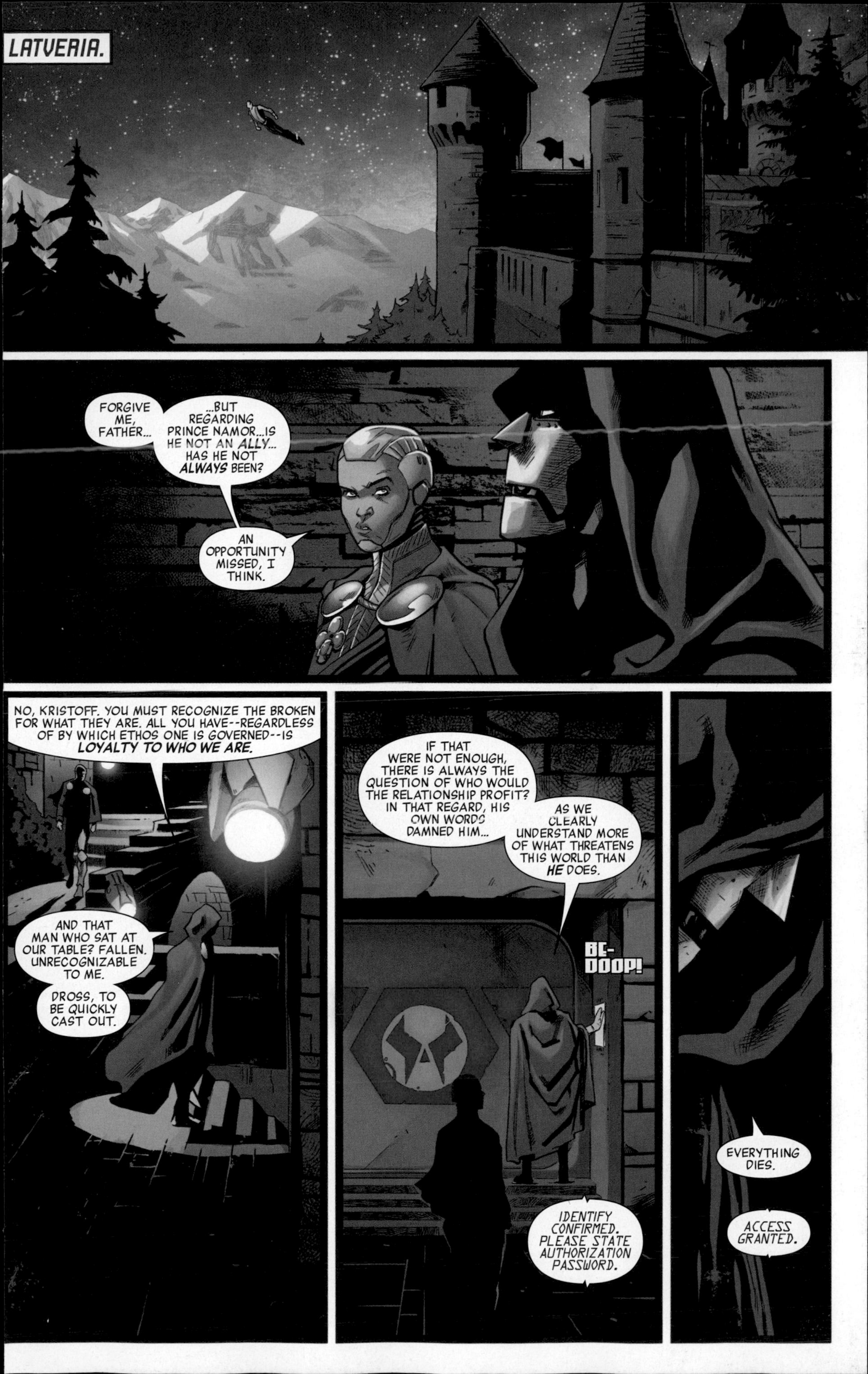
LATVERIA.
FORGIVE ME, FATHER...
...BUT REGARDING PRINCE NAMOR...IS HE NOT AN ALLY... HAS HE NOT ALWAYS BEEN?
AN OPPORTUNITY MISSED, I THINK.
NO, KRISTOFF. YOU MUST RECOGNIZE THE BROKEN FOR WHAT THEY ARE. ALL YOU HAVE--REGARDLESS OF BY WHICH ETHOS ONE IS GOVERNED--IS LOYALTY TO WHO WE ARE.
AND THAT MAN WHO SAT AT OUR TABLE? FALLEN. UNRECOGNIZABLE TO ME.
DROSS, TO BE QUICKLY CAST OUT.
IF THAT WERE NOT ENOUGH, THERE IS ALWAYS THE QUESTION OF WHO WOULD THE RELATIONSHIP PROFIT? IN THAT REGARD, HIS OWN WORDS DAMNED HIM...
AS WE CLEARLY UNDERSTAND MORE OF WHAT THREATENS THIS WORLD THAN HE DOES.
BE-DOOP!
IDENTIFY CONFIRMED. PLEASE STATE AUTHORIZATION PASSWORD.
EVERYTHING DIES.
ACCESS GRANTED.

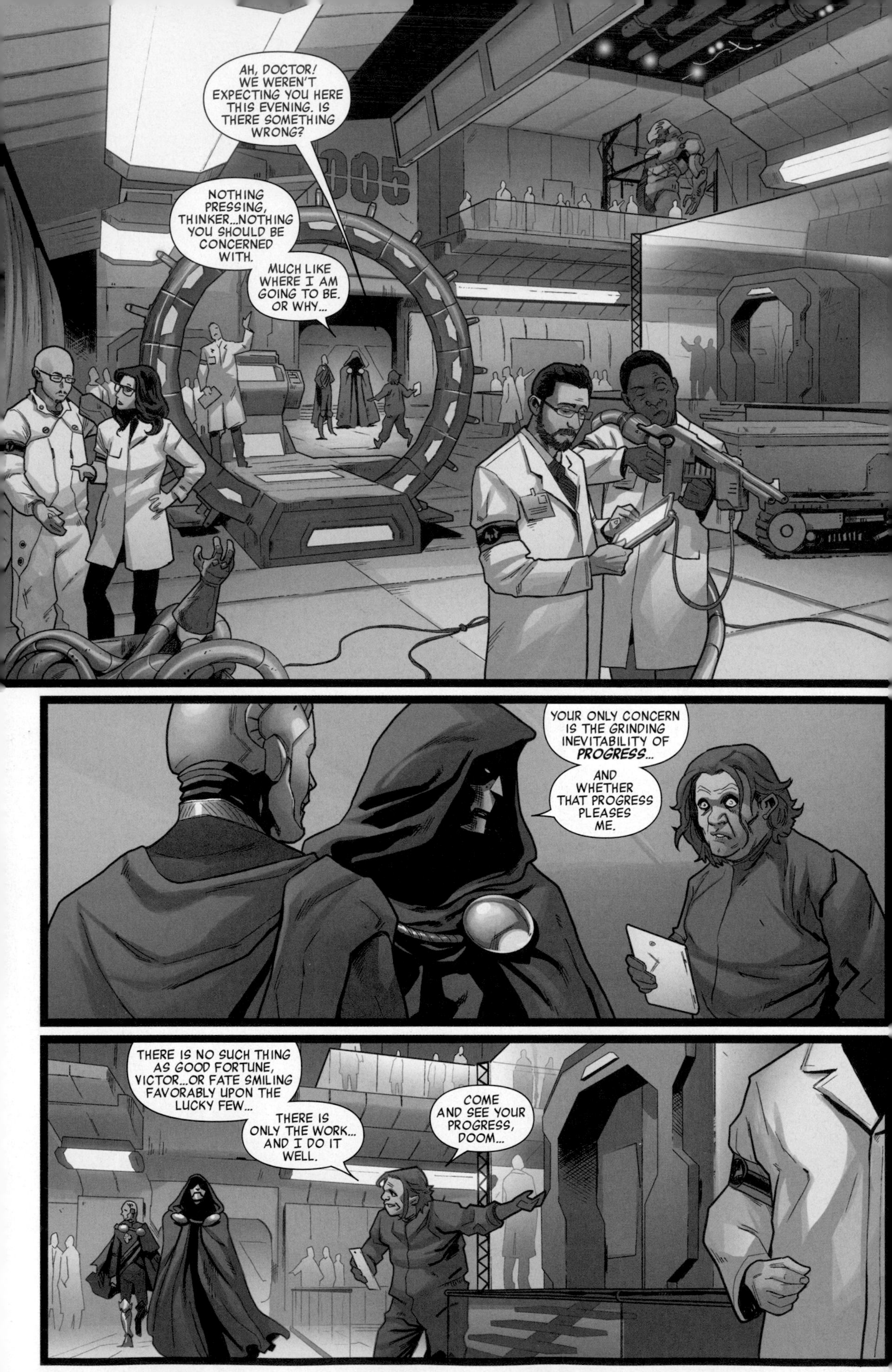
AH, DOCTOR! WE WEREN'T EXPECTING YOU HERE THIS EVENING. IS THERE SOMETHING WRONG?
NOTHING PRESSING, THINKER...NOTHING YOU SHOULD BE CONCERNED WITH.
MUCH LIKE WHERE I AM GOING TO BE. OR WHY...
YOUR ONLY CONCERN IS THE GRINDING INEVITABILITY OF PROGRESS...
AND WHETHER THAT PROGRESS PLEASES ME.
THERE IS NO SUCH THING AS GOOD FORTUNE, VICTOR...OR FATE SMILING FAVORABLY UPON THE LUCKY FEW...
THERE IS ONLY THE WORK... AND I DO IT WELL.
COME AND SEE YOUR PROGRESS, DOOM...

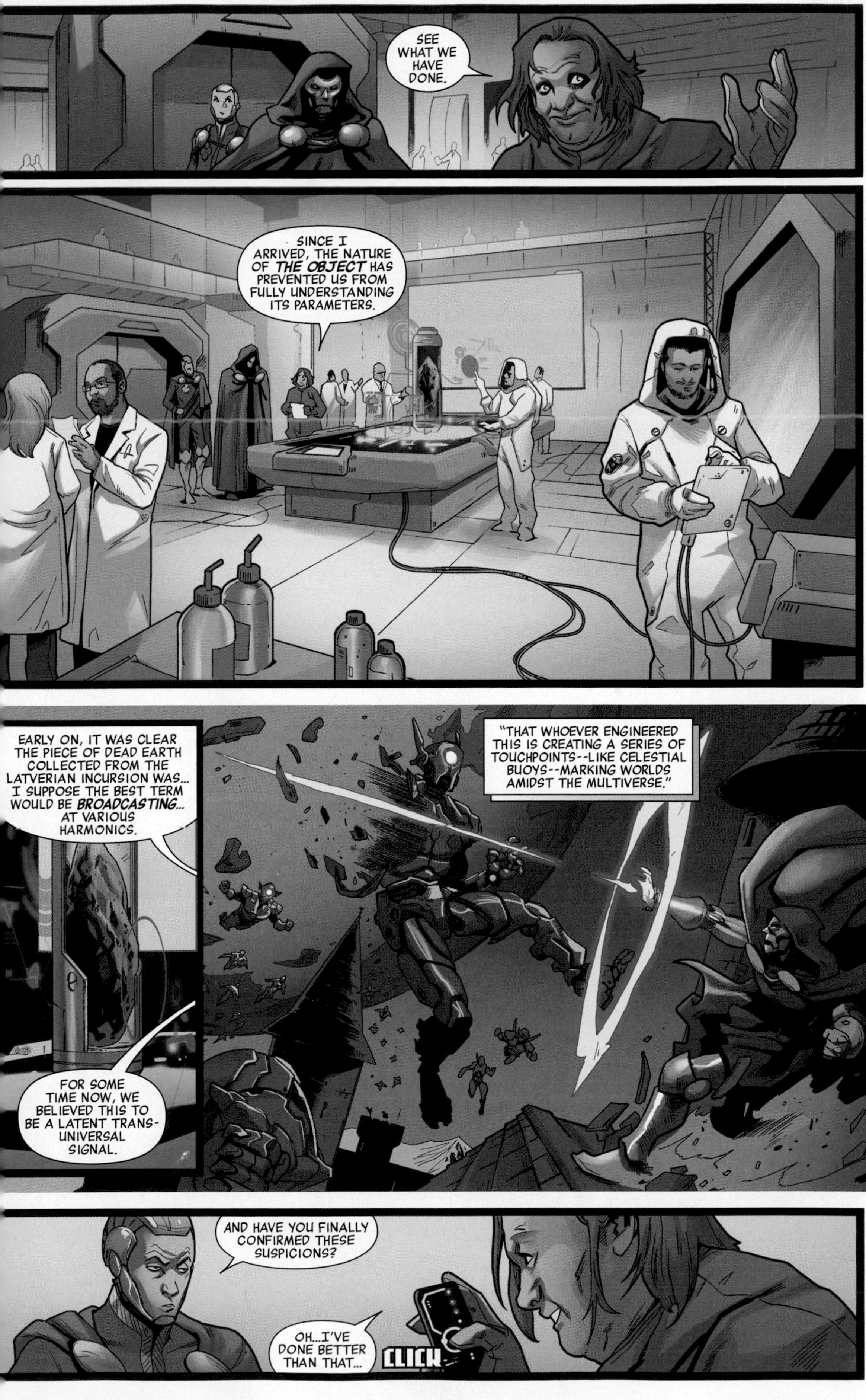
SEE WHAT WE HAVE DONE.
SINCE I ARRIVED, THE NATURE OF THE OBJECT HAS PREVENTED US FROM FULLY UNDERSTANDING ITS PARAMETERS.
EARLY ON, IT WAS CLEAR THE PIECE OF DEAD EARTH COLLECTED FROM THE LATVERIAN INCURSION WAS... I SUPPOSE THE BEST TERM WOULD BE BROADCASTING... AT VARIOUS HARMONICS.
FOR SOME TIME NOW, WE BELIEVED THIS TO BE A LATENT TRANS-UNIVERSAL SIGNAL.
"THAT WHOEVER ENGINEERED THIS IS CREATING A SERIES OF TOUCHPOINTS--LIKE CELESTIAL BUOYS--MARKING WORLDS AMIDST THE MULTIVERSE."
AND HAVE YOU FINALLY CONFIRMED THESE SUSPICIONS?
OH...I'VE DONE BETTER THAN THAT...
CLICK

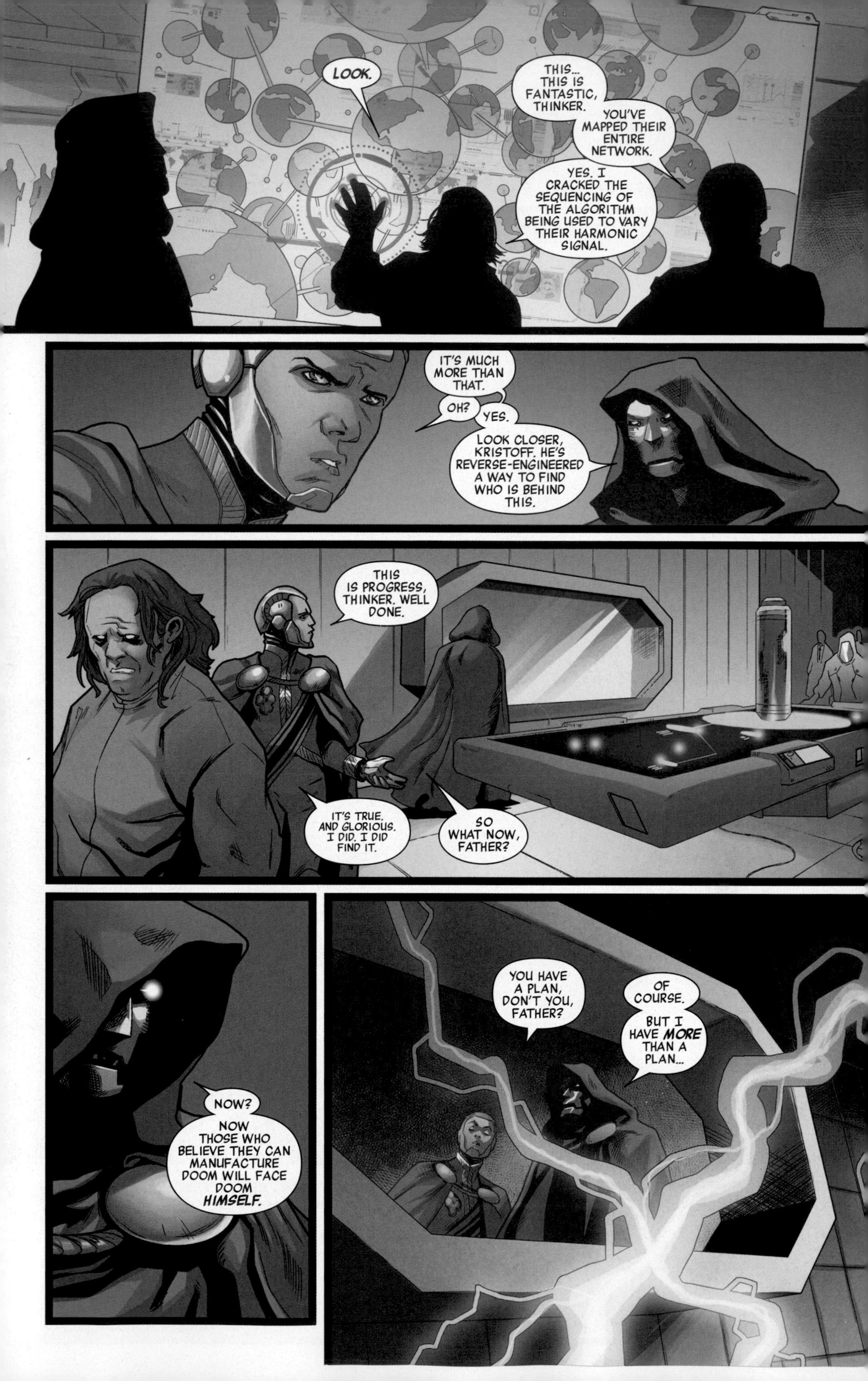
LOOK.
THIS... THIS IS FANTASTIC, THINKER.
YOU'VE MAPPED THEIR ENTIRE NETWORK.
YES. I CRACKED THE SEQUENCING OF THE ALGORITHM BEING USED TO VARY THEIR HARMONIC SIGNAL.
IT'S MUCH MORE THAN THAT.
OH?
YES.
LOOK CLOSER, KRISTOFF. HE'S REVERSE-ENGINEERED A WAY TO FIND WHO IS BEHIND THIS.
THIS IS PROGRESS, THINKER. WELL DONE.
IT'S TRUE. AND GLORIOUS. I DID. I DID FIND IT.
SO WHAT NOW, FATHER?
NOW?
NOW THOSE WHO BELIEVE THEY CAN MANUFACTURE DOOM WILL FACE DOOM HIMSELF.
YOU HAVE A PLAN, DON'T YOU, FATHER?
OF COURSE.
BUT I HAVE MORE THAN A PLAN...

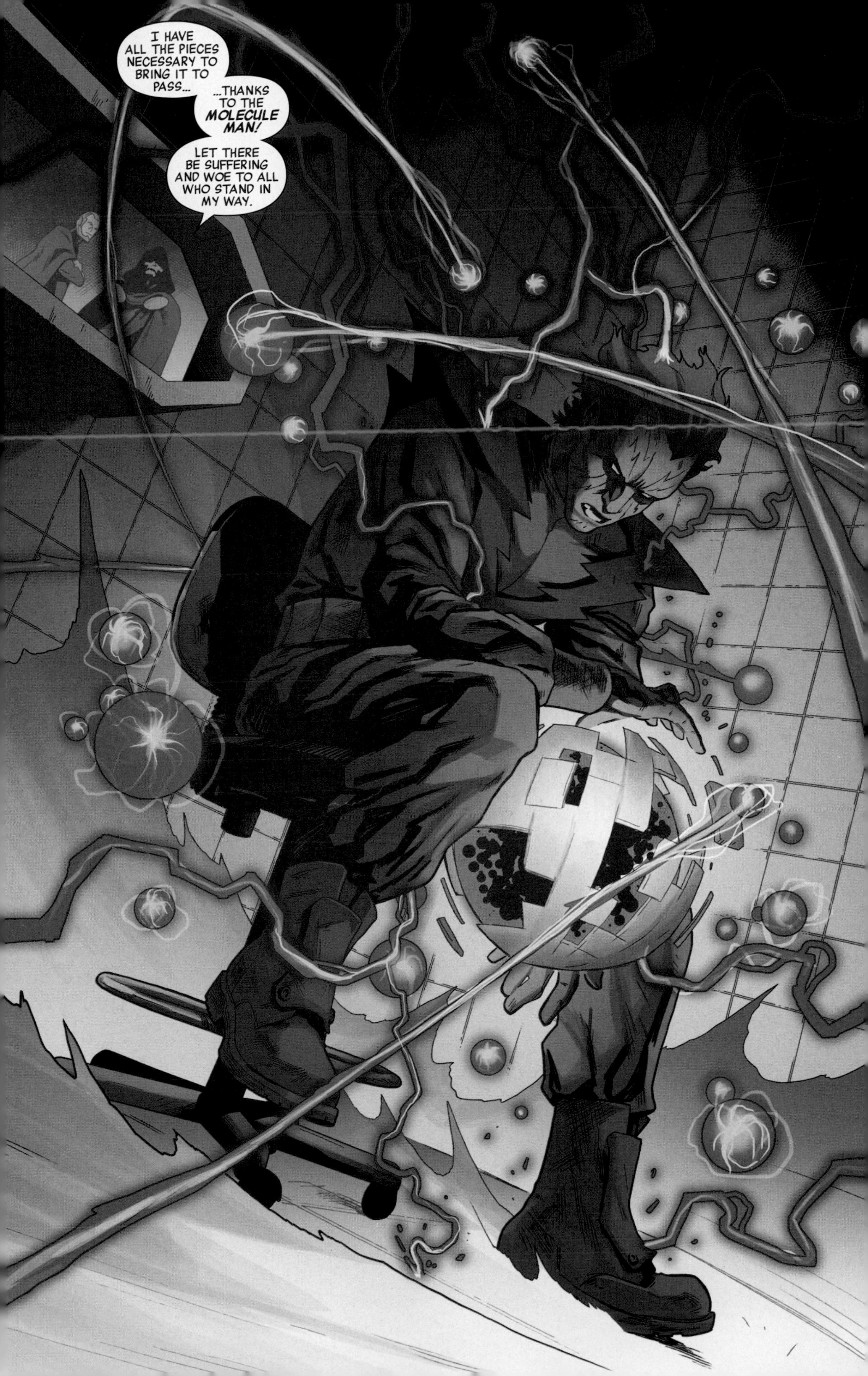
I HAVE ALL THE PIECES NECESSARY TO BRING IT TO PASS...
...THANKS TO THE ***MOLECULE MAN!***
LET THERE BE SUFFERING AND WOE TO ALL WHO STAND IN MY WAY.

"UNIVERSAL AVENGERS"

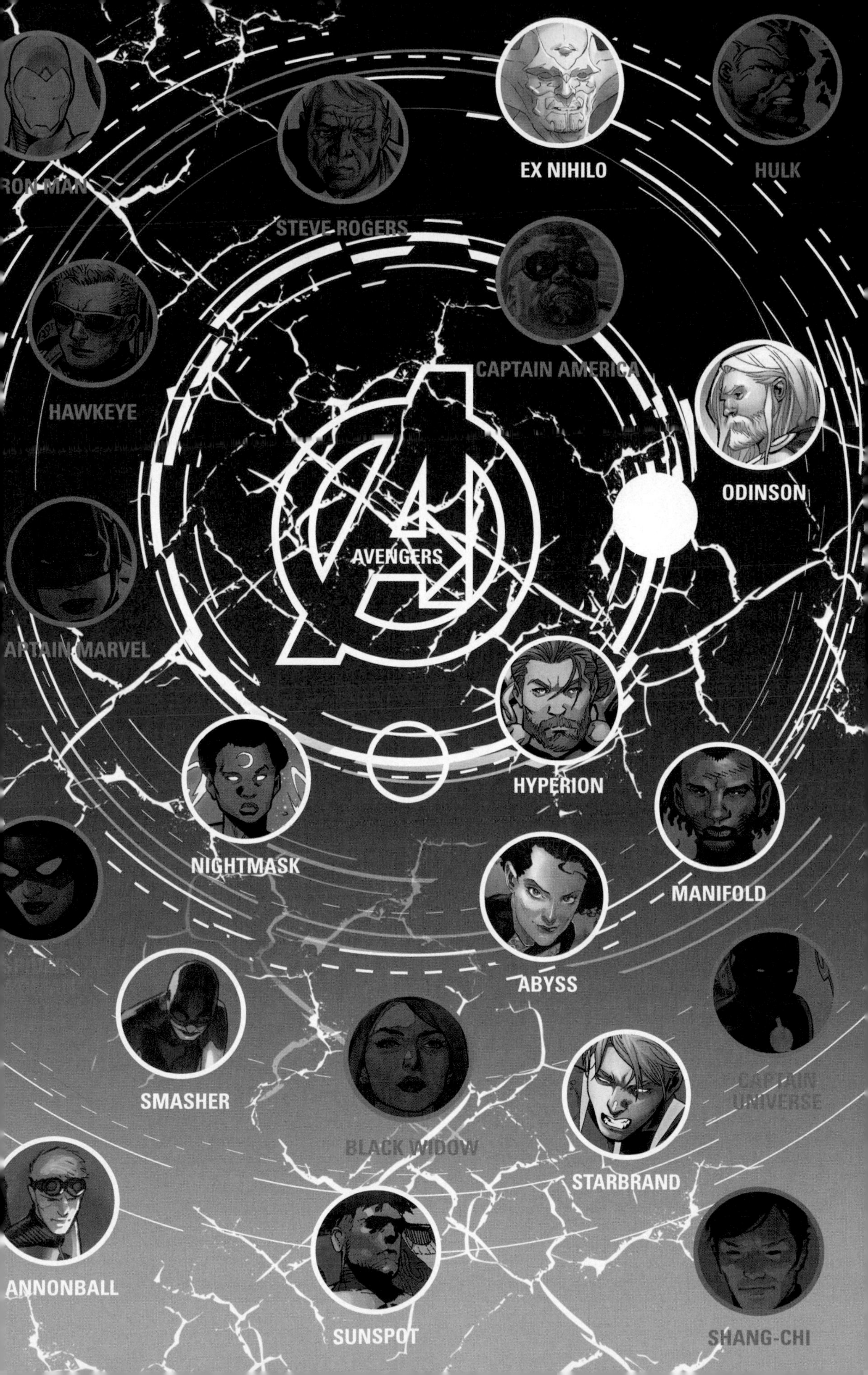
IRON MAN
STEVE ROGERS
EX NIHILO
HULK
HAWKEYE
CAPTAIN AMERICA
ODINSON
AVENGERS
CAPTAIN MARVEL
HYPERION
NIGHTMASK
MANIFOLD
SPIDER-WOMAN
ABYSS
SMASHER
CAPTAIN UNIVERSE
BLACK WIDOW
STARBRAND
CANNONBALL
SUNSPOT
SHANG-CHI

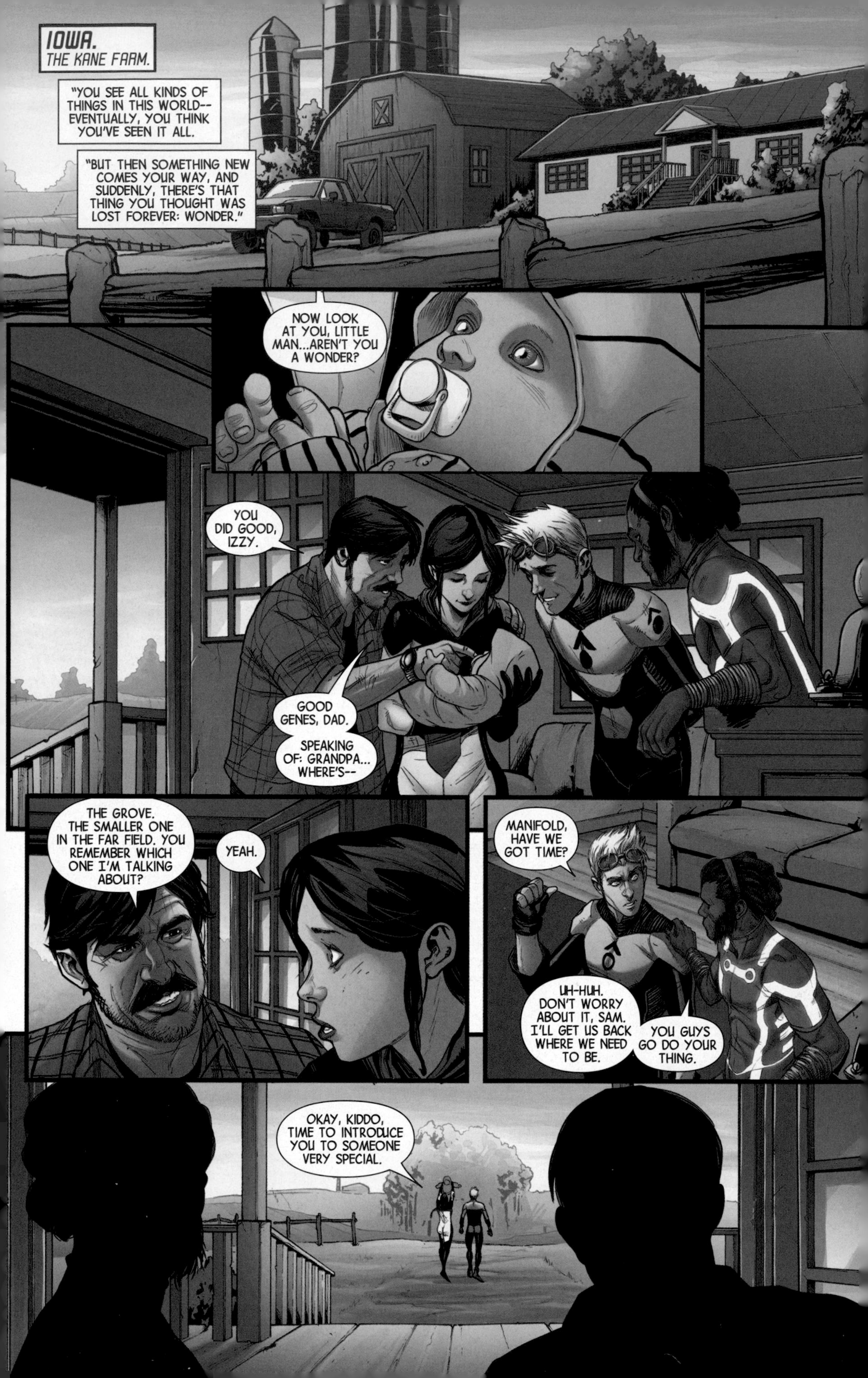
IOWA. THE KANE FARM.
"YOU SEE ALL KINDS OF THINGS IN THIS WORLD-- EVENTUALLY, YOU THINK YOU'VE SEEN IT ALL.
"BUT THEN SOMETHING NEW COMES YOUR WAY, AND SUDDENLY, THERE'S THAT THING YOU THOUGHT WAS LOST FOREVER: WONDER."
NOW LOOK AT YOU, LITTLE MAN...AREN'T YOU A WONDER?
YOU DID GOOD, IZZY.
GOOD GENES, DAD.
SPEAKING OF: GRANDPA... WHERE'S--
THE GROVE. THE SMALLER ONE IN THE FAR FIELD. YOU REMEMBER WHICH ONE I'M TALKING ABOUT?
YEAH.
MANIFOLD, HAVE WE GOT TIME?
UH-HUH. DON'T WORRY ABOUT IT, SAM. I'LL GET US BACK WHERE WE NEED TO BE.
YOU GUYS GO DO YOUR THING.
OKAY, KIDDO, TIME TO INTRODUCE YOU TO SOMEONE VERY SPECIAL.

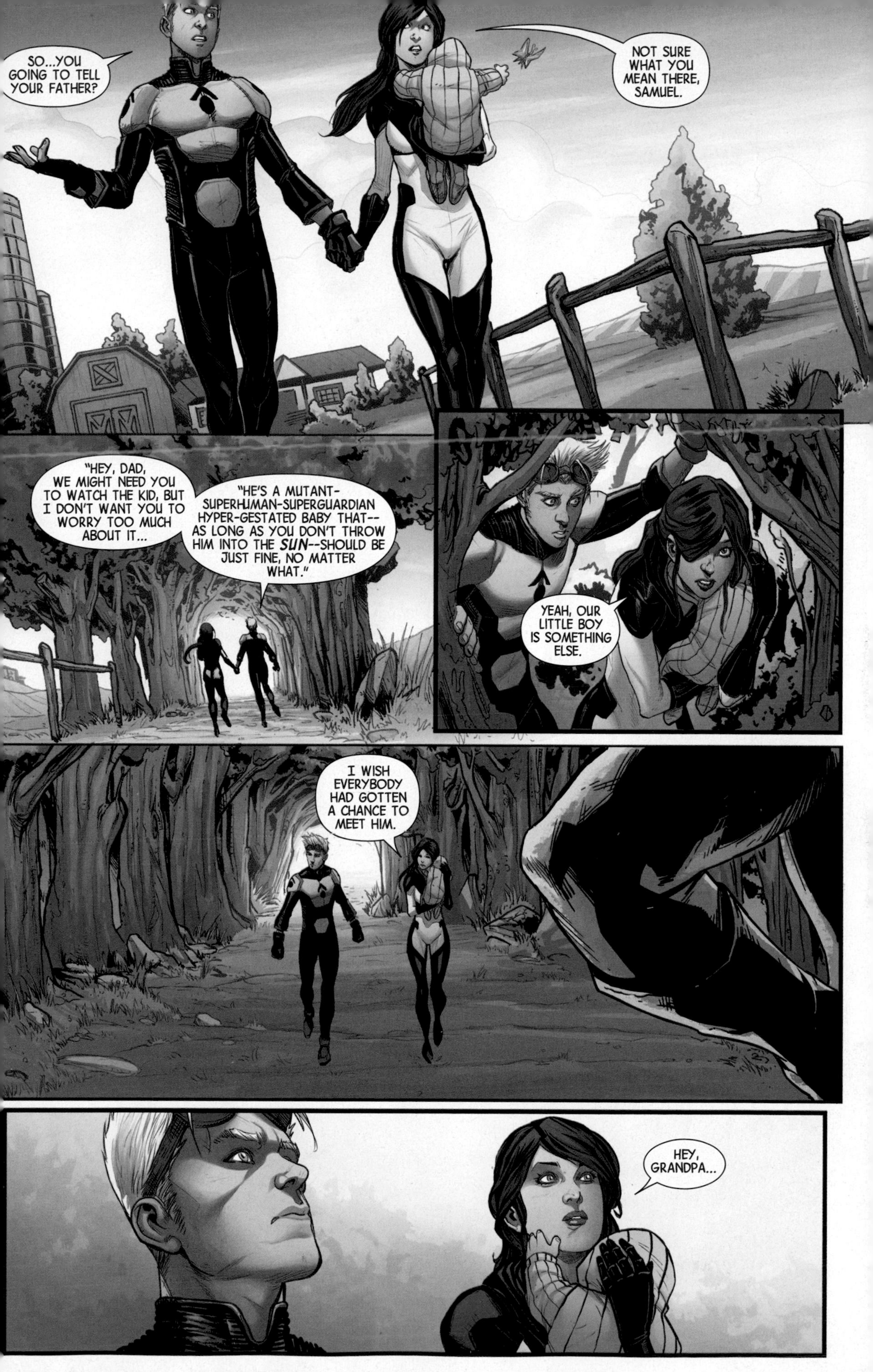
SO...YOU GOING TO TELL YOUR FATHER?
NOT SURE WHAT YOU MEAN THERE, SAMUEL.
"HEY, DAD, WE MIGHT NEED YOU TO WATCH THE KID, BUT I DON'T WANT YOU TO WORRY TOO MUCH ABOUT IT...
"HE'S A MUTANT-SUPERHUMAN-SUPERGUARDIAN HYPER-GESTATED BABY THAT--AS LONG AS YOU DON'T THROW HIM INTO THE *SUN*--SHOULD BE JUST FINE, NO MATTER WHAT."
YEAH, OUR LITTLE BOY IS SOMETHING ELSE.
I WISH EVERYBODY HAD GOTTEN A CHANCE TO MEET HIM.
HEY, GRANDPA...

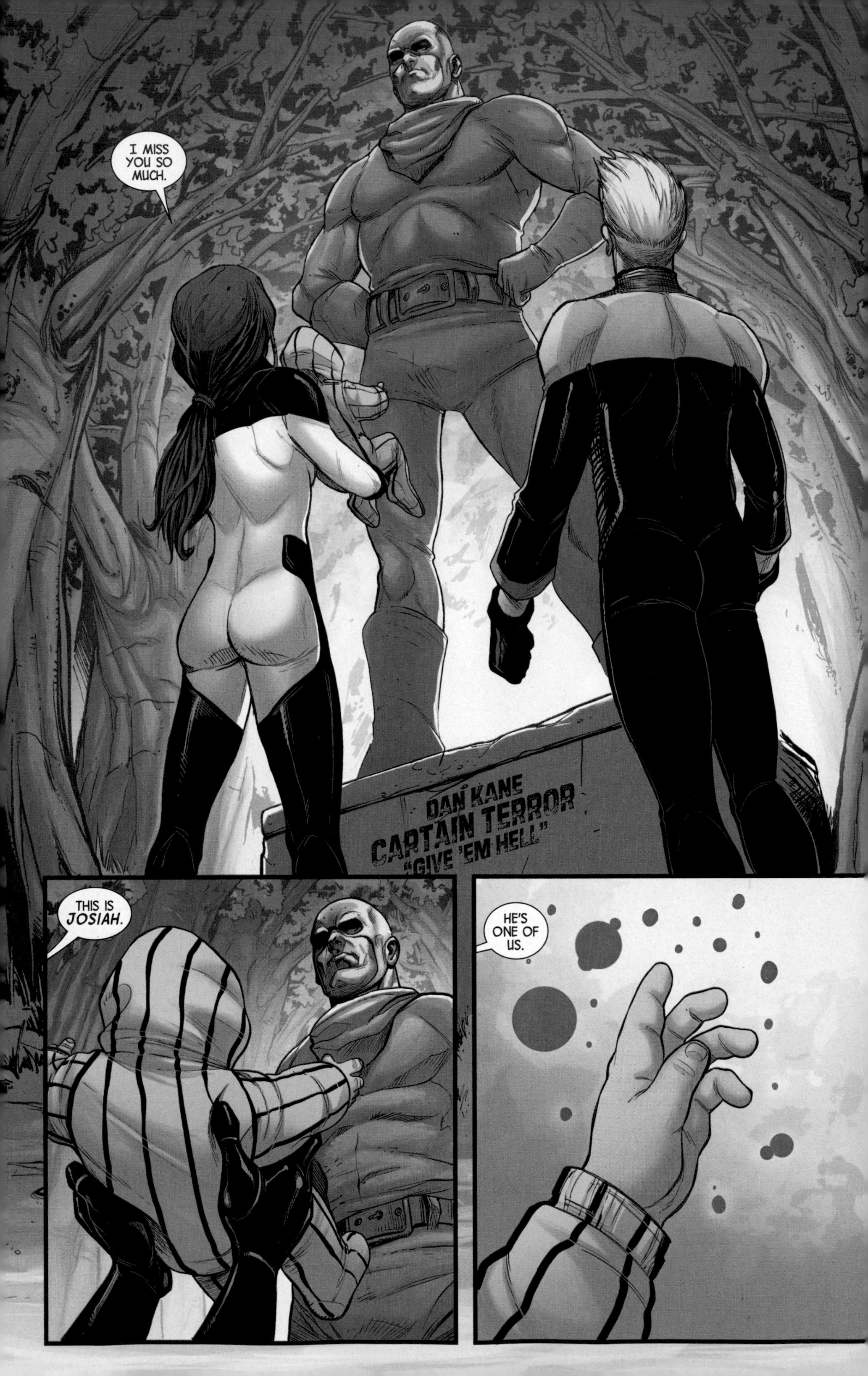
I MISS YOU SO MUCH.
DAN KANE
CAPTAIN TERROR
"GIVE 'EM HELL"
THIS IS JOSIAH.
HE'S ONE OF US.

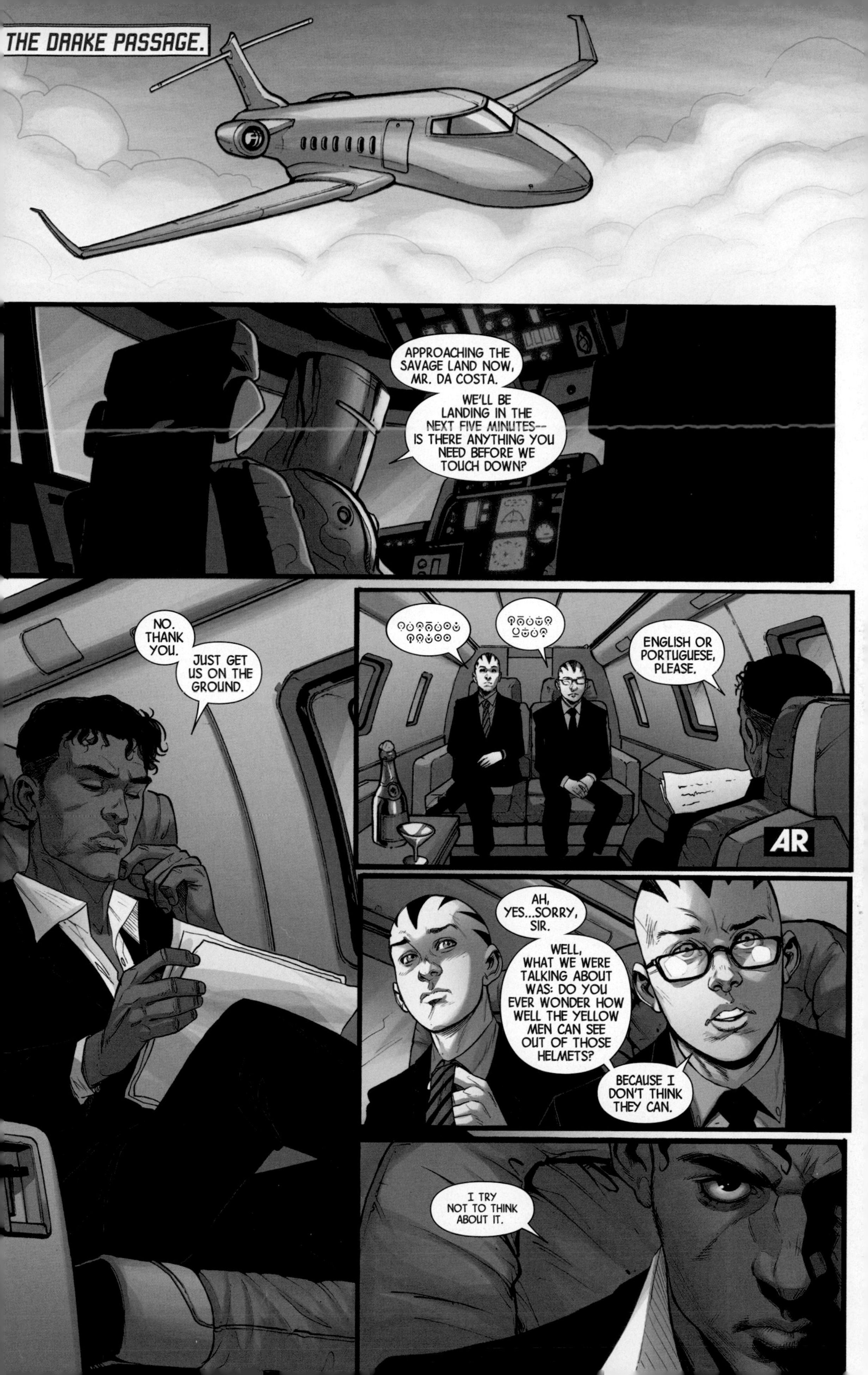
THE DRAKE PASSAGE.
APPROACHING THE SAVAGE LAND NOW, MR. DA COSTA.
WE'LL BE LANDING IN THE NEXT FIVE MINUTES-- IS THERE ANYTHING YOU NEED BEFORE WE TOUCH DOWN?
NO. THANK YOU.
JUST GET US ON THE GROUND.
ENGLISH OR PORTUGUESE, PLEASE.
AR
AH, YES...SORRY, SIR.
WELL, WHAT WE WERE TALKING ABOUT WAS: DO YOU EVER WONDER HOW WELL THE YELLOW MEN CAN SEE OUT OF THOSE HELMETS?
BECAUSE I DON'T THINK THEY CAN.
I TRY NOT TO THINK ABOUT IT.

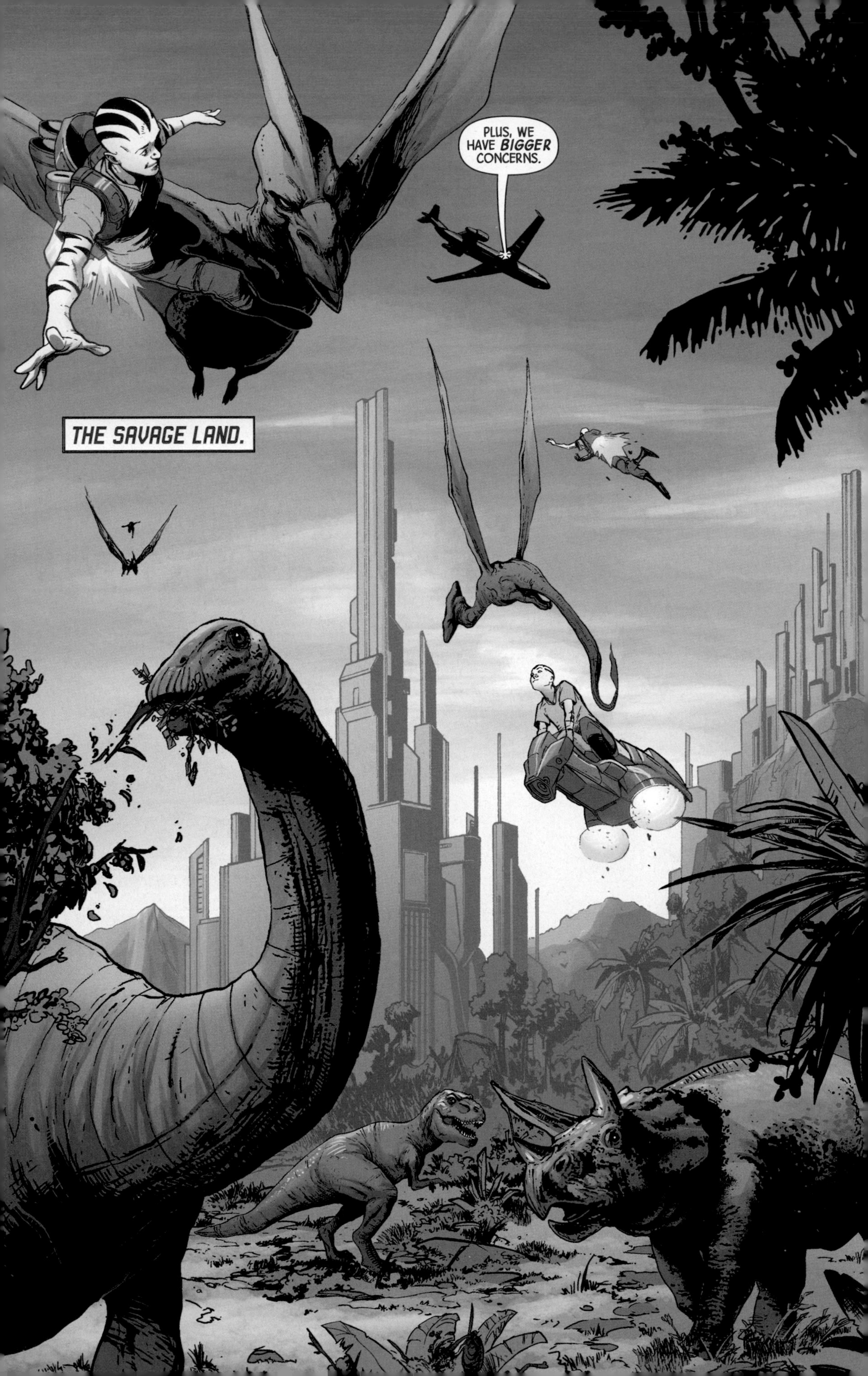
PLUS, WE HAVE BIGGER CONCERNS.
THE SAVAGE LAND.

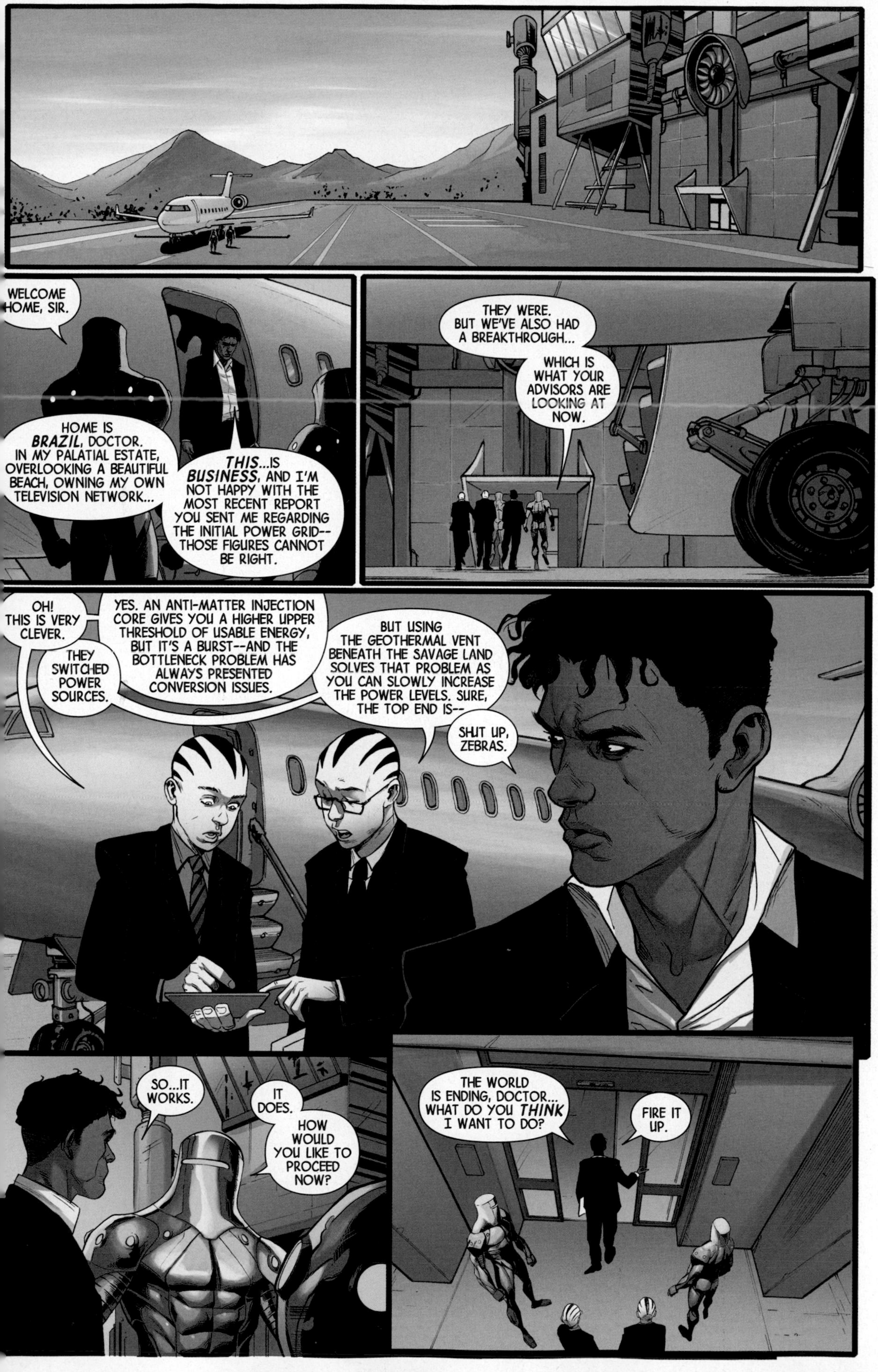
WELCOME HOME, SIR.
HOME IS BRAZIL, DOCTOR. IN MY PALATIAL ESTATE, OVERLOOKING A BEAUTIFUL BEACH, OWNING MY OWN TELEVISION NETWORK...
THIS...IS BUSINESS, AND I'M NOT HAPPY WITH THE MOST RECENT REPORT YOU SENT ME REGARDING THE INITIAL POWER GRID-- THOSE FIGURES CANNOT BE RIGHT.
THEY WERE. BUT WE'VE ALSO HAD A BREAKTHROUGH...
WHICH IS WHAT YOUR ADVISORS ARE LOOKING AT NOW.
OH! THIS IS VERY CLEVER.
YES. AN ANTI-MATTER INJECTION CORE GIVES YOU A HIGHER UPPER THRESHOLD OF USABLE ENERGY, BUT IT'S A BURST--AND THE BOTTLENECK PROBLEM HAS ALWAYS PRESENTED CONVERSION ISSUES.
THEY SWITCHED POWER SOURCES.
BUT USING THE GEOTHERMAL VENT BENEATH THE SAVAGE LAND SOLVES THAT PROBLEM AS YOU CAN SLOWLY INCREASE THE POWER LEVELS. SURE, THE TOP END IS--
SHUT UP, ZEBRAS.
SO...IT WORKS.
IT DOES.
HOW WOULD YOU LIKE TO PROCEED NOW?
THE WORLD IS ENDING, DOCTOR... WHAT DO YOU THINK I WANT TO DO?
FIRE IT UP.

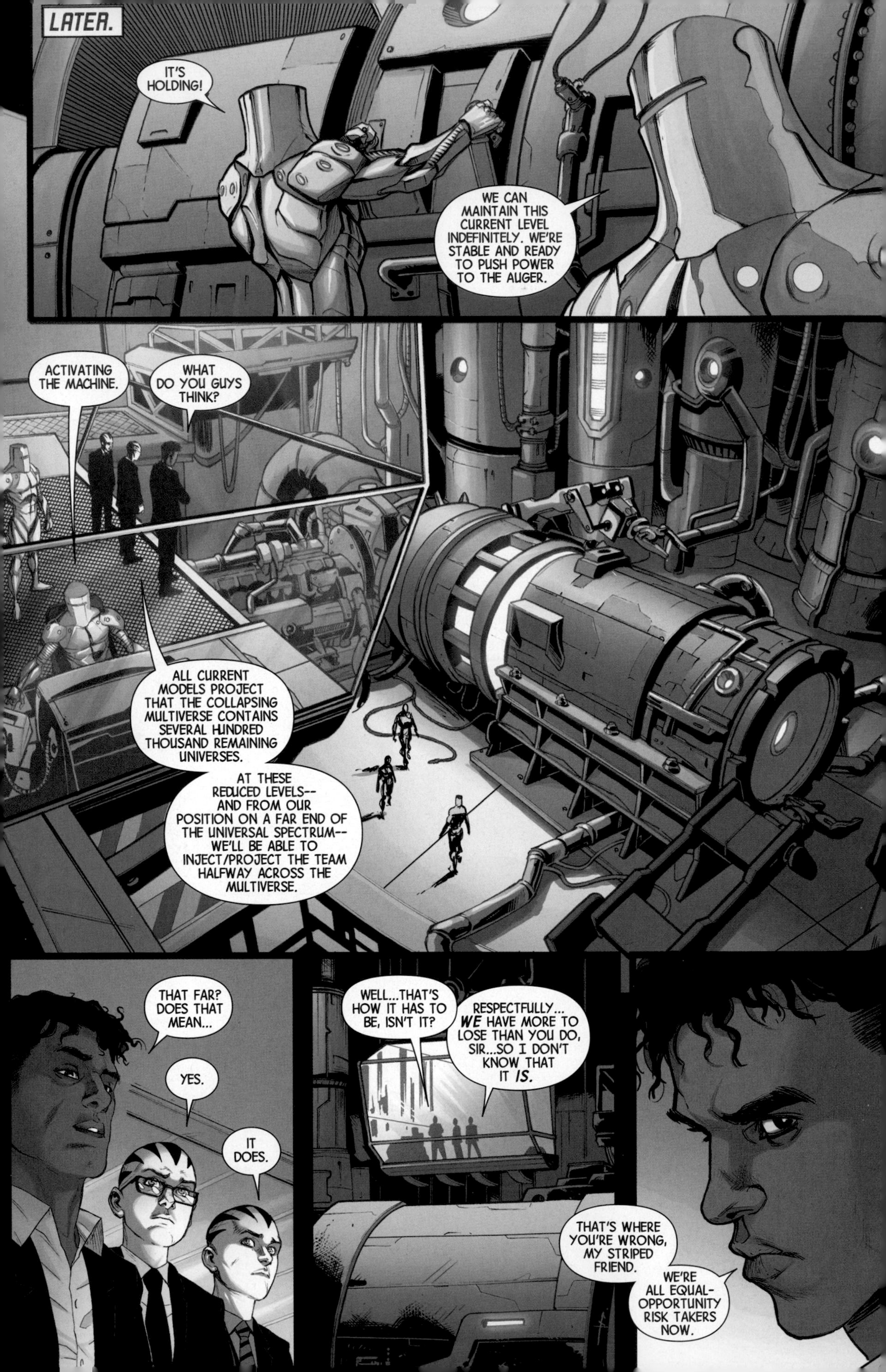
LATER.
IT'S HOLDING!
WE CAN MAINTAIN THIS CURRENT LEVEL INDEFINITELY. WE'RE STABLE AND READY TO PUSH POWER TO THE AUGER.
ACTIVATING THE MACHINE.
WHAT DO YOU GUYS THINK?
ALL CURRENT MODELS PROJECT THAT THE COLLAPSING MULTIVERSE CONTAINS SEVERAL HUNDRED THOUSAND REMAINING UNIVERSES.
AT THESE REDUCED LEVELS-- AND FROM OUR POSITION ON A FAR END OF THE UNIVERSAL SPECTRUM-- WE'LL BE ABLE TO INJECT/PROJECT THE TEAM HALFWAY ACROSS THE MULTIVERSE.
THAT FAR? DOES THAT MEAN...
YES.
IT DOES.
WELL...THAT'S HOW IT HAS TO BE, ISN'T IT?
RESPECTFULLY... *WE* HAVE MORE TO LOSE THAN YOU DO, SIR...SO I DON'T KNOW THAT IT *IS*.
THAT'S WHERE YOU'RE WRONG, MY STRIPED FRIEND.
WE'RE ALL EQUAL-OPPORTUNITY RISK TAKERS NOW.

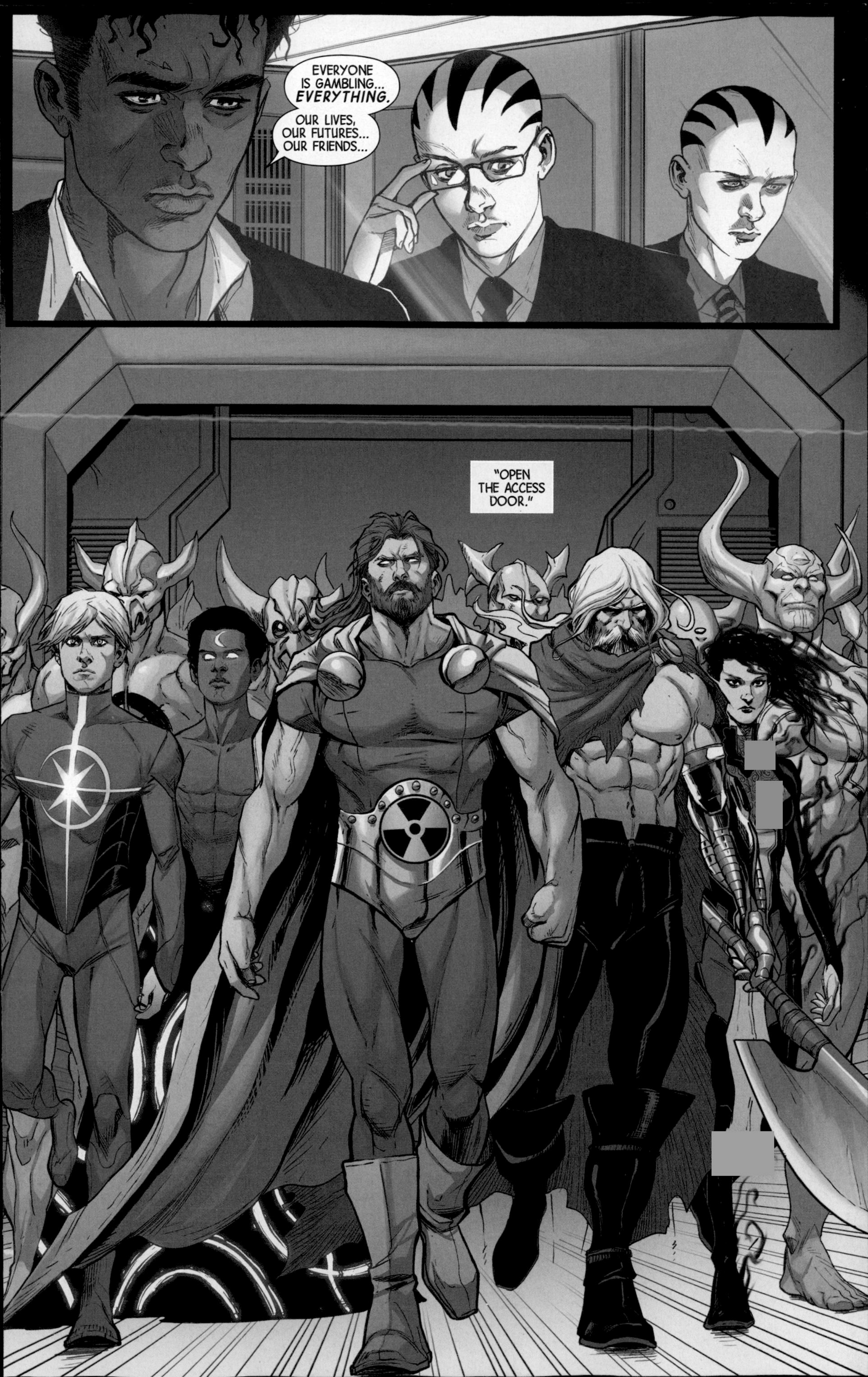
EVERYONE IS GAMBLING... EVERYTHING.
OUR LIVES, OUR FUTURES... OUR FRIENDS...
"OPEN THE ACCESS DOOR."

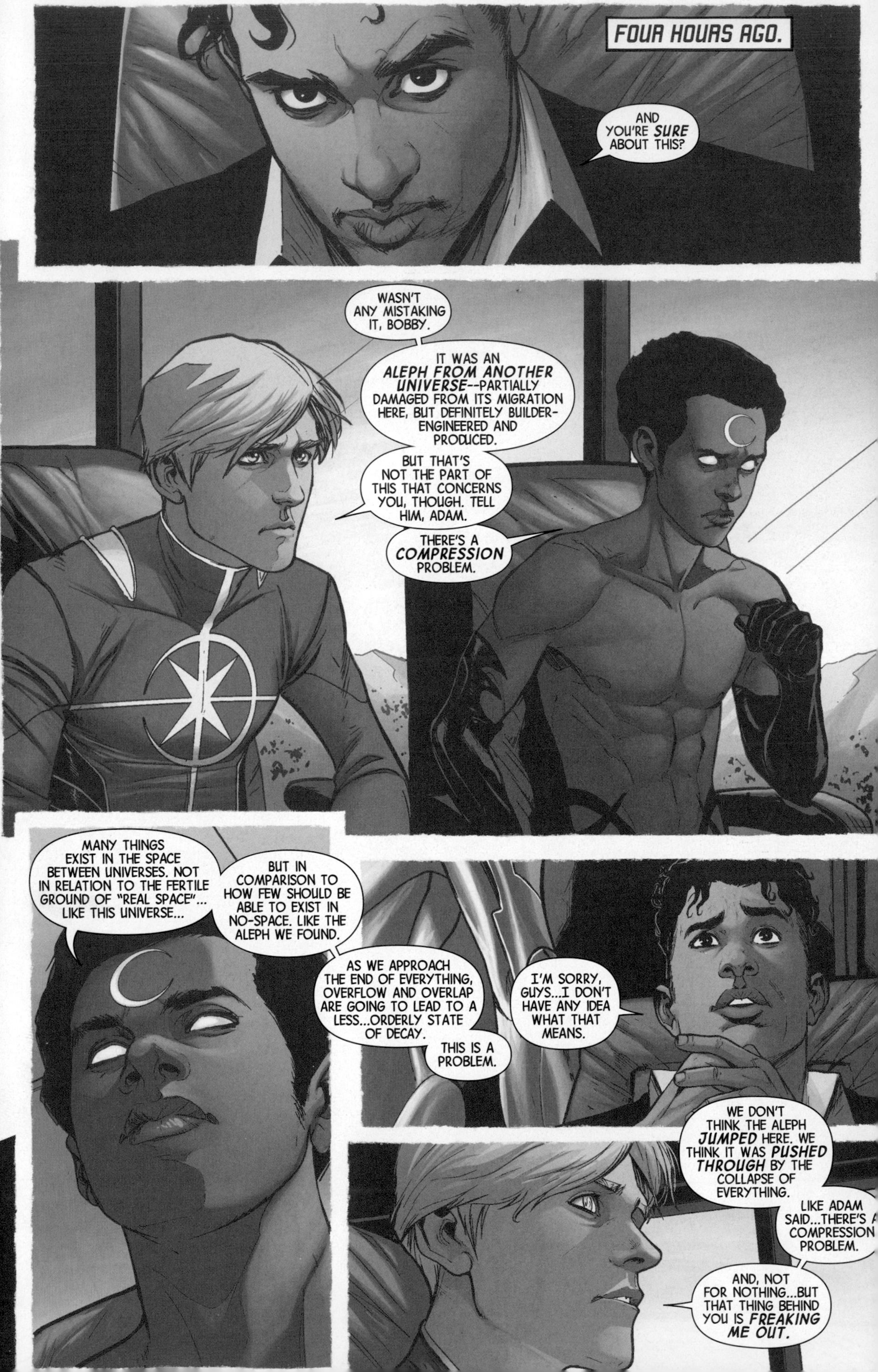

FOUR HOURS AGO.
AND YOU'RE SURE ABOUT THIS?
WASN'T ANY MISTAKING IT, BOBBY.
IT WAS AN ALEPH FROM ANOTHER UNIVERSE--PARTIALLY DAMAGED FROM ITS MIGRATION HERE, BUT DEFINITELY BUILDER-ENGINEERED AND PRODUCED.
BUT THAT'S NOT THE PART OF THIS THAT CONCERNS YOU, THOUGH. TELL HIM, ADAM.
THERE'S A COMPRESSION PROBLEM.
MANY THINGS EXIST IN THE SPACE BETWEEN UNIVERSES. NOT IN RELATION TO THE FERTILE GROUND OF "REAL SPACE"... LIKE THIS UNIVERSE...
BUT IN COMPARISON TO HOW FEW SHOULD BE ABLE TO EXIST IN NO-SPACE. LIKE THE ALEPH WE FOUND.
AS WE APPROACH THE END OF EVERYTHING, OVERFLOW AND OVERLAP ARE GOING TO LEAD TO A LESS...ORDERLY STATE OF DECAY.
THIS IS A PROBLEM.
I'M SORRY, GUYS...I DON'T HAVE ANY IDEA WHAT THAT MEANS.
WE DON'T THINK THE ALEPH JUMPED HERE. WE THINK IT WAS PUSHED THROUGH BY THE COLLAPSE OF EVERYTHING.
LIKE ADAM SAID...THERE'S A COMPRESSION PROBLEM.
AND, NOT FOR NOTHING...BUT THAT THING BEHIND YOU IS FREAKING ME OUT.

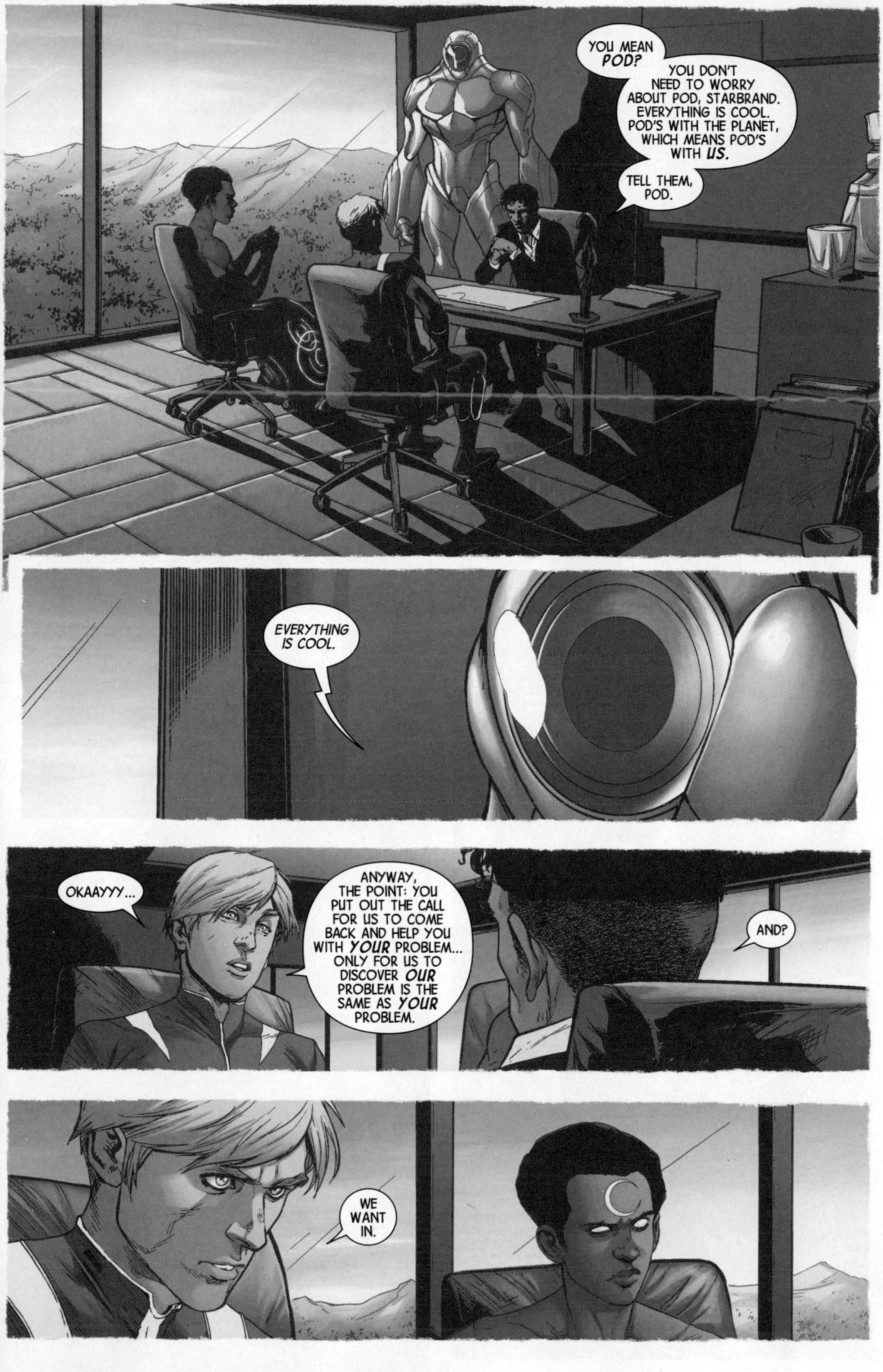
YOU MEAN *POD?*
YOU DON'T NEED TO WORRY ABOUT POD, STARBRAND. EVERYTHING IS COOL. POD'S WITH THE PLANET, WHICH MEANS POD'S WITH *US.*
TELL THEM, POD.
EVERYTHING IS COOL.
OKAAYYY...
ANYWAY, THE POINT: YOU PUT OUT THE CALL FOR US TO COME BACK AND HELP YOU WITH *YOUR* PROBLEM... ONLY FOR US TO DISCOVER *OUR* PROBLEM IS THE SAME AS *YOUR* PROBLEM.
AND?
WE WANT IN.

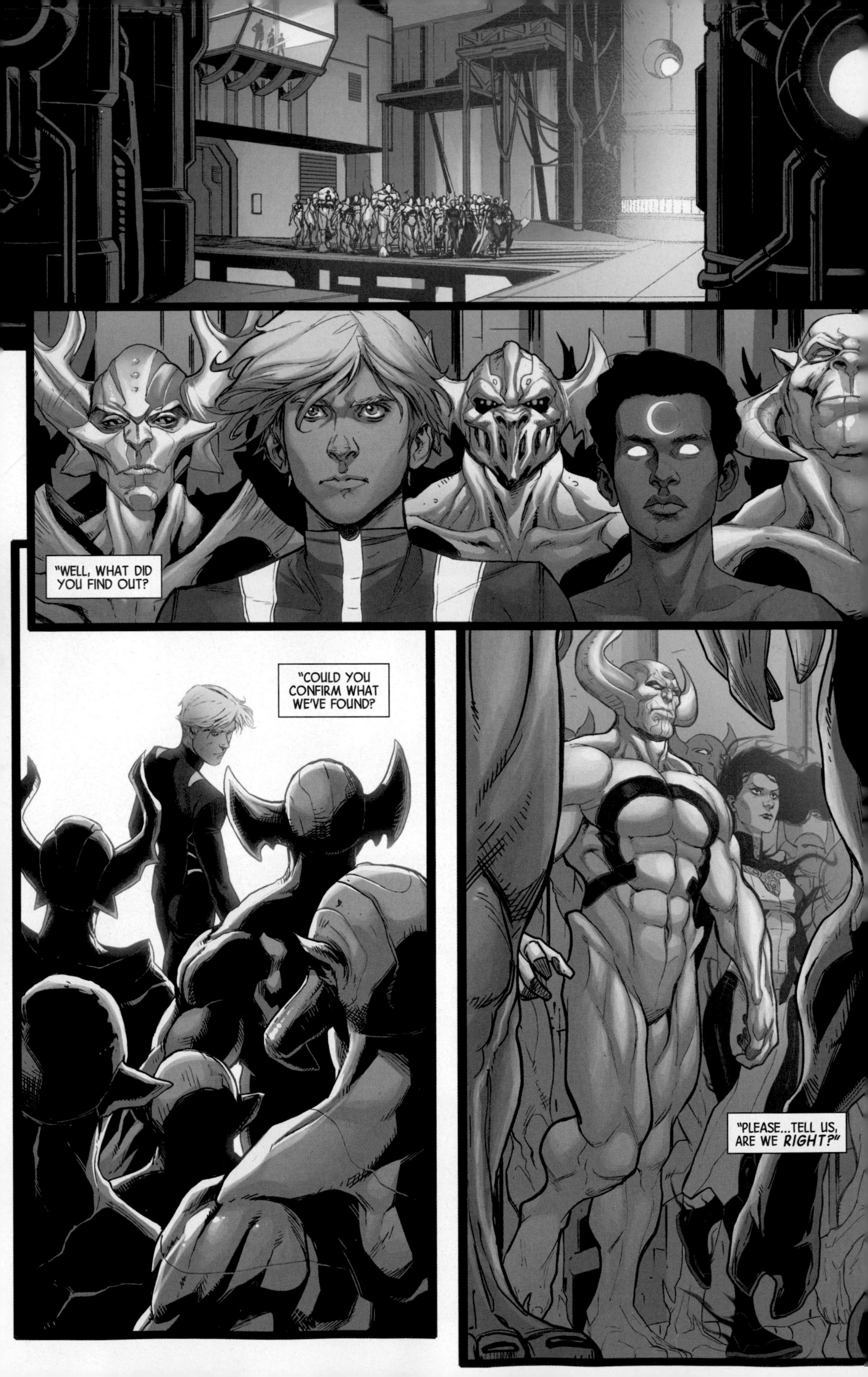
"WELL, WHAT DID YOU FIND OUT?
"COULD YOU CONFIRM WHAT WE'VE FOUND?
"PLEASE...TELL US, ARE WE *RIGHT?*"

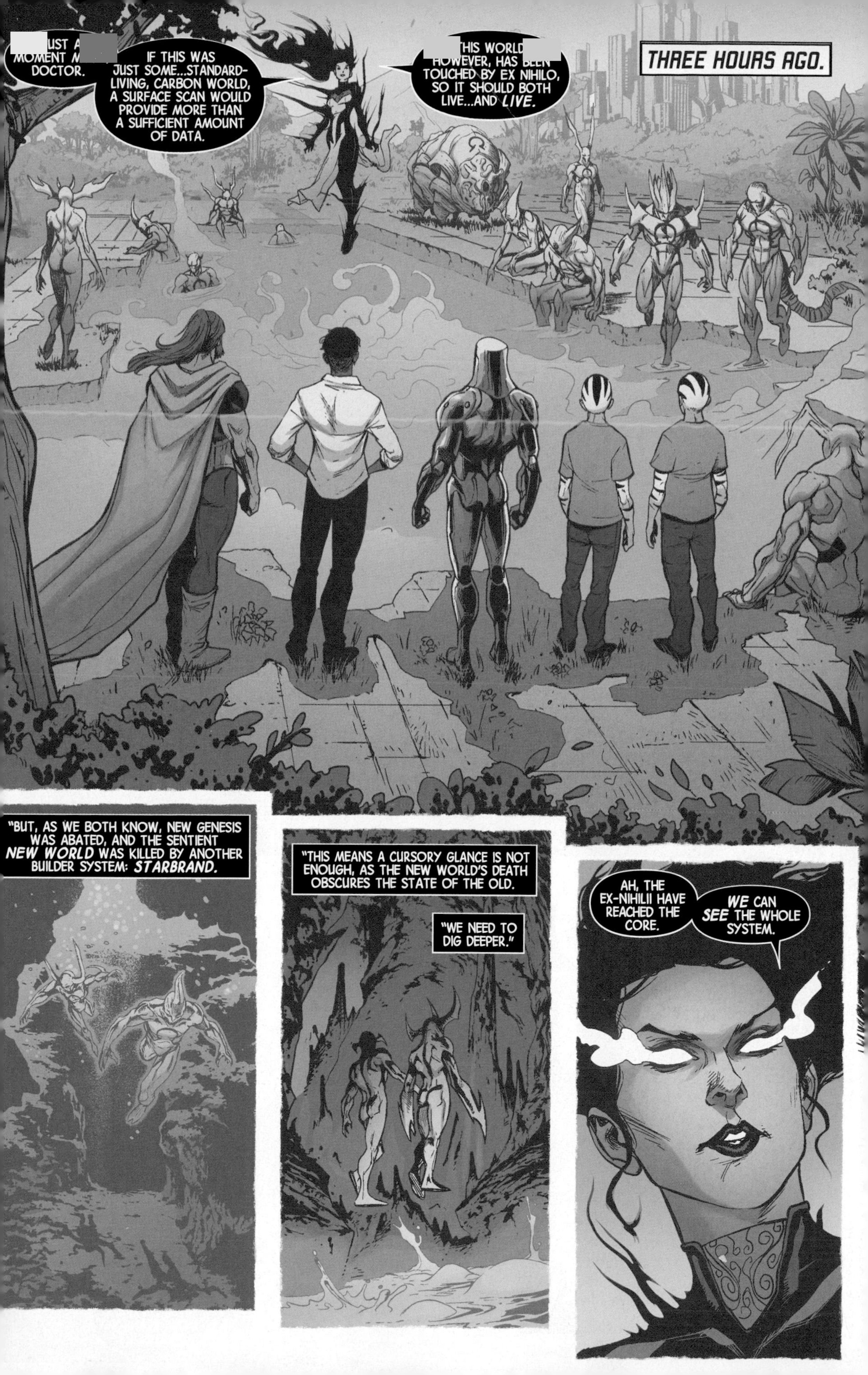
[redacted]UST A [redacted] MOMENT M[redacted] DOCTOR.
IF THIS WAS JUST SOME...STANDARD-LIVING, CARBON WORLD, A SURFACE SCAN WOULD PROVIDE MORE THAN A SUFFICIENT AMOUNT OF DATA.
[redacted] THIS WORLD[redacted] HOWEVER, HAS [redacted] TOUCHED BY EX NIHILO, SO IT SHOULD BOTH LIVE...AND LIVE.
THREE HOURS AGO.
"BUT, AS WE BOTH KNOW, NEW GENESIS WAS ABATED, AND THE SENTIENT NEW WORLD WAS KILLED BY ANOTHER BUILDER SYSTEM: STARBRAND.
"THIS MEANS A CURSORY GLANCE IS NOT ENOUGH, AS THE NEW WORLD'S DEATH OBSCURES THE STATE OF THE OLD.
"WE NEED TO DIG DEEPER."
AH, THE EX-NIHILII HAVE REACHED THE CORE.
WE CAN SEE THE WHOLE SYSTEM.

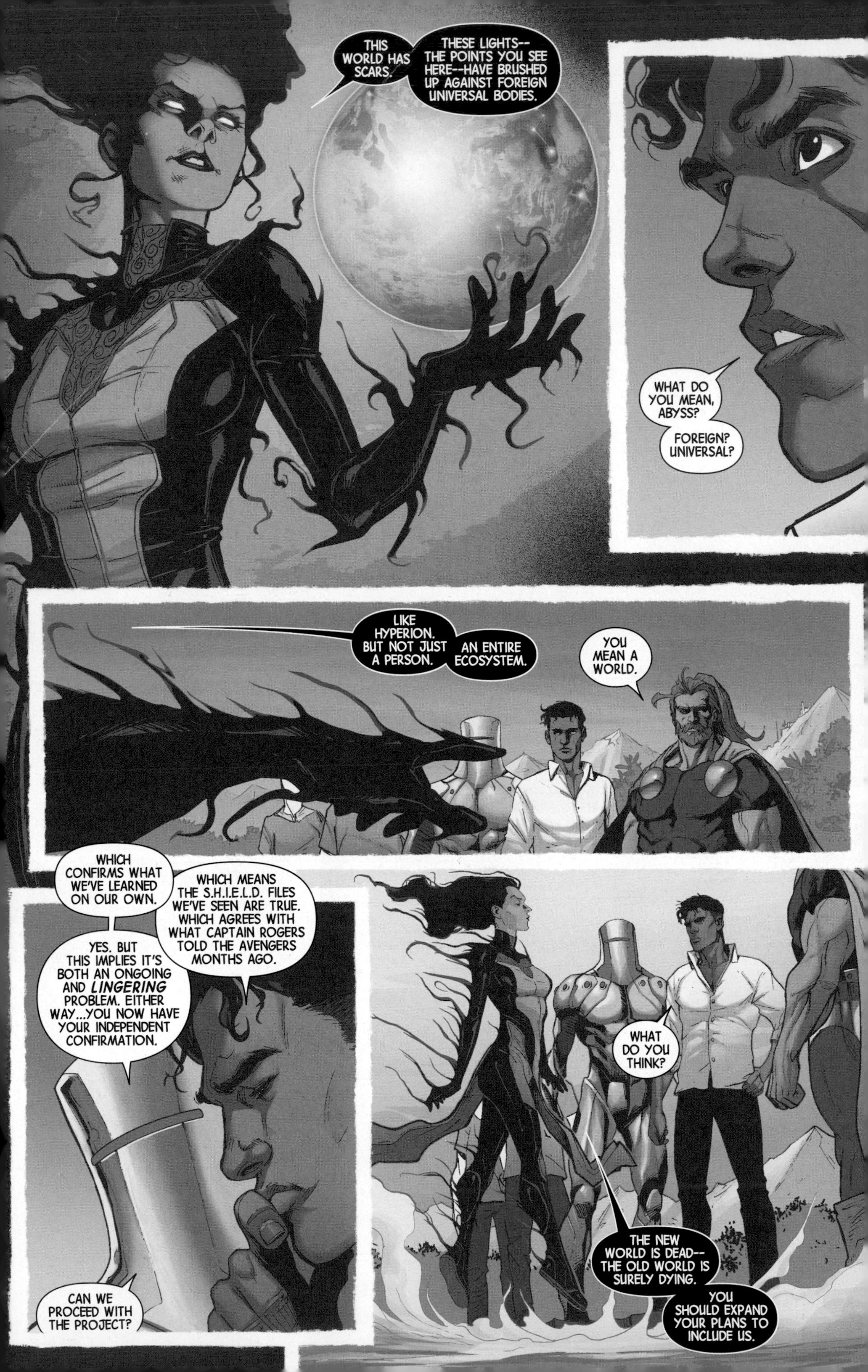

THIS WORLD HAS SCARS.
THESE LIGHTS-- THE POINTS YOU SEE HERE--HAVE BRUSHED UP AGAINST FOREIGN UNIVERSAL BODIES.
WHAT DO YOU MEAN, ABYSS?
FOREIGN? UNIVERSAL?
LIKE HYPERION. BUT NOT JUST A PERSON.
AN ENTIRE ECOSYSTEM.
YOU MEAN A WORLD.
WHICH CONFIRMS WHAT WE'VE LEARNED ON OUR OWN.
WHICH MEANS THE S.H.I.E.L.D. FILES WE'VE SEEN ARE TRUE. WHICH AGREES WITH WHAT CAPTAIN ROGERS TOLD THE AVENGERS MONTHS AGO.
YES. BUT THIS IMPLIES IT'S BOTH AN ONGOING AND *LINGERING* PROBLEM. EITHER WAY...YOU NOW HAVE YOUR INDEPENDENT CONFIRMATION.
CAN WE PROCEED WITH THE PROJECT?
WHAT DO YOU THINK?
THE NEW WORLD IS DEAD-- THE OLD WORLD IS SURELY DYING.
YOU SHOULD EXPAND YOUR PLANS TO INCLUDE US.

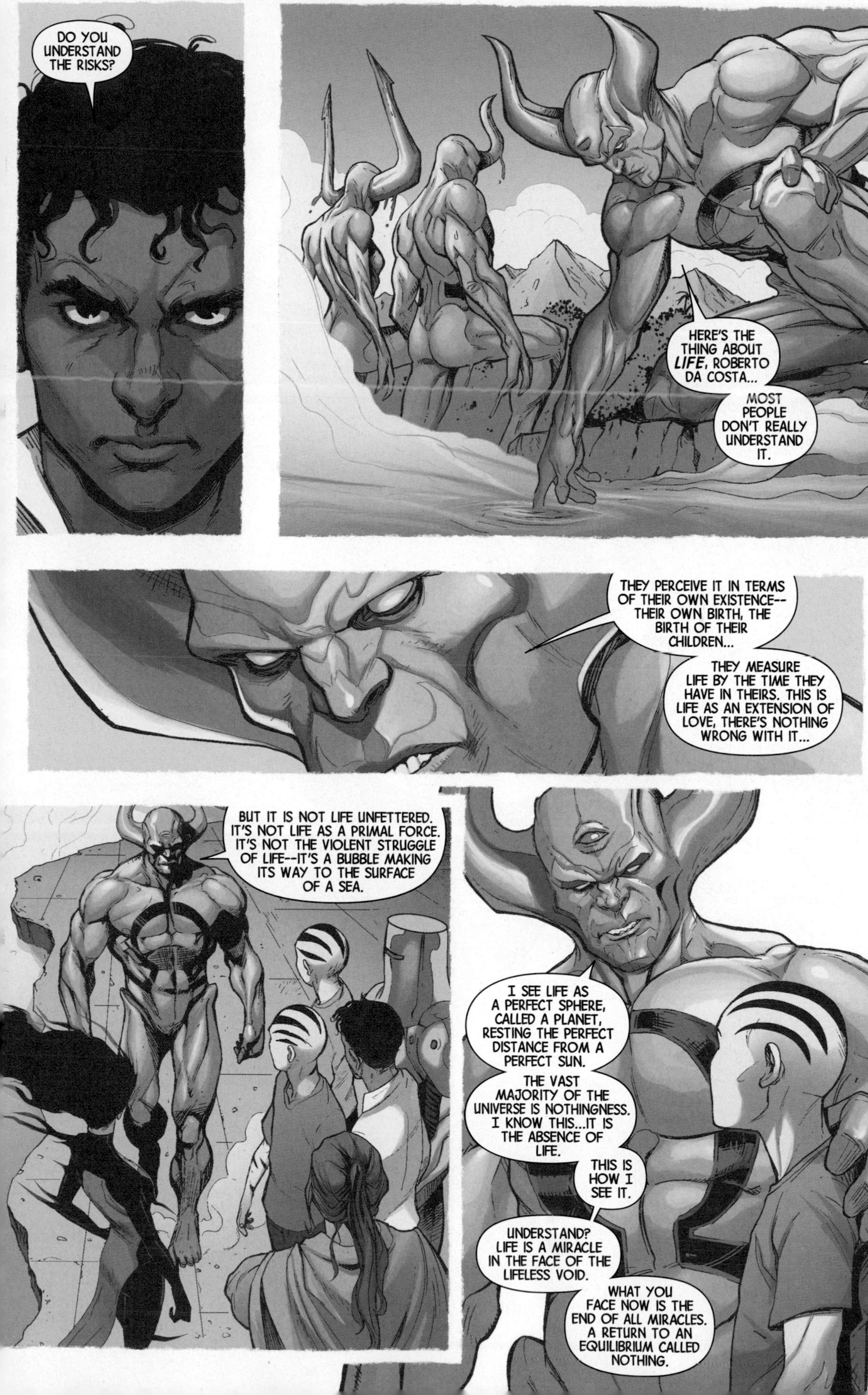
DO YOU UNDERSTAND THE RISKS?
HERE'S THE THING ABOUT *LIFE*, ROBERTO DA COSTA...
MOST PEOPLE DON'T REALLY UNDERSTAND IT.
THEY PERCEIVE IT IN TERMS OF THEIR OWN EXISTENCE-- THEIR OWN BIRTH, THE BIRTH OF THEIR CHILDREN...
THEY MEASURE LIFE BY THE TIME THEY HAVE IN THEIRS. THIS IS LIFE AS AN EXTENSION OF LOVE, THERE'S NOTHING WRONG WITH IT...
BUT IT IS NOT LIFE UNFETTERED. IT'S NOT LIFE AS A PRIMAL FORCE. IT'S NOT THE VIOLENT STRUGGLE OF LIFE--IT'S A BUBBLE MAKING ITS WAY TO THE SURFACE OF A SEA.
I SEE LIFE AS A PERFECT SPHERE, CALLED A PLANET, RESTING THE PERFECT DISTANCE FROM A PERFECT SUN.
THE VAST MAJORITY OF THE UNIVERSE IS NOTHINGNESS. I KNOW THIS...IT IS THE ABSENCE OF LIFE.
THIS IS HOW I SEE IT.
UNDERSTAND? LIFE IS A MIRACLE IN THE FACE OF THE LIFELESS VOID.
WHAT YOU FACE NOW IS THE END OF ALL MIRACLES. A RETURN TO AN EQUILIBRIUM CALLED NOTHING.

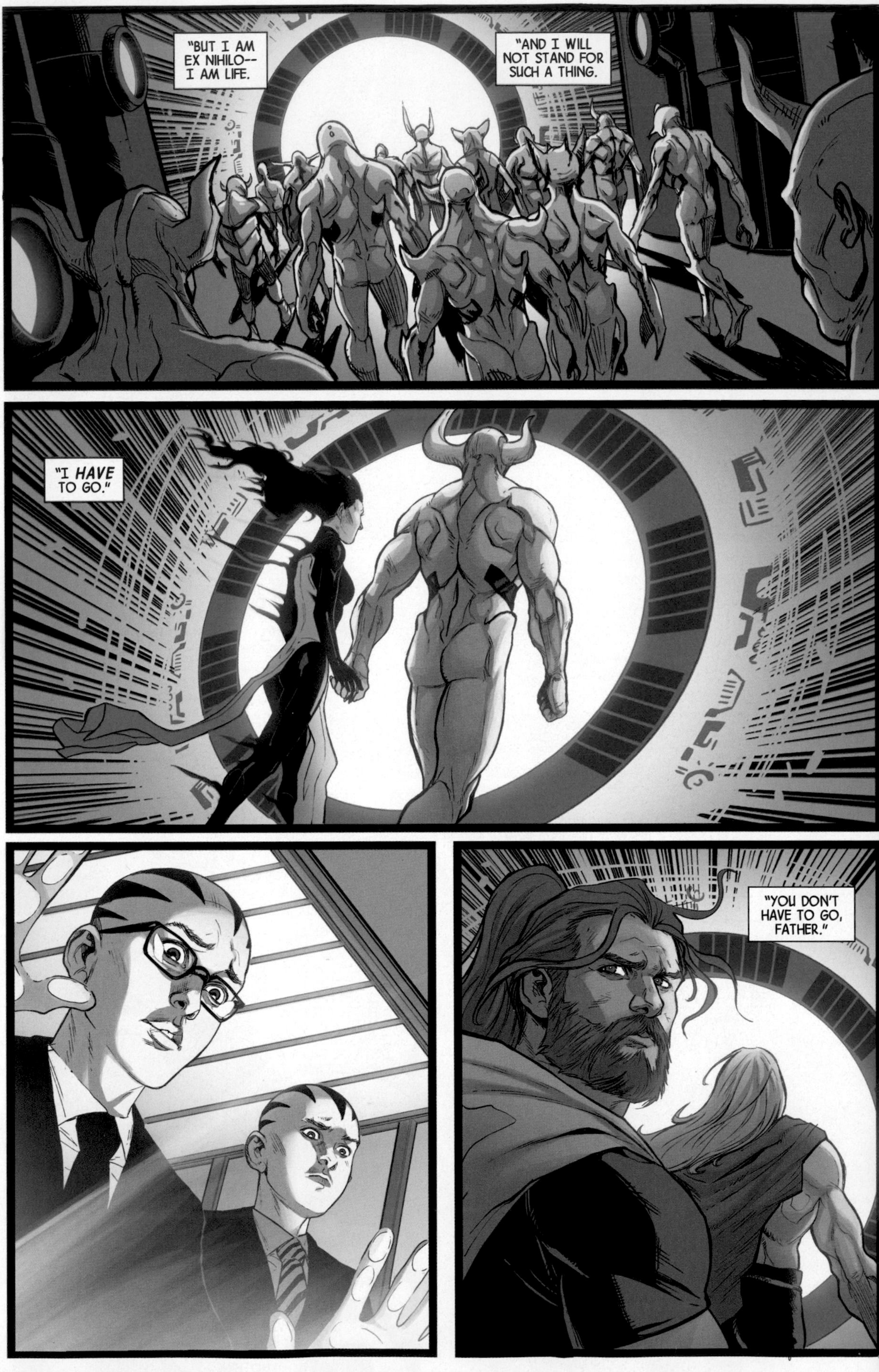
"BUT I AM EX NIHILO-- I AM LIFE.
"AND I WILL NOT STAND FOR SUCH A THING.
"I *HAVE* TO GO."
"YOU DON'T HAVE TO GO, FATHER."

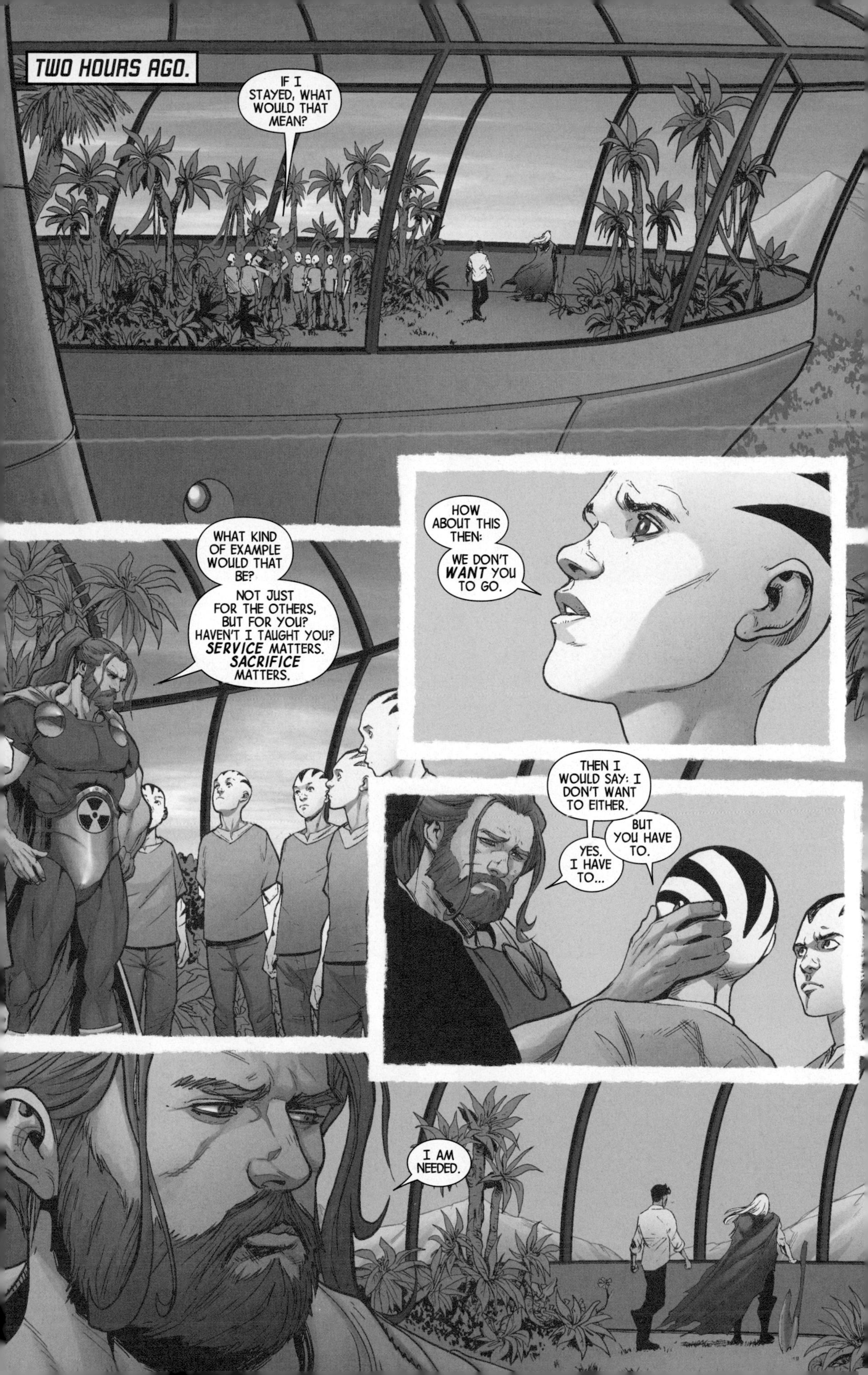

TWO HOURS AGO.
IF I STAYED, WHAT WOULD THAT MEAN?
HOW ABOUT THIS THEN:
WE DON'T WANT YOU TO GO.
WHAT KIND OF EXAMPLE WOULD THAT BE?
NOT JUST FOR THE OTHERS, BUT FOR YOU? HAVEN'T I TAUGHT YOU? SERVICE MATTERS. SACRIFICE MATTERS.
THEN I WOULD SAY: I DON'T WANT TO EITHER.
BUT YOU HAVE TO.
YES. I HAVE TO...
I AM NEEDED.

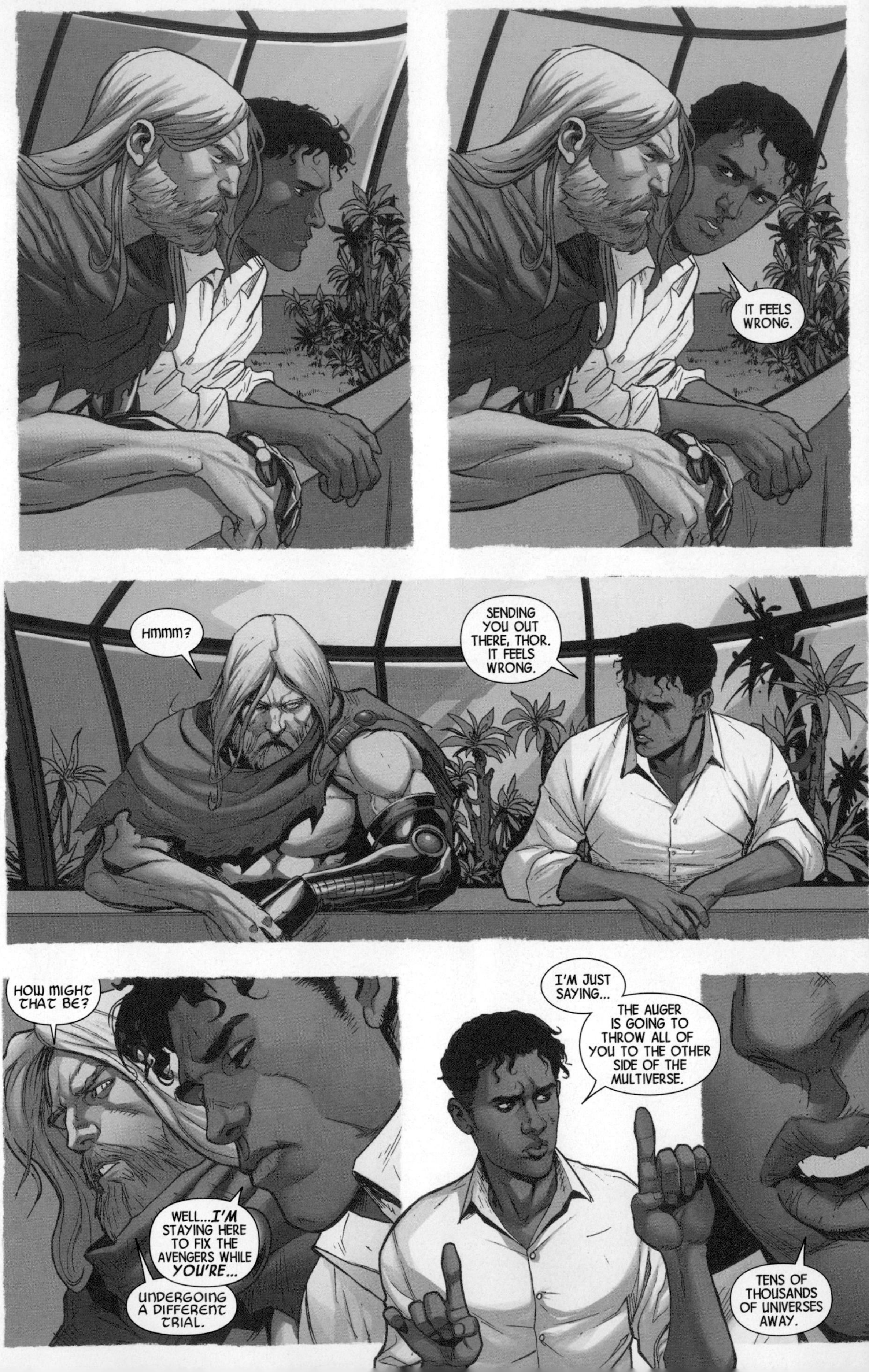
IT FEELS WRONG.
HMMM?
SENDING YOU OUT THERE, THOR. IT FEELS WRONG.
HOW MIGHT THAT BE?
WELL...I'M STAYING HERE TO FIX THE AVENGERS WHILE YOU'RE...
UNDERGOING A DIFFERENT TRIAL.
I'M JUST SAYING...
THE AUGER IS GOING TO THROW ALL OF YOU TO THE OTHER SIDE OF THE MULTIVERSE.
TENS OF THOUSANDS OF UNIVERSES AWAY.

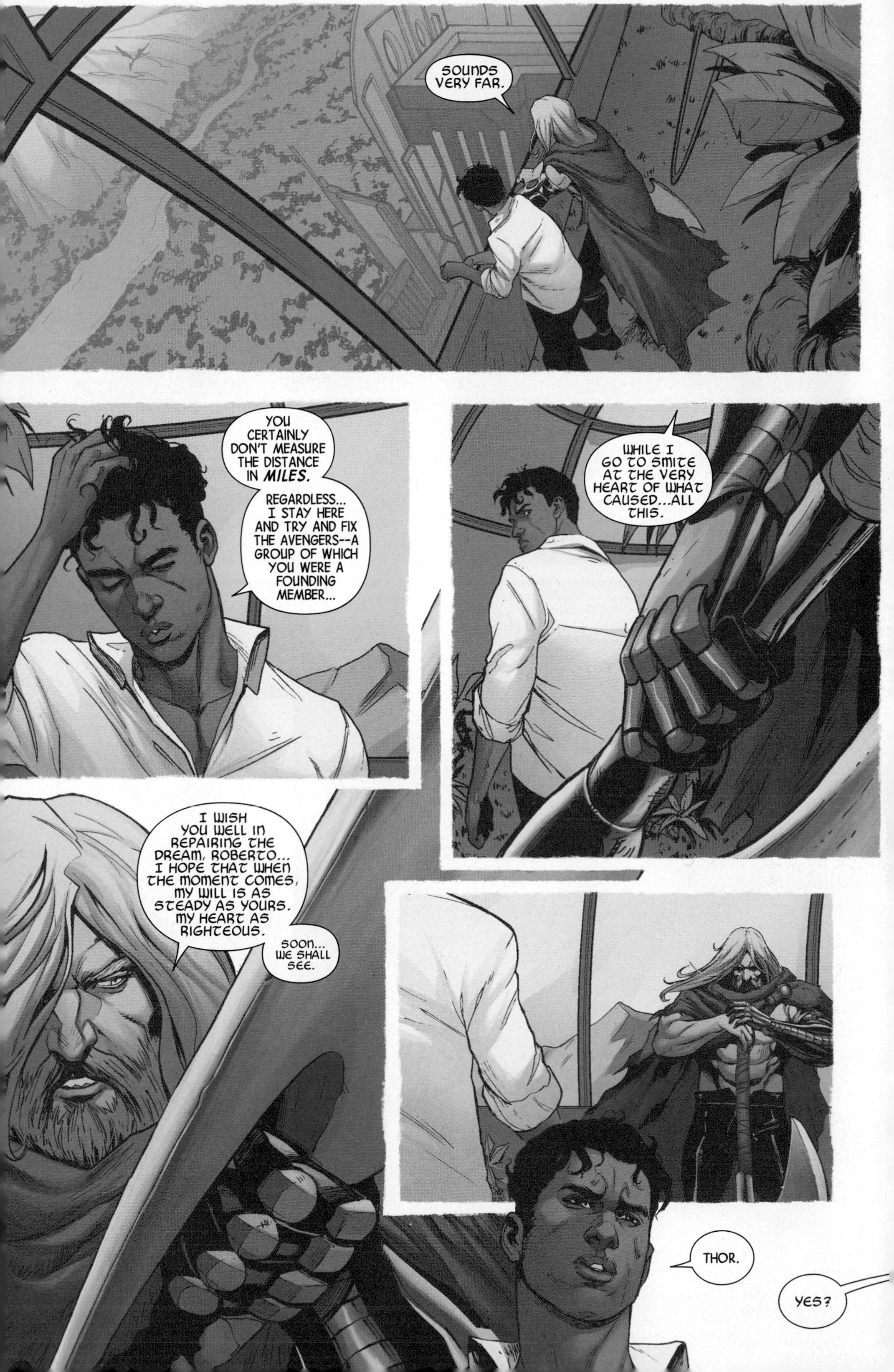
SOUNDS VERY FAR.
YOU CERTAINLY DON'T MEASURE THE DISTANCE IN MILES.
REGARDLESS... I STAY HERE AND TRY AND FIX THE AVENGERS--A GROUP OF WHICH YOU WERE A FOUNDING MEMBER...
WHILE I GO TO SMITE AT THE VERY HEART OF WHAT CAUSED...ALL THIS.
I WISH YOU WELL IN REPAIRING THE DREAM, ROBERTO... I HOPE THAT WHEN THE MOMENT COMES, MY WILL IS AS STEADY AS YOURS. MY HEART AS RIGHTEOUS.
SOON... WE SHALL SEE.
THOR.
YES?

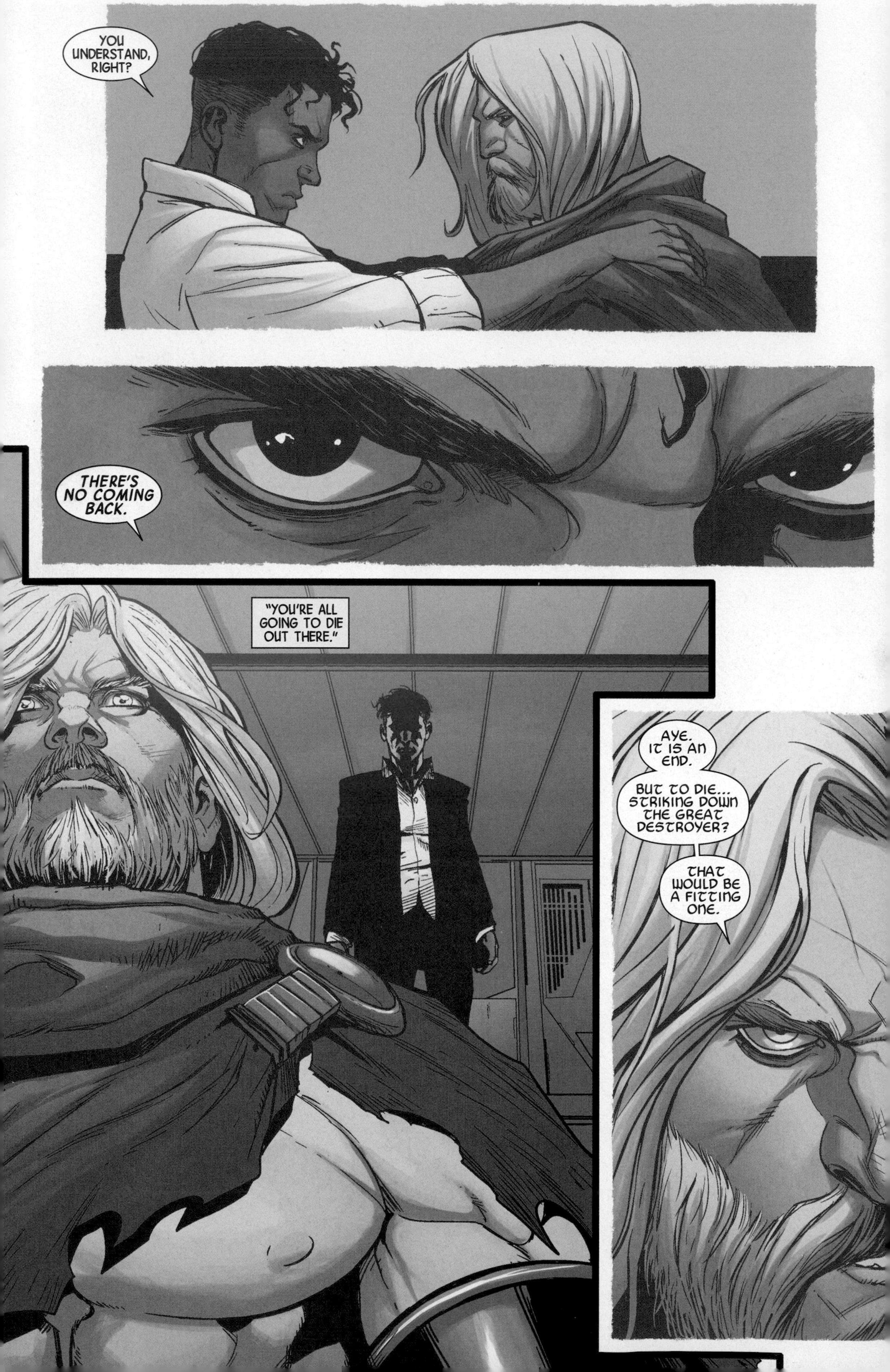
YOU UNDERSTAND, RIGHT?
THERE'S NO COMING BACK.
"YOU'RE ALL GOING TO DIE OUT THERE."
AYE. IT IS AN END.
BUT TO DIE... STRIKING DOWN THE GREAT DESTROYER?
THAT WOULD BE A FITTING ONE.

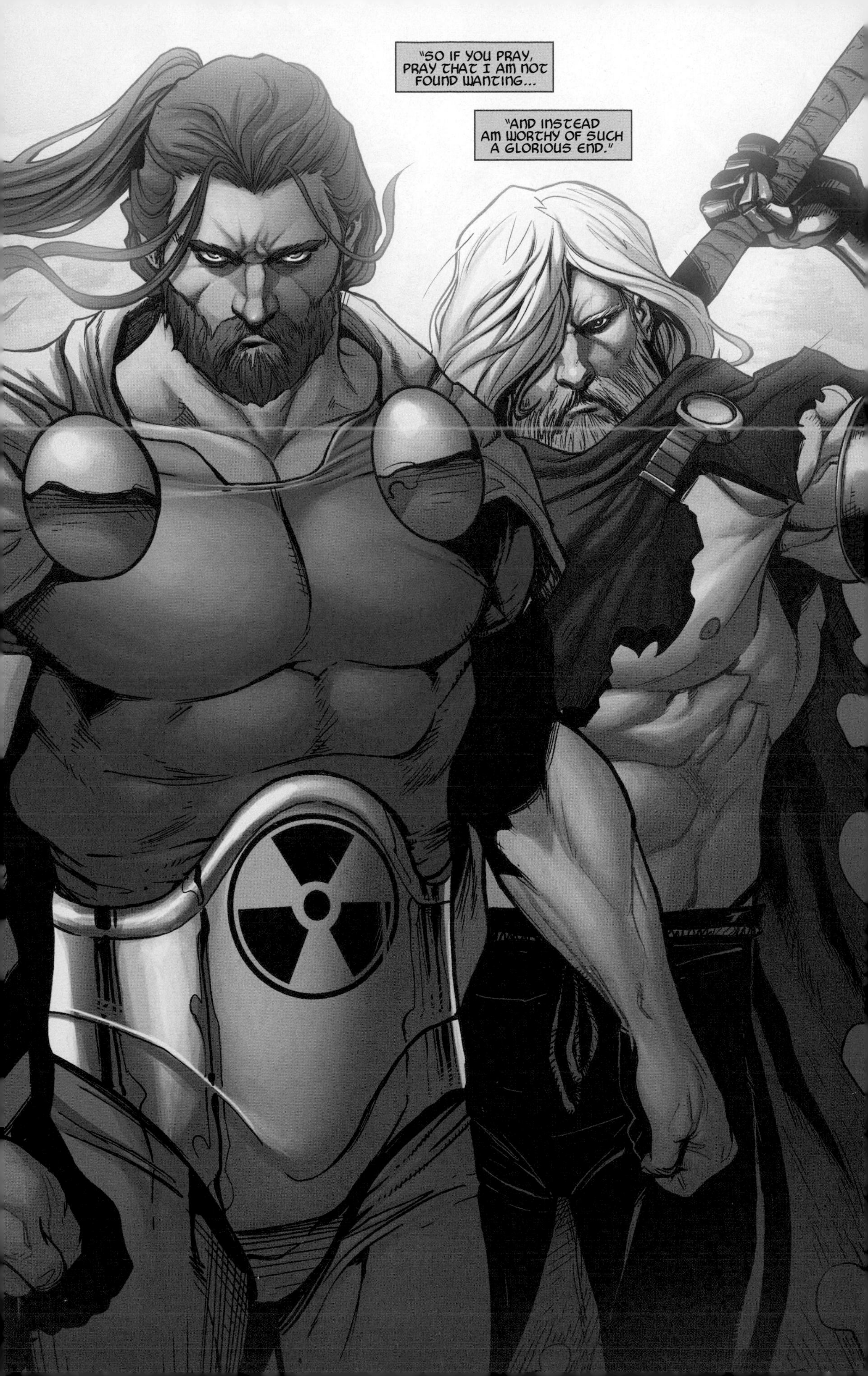
"SO IF YOU PRAY, PRAY THAT I AM NOT FOUND WANTING...
"AND INSTEAD AM WORTHY OF SUCH A GLORIOUS END."

"WHAT HAPPENED WHEN THE
WORLD WOKE UP"

THE ILLUMINATI

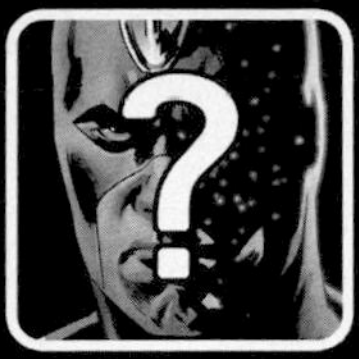

BLACK BOLT
Celestial Messiah

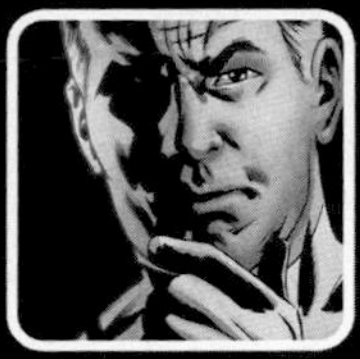

REED RICHARDS
Universal Builder

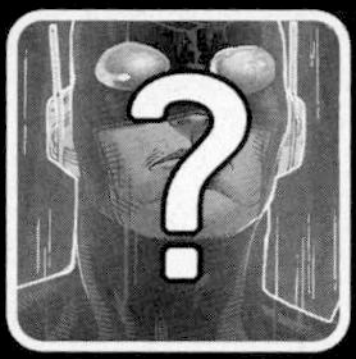

YELLOWJACKET
Size-Shifting Scientist

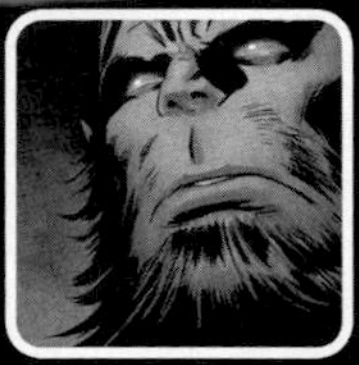

BEAST
Mutant Genius

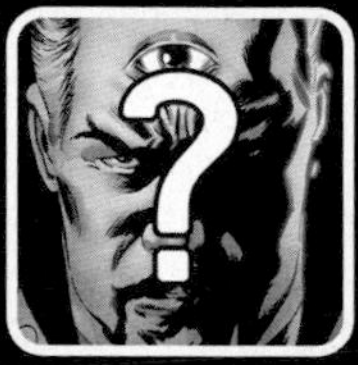

DOCTOR STRANGE
Sorcerer Supreme

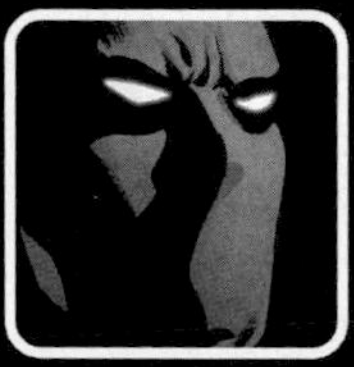

BLACK PANTHER
King of the Dead

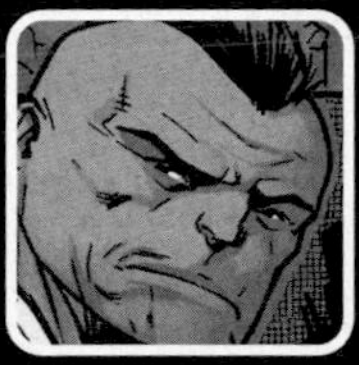

THE HULK/ "DOC GREEN"
Strongest There Is

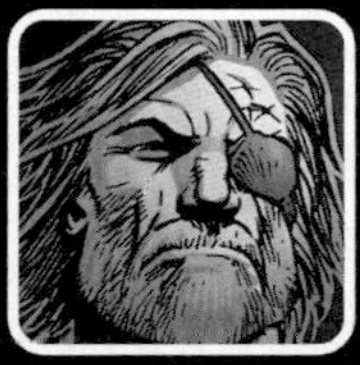

CAPTAIN BRITAIN
Multiverse Protector

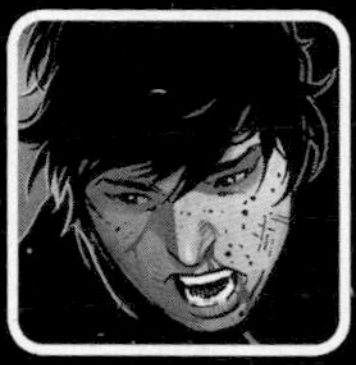

AMADEUS CHO
Mathematics Wunderkind

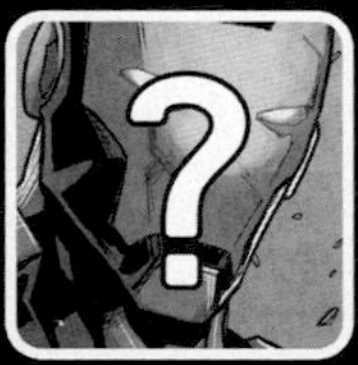

IRON MAN
Master of Machines

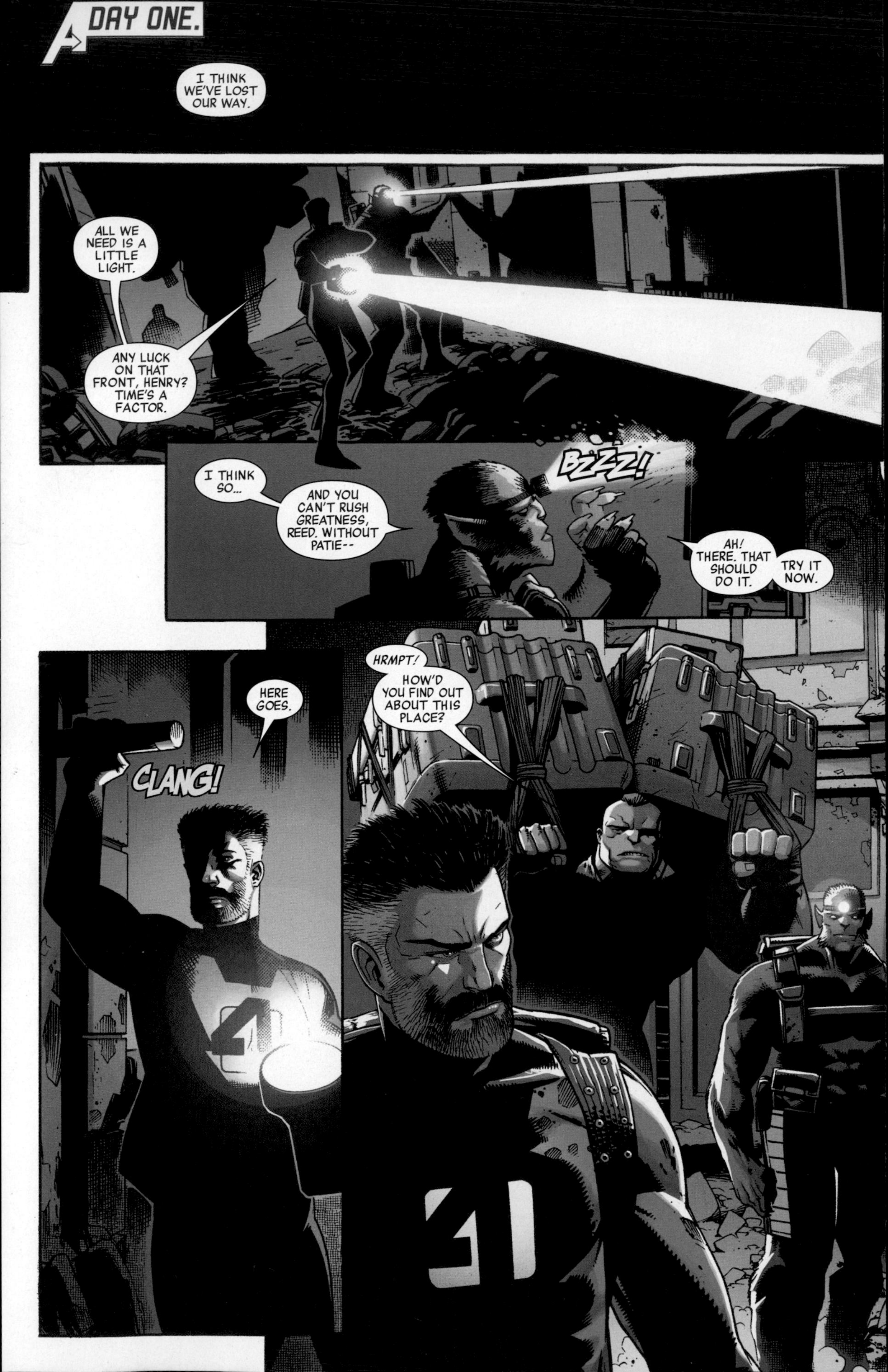
DAY ONE.
I THINK WE'VE LOST OUR WAY.
ALL WE NEED IS A LITTLE LIGHT.
ANY LUCK ON THAT FRONT, HENRY? TIME'S A FACTOR.
BZZZ!
I THINK SO...
AND YOU CAN'T RUSH GREATNESS, REED. WITHOUT PATIE--
AH! THERE. THAT SHOULD DO IT.
TRY IT NOW.
HERE GOES.
CLANG!
HRMPT!
HOW'D YOU FIND OUT ABOUT THIS PLACE?

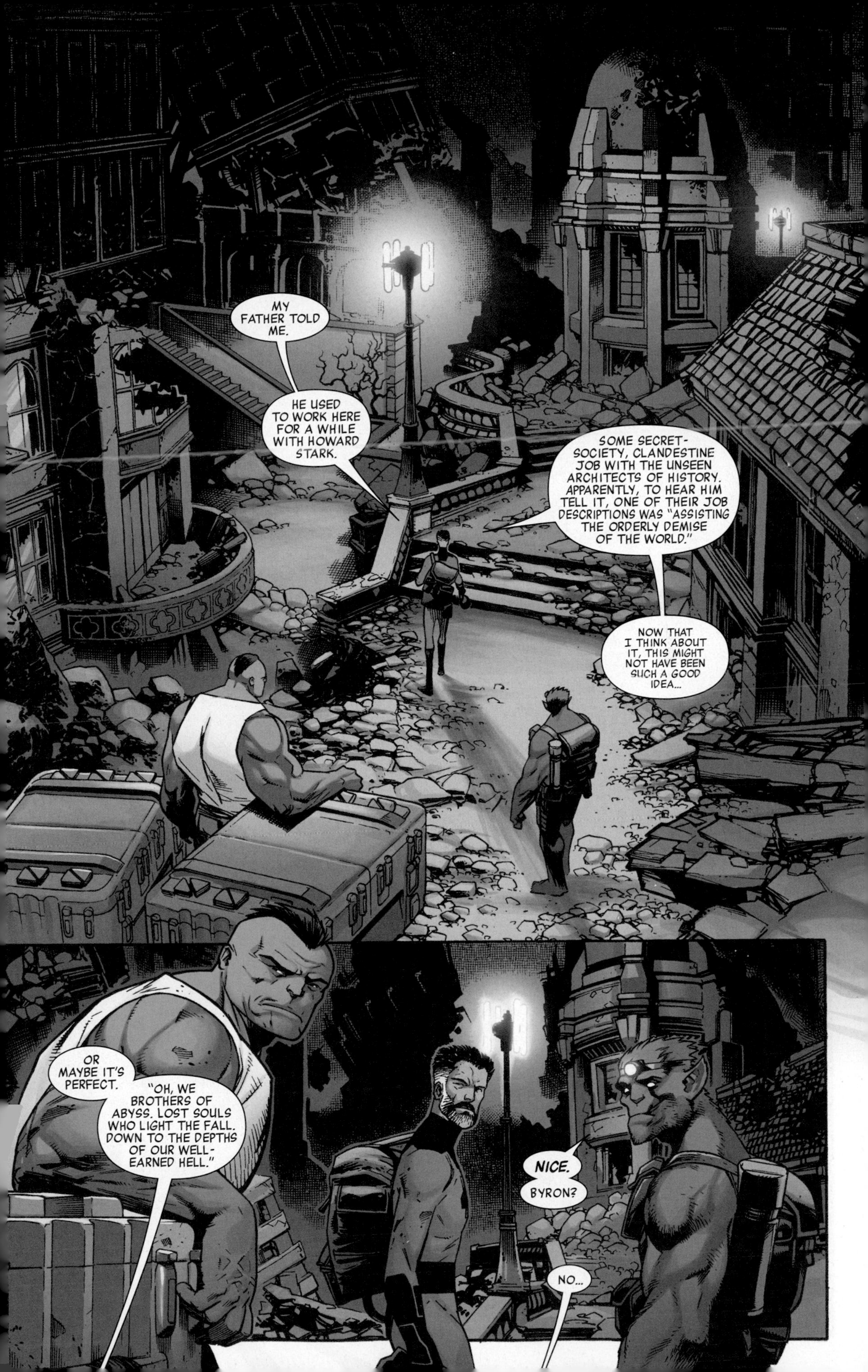
MY FATHER TOLD ME.
HE USED TO WORK HERE FOR A WHILE WITH HOWARD STARK.
SOME SECRET-SOCIETY, CLANDESTINE JOB WITH THE UNSEEN ARCHITECTS OF HISTORY. APPARENTLY, TO HEAR HIM TELL IT, ONE OF THEIR JOB DESCRIPTIONS WAS "ASSISTING THE ORDERLY DEMISE OF THE WORLD."
NOW THAT I THINK ABOUT IT, THIS MIGHT NOT HAVE BEEN SUCH A GOOD IDEA...
OR MAYBE IT'S PERFECT.
"OH, WE BROTHERS OF ABYSS. LOST SOULS WHO LIGHT THE FALL. DOWN TO THE DEPTHS OF OUR WELL-EARNED HELL."
NICE.
BYRON?
NO...

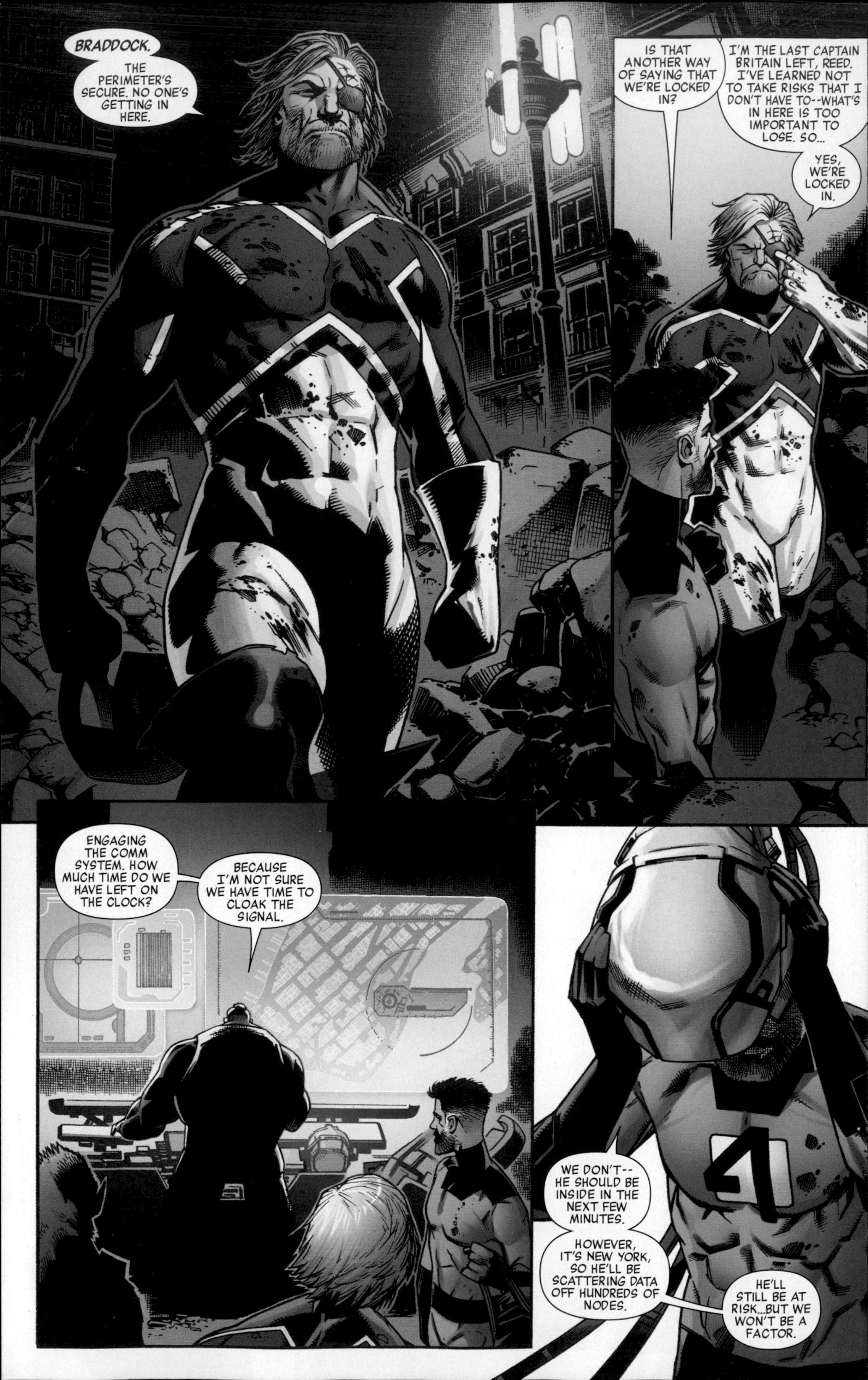
BRADDOCK.
THE PERIMETER'S SECURE. NO ONE'S GETTING IN HERE.
IS THAT ANOTHER WAY OF SAYING THAT WE'RE LOCKED IN?
I'M THE LAST CAPTAIN BRITAIN LEFT, REED. I'VE LEARNED NOT TO TAKE RISKS THAT I DON'T HAVE TO--WHAT'S IN HERE IS TOO IMPORTANT TO LOSE. SO...
YES, WE'RE LOCKED IN.
ENGAGING THE COMM SYSTEM. HOW MUCH TIME DO WE HAVE LEFT ON THE CLOCK?
BECAUSE I'M NOT SURE WE HAVE TIME TO CLOAK THE SIGNAL.
WE DON'T--HE SHOULD BE INSIDE IN THE NEXT FEW MINUTES.
HOWEVER, IT'S NEW YORK, SO HE'LL BE SCATTERING DATA OFF HUNDREDS OF NODES.
HE'LL STILL BE AT RISK...BUT WE WON'T BE A FACTOR.

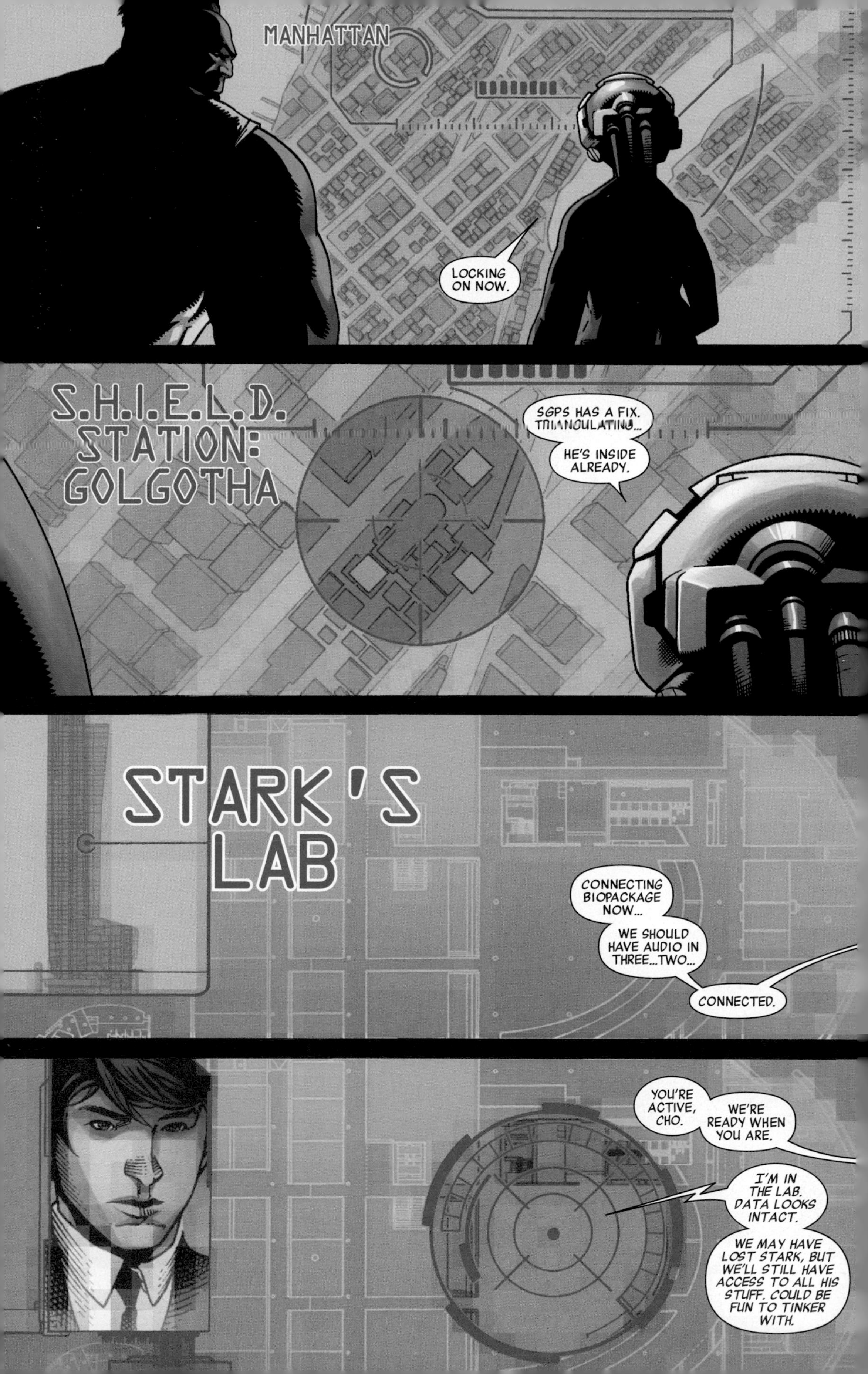
MANHATTAN
LOCKING ON NOW.
S.H.I.E.L.D. STATION: GOLGOTHA
SGPS HAS A FIX. TRIANGULATING...
HE'S INSIDE ALREADY.
STARK'S LAB
CONNECTING BIOPACKAGE NOW...
WE SHOULD HAVE AUDIO IN THREE...TWO...
CONNECTED.
YOU'RE ACTIVE, CHO.
WE'RE READY WHEN YOU ARE.
I'M IN THE LAB. DATA LOOKS INTACT.
WE MAY HAVE LOST STARK, BUT WE'LL STILL HAVE ACCESS TO ALL HIS STUFF. COULD BE FUN TO TINKER WITH.

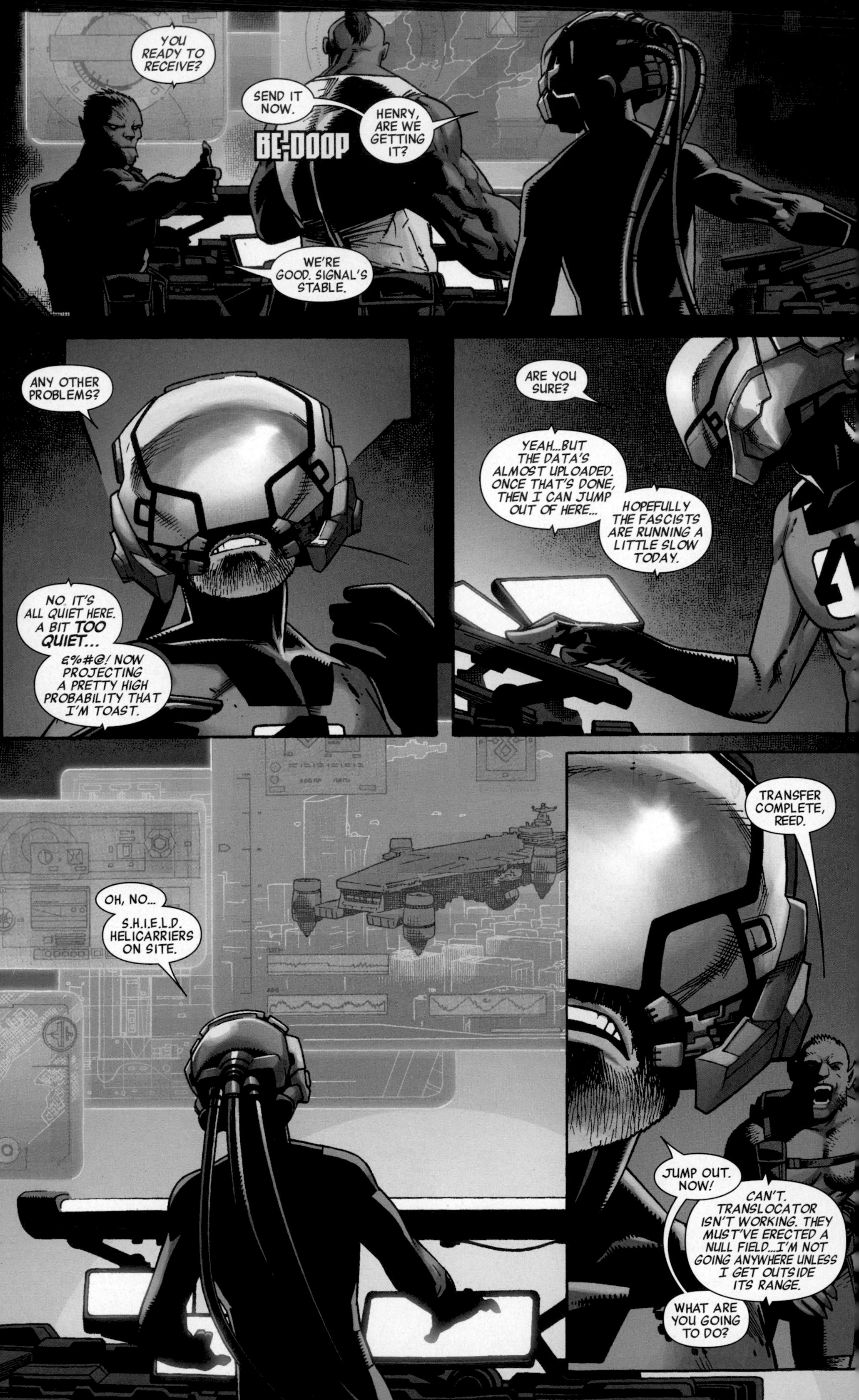
YOU READY TO RECEIVE?
SEND IT NOW.
BE-DOOP
HENRY, ARE WE GETTING IT?
WE'RE GOOD. SIGNAL'S STABLE.
ANY OTHER PROBLEMS?
NO. IT'S ALL QUIET HERE. A BIT TOO QUIET...
£%#@! NOW PROJECTING A PRETTY HIGH PROBABILITY THAT I'M TOAST.
ARE YOU SURE?
YEAH...BUT THE DATA'S ALMOST UPLOADED. ONCE THAT'S DONE, THEN I CAN JUMP OUT OF HERE...
HOPEFULLY THE FASCISTS ARE RUNNING A LITTLE SLOW TODAY.
OH, NO... S.H.I.E.L.D. HELICARRIERS ON SITE.
TRANSFER COMPLETE, REED.
JUMP OUT. NOW!
CAN'T. TRANSLOCATOR ISN'T WORKING. THEY MUST'VE ERECTED A NULL FIELD...I'M NOT GOING ANYWHERE UNLESS I GET OUTSIDE ITS RANGE.
WHAT ARE YOU GOING TO DO?

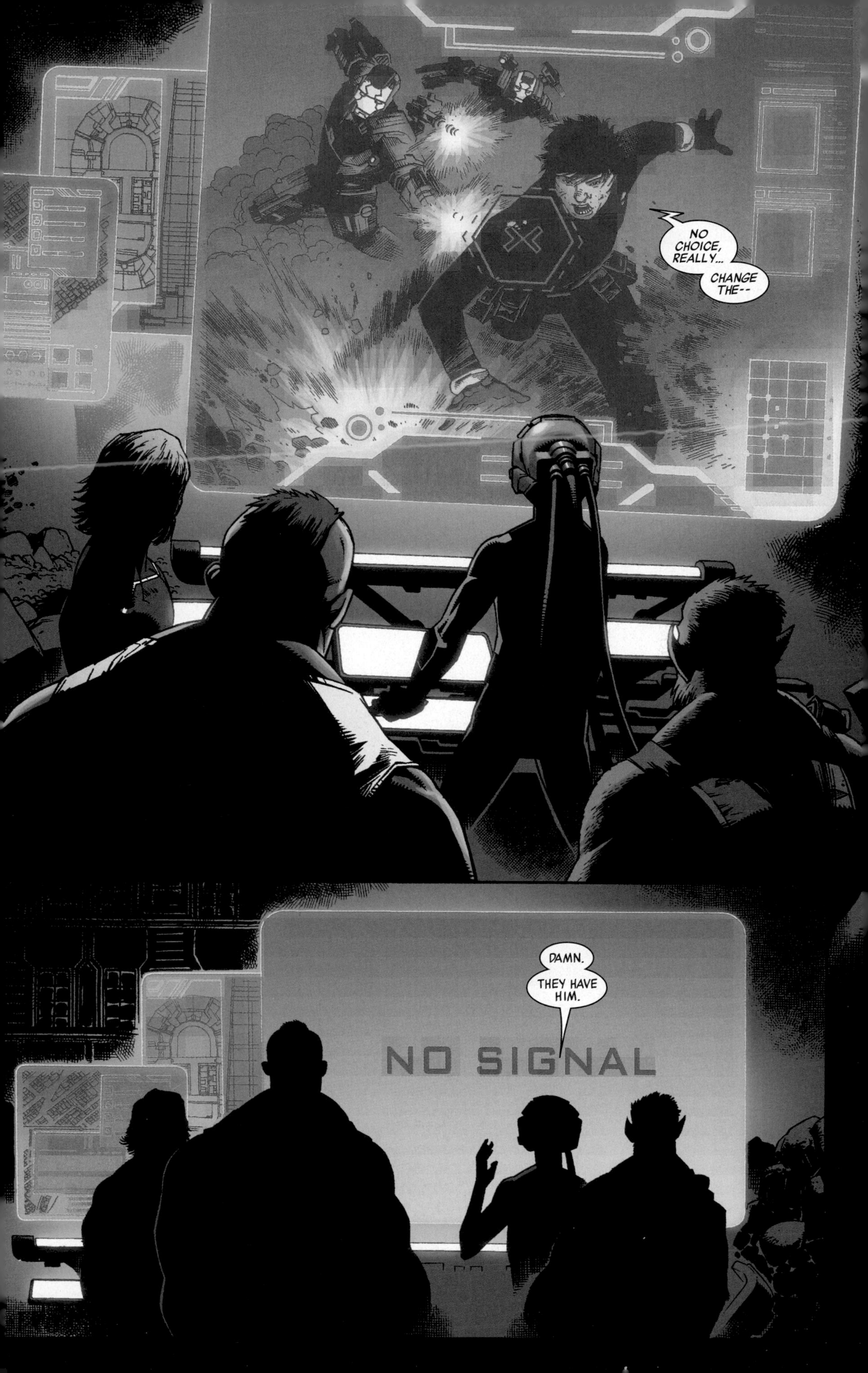
NO CHOICE, REALLY... CHANGE THE--
DAMN. THEY HAVE HIM.
NO SIGNAL

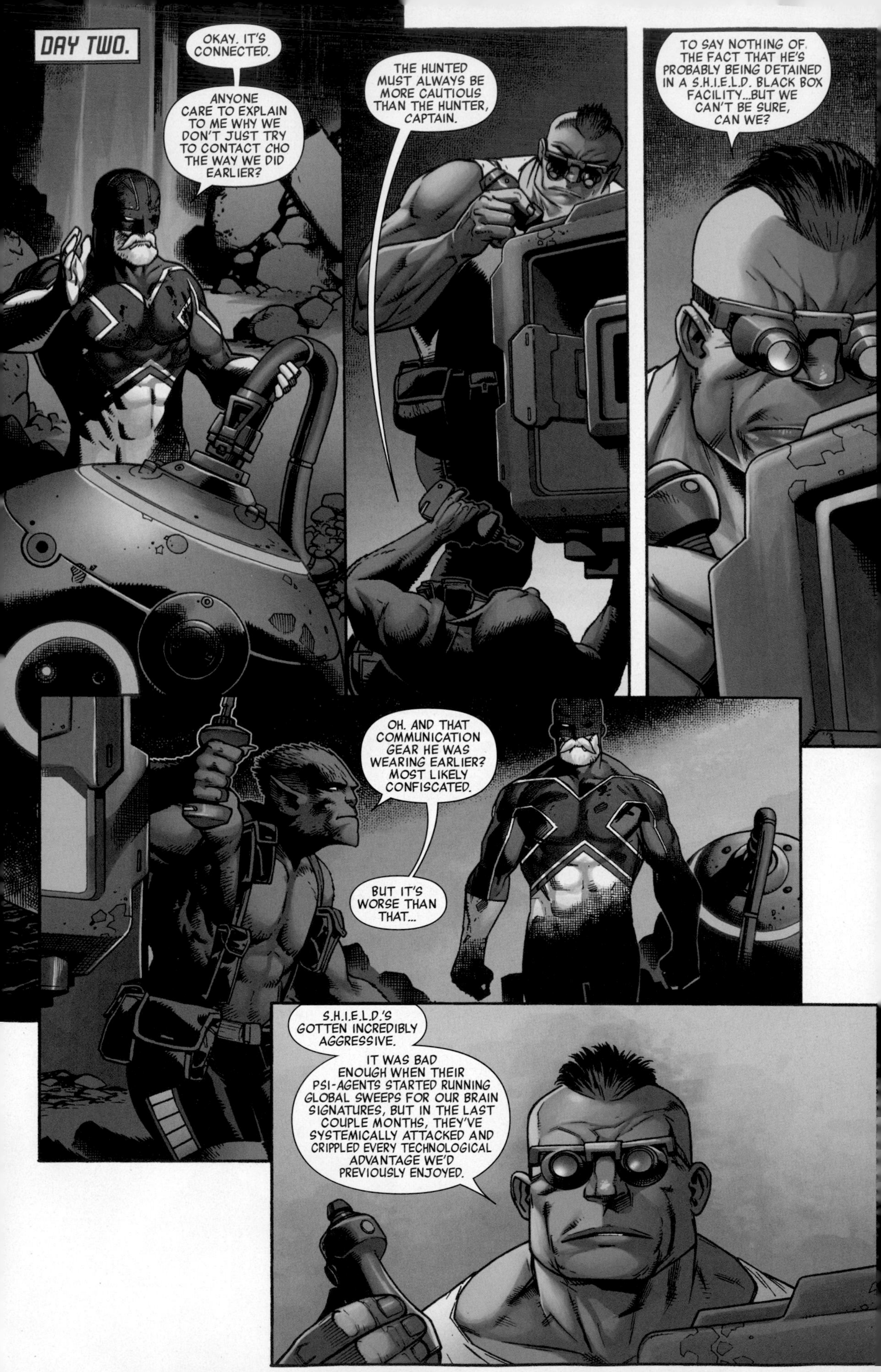
DAY TWO.
OKAY. IT'S CONNECTED.
ANYONE CARE TO EXPLAIN TO ME WHY WE DON'T JUST TRY TO CONTACT CHO THE WAY WE DID EARLIER?
THE HUNTED MUST ALWAYS BE MORE CAUTIOUS THAN THE HUNTER, CAPTAIN.
TO SAY NOTHING OF THE FACT THAT HE'S PROBABLY BEING DETAINED IN A S.H.I.E.L.D. BLACK BOX FACILITY...BUT WE CAN'T BE SURE, CAN WE?
OH. AND THAT COMMUNICATION GEAR HE WAS WEARING EARLIER? MOST LIKELY CONFISCATED.
BUT IT'S WORSE THAN THAT...
S.H.I.E.L.D.'S GOTTEN INCREDIBLY AGGRESSIVE.
IT WAS BAD ENOUGH WHEN THEIR PSI-AGENTS STARTED RUNNING GLOBAL SWEEPS FOR OUR BRAIN SIGNATURES, BUT IN THE LAST COUPLE MONTHS, THEY'VE SYSTEMICALLY ATTACKED AND CRIPPLED EVERY TECHNOLOGICAL ADVANTAGE WE'D PREVIOUSLY ENJOYED.

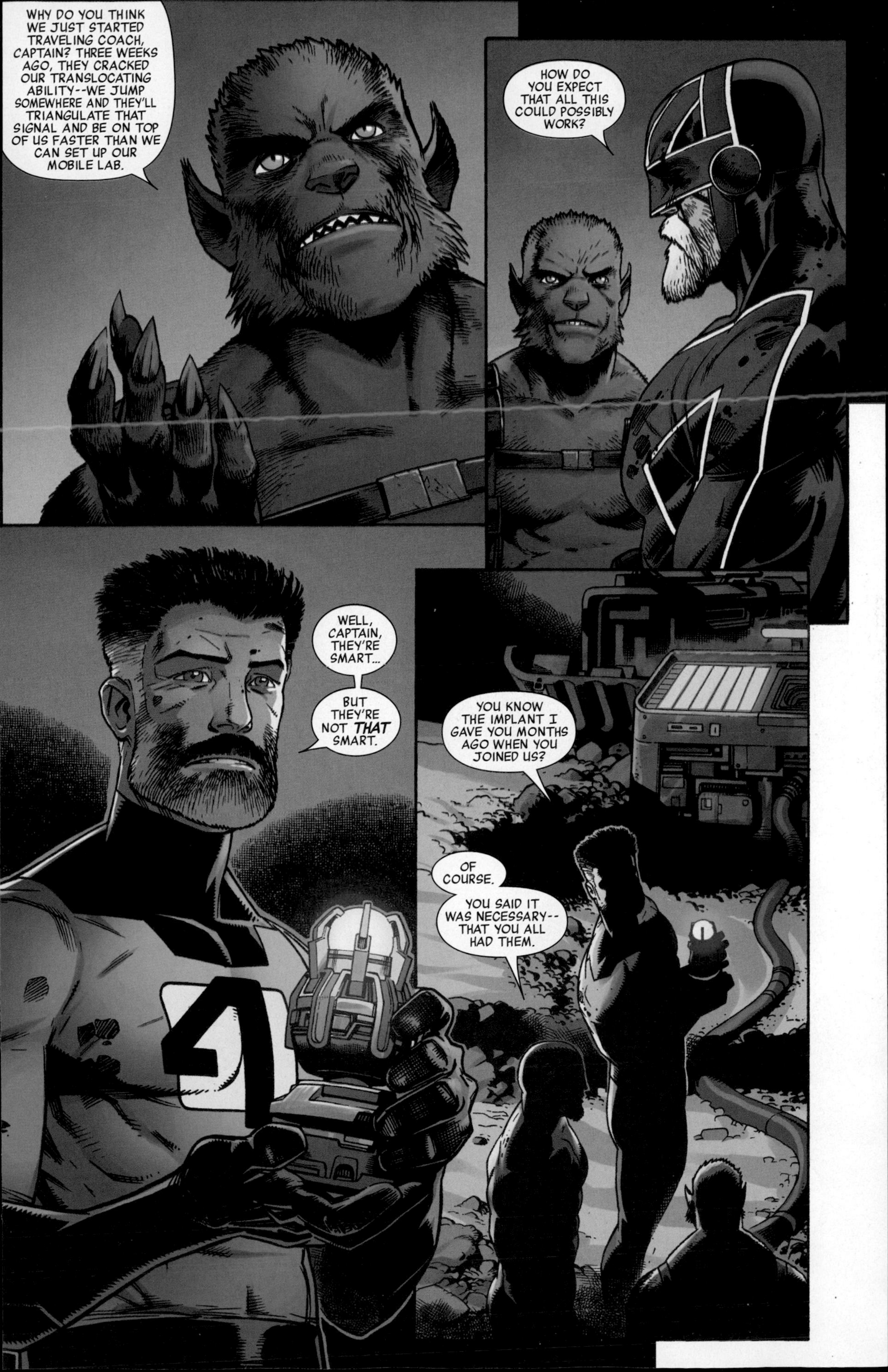
WHY DO YOU THINK WE JUST STARTED TRAVELING COACH, CAPTAIN? THREE WEEKS AGO, THEY CRACKED OUR TRANSLOCATING ABILITY--WE JUMP SOMEWHERE AND THEY'LL TRIANGULATE THAT SIGNAL AND BE ON TOP OF US FASTER THAN WE CAN SET UP OUR MOBILE LAB.
HOW DO YOU EXPECT THAT ALL THIS COULD POSSIBLY WORK?
WELL, CAPTAIN, THEY'RE SMART...
BUT THEY'RE NOT *THAT* SMART.
YOU KNOW THE IMPLANT I GAVE YOU MONTHS AGO WHEN YOU JOINED US?
OF COURSE.
YOU SAID IT WAS NECESSARY-- THAT YOU ALL HAD THEM.

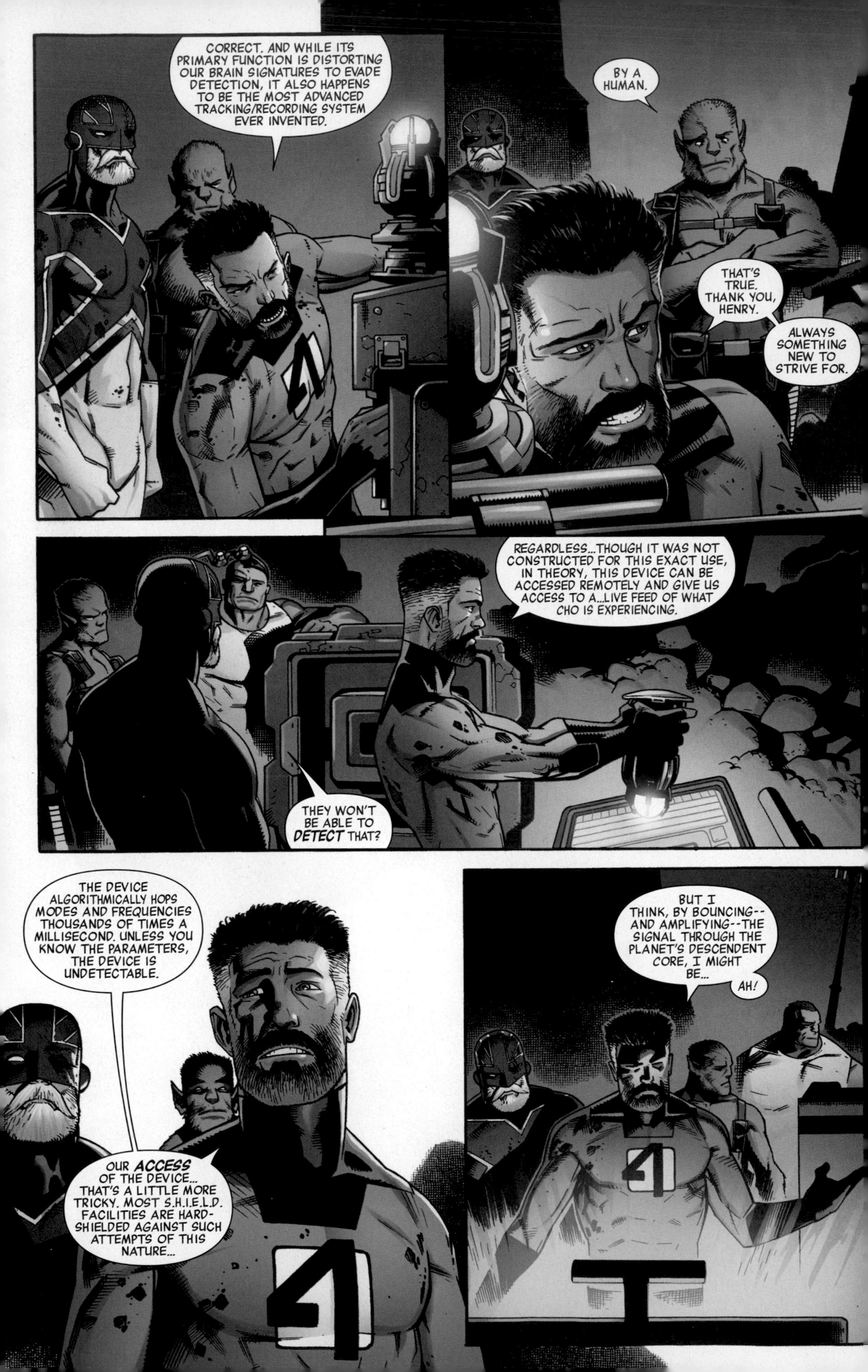
CORRECT. AND WHILE ITS PRIMARY FUNCTION IS DISTORTING OUR BRAIN SIGNATURES TO EVADE DETECTION, IT ALSO HAPPENS TO BE THE MOST ADVANCED TRACKING/RECORDING SYSTEM EVER INVENTED.
BY A HUMAN.
THAT'S TRUE. THANK YOU, HENRY.
ALWAYS SOMETHING NEW TO STRIVE FOR.
REGARDLESS...THOUGH IT WAS NOT CONSTRUCTED FOR THIS EXACT USE, IN THEORY, THIS DEVICE CAN BE ACCESSED REMOTELY AND GIVE US ACCESS TO A...LIVE FEED OF WHAT CHO IS EXPERIENCING.
THEY WON'T BE ABLE TO DETECT THAT?
THE DEVICE ALGORITHMICALLY HOPS MODES AND FREQUENCIES THOUSANDS OF TIMES A MILLISECOND. UNLESS YOU KNOW THE PARAMETERS, THE DEVICE IS UNDETECTABLE.
OUR ACCESS OF THE DEVICE... THAT'S A LITTLE MORE TRICKY. MOST S.H.I.E.L.D. FACILITIES ARE HARD-SHIELDED AGAINST SUCH ATTEMPTS OF THIS NATURE...
BUT I THINK, BY BOUNCING-- AND AMPLIFYING--THE SIGNAL THROUGH THE PLANET'S DESCENDENT CORE, I MIGHT BE...
AH!

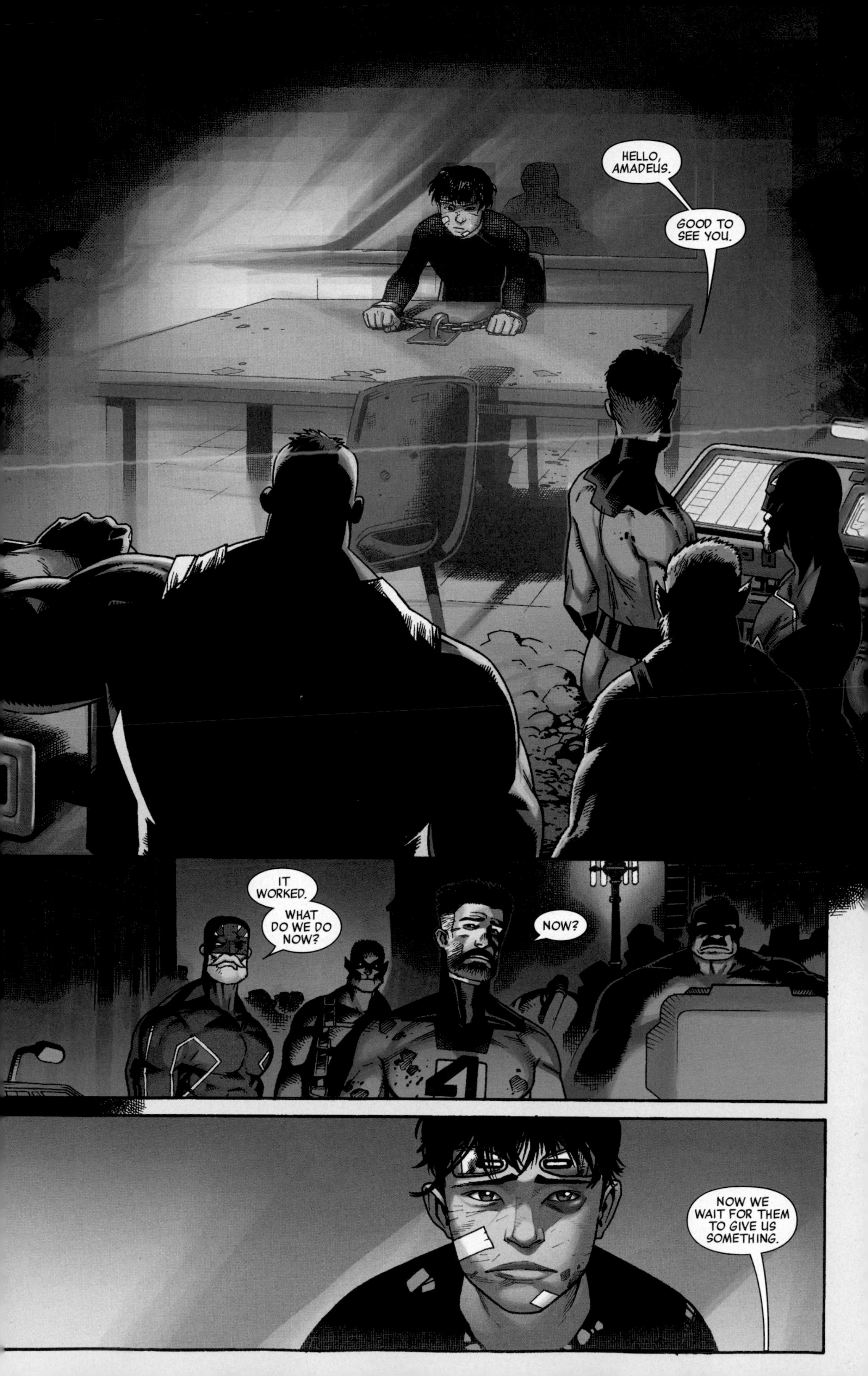
HELLO, AMADEUS.
GOOD TO SEE YOU.
IT WORKED.
WHAT DO WE DO NOW?
NOW?
NOW WE WAIT FOR THEM TO GIVE US SOMETHING.

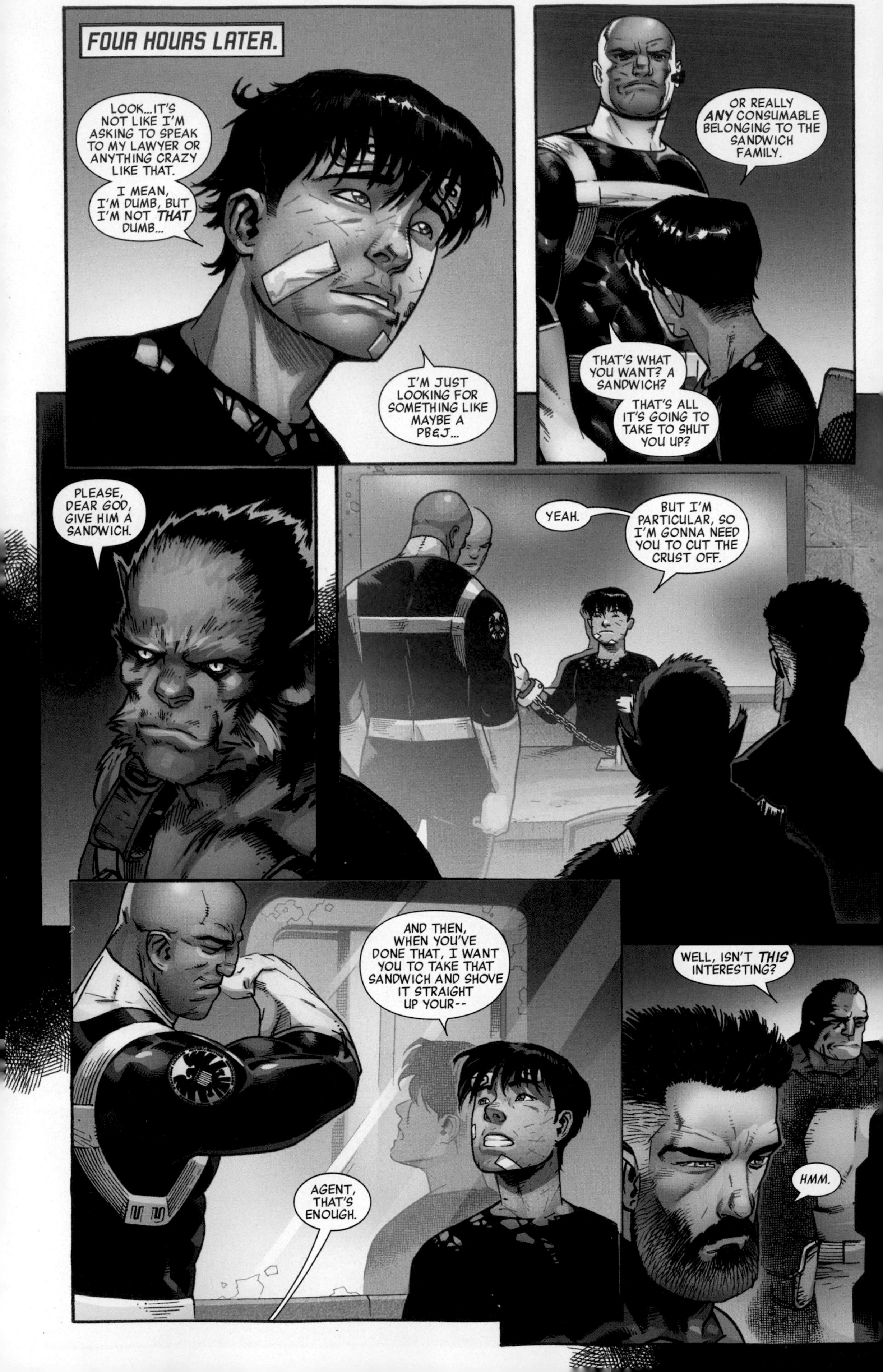
FOUR HOURS LATER.
LOOK...IT'S NOT LIKE I'M ASKING TO SPEAK TO MY LAWYER OR ANYTHING CRAZY LIKE THAT.
I MEAN, I'M DUMB, BUT I'M NOT THAT DUMB...
I'M JUST LOOKING FOR SOMETHING LIKE MAYBE A PB&J...
OR REALLY ANY CONSUMABLE BELONGING TO THE SANDWICH FAMILY.
THAT'S WHAT YOU WANT? A SANDWICH?
THAT'S ALL IT'S GOING TO TAKE TO SHUT YOU UP?
PLEASE, DEAR GOD, GIVE HIM A SANDWICH.
YEAH.
BUT I'M PARTICULAR, SO I'M GONNA NEED YOU TO CUT THE CRUST OFF.
AND THEN, WHEN YOU'VE DONE THAT, I WANT YOU TO TAKE THAT SANDWICH AND SHOVE IT STRAIGHT UP YOUR--
AGENT, THAT'S ENOUGH.
WELL, ISN'T THIS INTERESTING?
HMM.

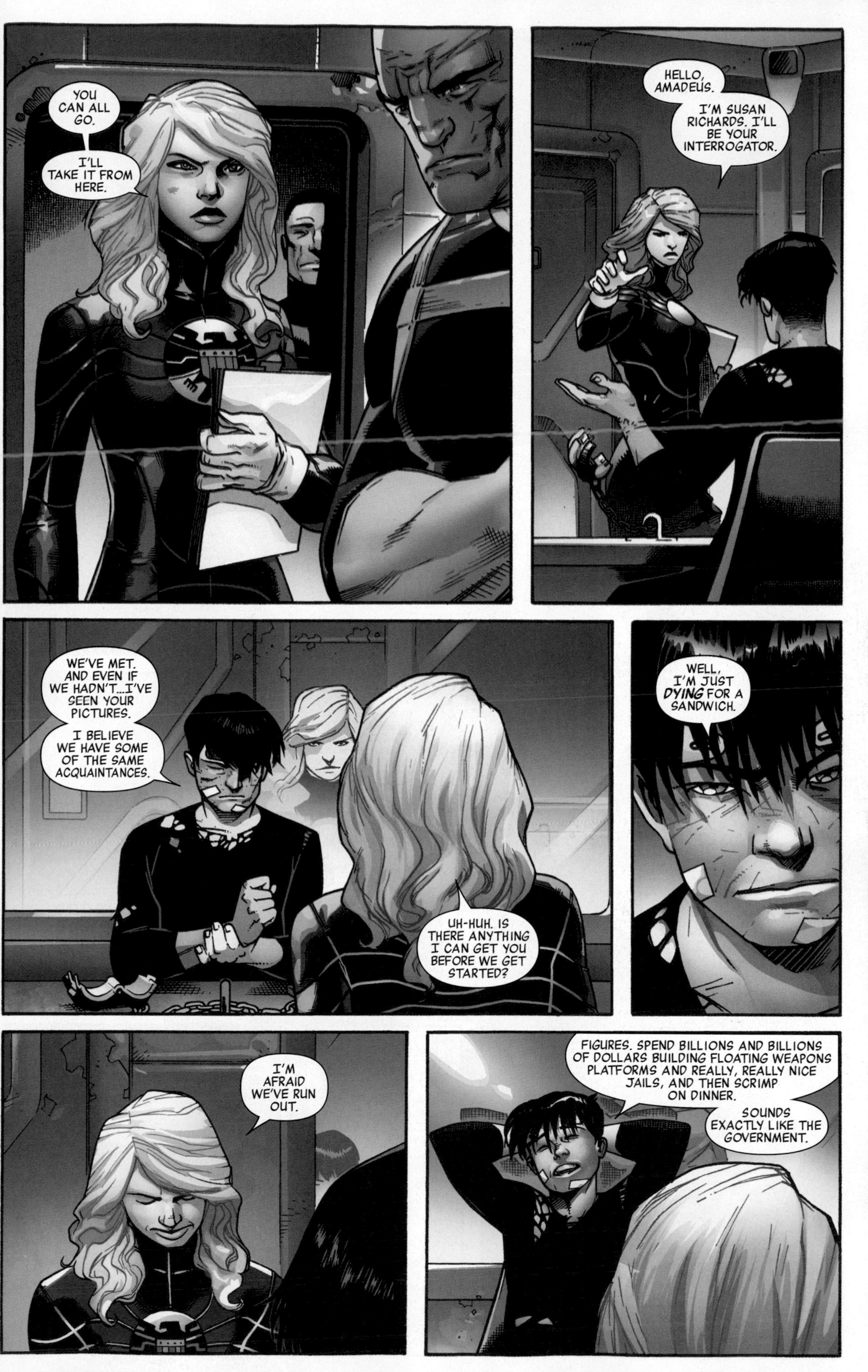
YOU CAN ALL GO.
I'LL TAKE IT FROM HERE.
HELLO, AMADEUS.
I'M SUSAN RICHARDS. I'LL BE YOUR INTERROGATOR.
WE'VE MET. AND EVEN IF WE HADN'T...I'VE SEEN YOUR PICTURES.
I BELIEVE WE HAVE SOME OF THE SAME ACQUAINTANCES.
UH-HUH. IS THERE ANYTHING I CAN GET YOU BEFORE WE GET STARTED?
WELL, I'M JUST DYING FOR A SANDWICH.
I'M AFRAID WE'VE RUN OUT.
FIGURES. SPEND BILLIONS AND BILLIONS OF DOLLARS BUILDING FLOATING WEAPONS PLATFORMS AND REALLY, REALLY NICE JAILS, AND THEN SCRIMP ON DINNER.
SOUNDS EXACTLY LIKE THE GOVERNMENT.

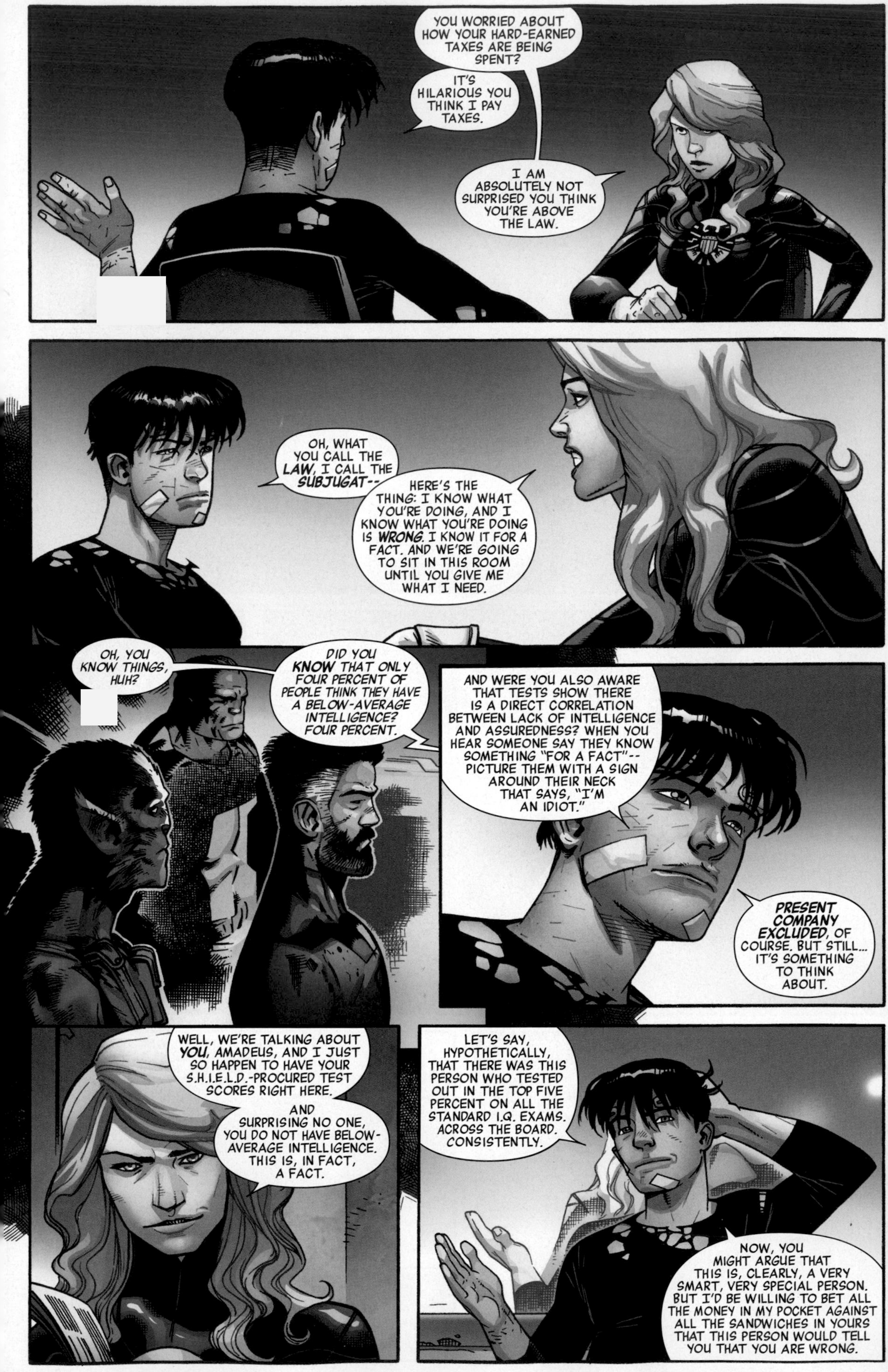
YOU WORRIED ABOUT HOW YOUR HARD-EARNED TAXES ARE BEING SPENT?
IT'S HILARIOUS YOU THINK I PAY TAXES.
I AM ABSOLUTELY NOT SURPRISED YOU THINK YOU'RE ABOVE THE LAW.
OH, WHAT YOU CALL THE LAW, I CALL THE SUBJUGAT--
HERE'S THE THING: I KNOW WHAT YOU'RE DOING, AND I KNOW WHAT YOU'RE DOING IS WRONG. I KNOW IT FOR A FACT. AND WE'RE GOING TO SIT IN THIS ROOM UNTIL YOU GIVE ME WHAT I NEED.
OH, YOU KNOW THINGS, HUH?
DID YOU KNOW THAT ONLY FOUR PERCENT OF PEOPLE THINK THEY HAVE A BELOW-AVERAGE INTELLIGENCE? FOUR PERCENT.
AND WERE YOU ALSO AWARE THAT TESTS SHOW THERE IS A DIRECT CORRELATION BETWEEN LACK OF INTELLIGENCE AND ASSUREDNESS? WHEN YOU HEAR SOMEONE SAY THEY KNOW SOMETHING "FOR A FACT"-- PICTURE THEM WITH A SIGN AROUND THEIR NECK THAT SAYS, "I'M AN IDIOT."
PRESENT COMPANY EXCLUDED, OF COURSE. BUT STILL... IT'S SOMETHING TO THINK ABOUT.
WELL, WE'RE TALKING ABOUT YOU, AMADEUS, AND I JUST SO HAPPEN TO HAVE YOUR S.H.I.E.L.D.-PROCURED TEST SCORES RIGHT HERE.
AND SURPRISING NO ONE, YOU DO NOT HAVE BELOW-AVERAGE INTELLIGENCE. THIS IS, IN FACT, A FACT.
LET'S SAY, HYPOTHETICALLY, THAT THERE WAS THIS PERSON WHO TESTED OUT IN THE TOP FIVE PERCENT ON ALL THE STANDARD I.Q. EXAMS. ACROSS THE BOARD. CONSISTENTLY.
NOW, YOU MIGHT ARGUE THAT THIS IS, CLEARLY, A VERY SMART, VERY SPECIAL PERSON. BUT I'D BE WILLING TO BET ALL THE MONEY IN MY POCKET AGAINST ALL THE SANDWICHES IN YOURS THAT THIS PERSON WOULD TELL YOU THAT YOU ARE WRONG.

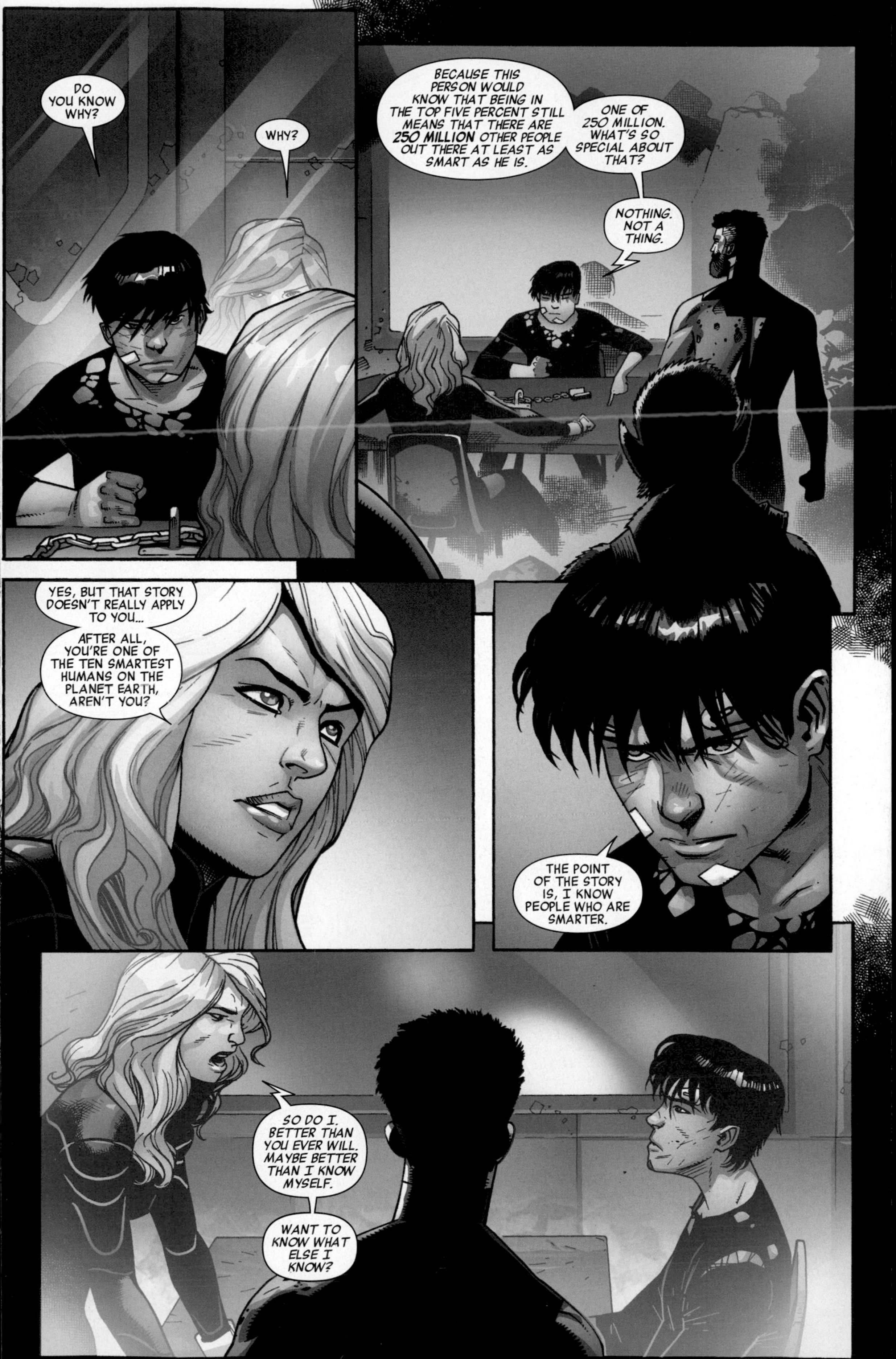
DO YOU KNOW WHY?
WHY?
BECAUSE THIS PERSON WOULD KNOW THAT BEING IN THE TOP FIVE PERCENT STILL MEANS THAT THERE ARE 250 MILLION OTHER PEOPLE OUT THERE AT LEAST AS SMART AS HE IS.
ONE OF 250 MILLION. WHAT'S SO SPECIAL ABOUT THAT?
NOTHING. NOT A THING.
YES, BUT THAT STORY DOESN'T REALLY APPLY TO YOU...
AFTER ALL, YOU'RE ONE OF THE TEN SMARTEST HUMANS ON THE PLANET EARTH, AREN'T YOU?
THE POINT OF THE STORY IS, I KNOW PEOPLE WHO ARE SMARTER.
SO DO I. BETTER THAN YOU EVER WILL. MAYBE BETTER THAN I KNOW MYSELF.
WANT TO KNOW WHAT ELSE I KNOW?

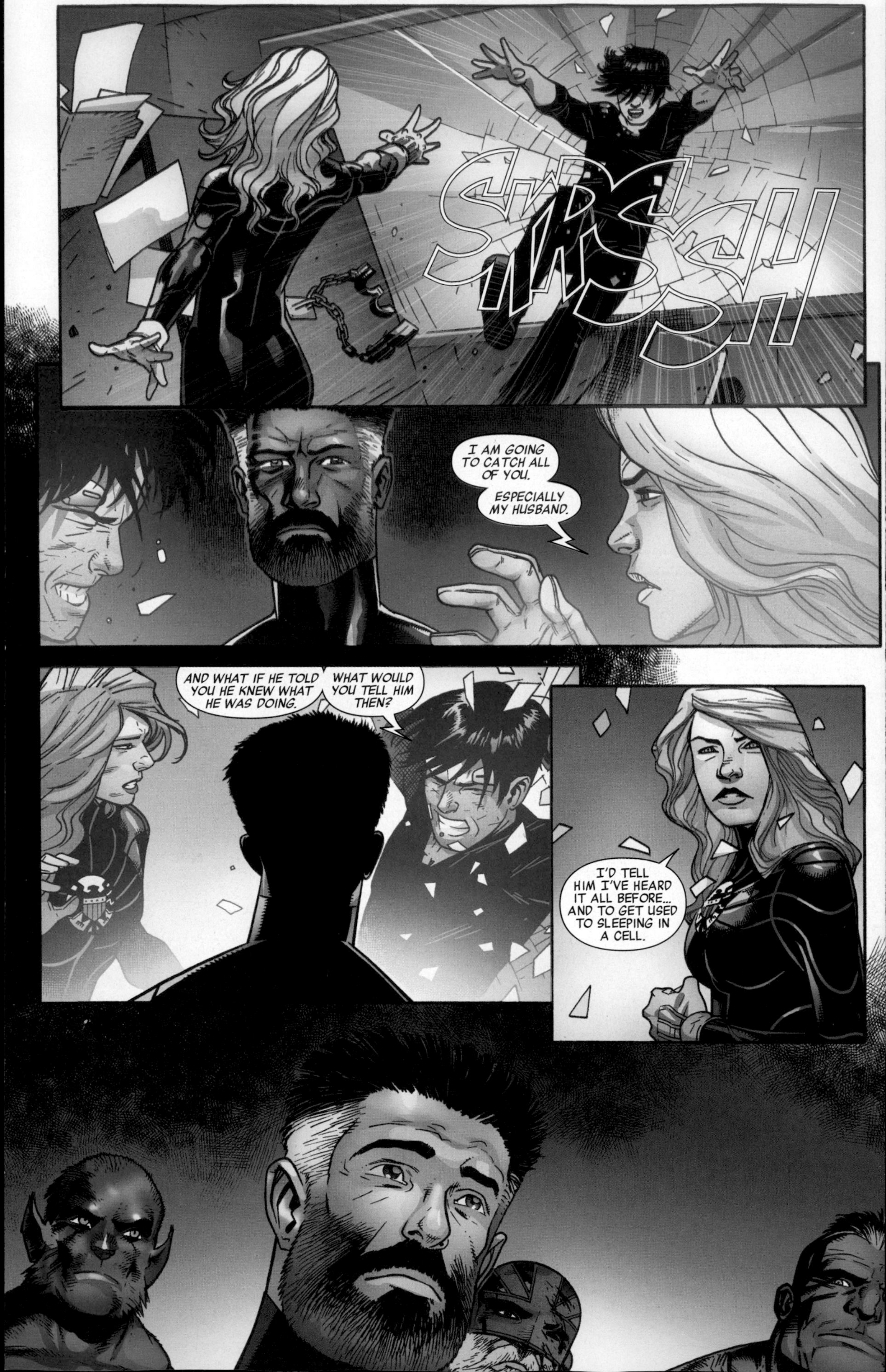
SHRASSH
I AM GOING TO CATCH ALL OF YOU.
ESPECIALLY MY HUSBAND.
AND WHAT IF HE TOLD YOU HE KNEW WHAT HE WAS DOING.
WHAT WOULD YOU TELL HIM THEN?
I'D TELL HIM I'VE HEARD IT ALL BEFORE... AND TO GET USED TO SLEEPING IN A CELL.

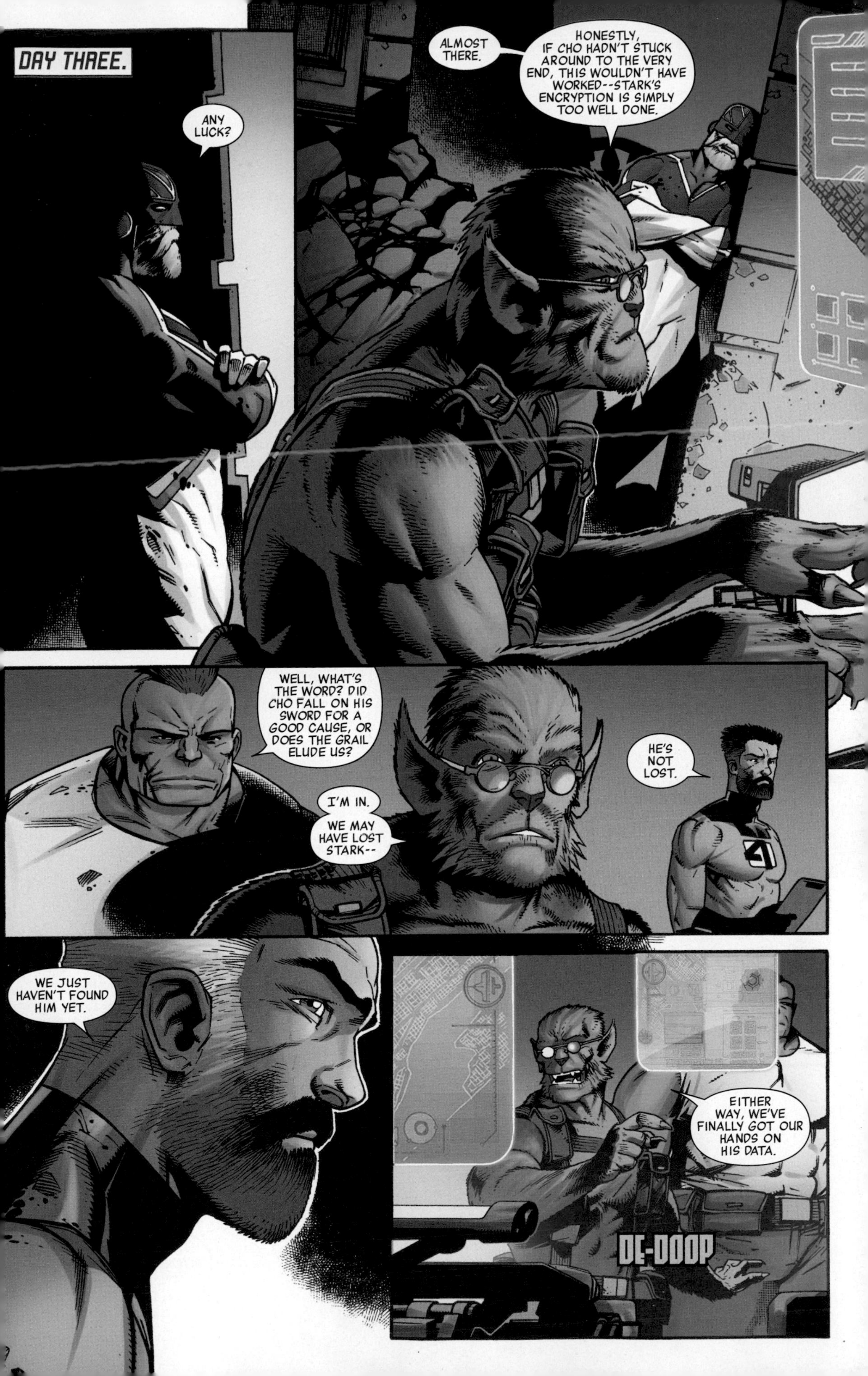
DAY THREE.
ANY LUCK?
ALMOST THERE.
HONESTLY, IF CHO HADN'T STUCK AROUND TO THE VERY END, THIS WOULDN'T HAVE WORKED--STARK'S ENCRYPTION IS SIMPLY TOO WELL DONE.
WELL, WHAT'S THE WORD? DID CHO FALL ON HIS SWORD FOR A GOOD CAUSE, OR DOES THE GRAIL ELUDE US?
I'M IN.
WE MAY HAVE LOST STARK--
HE'S NOT LOST.
WE JUST HAVEN'T FOUND HIM YET.
EITHER WAY, WE'VE FINALLY GOT OUR HANDS ON HIS DATA.
DE-DOOP

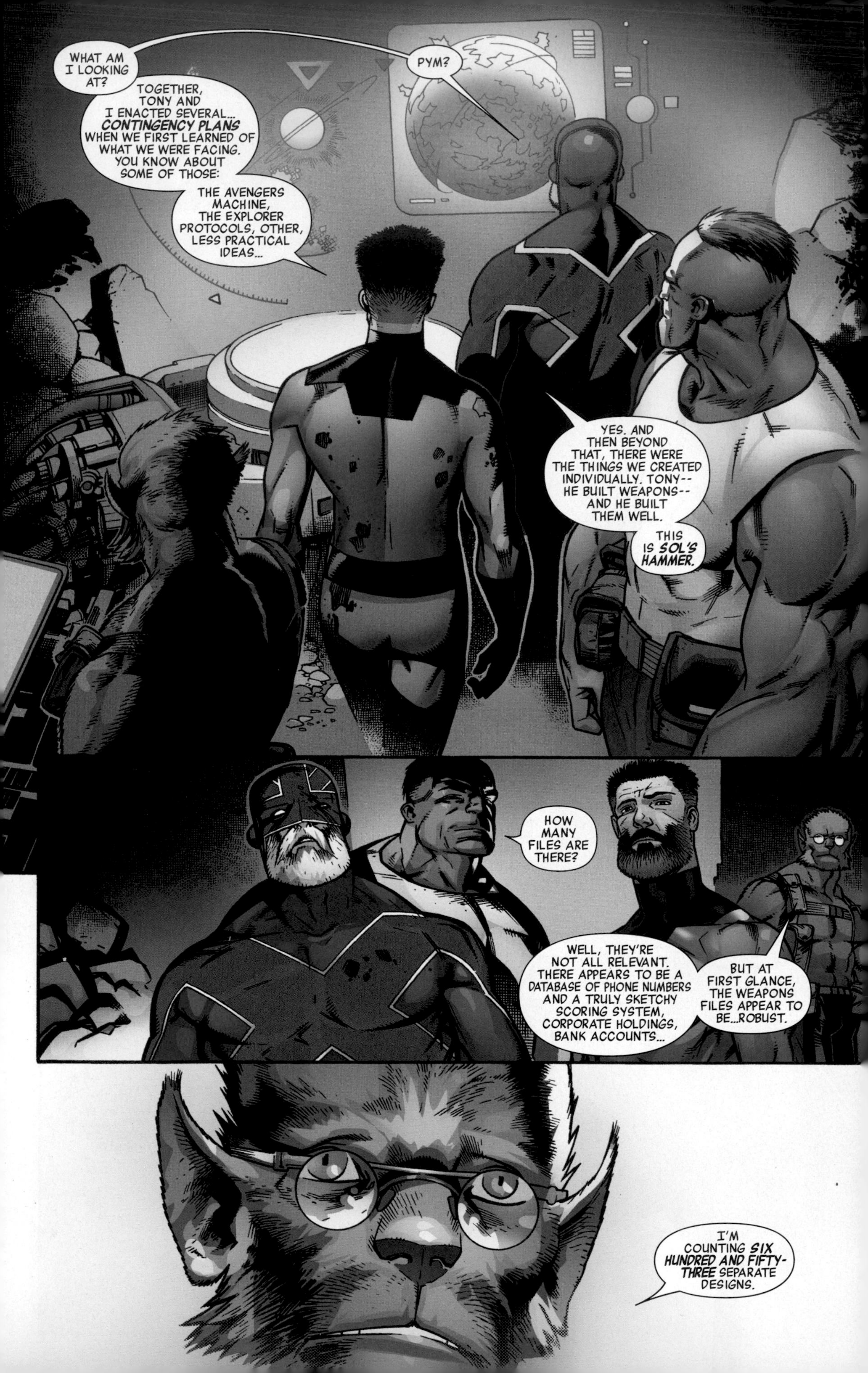
WHAT AM I LOOKING AT?
PYM?
TOGETHER, TONY AND I ENACTED SEVERAL... CONTINGENCY PLANS WHEN WE FIRST LEARNED OF WHAT WE WERE FACING. YOU KNOW ABOUT SOME OF THOSE:
THE AVENGERS MACHINE, THE EXPLORER PROTOCOLS, OTHER, LESS PRACTICAL IDEAS...
YES. AND THEN BEYOND THAT, THERE WERE THE THINGS WE CREATED INDIVIDUALLY. TONY-- HE BUILT WEAPONS-- AND HE BUILT THEM WELL.
THIS IS SOL'S HAMMER.
HOW MANY FILES ARE THERE?
WELL, THEY'RE NOT ALL RELEVANT. THERE APPEARS TO BE A DATABASE OF PHONE NUMBERS AND A TRULY SKETCHY SCORING SYSTEM, CORPORATE HOLDINGS, BANK ACCOUNTS...
BUT AT FIRST GLANCE, THE WEAPONS FILES APPEAR TO BE...ROBUST.
I'M COUNTING SIX HUNDRED AND FIFTY-THREE SEPARATE DESIGNS.

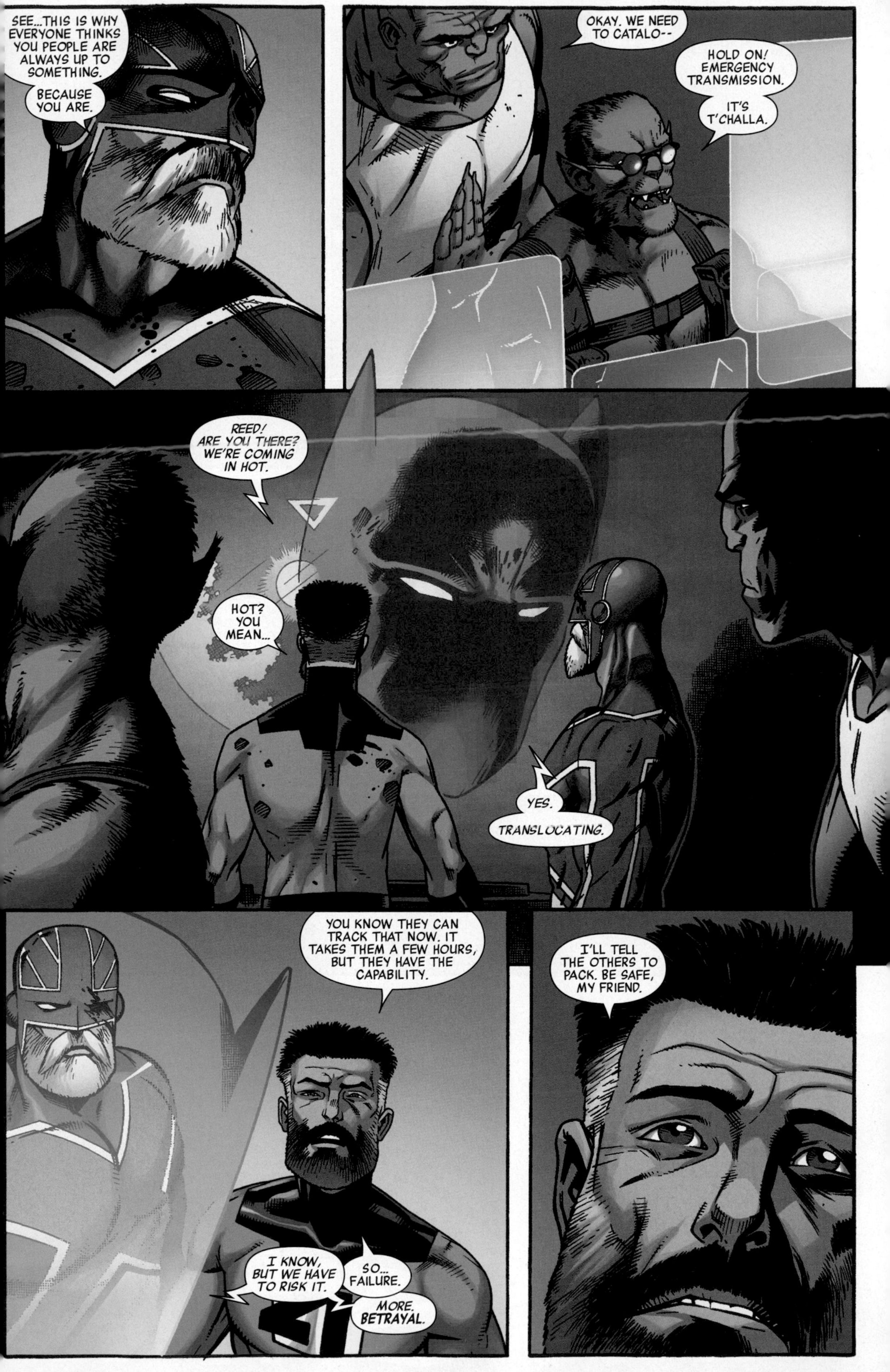
SEE...THIS IS WHY EVERYONE THINKS YOU PEOPLE ARE ALWAYS UP TO SOMETHING.
BECAUSE YOU ARE.
OKAY. WE NEED TO CATALO--
HOLD ON! EMERGENCY TRANSMISSION.
IT'S T'CHALLA.
REED! ARE YOU THERE? WE'RE COMING IN HOT.
HOT? YOU MEAN...
YES.
TRANSLOCATING.
YOU KNOW THEY CAN TRACK THAT NOW. IT TAKES THEM A FEW HOURS, BUT THEY HAVE THE CAPABILITY.
I KNOW, BUT WE HAVE TO RISK IT.
SO... FAILURE.
MORE. BETRAYAL.
I'LL TELL THE OTHERS TO PACK. BE SAFE, MY FRIEND.

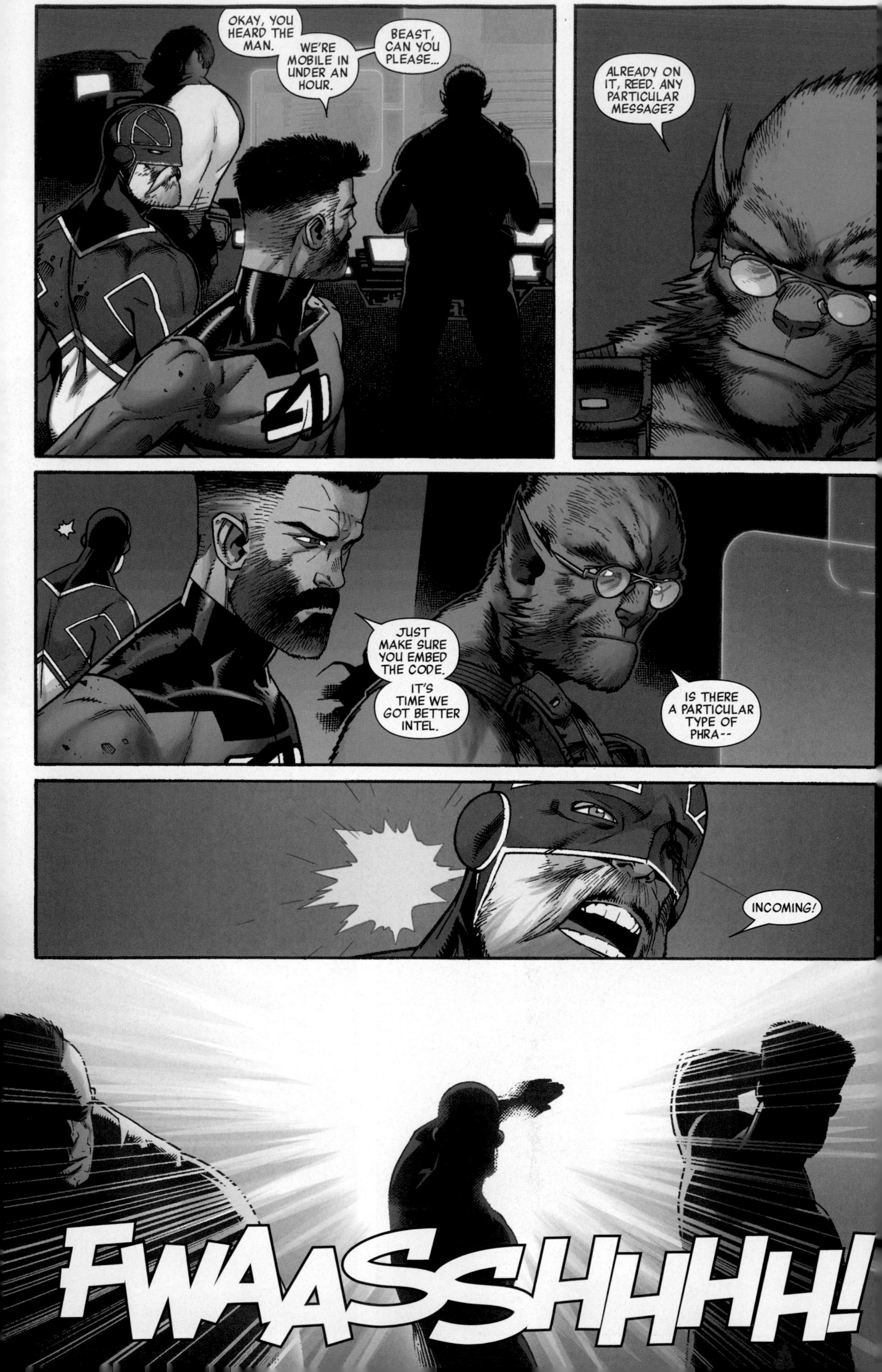
OKAY, YOU HEARD THE MAN.
WE'RE MOBILE IN UNDER AN HOUR.
BEAST, CAN YOU PLEASE...
ALREADY ON IT, REED. ANY PARTICULAR MESSAGE?
JUST MAKE SURE YOU EMBED THE CODE.
IT'S TIME WE GOT BETTER INTEL.
IS THERE A PARTICULAR TYPE OF PHRA--
INCOMING!
FWAASSHHHH!

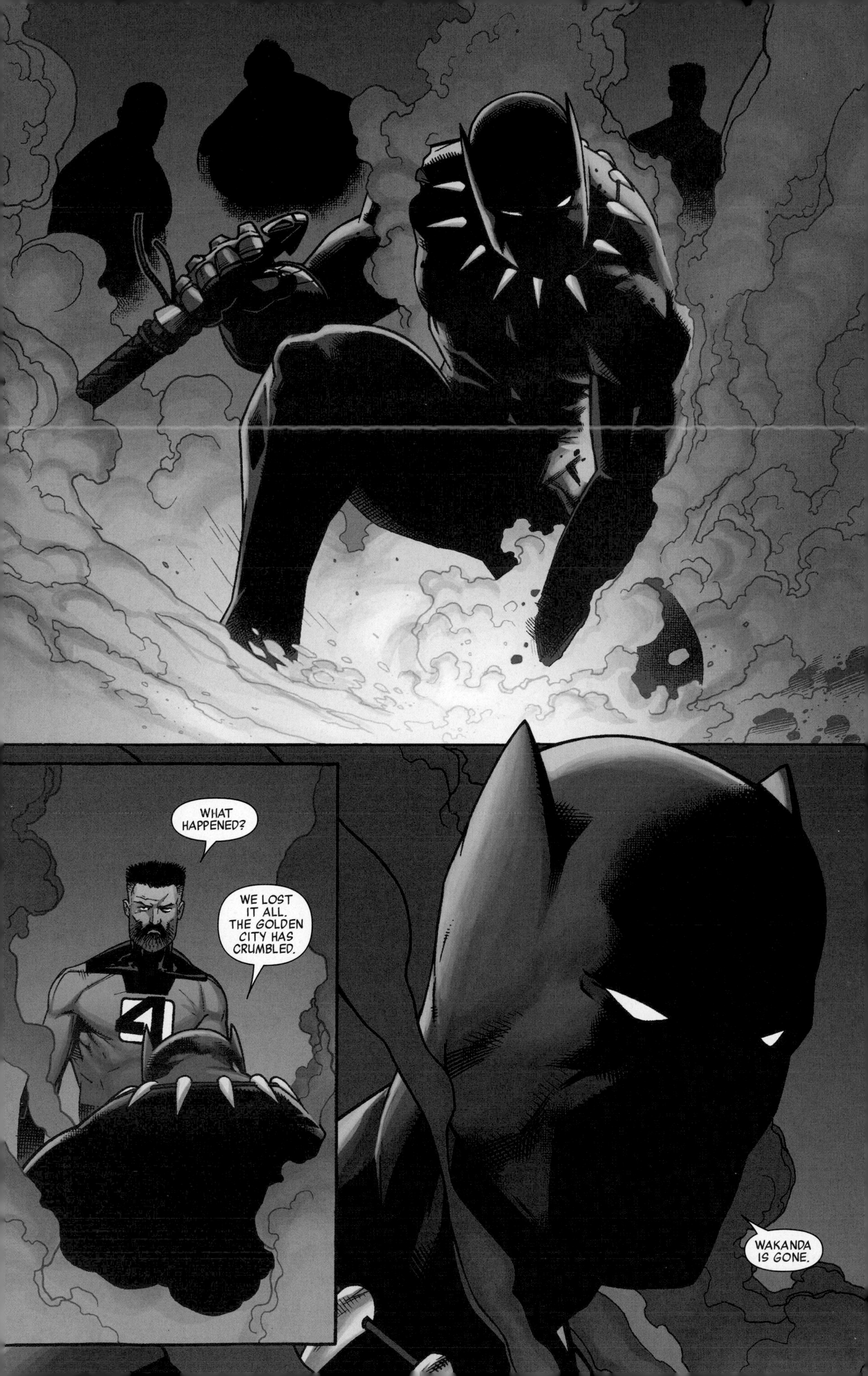
WHAT HAPPENED?
WE LOST IT ALL. THE GOLDEN CITY HAS CRUMBLED.
WAKANDA IS GONE.

"ARCHANGEL"

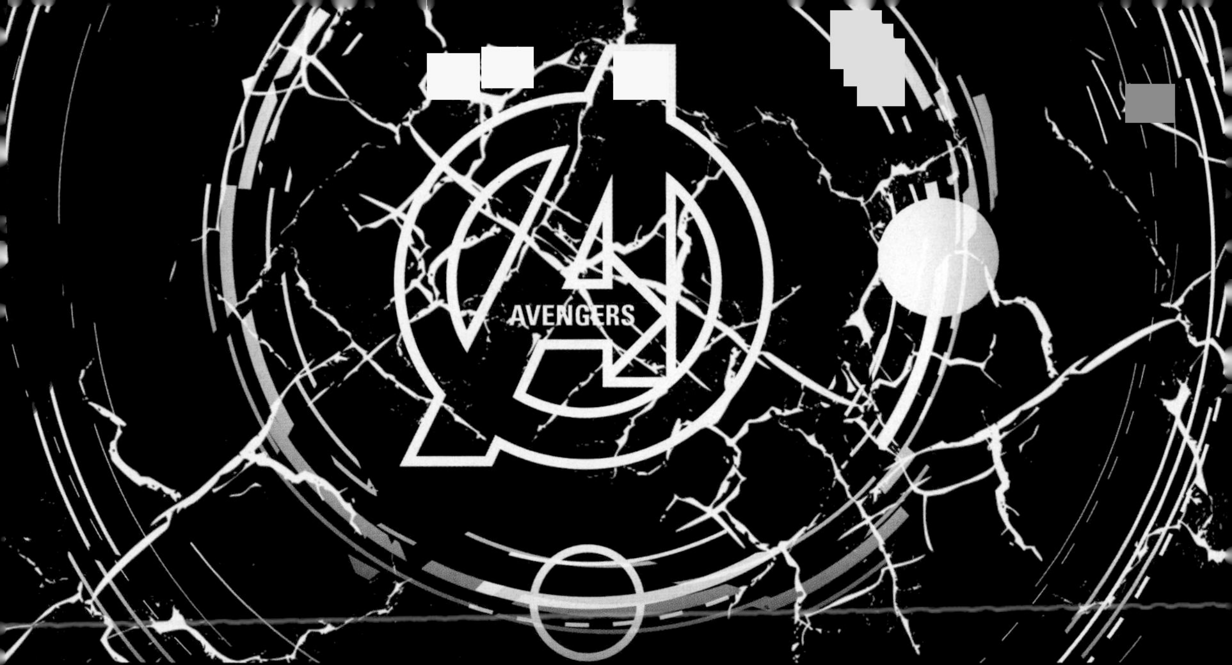
AVENGERS

S.H.I.E.L.D. AVENGERS

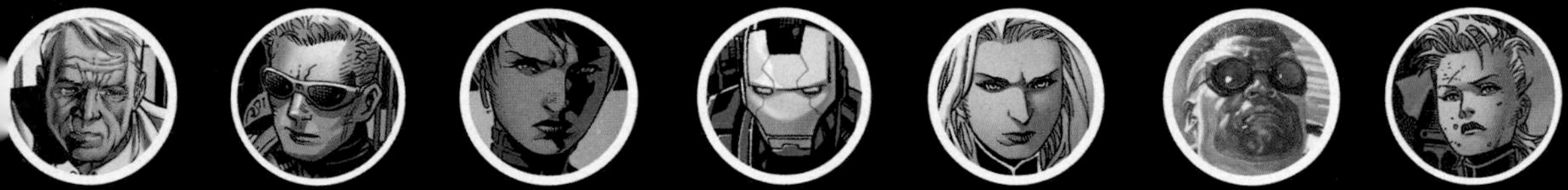

STEVE ROGERS | HAWKEYE | MARIA HILL | WAR MACHINE DRONES | INVISIBLE WOMAN | CAPTAIN AMERICA | CAPTAIN MARVEL

MULTIVERSAL AVENGERS

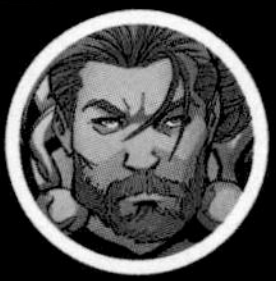

HYPERION

NEW AVENGERS

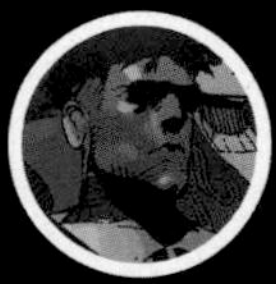

SUNSPOT

THE ILLUMINATI

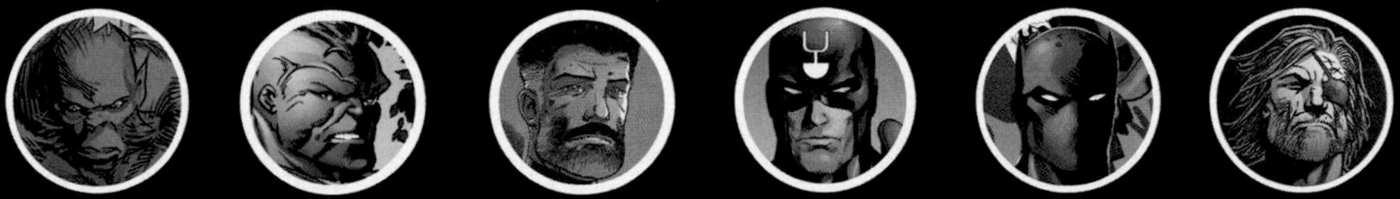

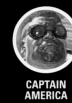

BEAST | HULK/ DOC GREEN | MISTER FANTASTIC | BLACK BOLT | BLACK PANTHER | CAPTAIN BRITAIN

THE CABAL

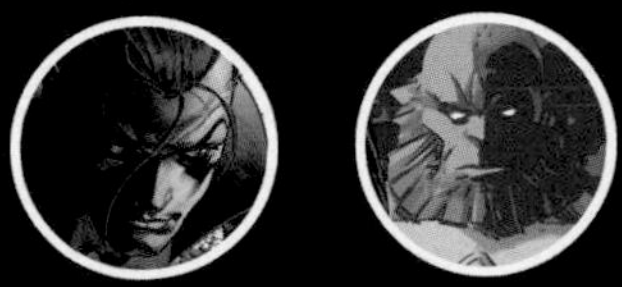

NAMOR | TERRAX

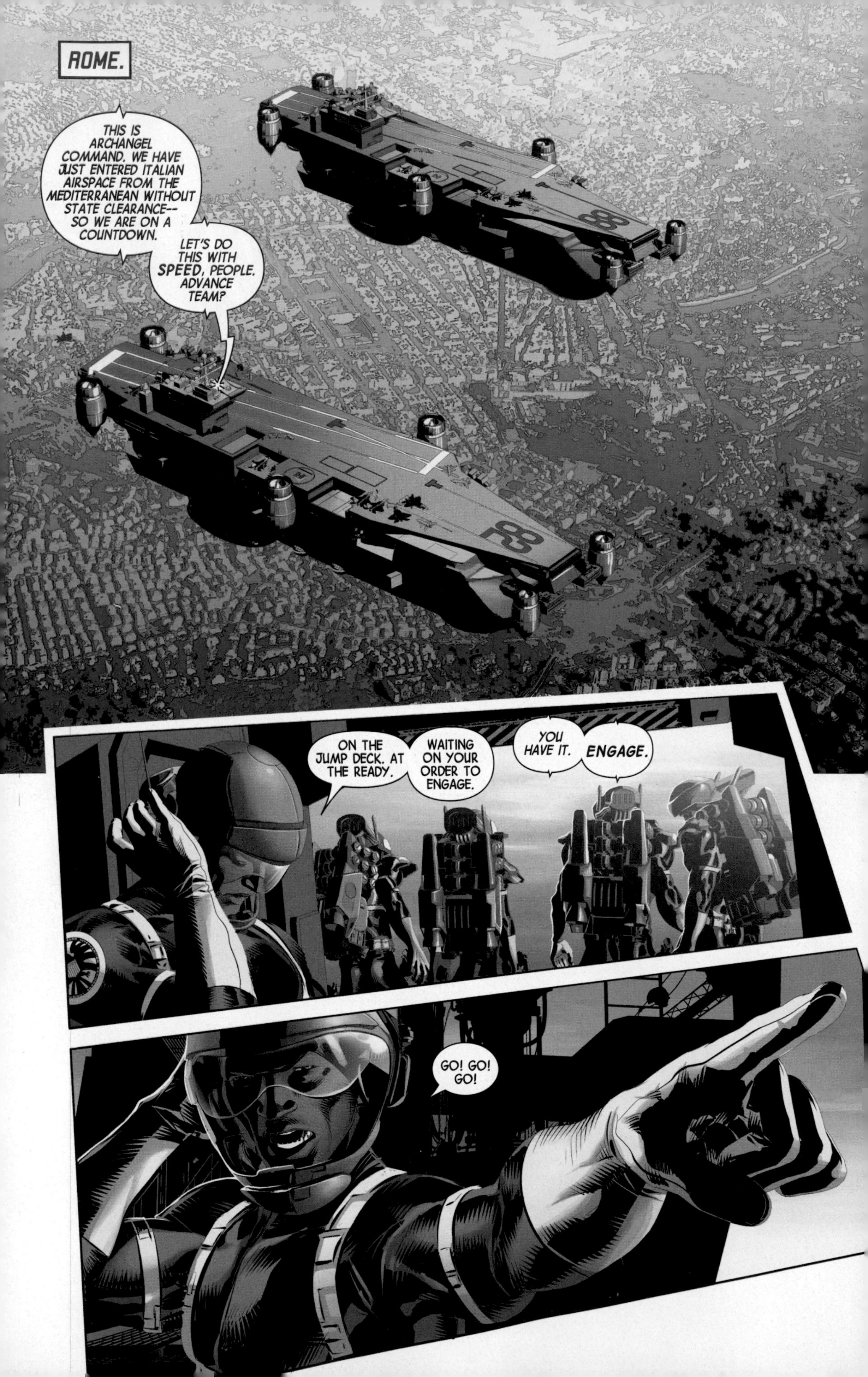
ROME.
THIS IS ARCHANGEL COMMAND. WE HAVE JUST ENTERED ITALIAN AIRSPACE FROM THE MEDITERRANEAN WITHOUT STATE CLEARANCE-- SO WE ARE ON A COUNTDOWN.
LET'S DO THIS WITH SPEED, PEOPLE. ADVANCE TEAM?
ON THE JUMP DECK. AT THE READY.
WAITING ON YOUR ORDER TO ENGAGE.
YOU HAVE IT.
ENGAGE.
GO! GO! GO!

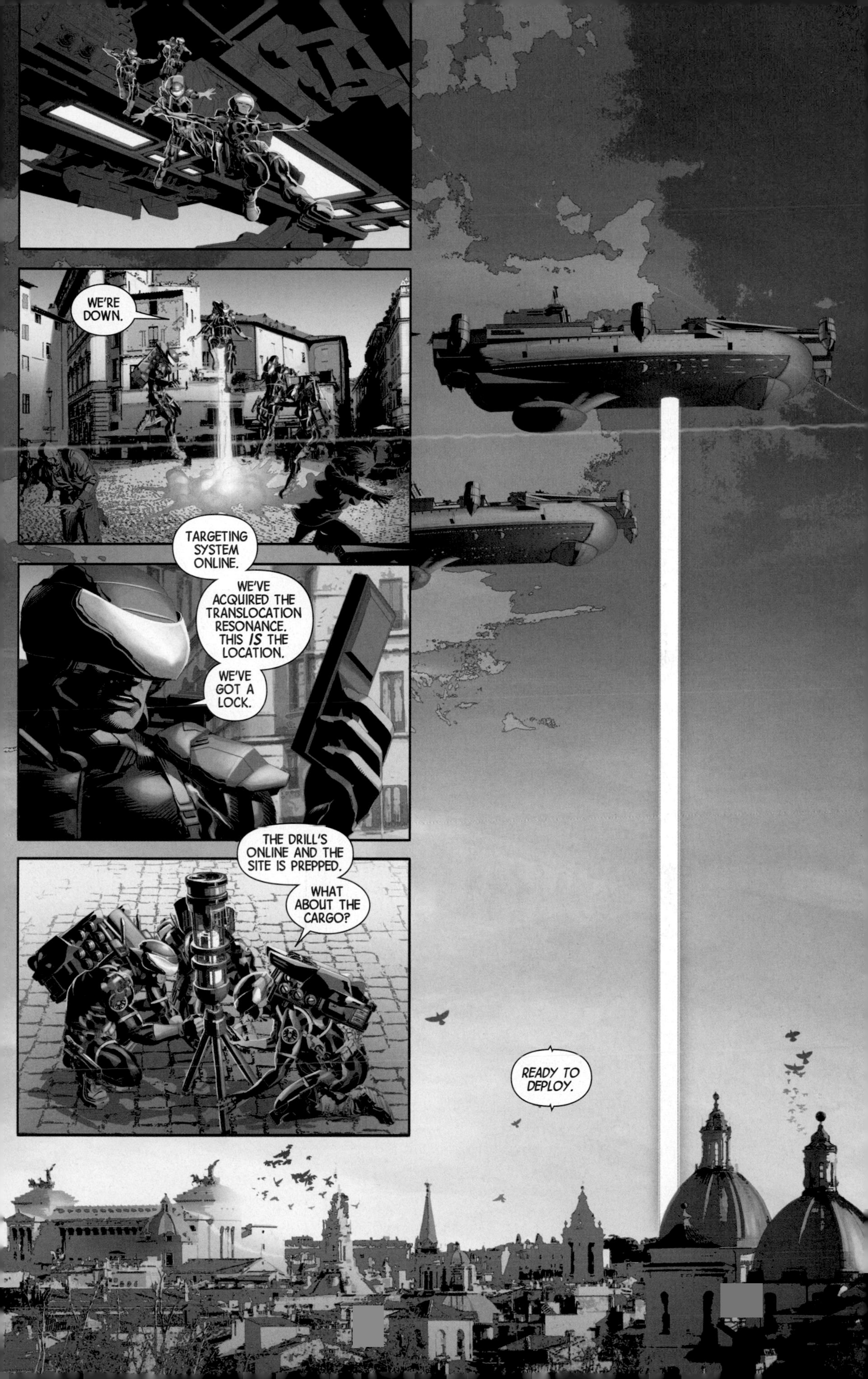
WE'RE DOWN.
TARGETING SYSTEM ONLINE.
WE'VE ACQUIRED THE TRANSLOCATION RESONANCE. THIS *IS* THE LOCATION.
WE'VE GOT A LOCK.
THE DRILL'S ONLINE AND THE SITE IS PREPPED.
WHAT ABOUT THE CARGO?
READY TO DEPLOY.

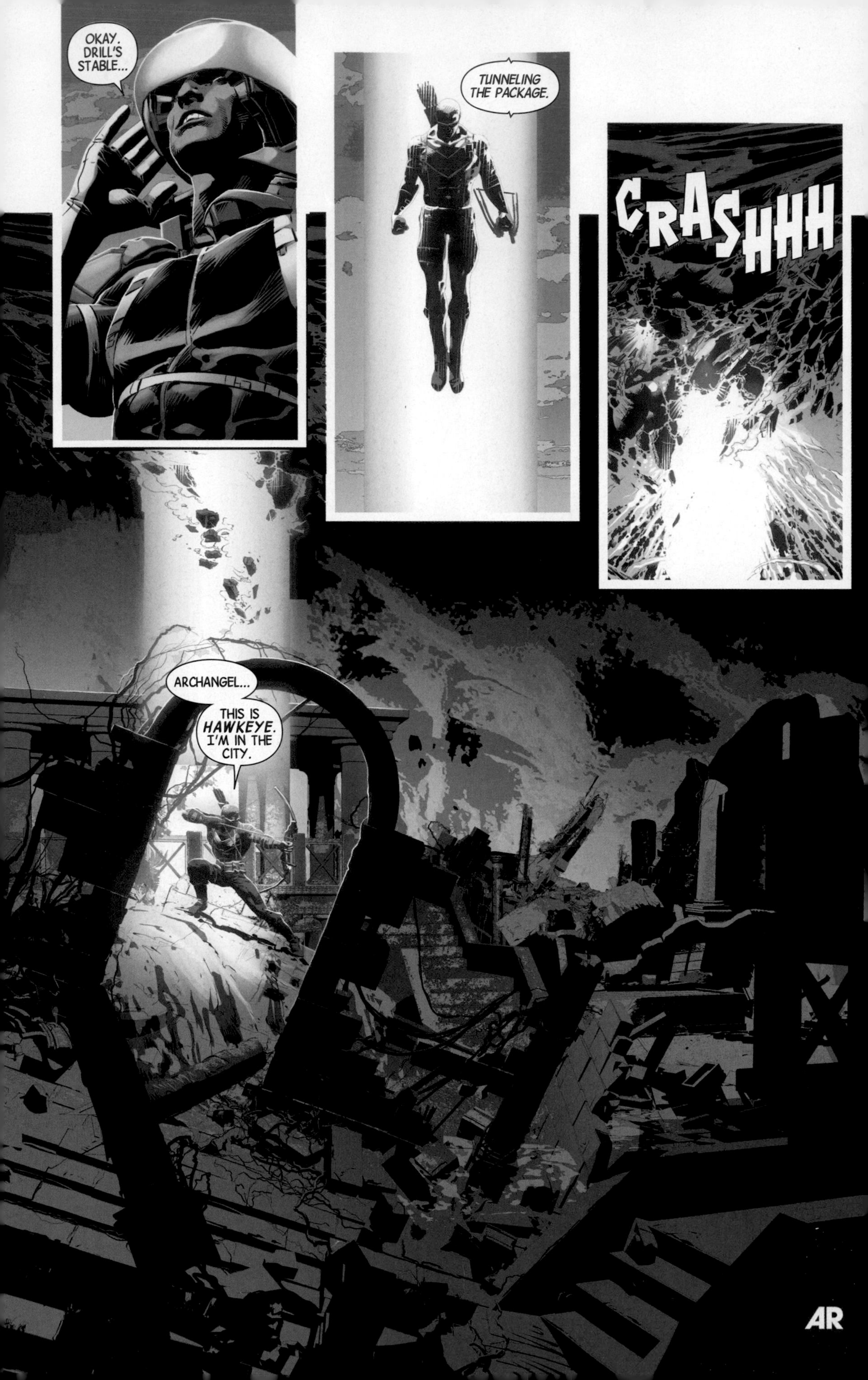
OKAY. DRILL'S STABLE...
TUNNELING THE PACKAGE.
CRASHHH
ARCHANGEL...
THIS IS HAWKEYE. I'M IN THE CITY.
AR

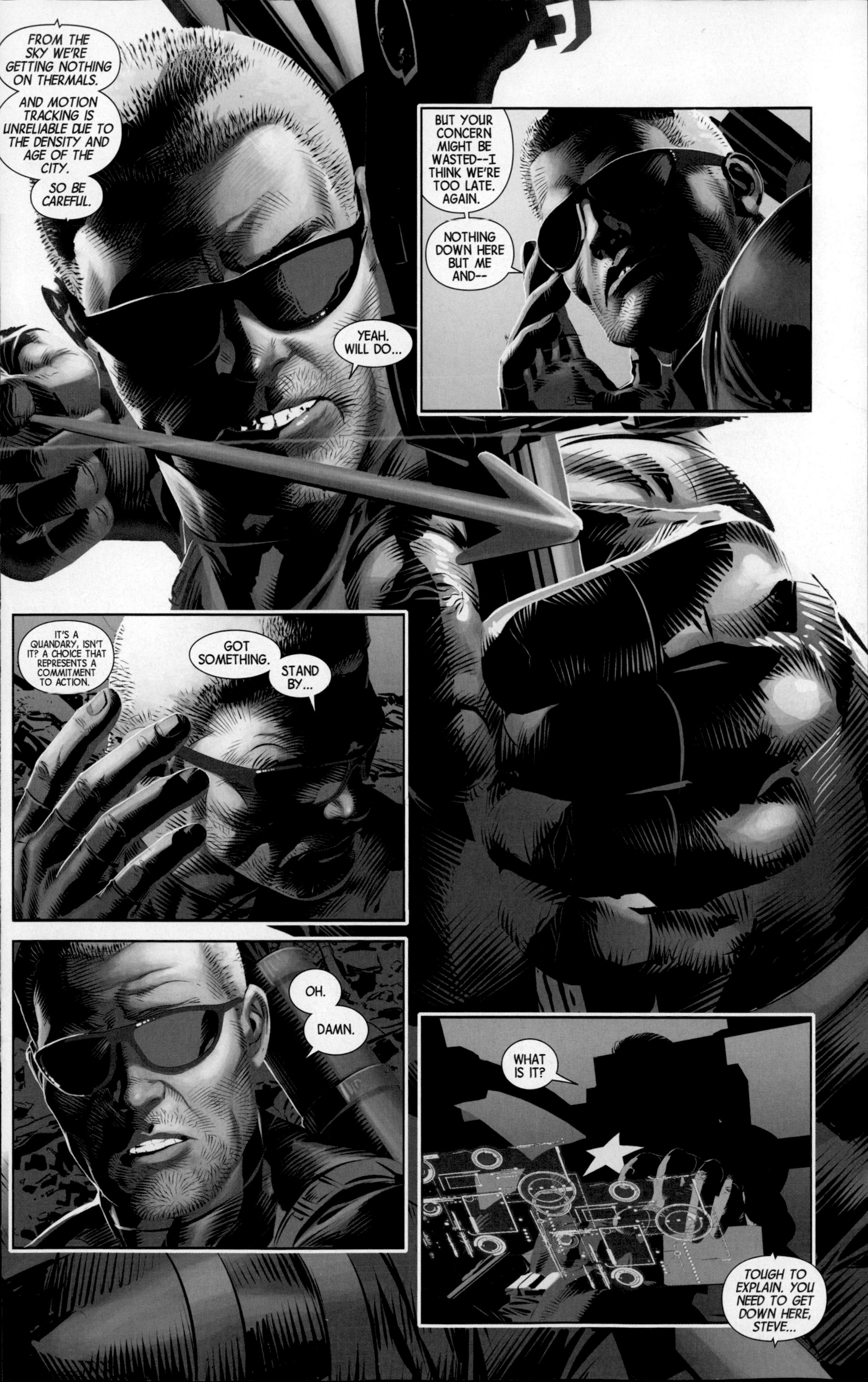
FROM THE SKY WE'RE GETTING NOTHING ON THERMALS.
AND MOTION TRACKING IS UNRELIABLE DUE TO THE DENSITY AND AGE OF THE CITY.
SO BE CAREFUL.
YEAH. WILL DO...
BUT YOUR CONCERN MIGHT BE WASTED--I THINK WE'RE TOO LATE. AGAIN.
NOTHING DOWN HERE BUT ME AND--
IT'S A QUANDARY, ISN'T IT? A CHOICE THAT REPRESENTS A COMMITMENT TO ACTION.
GOT SOMETHING.
STAND BY...
OH.
DAMN.
WHAT IS IT?
TOUGH TO EXPLAIN. YOU NEED TO GET DOWN HERE, STEVE...

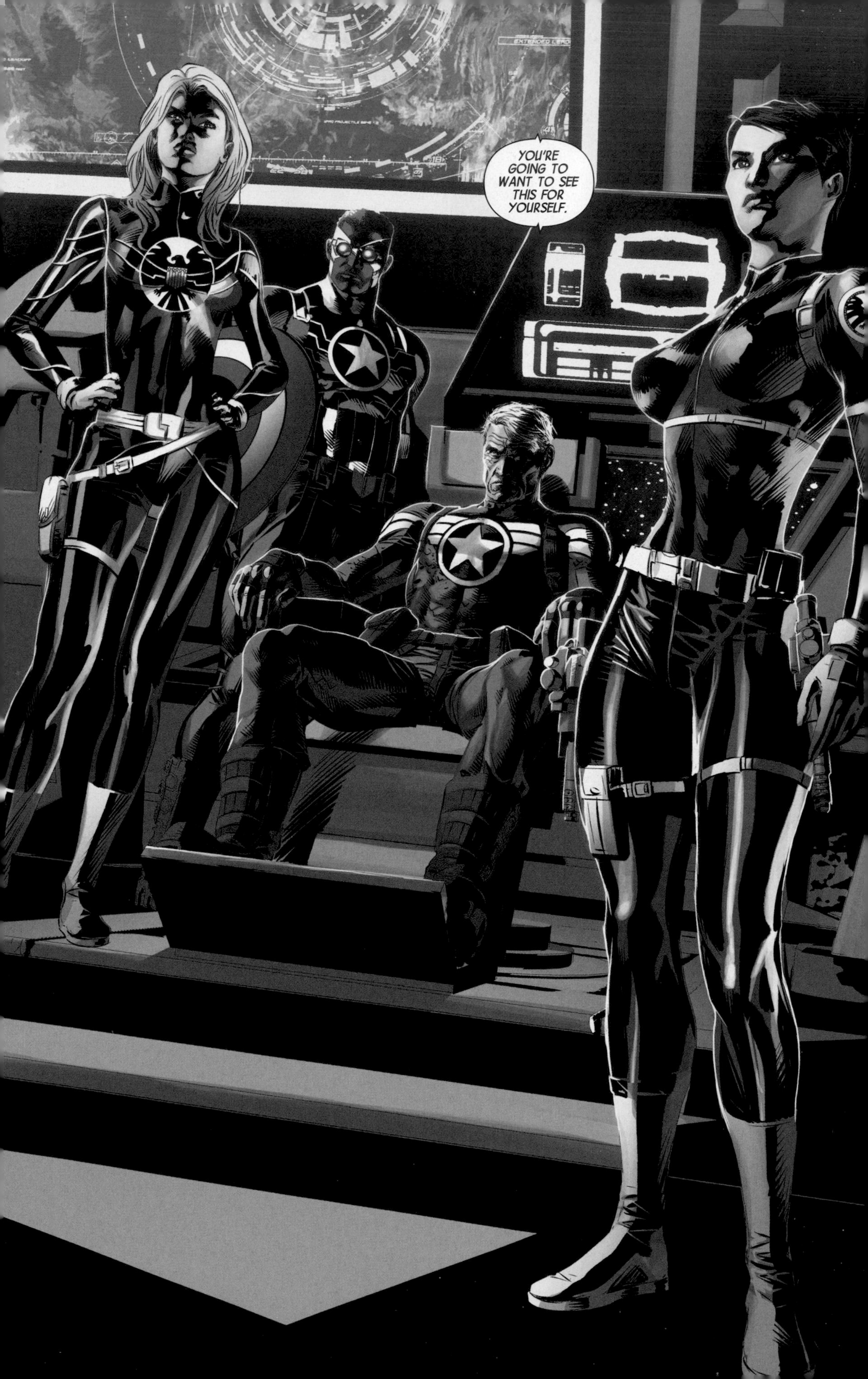
YOU'RE GOING TO WANT TO SEE THIS FOR YOURSELF.

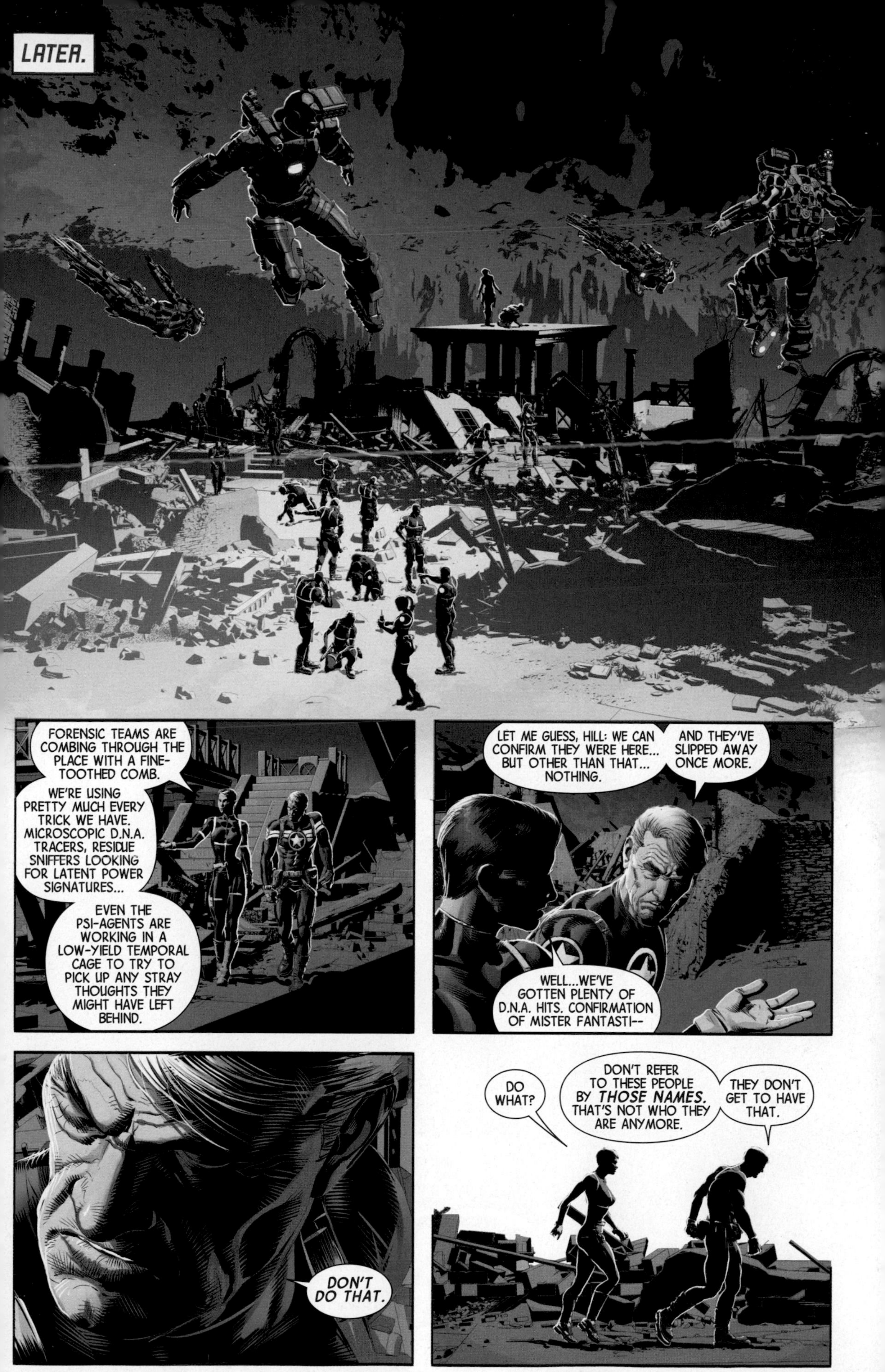
LATER.
FORENSIC TEAMS ARE COMBING THROUGH THE PLACE WITH A FINE-TOOTHED COMB.
WE'RE USING PRETTY MUCH EVERY TRICK WE HAVE. MICROSCOPIC D.N.A. TRACERS, RESIDUE SNIFFERS LOOKING FOR LATENT POWER SIGNATURES...
EVEN THE PSI-AGENTS ARE WORKING IN A LOW-YIELD TEMPORAL CAGE TO TRY TO PICK UP ANY STRAY THOUGHTS THEY MIGHT HAVE LEFT BEHIND.
LET ME GUESS, HILL: WE CAN CONFIRM THEY WERE HERE... BUT OTHER THAN THAT... NOTHING.
AND THEY'VE SLIPPED AWAY ONCE MORE.
WELL...WE'VE GOTTEN PLENTY OF D.N.A. HITS. CONFIRMATION OF MISTER FANTASTI--
DON'T DO THAT.
DO WHAT?
DON'T REFER TO THESE PEOPLE BY *THOSE NAMES.* THAT'S NOT WHO THEY ARE ANYMORE.
THEY DON'T GET TO HAVE THAT.

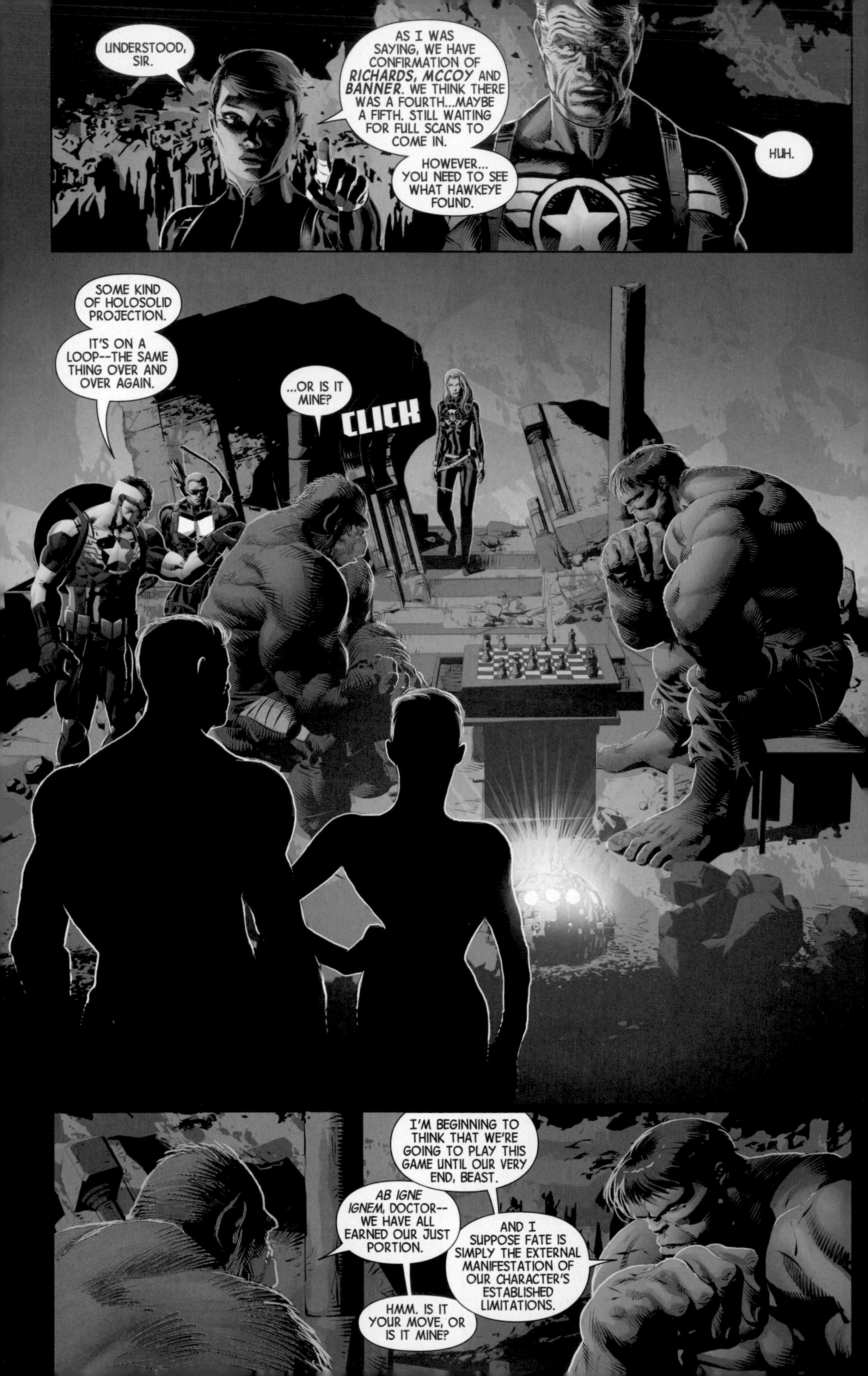

UNDERSTOOD, SIR.
AS I WAS SAYING, WE HAVE CONFIRMATION OF RICHARDS, MCCOY AND BANNER. WE THINK THERE WAS A FOURTH...MAYBE A FIFTH. STILL WAITING FOR FULL SCANS TO COME IN.
HOWEVER... YOU NEED TO SEE WHAT HAWKEYE FOUND.
HUH.
SOME KIND OF HOLOSOLID PROJECTION.
IT'S ON A LOOP--THE SAME THING OVER AND OVER AGAIN.
...OR IS IT MINE?
CLICK
I'M BEGINNING TO THINK THAT WE'RE GOING TO PLAY THIS GAME UNTIL OUR VERY END, BEAST.
AB IGNE IGNEM, DOCTOR--WE HAVE ALL EARNED OUR JUST PORTION.
AND I SUPPOSE FATE IS SIMPLY THE EXTERNAL MANIFESTATION OF OUR CHARACTER'S ESTABLISHED LIMITATIONS.
HMM. IS IT YOUR MOVE, OR IS IT MINE?

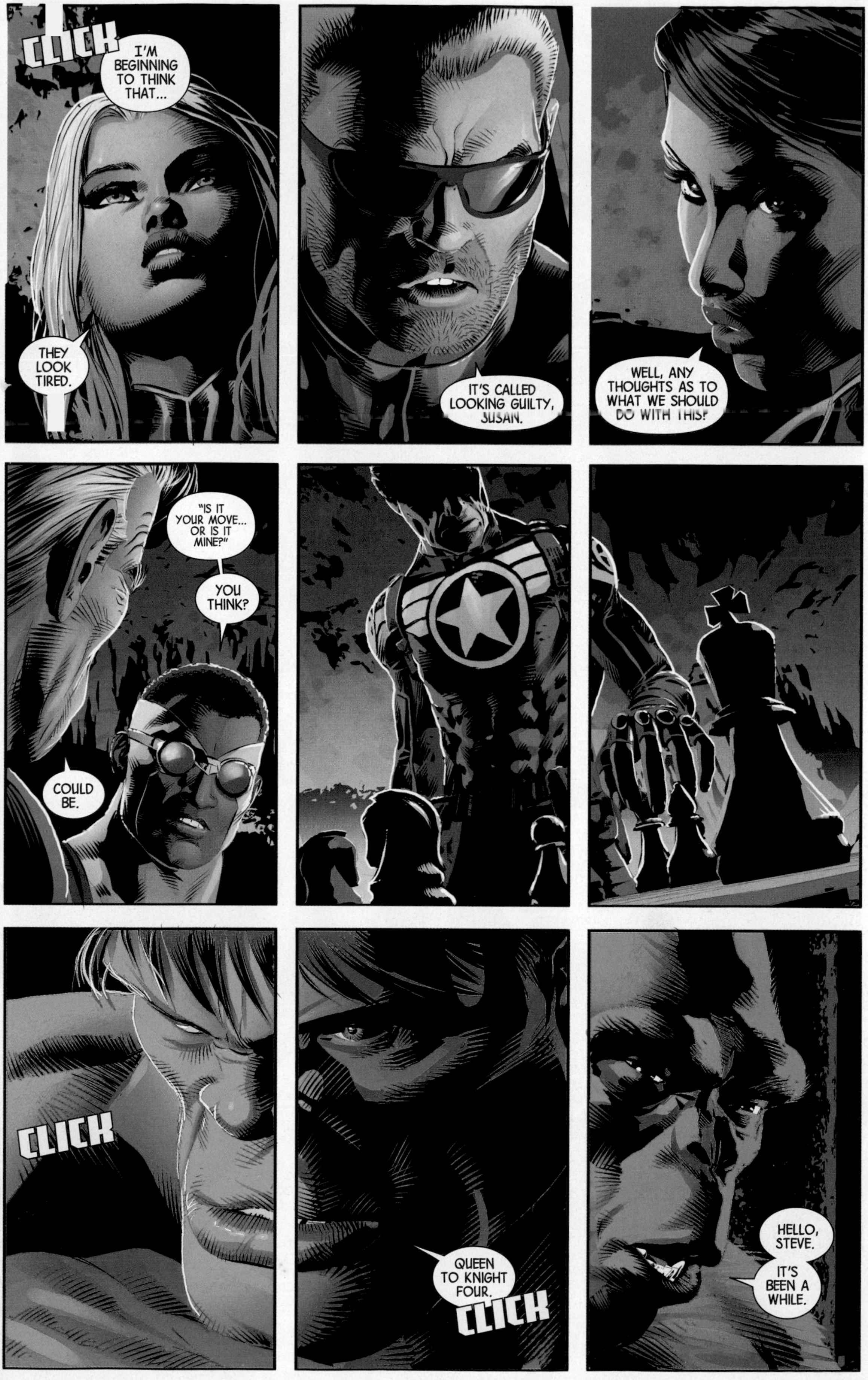
CLICK
I'M BEGINNING TO THINK THAT...
THEY LOOK TIRED.
IT'S CALLED LOOKING GUILTY, SUSAN.
WELL, ANY THOUGHTS AS TO WHAT WE SHOULD DO WITH THIS?
"IS IT YOUR MOVE... OR IS IT MINE?"
YOU THINK?
COULD BE.
CLICK
QUEEN TO KNIGHT FOUR.
CLICK
HELLO, STEVE.
IT'S BEEN A WHILE.

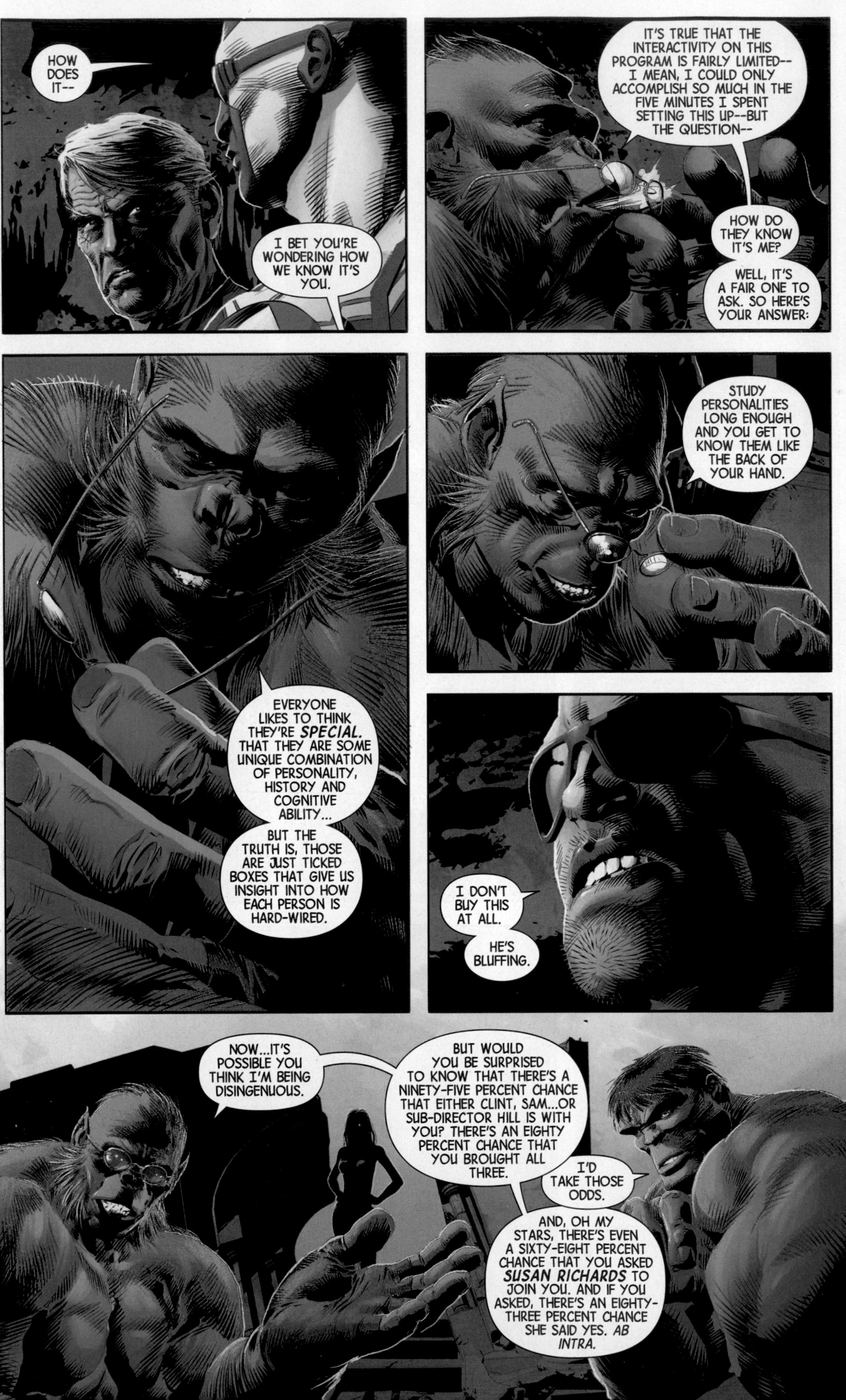
HOW DOES IT--
I BET YOU'RE WONDERING HOW WE KNOW IT'S YOU.
IT'S TRUE THAT THE INTERACTIVITY ON THIS PROGRAM IS FAIRLY LIMITED-- I MEAN, I COULD ONLY ACCOMPLISH SO MUCH IN THE FIVE MINUTES I SPENT SETTING THIS UP--BUT THE QUESTION--
HOW DO THEY KNOW IT'S ME?
WELL, IT'S A FAIR ONE TO ASK. SO HERE'S YOUR ANSWER:
STUDY PERSONALITIES LONG ENOUGH AND YOU GET TO KNOW THEM LIKE THE BACK OF YOUR HAND.
EVERYONE LIKES TO THINK THEY'RE *SPECIAL.* THAT THEY ARE SOME UNIQUE COMBINATION OF PERSONALITY, HISTORY AND COGNITIVE ABILITY...
BUT THE TRUTH IS, THOSE ARE JUST TICKED BOXES THAT GIVE US INSIGHT INTO HOW EACH PERSON IS HARD-WIRED.
I DON'T BUY THIS AT ALL.
HE'S BLUFFING.
NOW...IT'S POSSIBLE YOU THINK I'M BEING DISINGENUOUS.
BUT WOULD YOU BE SURPRISED TO KNOW THAT THERE'S A NINETY-FIVE PERCENT CHANCE THAT EITHER CLINT, SAM...OR SUB-DIRECTOR HILL IS WITH YOU? THERE'S AN EIGHTY PERCENT CHANCE THAT YOU BROUGHT ALL THREE.
I'D TAKE THOSE ODDS.
AND, OH MY STARS, THERE'S EVEN A SIXTY-EIGHT PERCENT CHANCE THAT YOU ASKED *SUSAN RICHARDS* TO JOIN YOU. AND IF YOU ASKED, THERE'S AN EIGHTY-THREE PERCENT CHANCE SHE SAID YES. *AB INTRA.*

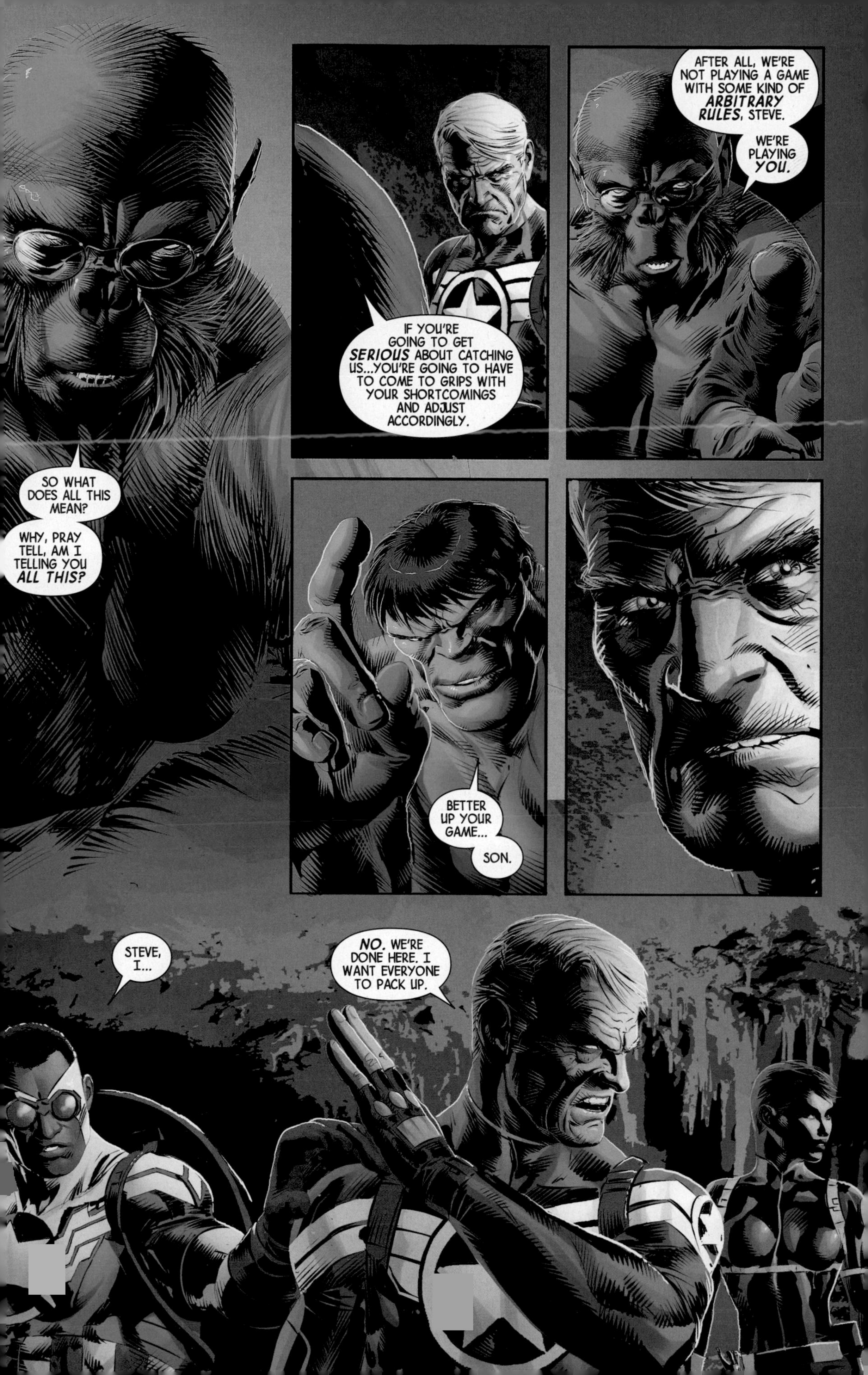

IF YOU'RE GOING TO GET SERIOUS ABOUT CATCHING US...YOU'RE GOING TO HAVE TO COME TO GRIPS WITH YOUR SHORTCOMINGS AND ADJUST ACCORDINGLY.
AFTER ALL, WE'RE NOT PLAYING A GAME WITH SOME KIND OF ARBITRARY RULES, STEVE.
WE'RE PLAYING YOU.
SO WHAT DOES ALL THIS MEAN?
WHY, PRAY TELL, AM I TELLING YOU ALL THIS?
BETTER UP YOUR GAME...
SON.
STEVE, I...
NO. WE'RE DONE HERE. I WANT EVERYONE TO PACK UP.

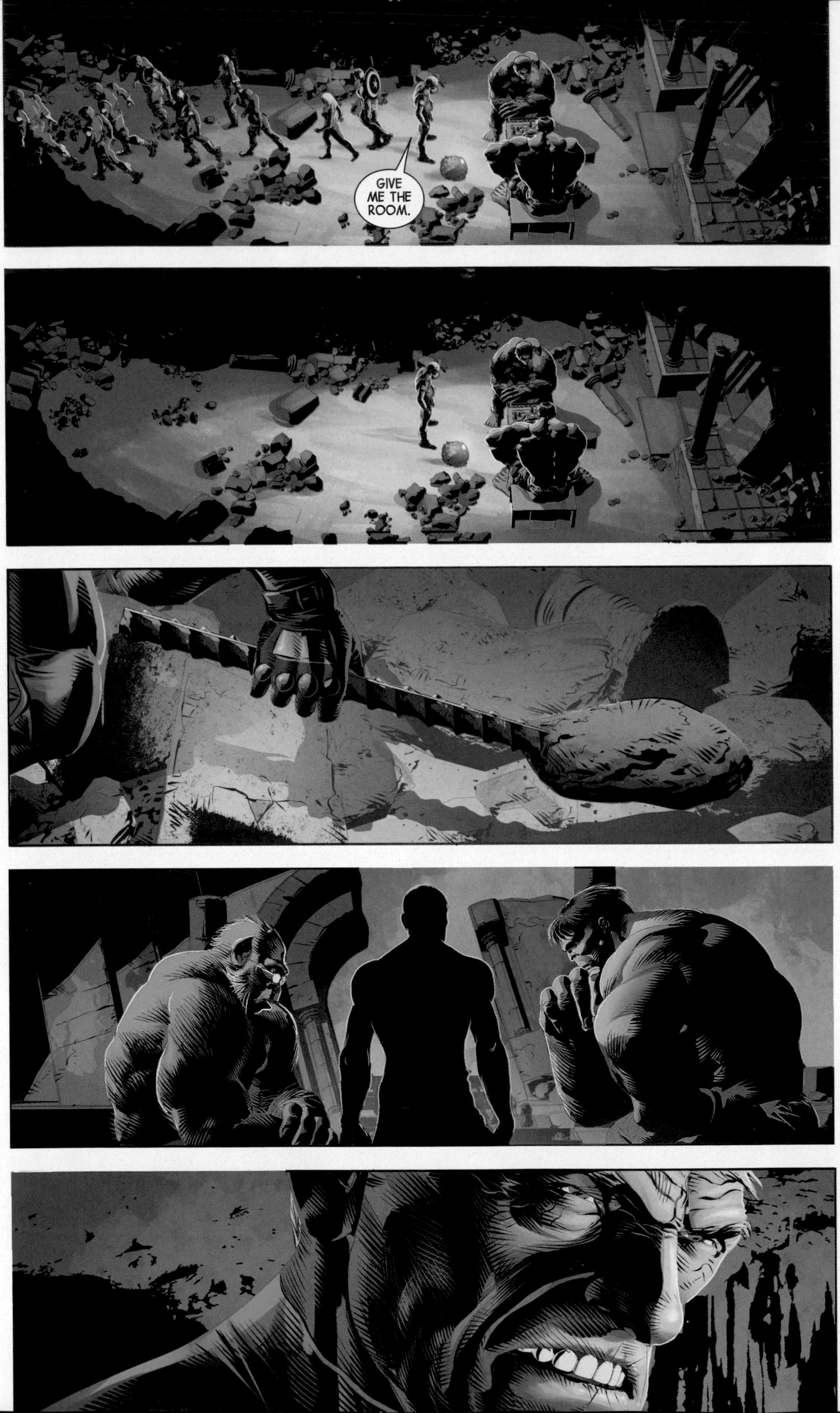
GIVE ME THE ROOM.

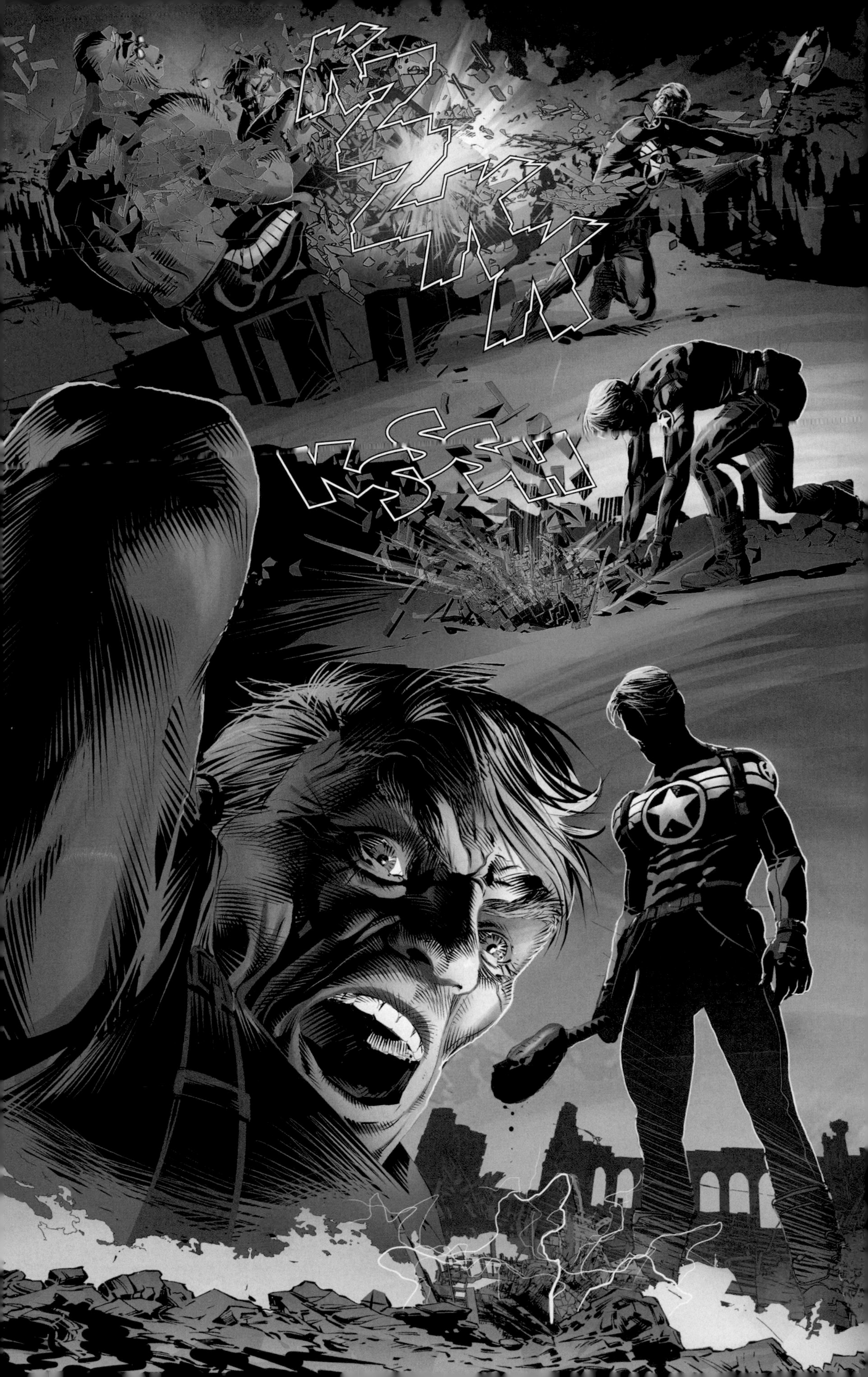
KSSSH

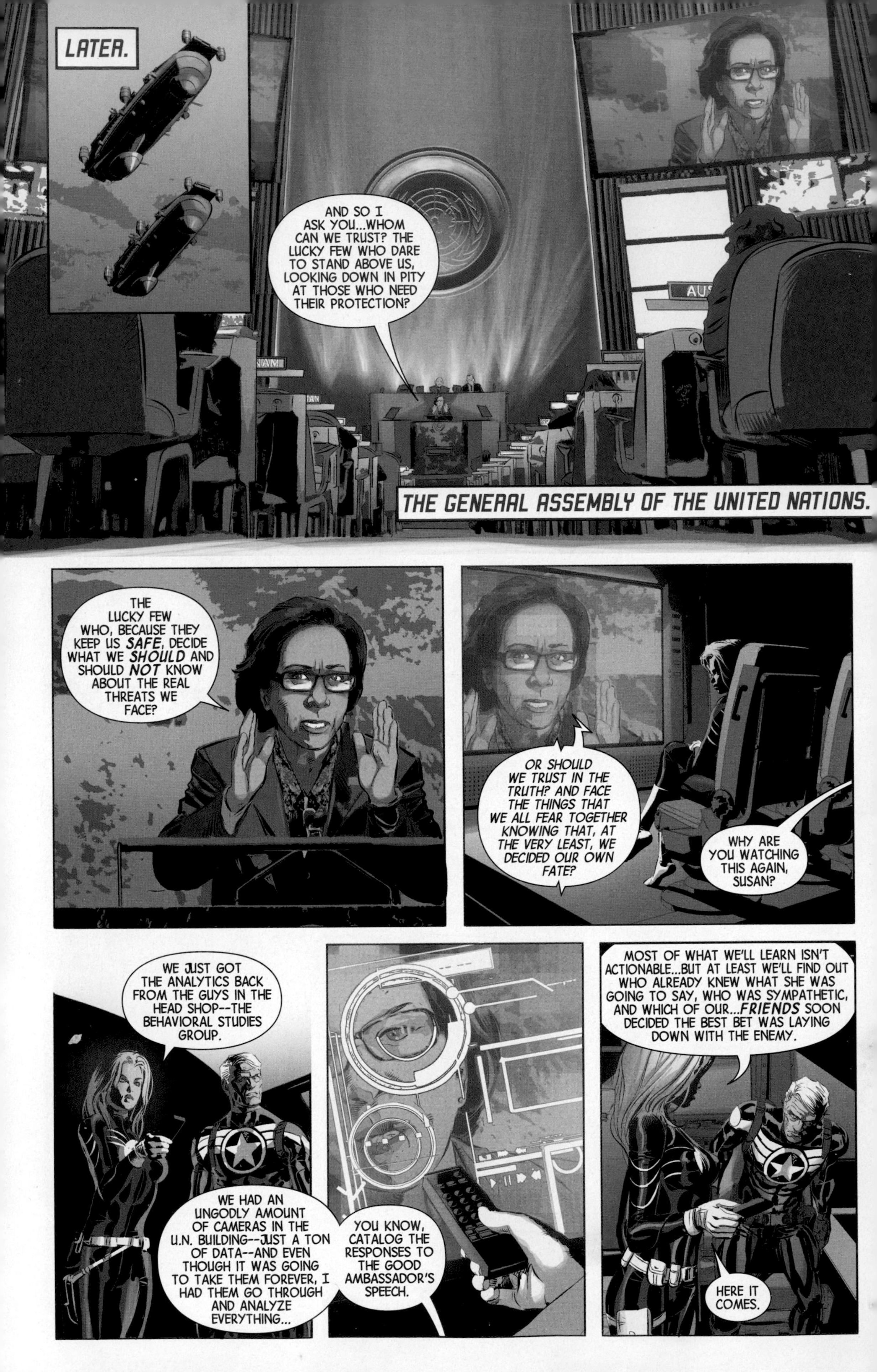
LATER.
AND SO I ASK YOU...WHOM CAN WE TRUST? THE LUCKY FEW WHO DARE TO STAND ABOVE US, LOOKING DOWN IN PITY AT THOSE WHO NEED THEIR PROTECTION?
THE GENERAL ASSEMBLY OF THE UNITED NATIONS.
THE LUCKY FEW WHO, BECAUSE THEY KEEP US SAFE, DECIDE WHAT WE SHOULD AND SHOULD NOT KNOW ABOUT THE REAL THREATS WE FACE?
OR SHOULD WE TRUST IN THE TRUTH? AND FACE THE THINGS THAT WE ALL FEAR TOGETHER KNOWING THAT, AT THE VERY LEAST, WE DECIDED OUR OWN FATE?
WHY ARE YOU WATCHING THIS AGAIN, SUSAN?
WE JUST GOT THE ANALYTICS BACK FROM THE GUYS IN THE HEAD SHOP--THE BEHAVIORAL STUDIES GROUP.
WE HAD AN UNGODLY AMOUNT OF CAMERAS IN THE U.N. BUILDING--JUST A TON OF DATA--AND EVEN THOUGH IT WAS GOING TO TAKE THEM FOREVER, I HAD THEM GO THROUGH AND ANALYZE EVERYTHING...
YOU KNOW, CATALOG THE RESPONSES TO THE GOOD AMBASSADOR'S SPEECH.
MOST OF WHAT WE'LL LEARN ISN'T ACTIONABLE...BUT AT LEAST WE'LL FIND OUT WHO ALREADY KNEW WHAT SHE WAS GOING TO SAY, WHO WAS SYMPATHETIC, AND WHICH OF OUR...FRIENDS SOON DECIDED THE BEST BET WAS LAYING DOWN WITH THE ENEMY.
HERE IT COMES.

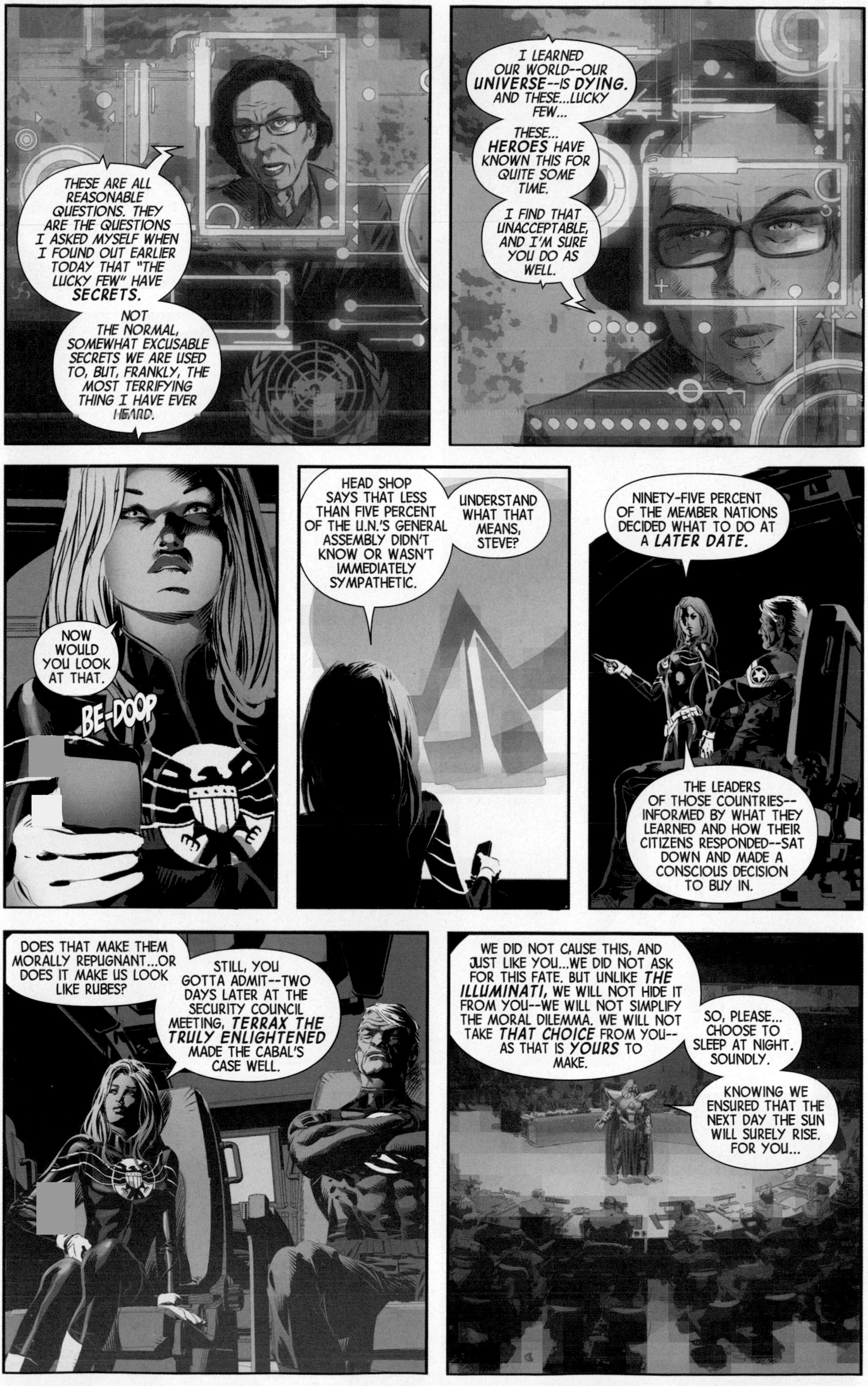
THESE ARE ALL REASONABLE QUESTIONS. THEY ARE THE QUESTIONS I ASKED MYSELF WHEN I FOUND OUT EARLIER TODAY THAT "THE LUCKY FEW" HAVE SECRETS.
NOT THE NORMAL, SOMEWHAT EXCUSABLE SECRETS WE ARE USED TO, BUT, FRANKLY, THE MOST TERRIFYING THING I HAVE EVER HEARD.
I LEARNED OUR WORLD--OUR UNIVERSE--IS DYING. AND THESE...LUCKY FEW...
THESE... HEROES HAVE KNOWN THIS FOR QUITE SOME TIME.
I FIND THAT UNACCEPTABLE, AND I'M SURE YOU DO AS WELL.
NOW WOULD YOU LOOK AT THAT.
BE-DOOP
HEAD SHOP SAYS THAT LESS THAN FIVE PERCENT OF THE U.N.'S GENERAL ASSEMBLY DIDN'T KNOW OR WASN'T IMMEDIATELY SYMPATHETIC.
UNDERSTAND WHAT THAT MEANS, STEVE?
NINETY-FIVE PERCENT OF THE MEMBER NATIONS DECIDED WHAT TO DO AT A LATER DATE.
THE LEADERS OF THOSE COUNTRIES--INFORMED BY WHAT THEY LEARNED AND HOW THEIR CITIZENS RESPONDED--SAT DOWN AND MADE A CONSCIOUS DECISION TO BUY IN.
DOES THAT MAKE THEM MORALLY REPUGNANT...OR DOES IT MAKE US LOOK LIKE RUBES?
STILL, YOU GOTTA ADMIT--TWO DAYS LATER AT THE SECURITY COUNCIL MEETING, TERRAX THE TRULY ENLIGHTENED MADE THE CABAL'S CASE WELL.
WE DID NOT CAUSE THIS, AND JUST LIKE YOU...WE DID NOT ASK FOR THIS FATE. BUT UNLIKE THE ILLUMINATI, WE WILL NOT HIDE IT FROM YOU--WE WILL NOT SIMPLIFY THE MORAL DILEMMA. WE WILL NOT TAKE THAT CHOICE FROM YOU--AS THAT IS YOURS TO MAKE.
SO, PLEASE... CHOOSE TO SLEEP AT NIGHT. SOUNDLY.
KNOWING WE ENSURED THAT THE NEXT DAY THE SUN WILL SURELY RISE. FOR YOU...

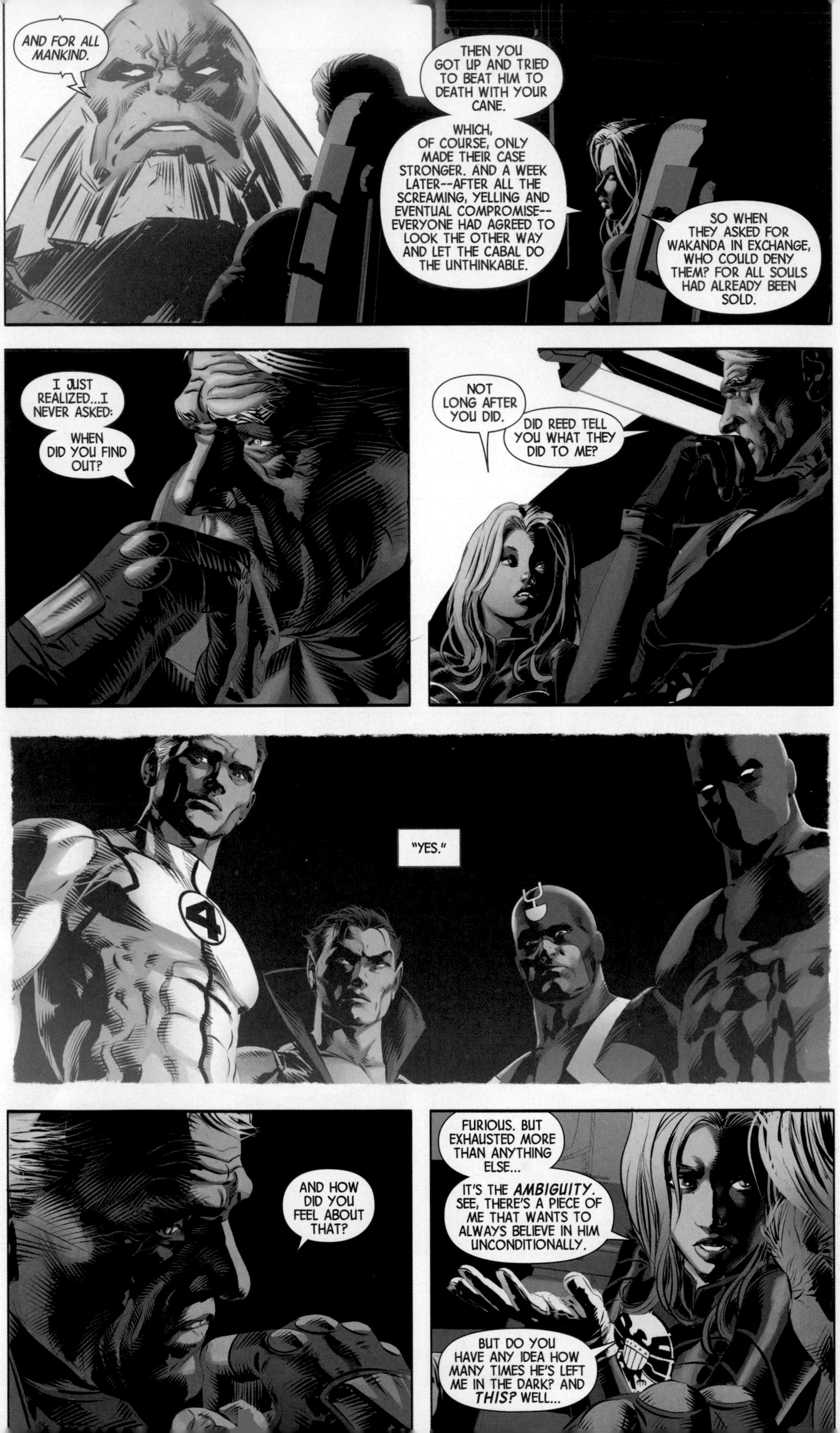
AND FOR ALL MANKIND.
THEN YOU GOT UP AND TRIED TO BEAT HIM TO DEATH WITH YOUR CANE.
WHICH, OF COURSE, ONLY MADE THEIR CASE STRONGER. AND A WEEK LATER--AFTER ALL THE SCREAMING, YELLING AND EVENTUAL COMPROMISE--EVERYONE HAD AGREED TO LOOK THE OTHER WAY AND LET THE CABAL DO THE UNTHINKABLE.
SO WHEN THEY ASKED FOR WAKANDA IN EXCHANGE, WHO COULD DENY THEM? FOR ALL SOULS HAD ALREADY BEEN SOLD.
I JUST REALIZED...I NEVER ASKED:
WHEN DID YOU FIND OUT?
NOT LONG AFTER YOU DID.
DID REED TELL YOU WHAT THEY DID TO ME?
"YES."
AND HOW DID YOU FEEL ABOUT THAT?
FURIOUS. BUT EXHAUSTED MORE THAN ANYTHING ELSE...
IT'S THE AMBIGUITY. SEE, THERE'S A PIECE OF ME THAT WANTS TO ALWAYS BELIEVE IN HIM UNCONDITIONALLY.
BUT DO YOU HAVE ANY IDEA HOW MANY TIMES HE'S LEFT ME IN THE DARK? AND THIS? WELL...

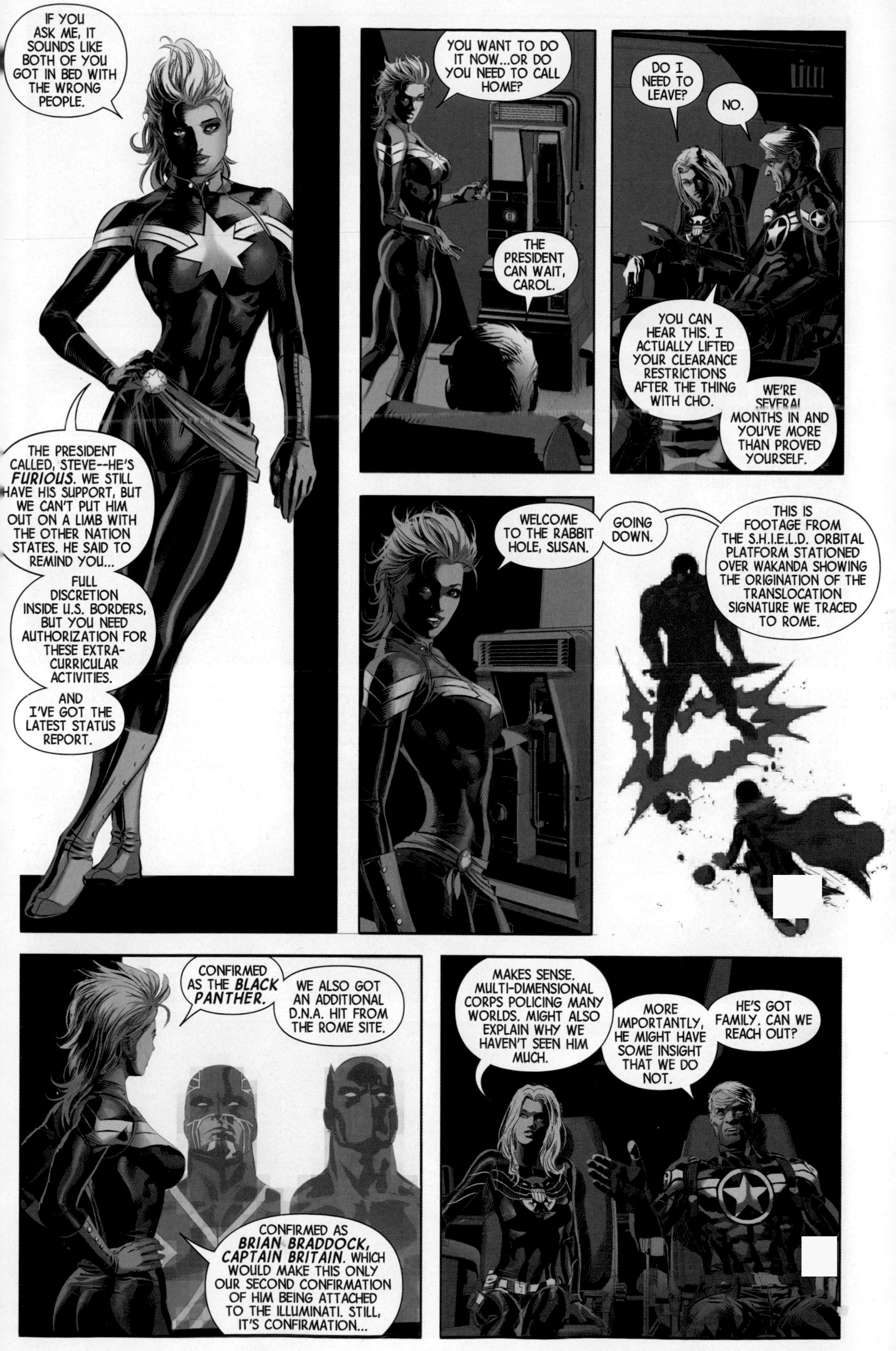

IF YOU ASK ME, IT SOUNDS LIKE BOTH OF YOU GOT IN BED WITH THE WRONG PEOPLE.
THE PRESIDENT CALLED, STEVE--HE'S *FURIOUS*. WE STILL HAVE HIS SUPPORT, BUT WE CAN'T PUT HIM OUT ON A LIMB WITH THE OTHER NATION STATES. HE SAID TO REMIND YOU...
FULL DISCRETION INSIDE U.S. BORDERS, BUT YOU NEED AUTHORIZATION FOR THESE EXTRA-CURRICULAR ACTIVITIES.
AND I'VE GOT THE LATEST STATUS REPORT.
YOU WANT TO DO IT NOW...OR DO YOU NEED TO CALL HOME?
THE PRESIDENT CAN WAIT, CAROL.
DO I NEED TO LEAVE?
NO.
YOU CAN HEAR THIS. I ACTUALLY LIFTED YOUR CLEARANCE RESTRICTIONS AFTER THE THING WITH CHO.
WE'RE SEVERAL MONTHS IN AND YOU'VE MORE THAN PROVED YOURSELF.
WELCOME TO THE RABBIT HOLE, SUSAN.
GOING DOWN.
THIS IS FOOTAGE FROM THE S.H.I.E.L.D. ORBITAL PLATFORM STATIONED OVER WAKANDA SHOWING THE ORIGINATION OF THE TRANSLOCATION SIGNATURE WE TRACED TO ROME.
CONFIRMED AS THE *BLACK PANTHER*.
WE ALSO GOT AN ADDITIONAL D.N.A. HIT FROM THE ROME SITE.
CONFIRMED AS *BRIAN BRADDOCK, CAPTAIN BRITAIN*. WHICH WOULD MAKE THIS ONLY OUR SECOND CONFIRMATION OF HIM BEING ATTACHED TO THE ILLUMINATI. STILL, IT'S CONFIRMATION...
MAKES SENSE. MULTI-DIMENSIONAL CORPS POLICING MANY WORLDS. MIGHT ALSO EXPLAIN WHY WE HAVEN'T SEEN HIM MUCH.
MORE IMPORTANTLY, HE MIGHT HAVE SOME INSIGHT THAT WE DO NOT.
HE'S GOT FAMILY. CAN WE REACH OUT?

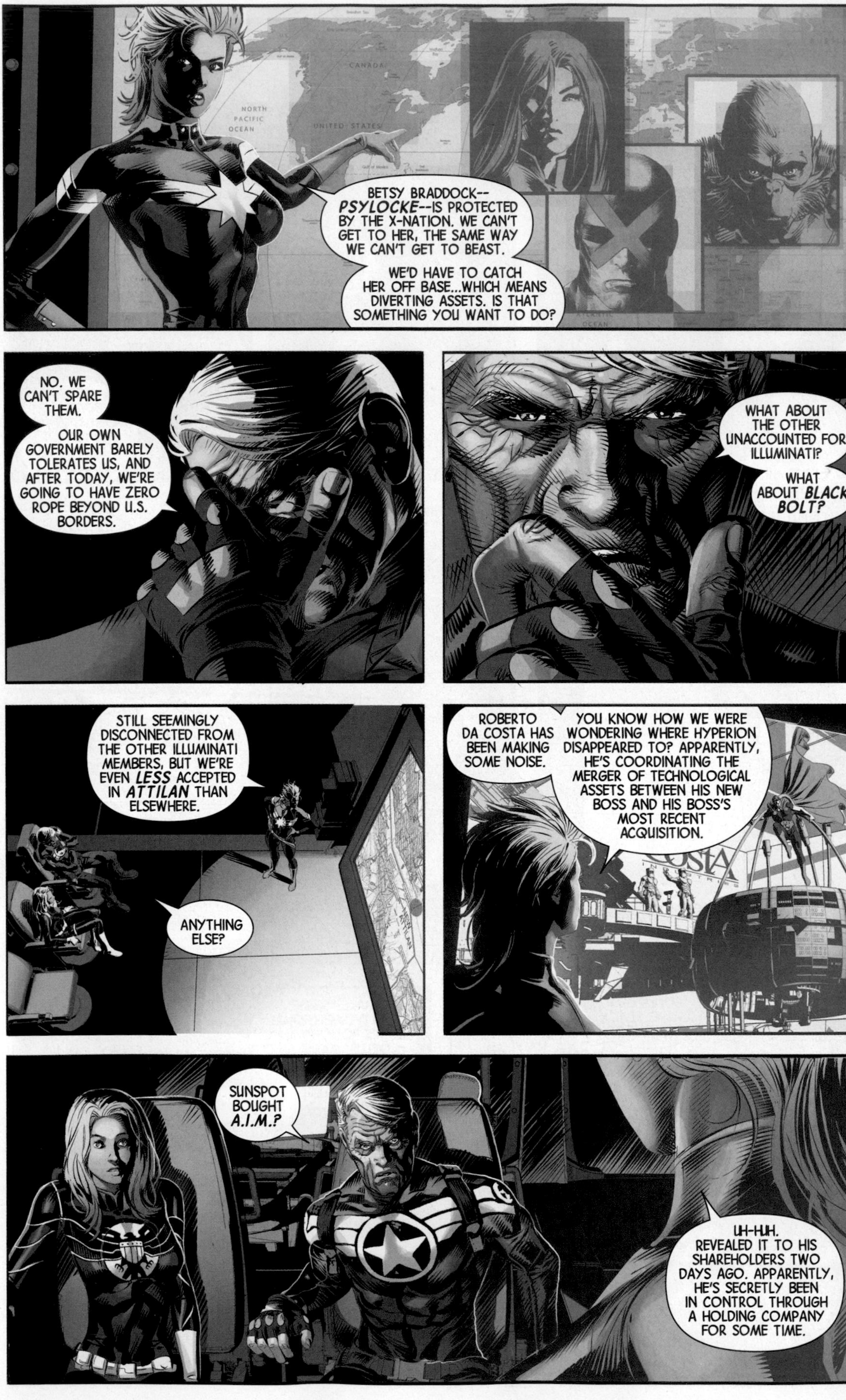
BETSY BRADDOCK--PSYLOCKE--IS PROTECTED BY THE X-NATION. WE CAN'T GET TO HER, THE SAME WAY WE CAN'T GET TO BEAST.
WE'D HAVE TO CATCH HER OFF BASE...WHICH MEANS DIVERTING ASSETS. IS THAT SOMETHING YOU WANT TO DO?
NO. WE CAN'T SPARE THEM.
OUR OWN GOVERNMENT BARELY TOLERATES US, AND AFTER TODAY, WE'RE GOING TO HAVE ZERO ROPE BEYOND U.S. BORDERS.
WHAT ABOUT THE OTHER UNACCOUNTED FOR ILLUMINATI?
WHAT ABOUT BLACK BOLT?
STILL SEEMINGLY DISCONNECTED FROM THE OTHER ILLUMINATI MEMBERS, BUT WE'RE EVEN LESS ACCEPTED IN ATTILAN THAN ELSEWHERE.
ANYTHING ELSE?
ROBERTO DA COSTA HAS BEEN MAKING SOME NOISE.
YOU KNOW HOW WE WERE WONDERING WHERE HYPERION DISAPPEARED TO? APPARENTLY, HE'S COORDINATING THE MERGER OF TECHNOLOGICAL ASSETS BETWEEN HIS NEW BOSS AND HIS BOSS'S MOST RECENT ACQUISITION.
SUNSPOT BOUGHT A.I.M.?
UH-HUH. REVEALED IT TO HIS SHAREHOLDERS TWO DAYS AGO. APPARENTLY, HE'S SECRETLY BEEN IN CONTROL THROUGH A HOLDING COMPANY FOR SOME TIME.

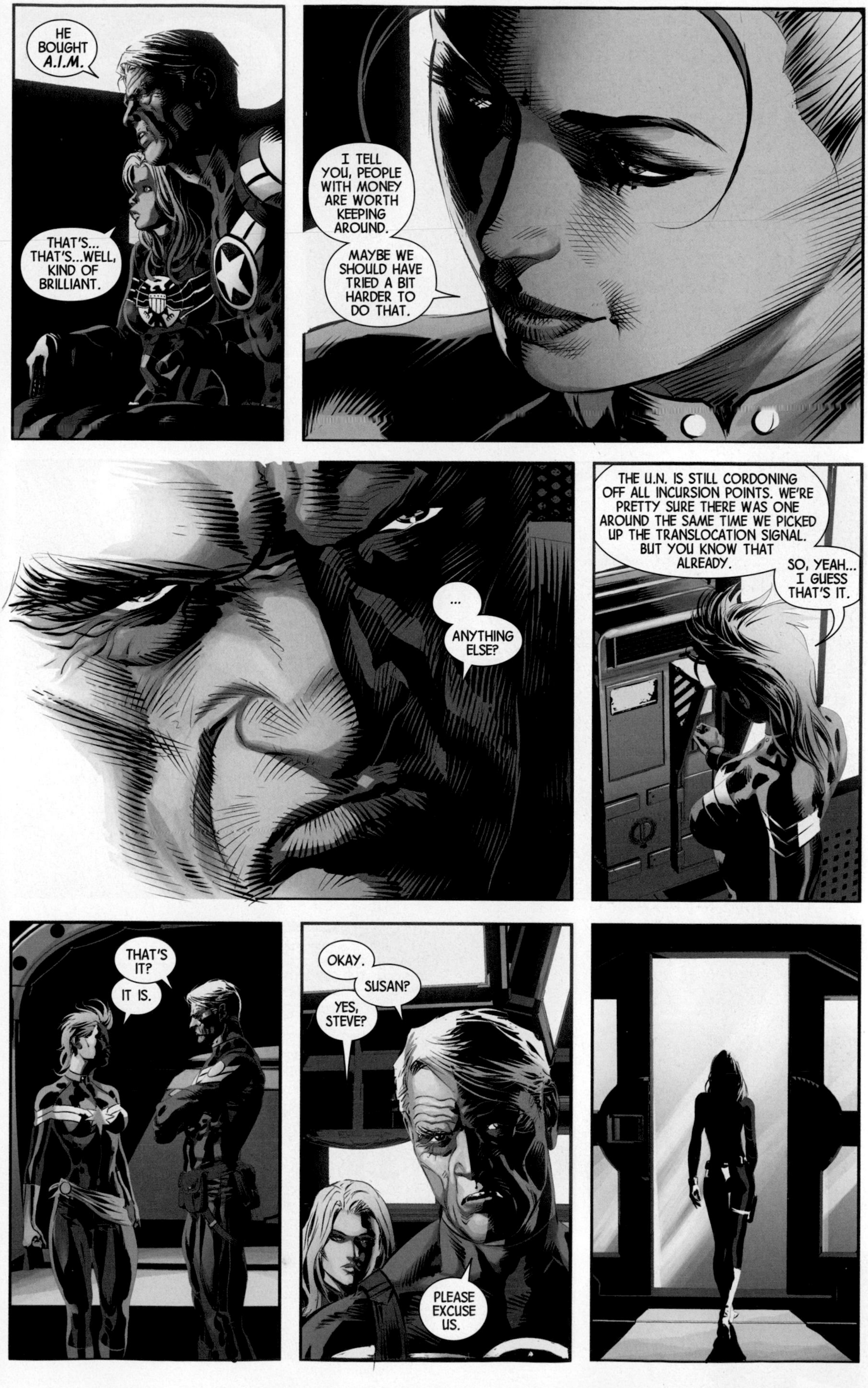
HE BOUGHT A.I.M.
THAT'S... THAT'S...WELL, KIND OF BRILLIANT.
I TELL YOU, PEOPLE WITH MONEY ARE WORTH KEEPING AROUND.
MAYBE WE SHOULD HAVE TRIED A BIT HARDER TO DO THAT.
...
ANYTHING ELSE?
THE U.N. IS STILL CORDONING OFF ALL INCURSION POINTS. WE'RE PRETTY SURE THERE WAS ONE AROUND THE SAME TIME WE PICKED UP THE TRANSLOCATION SIGNAL. BUT YOU KNOW THAT ALREADY.
SO, YEAH... I GUESS THAT'S IT.
THAT'S IT?
IT IS.
OKAY.
SUSAN?
YES, STEVE?
PLEASE EXCUSE US.

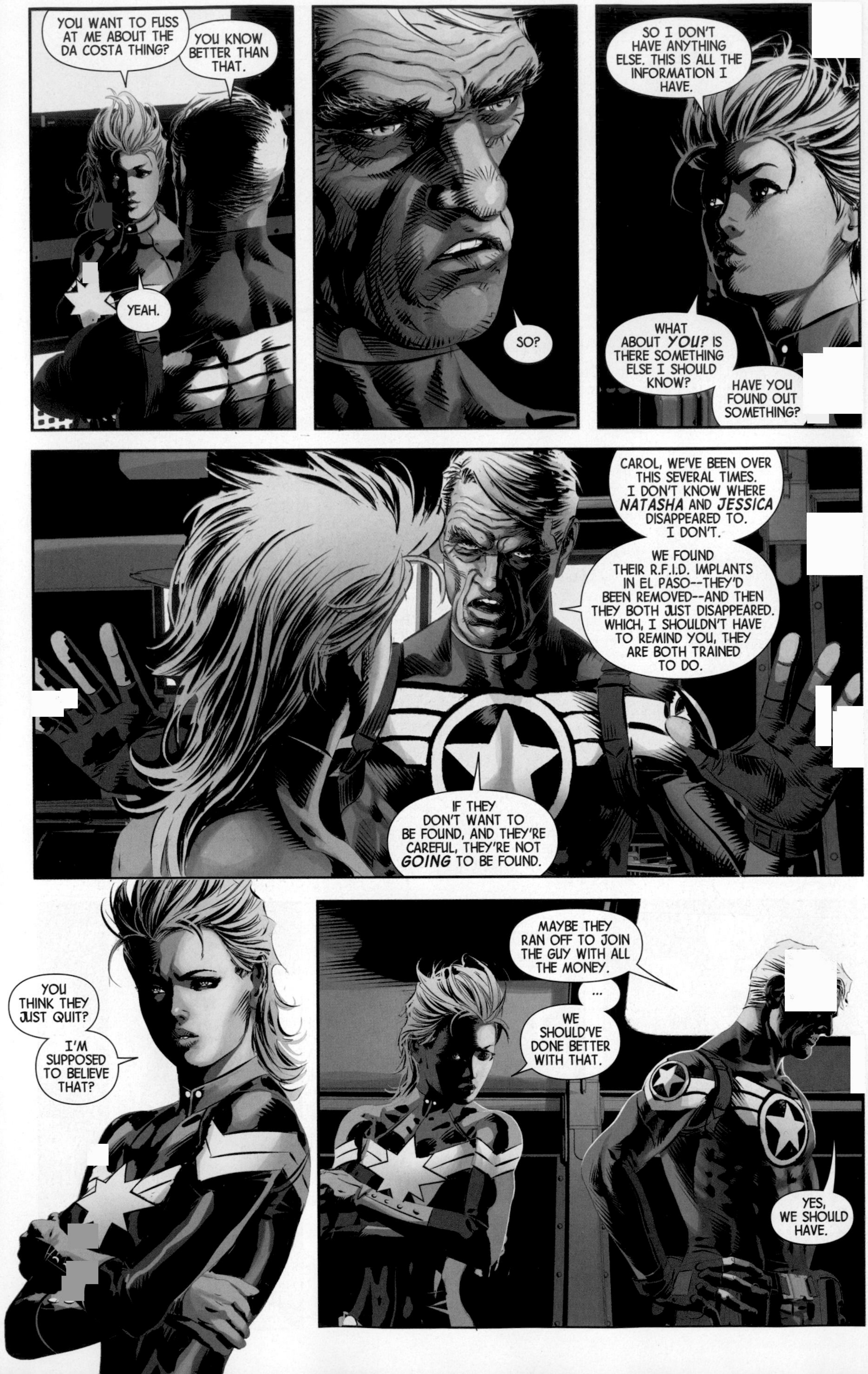
YOU WANT TO FUSS AT ME ABOUT THE DA COSTA THING?
YOU KNOW BETTER THAN THAT.
YEAH.
SO?
SO I DON'T HAVE ANYTHING ELSE. THIS IS ALL THE INFORMATION I HAVE.
WHAT ABOUT YOU? IS THERE SOMETHING ELSE I SHOULD KNOW?
HAVE YOU FOUND OUT SOMETHING?
CAROL, WE'VE BEEN OVER THIS SEVERAL TIMES. I DON'T KNOW WHERE NATASHA AND JESSICA DISAPPEARED TO. I DON'T.
WE FOUND THEIR R.F.I.D. IMPLANTS IN EL PASO--THEY'D BEEN REMOVED--AND THEN THEY BOTH JUST DISAPPEARED. WHICH, I SHOULDN'T HAVE TO REMIND YOU, THEY ARE BOTH TRAINED TO DO.
IF THEY DON'T WANT TO BE FOUND, AND THEY'RE CAREFUL, THEY'RE NOT GOING TO BE FOUND.
YOU THINK THEY JUST QUIT?
I'M SUPPOSED TO BELIEVE THAT?
MAYBE THEY RAN OFF TO JOIN THE GUY WITH ALL THE MONEY.
...
WE SHOULD'VE DONE BETTER WITH THAT.
YES, WE SHOULD HAVE.

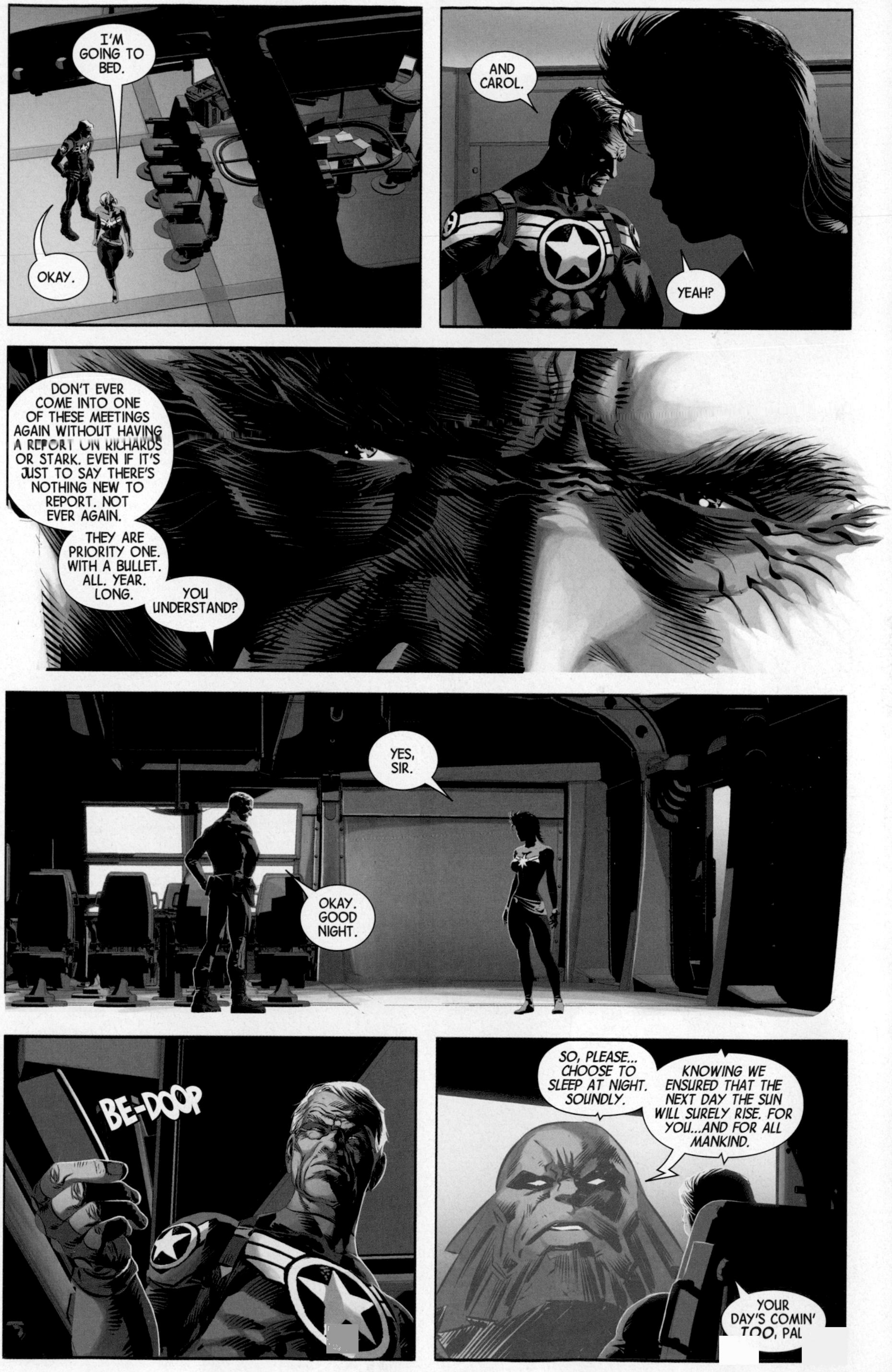

I'M GOING TO BED.
OKAY.
AND CAROL.
YEAH?
DON'T EVER COME INTO ONE OF THESE MEETINGS AGAIN WITHOUT HAVING A REPORT ON RICHARDS OR STARK. EVEN IF IT'S JUST TO SAY THERE'S NOTHING NEW TO REPORT. NOT EVER AGAIN.
THEY ARE PRIORITY ONE. WITH A BULLET. ALL. YEAR. LONG.
YOU UNDERSTAND?
YES, SIR.
OKAY. GOOD NIGHT.
BE-DOOP
SO, PLEASE... CHOOSE TO SLEEP AT NIGHT. SOUNDLY.
KNOWING WE ENSURED THAT THE NEXT DAY THE SUN WILL SURELY RISE. FOR YOU...AND FOR ALL MANKIND.
YOUR DAY'S COMIN' TOO, PAL

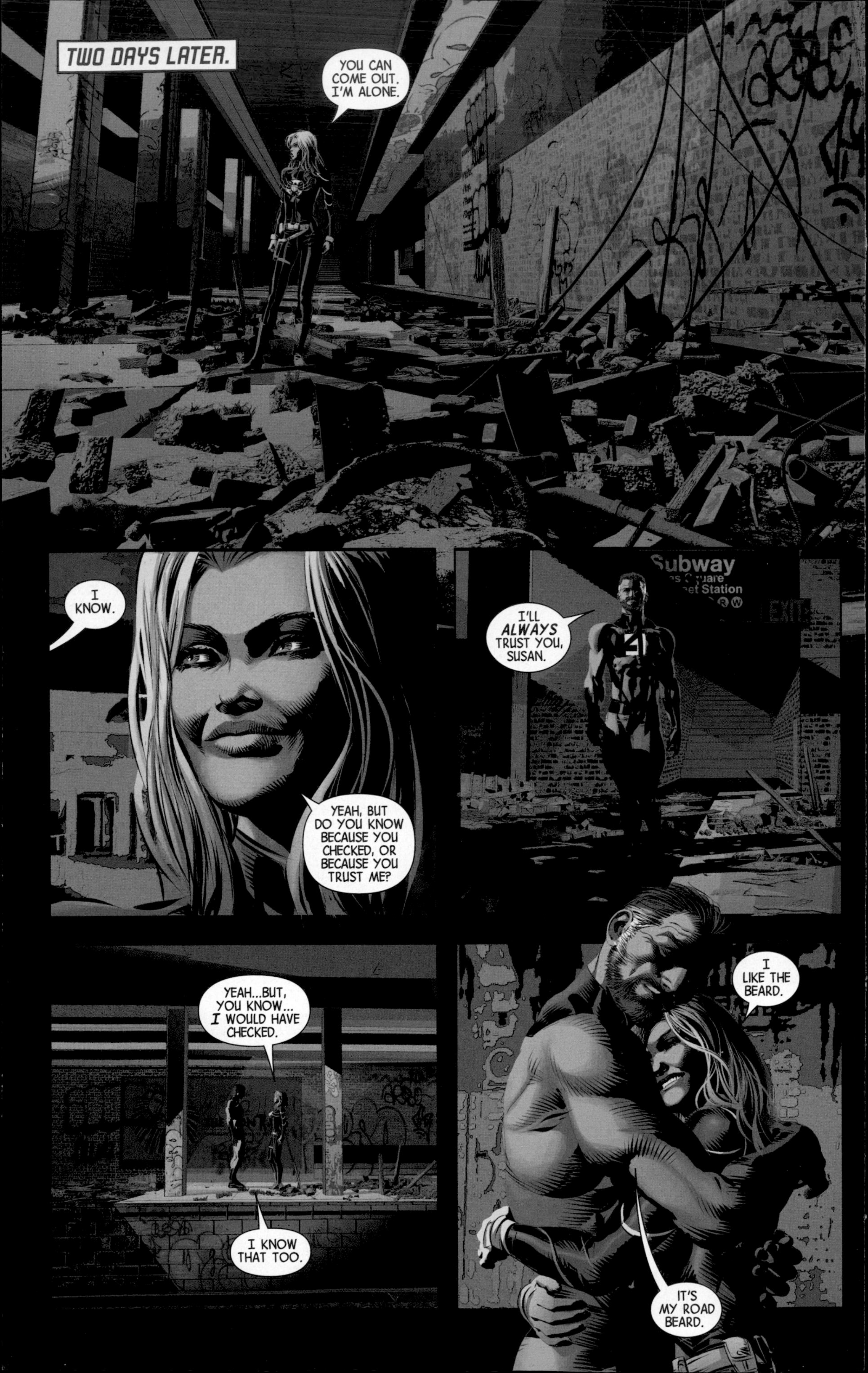
TWO DAYS LATER.
YOU CAN COME OUT. I'M ALONE.
I KNOW.
YEAH, BUT DO YOU KNOW BECAUSE YOU CHECKED, OR BECAUSE YOU TRUST ME?
Subway
Station
EXIT
I'LL ALWAYS TRUST YOU, SUSAN.
YEAH...BUT, YOU KNOW... I WOULD HAVE CHECKED.
I KNOW THAT TOO.
I LIKE THE BEARD.
IT'S MY ROAD BEARD.

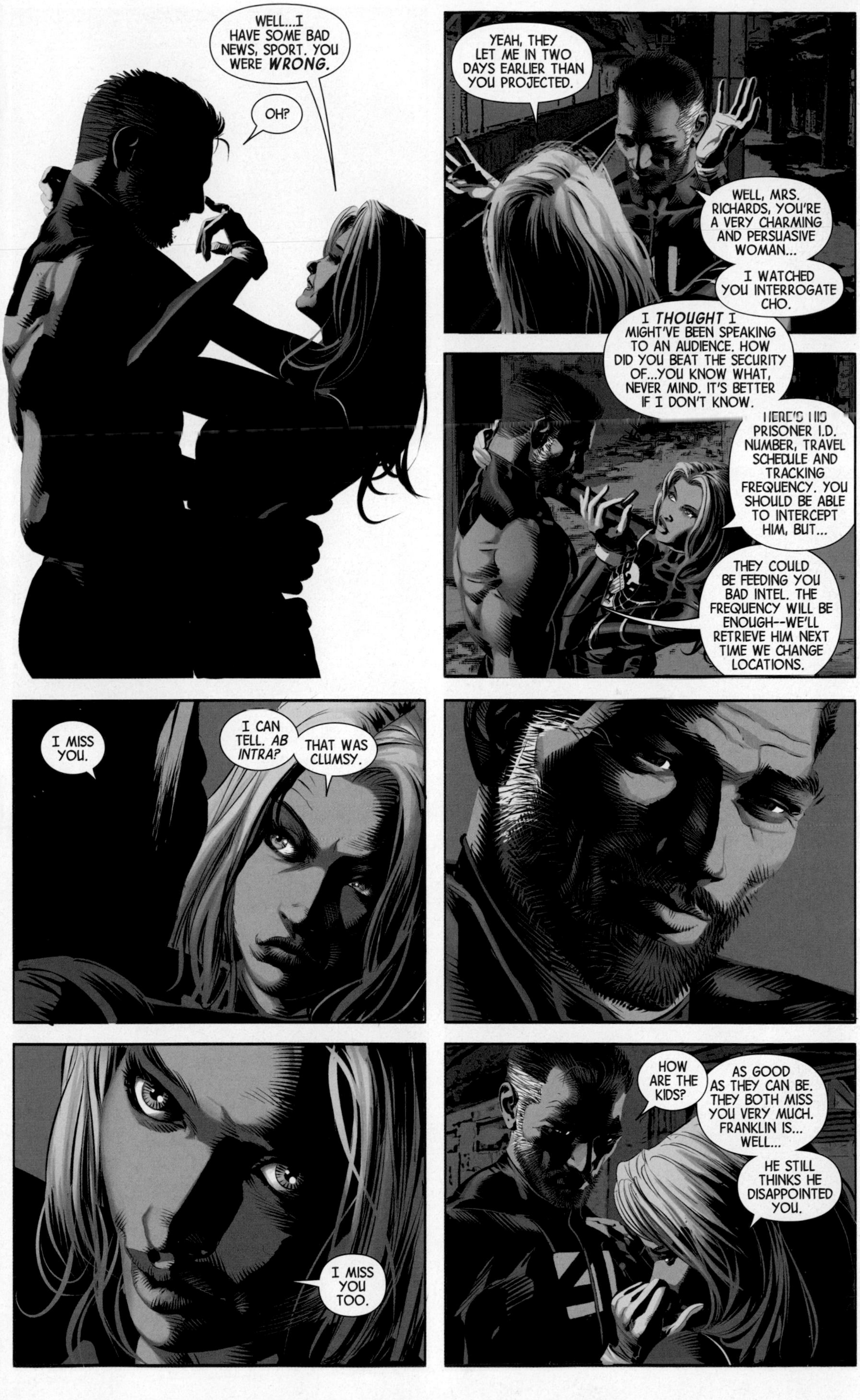

WELL...I HAVE SOME BAD NEWS, SPORT. YOU WERE **WRONG.**
OH?
YEAH, THEY LET ME IN TWO DAYS EARLIER THAN YOU PROJECTED.
WELL, MRS. RICHARDS, YOU'RE A VERY CHARMING AND PERSUASIVE WOMAN...
I WATCHED YOU INTERROGATE CHO.
I *THOUGHT* I MIGHT'VE BEEN SPEAKING TO AN AUDIENCE. HOW DID YOU BEAT THE SECURITY OF...YOU KNOW WHAT, NEVER MIND. IT'S BETTER IF I DON'T KNOW.
PRISONER I.D. NUMBER, TRAVEL SCHEDULE AND TRACKING FREQUENCY. YOU SHOULD BE ABLE TO INTERCEPT HIM, BUT...
THEY COULD BE FEEDING YOU BAD INTEL. THE FREQUENCY WILL BE ENOUGH--WE'LL RETRIEVE HIM NEXT TIME WE CHANGE LOCATIONS.
I MISS YOU.
I CAN TELL. *AB INTRA?*
THAT WAS CLUMSY.
I MISS YOU TOO.
HOW ARE THE KIDS?
AS GOOD AS THEY CAN BE. THEY BOTH MISS YOU VERY MUCH. FRANKLIN IS... WELL...
HE STILL THINKS HE DISAPPOINTED YOU.

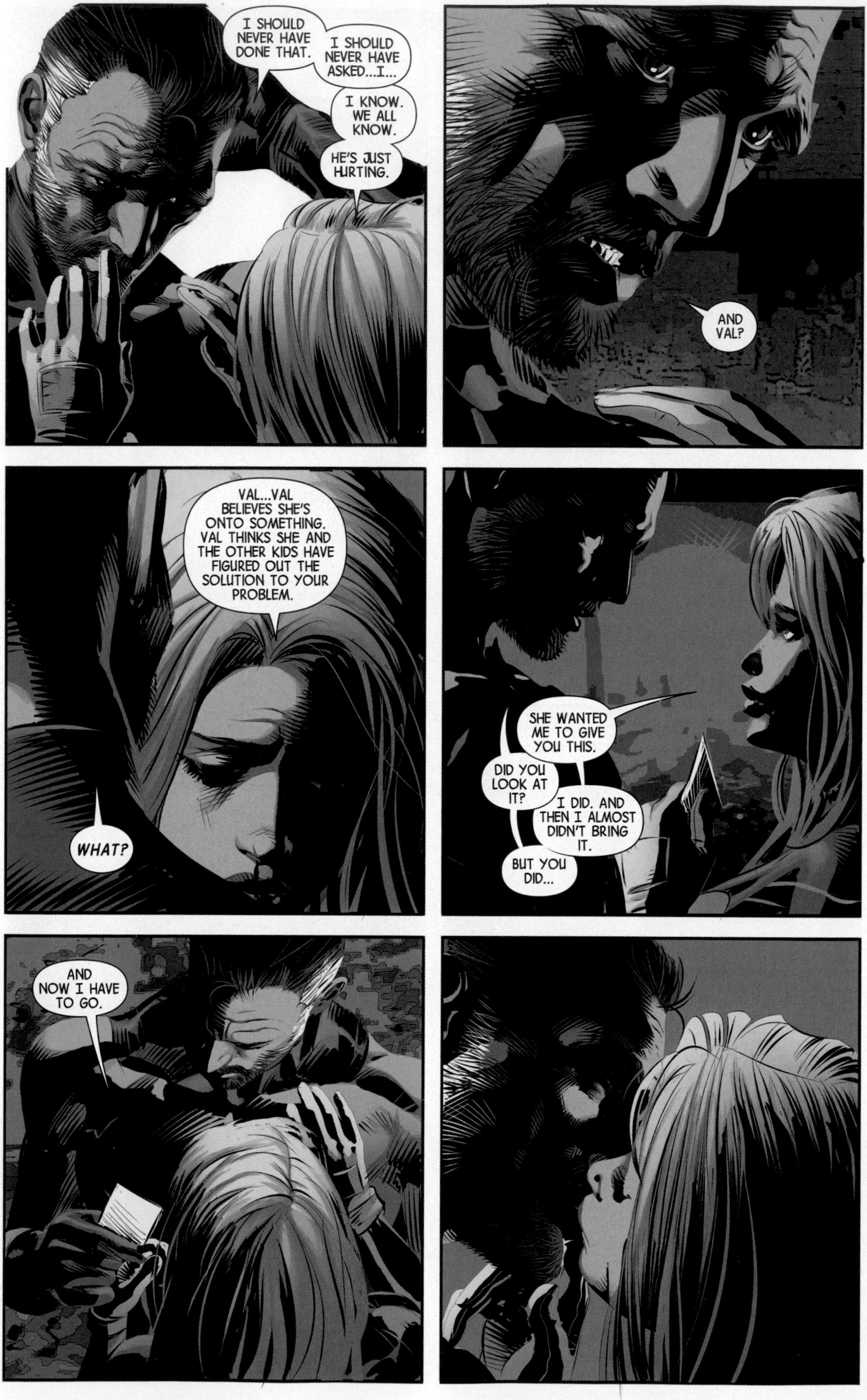
I SHOULD NEVER HAVE DONE THAT.
I SHOULD NEVER HAVE ASKED...I...
I KNOW. WE ALL KNOW.
HE'S JUST HURTING.
AND VAL?
VAL...VAL BELIEVES SHE'S ONTO SOMETHING. VAL THINKS SHE AND THE OTHER KIDS HAVE FIGURED OUT THE SOLUTION TO YOUR PROBLEM.
WHAT?
SHE WANTED ME TO GIVE YOU THIS.
DID YOU LOOK AT IT?
I DID. AND THEN I ALMOST DIDN'T BRING IT.
BUT YOU DID...
AND NOW I HAVE TO GO.

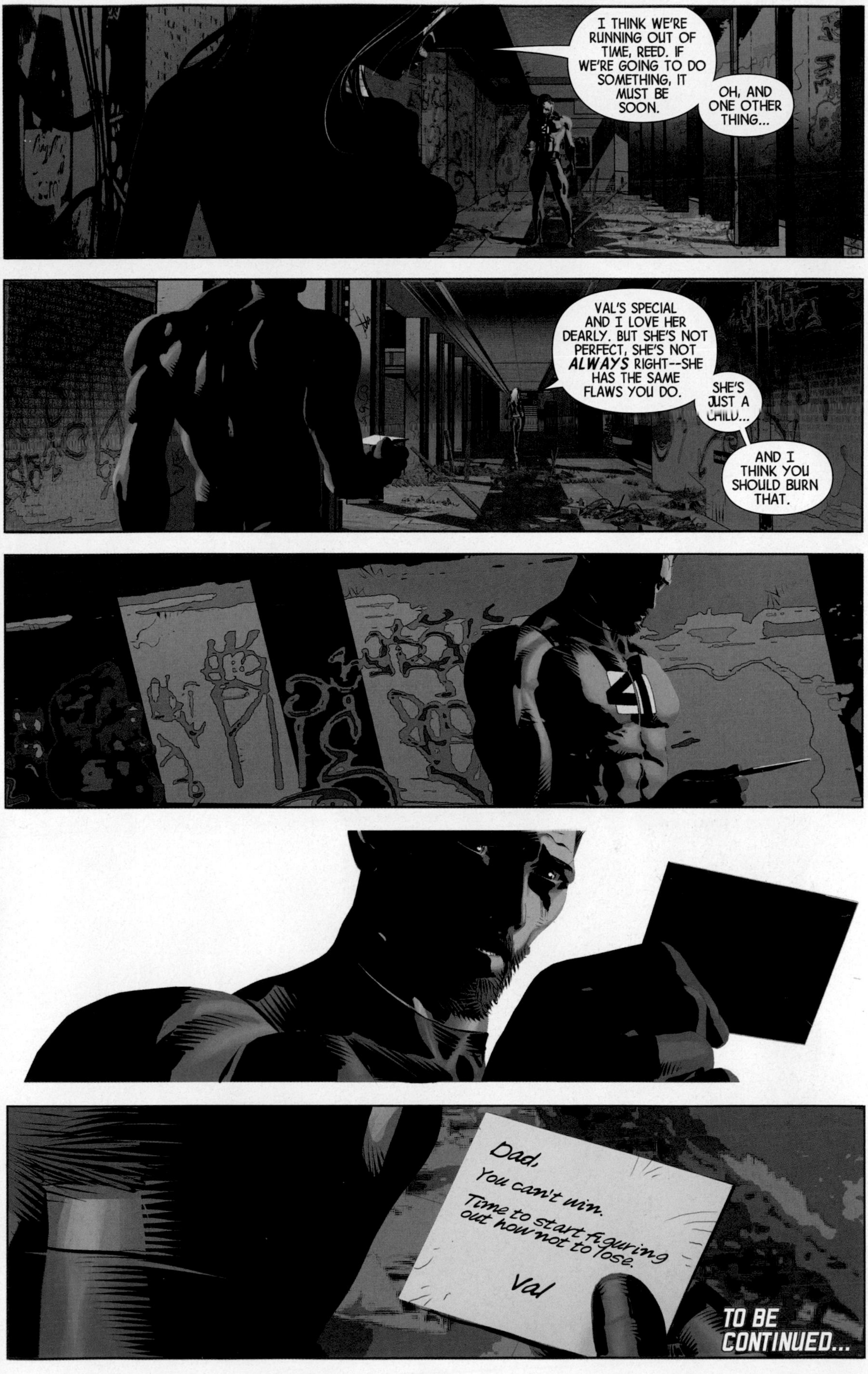
I THINK WE'RE RUNNING OUT OF TIME, REED. IF WE'RE GOING TO DO SOMETHING, IT MUST BE SOON.
OH, AND ONE OTHER THING...
VAL'S SPECIAL AND I LOVE HER DEARLY. BUT SHE'S NOT PERFECT, SHE'S NOT ALWAYS RIGHT--SHE HAS THE SAME FLAWS YOU DO.
SHE'S JUST A CHILD...
AND I THINK YOU SHOULD BURN THAT.
Dad,
You can't win.
Time to start figuring out how not to lose.
Val
TO BE CONTINUED...

AVENGERS #35

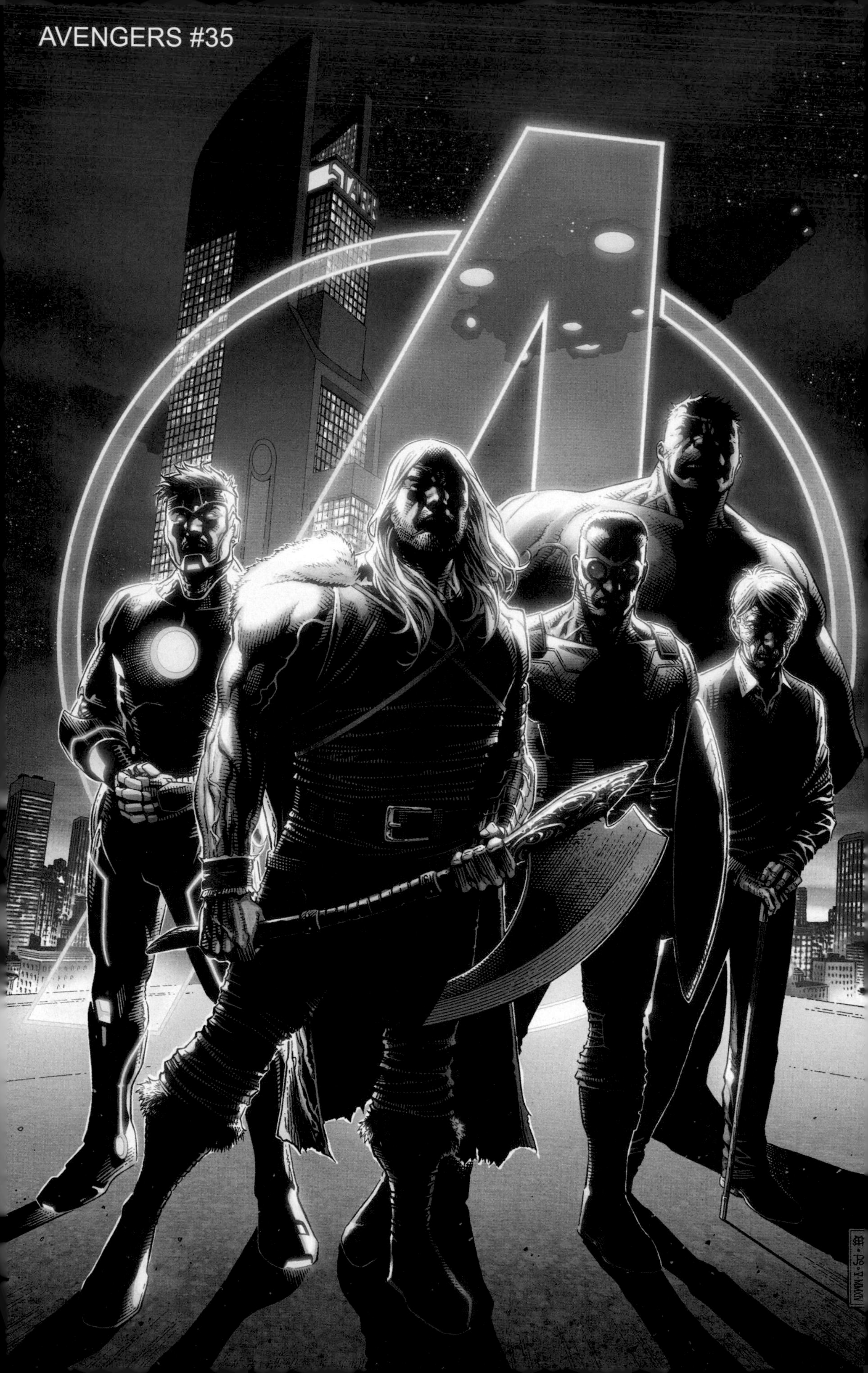

AVENGERS #36

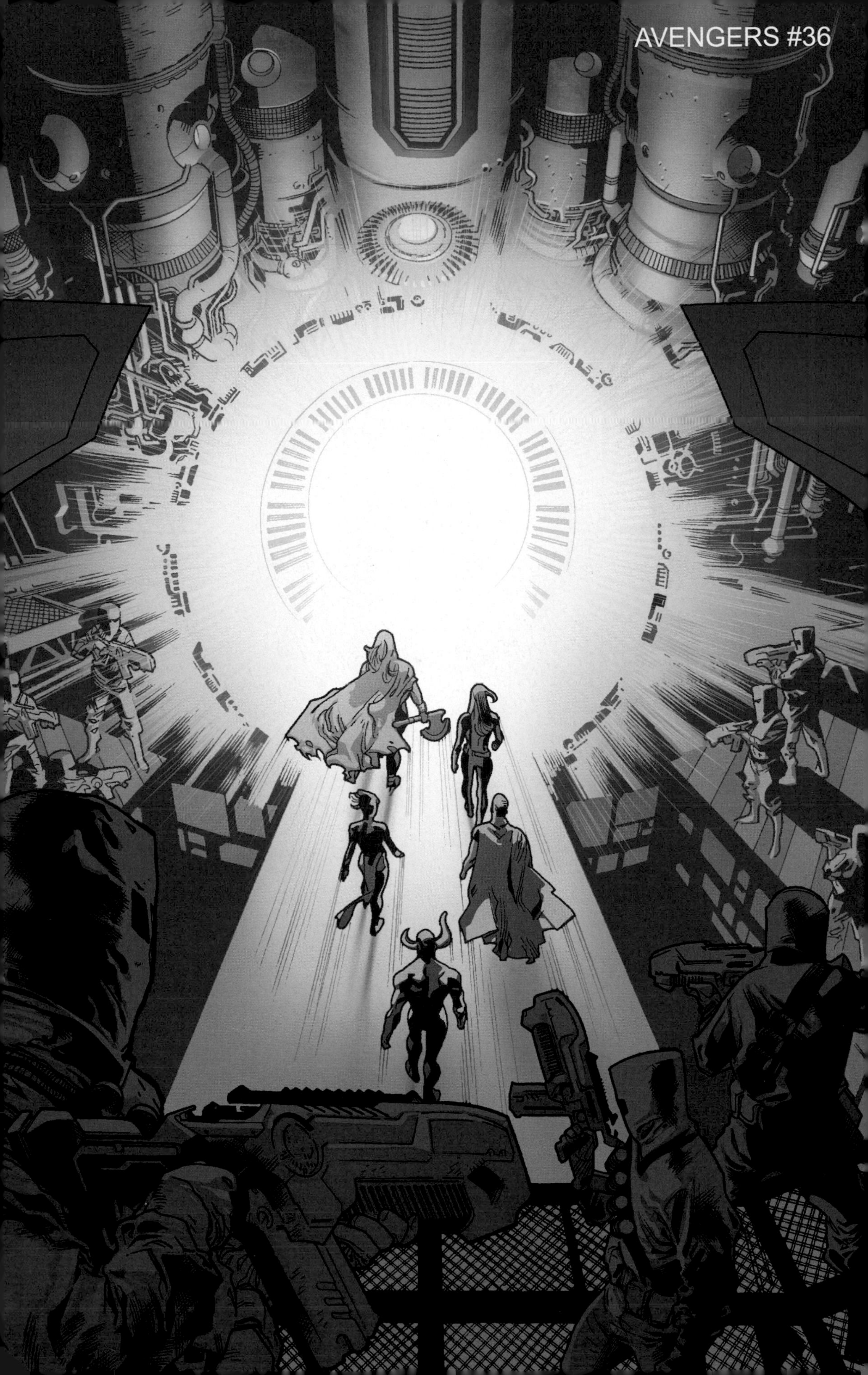

AVENGERS #37

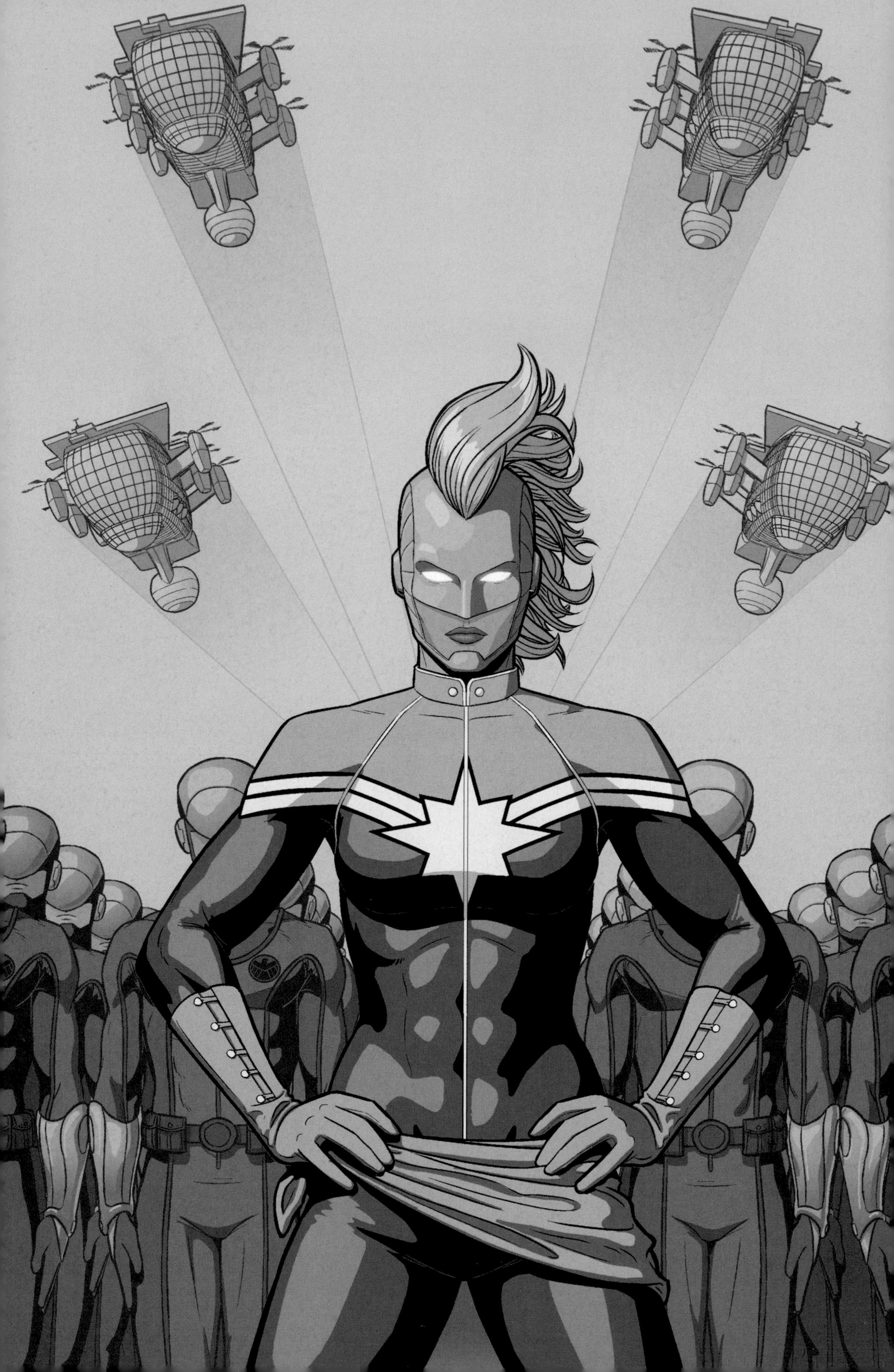

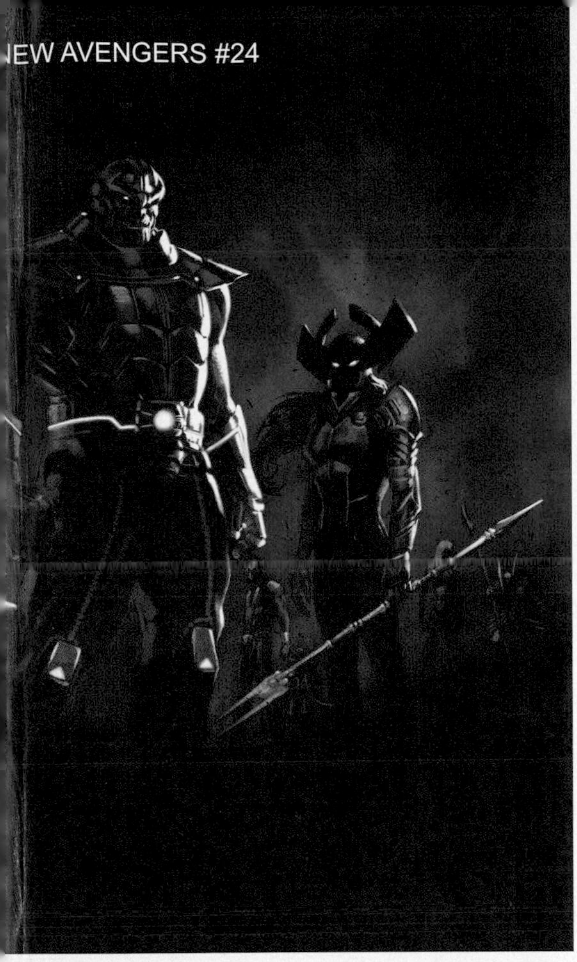

NEW AVENGERS #24

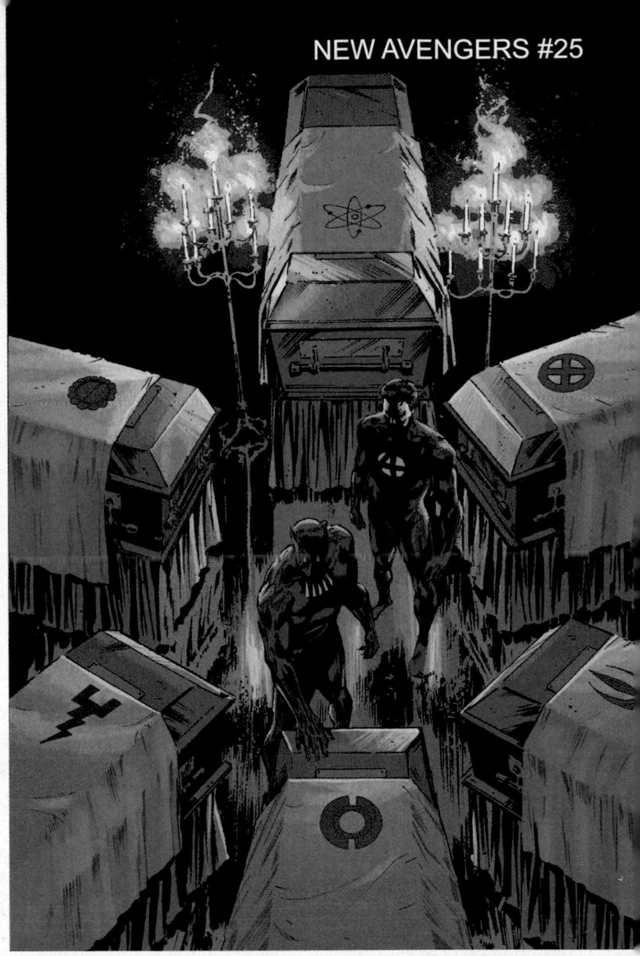

NEW AVENGERS #25

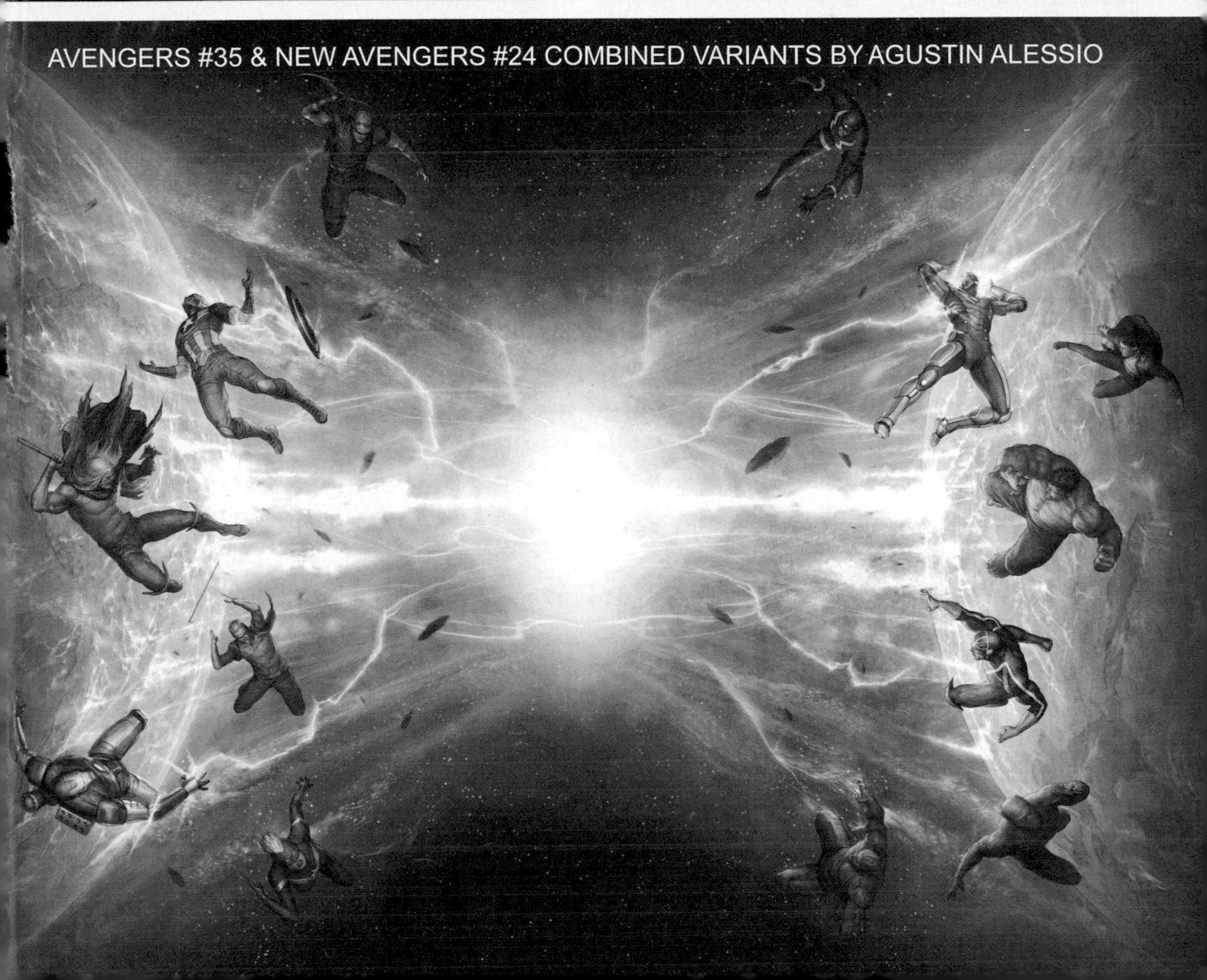

AVENGERS #35 & NEW AVENGERS #24 COMBINED VARIANTS BY AGUSTIN ALESSIO

MARVEL AUGMENTED REALITY (AR) ENHANCES AND CHANGES THE WAY YOU EXPERIENCE COMICS!

TO ACCESS THE FREE MARVEL AR CONTENT IN THIS BOOK*:

1. Locate the **AR** logo within the comic.
2. Go to Marvel.com/AR in your web browser.
3. Search by series title to find the corresponding AR.
4. Enjoy Marvel AR!

*All AR content that appears in this book has been archived and will be available only at Marvel.com/AR — no longer in the Marvel AR App. Content subject to change and availability.

AR INDEX

TO REDEEM YOUR CODE FOR A FREE DIGITAL COPY:

1. GO TO MARVEL.COM/REDEEM. OFFER EXPIRES ON 1/14/17.
2. FOLLOW THE ON-SCREEN INSTRUCTIONS TO REDEEM YOUR DIGITAL COPY.
3. LAUNCH THE MARVEL COMICS APP TO READ YOUR COMIC NOW!
4. YOUR DIGITAL COPY WILL BE FOUND UNDER THE *MY COMICS* TAB.
5. READ & ENJOY!

YOUR FREE DIGITAL COPY WILL BE AVAILABLE ON

| MARVEL COMICS APP FOR APPLE® iOS DEVICES | MARVEL COMICS APP FOR ANDROID™ DEVICES |